"Everyone loves a good story. Even more, everyone loves a good story that is true. *Ocean of Stars and Dreams* is a compelling true story that will draw you in and have you emotionally connected to the characters and their journey. Read it, enjoy it, and be reminded to celebrate your own journey."

—DR. JASON YOUNG
Author, Keynote Speaker, Executive Coach

"Maday Martínez de Osaba has provided the reader with a passionate and detailed history of her Cuban American family and their amazing journey through life and their eventual immigration to the United States. I was both educated and encouraged through this writing. It shows us that anything is possible in life. The perseverance and determination showcased in these pages are truly inspiring."

—TIM DRAKE
Author of *Inherited Freedom*, *Solitary Vigilance*, and *Death Is the Final Reckoning*

"In reading the compelling stories of Maday Martínez de Osaba's family's journey, I found striking similarities between immigrants overcoming adversity to follow their dreams and world-class athletes overcoming obstacles to achieve their goals. *Ocean of Stars and Dreams* made the resilient part of my spirit rise up—the part that perseveres, works hard, and never gives up, knowing that endurance will be rewarded—and it will do the same for all who read it!"

—ROBYN BENINCASA
CNN Hero, American Endurance Racer, World Champion Adventure Racer, New York Times Best-Selling Author, Award-Winning Motivational Speaker

OCEAN of STARS and DREAMS

OCEAN
of
STARS
and
DREAMS

MAR DE ESTRELLAS Y SUEÑOS

MADAY MARTÍNEZ DE OSABA

Copyright © 2022 by Maday Martínez de Osaba

All rights reserved. No part of this book may be reproduced or used in any manner without the prior written permission of the copyright owner, except for the use of brief quotations in a book review.

Some names and identifying details have been changed to protect the privacy of individuals.

Consulting by Freedom Press.

Editing by Steph Spector.

Cover and interior design by Charissa Newell, twolineSTUDIO.

Additional works cited:
Coelho, Paulo. The Alchemist. HarperOne,1993.
Martí, José. Los Zapaticos de Rosa. Cuba. 1889.

Printed in the United States of America.

ebook ISBN: 979-8-9854105-2-5
paperback ISBN: 979-8-9854105-0-1
hardcover ISBN: 979-8-9854105-1-8

DEDICATION

With all my love,

To my parents, Loida and Roberto.
Your sacrifices were innumerable.
My love and gratitude are immeasurable.

To my daughter, Lindsey.
Te amo . . . eres mi luna y mis estrellas.

To my brother, Robb.
A million thank yous could never be enough
for your priceless gift of life. You are my hero.

To my sister, Suzette.
You are a beautiful soul and a gift to this world.

To my entire family.
It has been the privilege of my life to be
in your presence, to soak in your joy.

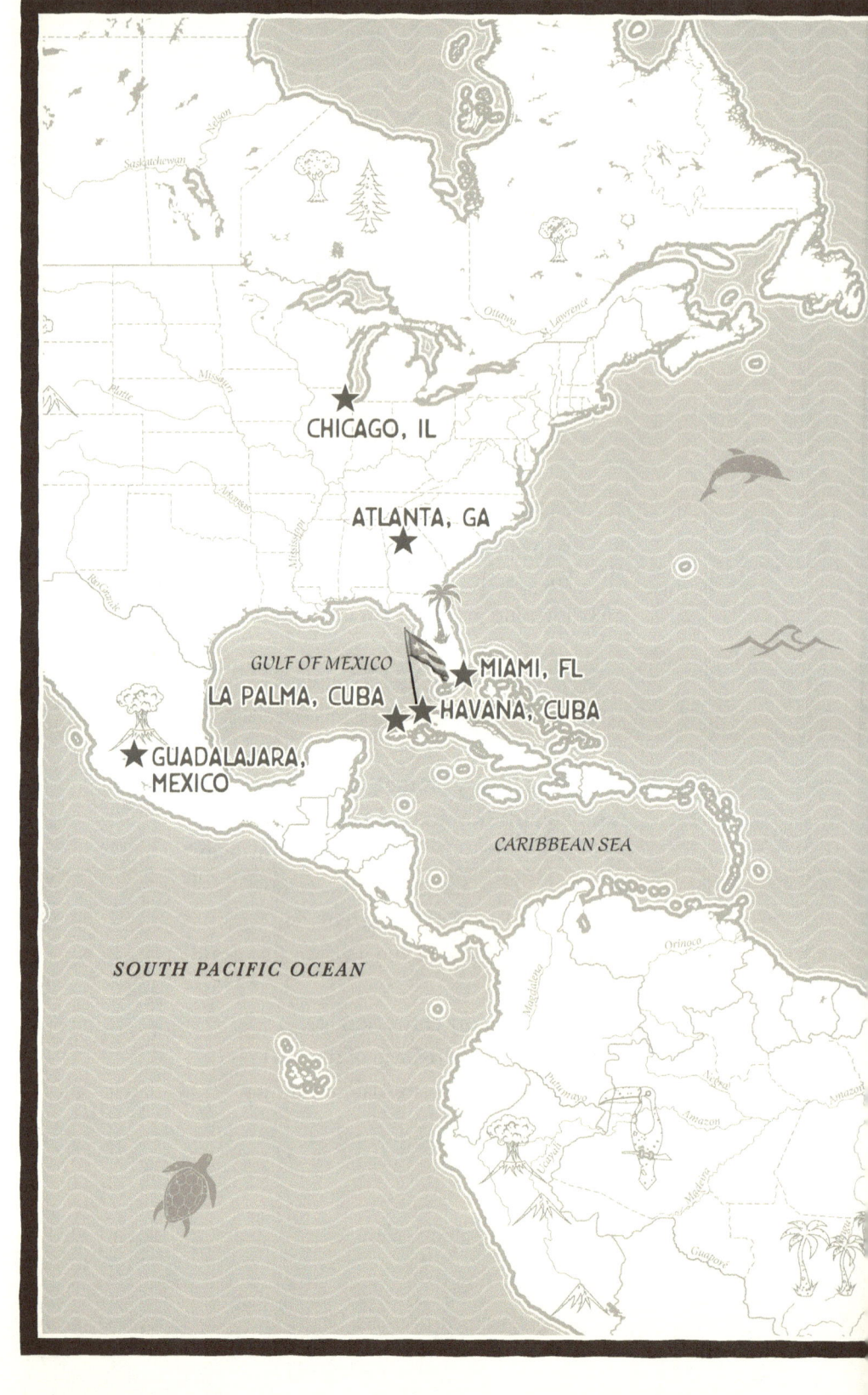

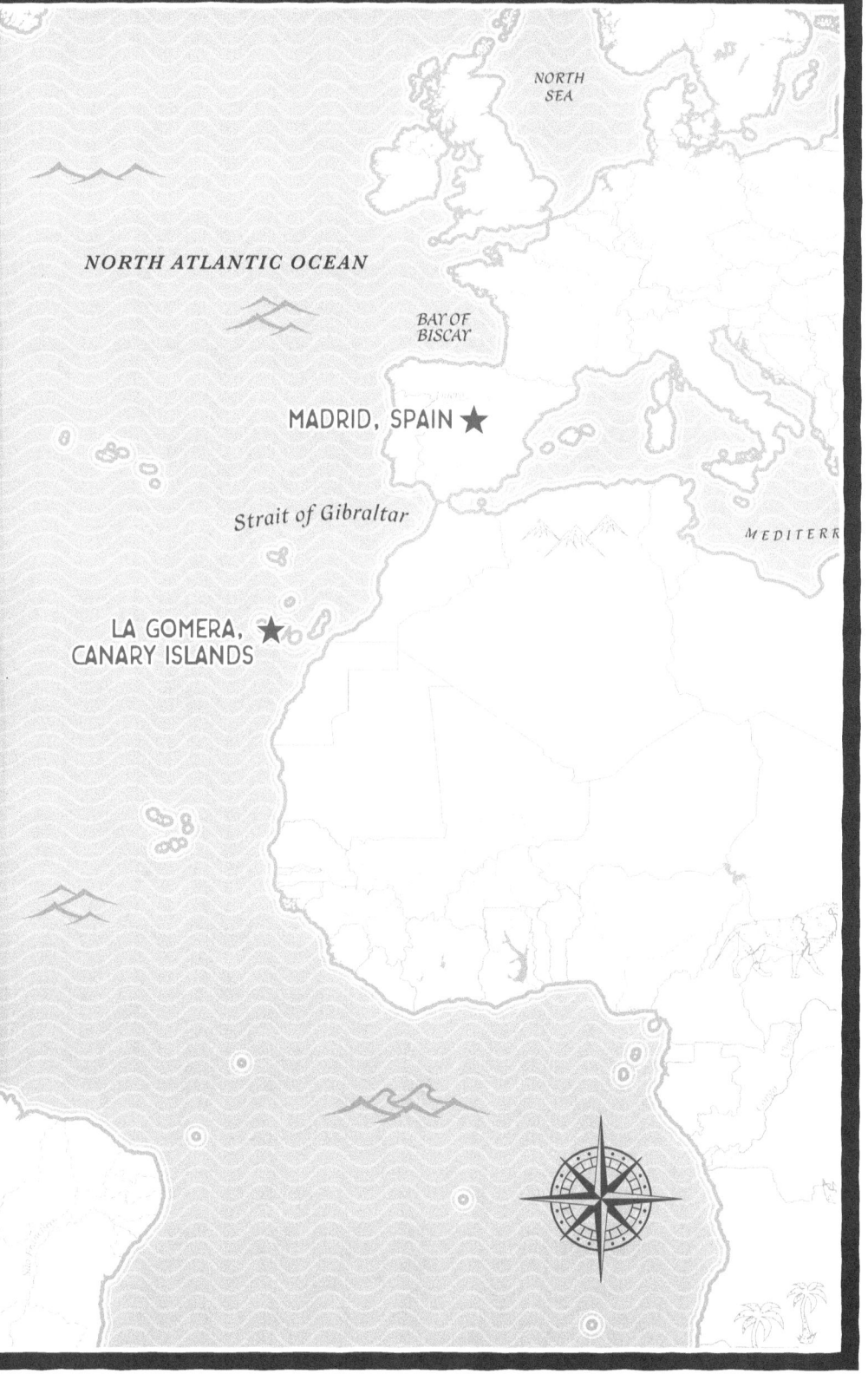

*"Life is not what one lived,
but rather what one remembers,
and how it is remembered
to tell the tale."*

— GABRIEL GARCÍA MÁRQUEZ

*"Yours is the light by
which my spirit's born:
— you are
my sun, my moon, and all my stars."*

— E.E. CUMMINGS

CHAPTER ONE

ATLANTA, GEORGIA

2022

"Cristina, Cristina..."

The door swung open with a bang, shaking the entire room. Cristina's mother, Lolita, stared down at her tear-stained face. Lolita took a deep breath and with a heavy heart reached out to place her hand gently on the soft fleece blanket draped over Cristina's shoulder. "How are you feeling?"

"Please, just leave," whispered Cristina. She lay curled up, facing the window, in the center of the twin bed. The early morning sunlight, streaming through the sheer Wedgewood-blue curtains of her childhood bedroom, blinded her exhausted eyes. She had barely slept, falling in and out of a restless sleep throughout the night. Cristina had been home six days, and each morning, she tried to go back to sleep at daybreak but never could. The moment she awoke, her mind began to ruminate and replay the conversations and arguments she had with the man she loved—which is what brought her back to her parent's home. *I just want to hide from the world*, thought Cristina.

It pained Lolita to see her oldest daughter crushed and wallowing in her anguish. She wanted so badly to be there for her daughter. Lolita never imagined Cristina would be back home at fifty-four years old. Certainly not under these life-shattering conditions. Over the past few years, Cristina had been filled with increasing resentment in her marriage to Andrés, and she finally reached a breaking point. The fights she and Andrés had were about nothing, and at the same time, they were about everything. They had grown apart. Even their daughter, Alejandra, wasn't enough of a reason to stay together—the fractures were far too deep. Though they both adored her, they knew it would be more harmful to stay in an empty marriage.

Sometimes, when you marry at a young age, you wake up one day next to a stranger you thought you knew, thought Cristina. She was filled with regret, depression, and confusion.

Andrés had checked out long before the relationship began to unravel. *Even when surrounded by family and friends*, Cristina thought, *feeling utterly alone in a marriage is the loneliest place in the world.*

Where will I go from here?

Am I ever going to feel okay again?

Lolita sat on the edge of the small bed, close to Cristina. She softly ran her fingers over Cristina's long dark hair, tucking a strand of hair behind her ear, just as she did when Cristina was a little girl.

"You can't stay in this bed all day," said Lolita.

"I will get up a little later," said Cristina, "I promise. I just can't right now."

"Can I bring you breakfast?"

"No, thank you. I'm not hungry—my stomach is in knots."

"How about some coffee or juice?"

"No, thank you. I just want to be alone. I will drink something when I get up," said Cristina.

"Do you feel like talking? It could help you start to untangle your thoughts and feelings," offered Lolita.

"I'm not ready to talk," said a distraught, broken-hearted Cristina.

Lolita wanted to be supportive but also give Cristina some space to think. Standing up from the bed, Lolita gently pulled the covers over Cristina. For a moment, she felt as if she were putting eight-year-old Cristina to bed. *Where did the time go? It feels like my little girl was sleeping in this bed just yesterday,* thought Lolita. She stepped out of the room and quietly closed the door.

Cristina turned to face the wall. Hanging perfectly in a straight line were the shelves with trophies and ribbons from her days competing in piano while at Peachtree Springs High School. She had started playing the piano when she was five years old and continued developing into an excellent pianist. When she was playing, she felt she could do anything and knew she would be successful in her life. This was the opposite of how she was feeling now—she felt more defeated than after any loss she'd had in a piano competition.

Cristina stared at the ceiling, racking her exhausted brain, trying to think back to when she and Andrés had started drifting apart. A few years ago, there had been several big disappointments in his life that cut him off at the knees. He had been up for a huge promotion at work—a position he had always dreamed of—only to find out his colleague would be awarded the position, even though Andrés was more qualified.

Andrés was in his early fifties but knew his opportunities would become more competitive as new, younger executives with Ivy League educations joined the company. This rejection devastated him, leading him to distance himself from Cristina.

Shutting someone out and making them feel invisible in a marriage is the most painful way to push them away, thought Cristina. She never thought this would happen to them. Andrés was her soulmate and her first love. *How could he throw their family away?* She tried and tried to make things right, but Andrés was unwilling and unable to meet her halfway. Sadly, this is where she found herself now—alone and heartbroken for the life she thought she would have.

After about an hour, Cristina knew she needed to get up. Drowning in her misery for almost a week would have to be enough for now. She had never been the type to dwell in her sadness without eventually coming up for air.

Grieving the end of her marriage had been overwhelming in the first few days back at home with her parents. Today, she was ready to get out of bed, shower, put on some fresh clothes, a little makeup, and finally leave her room to be with her family. Ever since she was a little girl, Cristina liked dressing up and looking pretty. In the middle of the storm, she needed something to feel familiar and comforting.

Cristina's closet in her and Andrés's home was a dream. Her stylish clothes and designer shoes had always been the envy of her friends. Cristina's classic pieces were timeless, and the colorful, trendy accessories she added each season kept her looks in step with the latest fashion. Her long locks were always styled in a modern, face-framing shape, making her appear years younger than her true age. Every few months, she would add caramel highlights for the warmth it gave her hair. For her signature look, she wore natural makeup, and a lovely scent would finish out the polished image she presented to the world.

When she left to spend a few days at her parents' house, Cristina had been in a panic, packing in a hurry. She didn't take any of her tailored shirts or trousers and left her elegant dresses behind. The expensive shoes she loved so much sat in her closet at home, untouched.

None of the material things mattered now. Her life was in pieces, and she couldn't fathom moving past her searing heartache. Cristina had only taken the most basic of pieces to get her through the next days or weeks—she wasn't sure how long she would be home, but it seemed that her simple, worn-in jeans, soft cotton T-shirts, and black leather booties would be fine to start figuring out her new life.

Without Andrés.

Cristina thought, *Enough of this. I need to pull myself together and get out of bed.* Pushing back the covers, she slowly sat up. Her emotions were a jumbled mess, and it felt incredibly strange to be in her childhood bedroom. With a downward gaze, she laced her fingers around the back of her neck, lifting her head and shrugging her shoulders in an attempt to work out the soreness she felt from the last week of lying in bed. As she moved her head around from side to side, the tension began to ease. She slipped her tired feet into sheepskin-lined slippers and shuffled to the bathroom to get ready for the day—which involved later facing the inevitable litany of questions from her concerned parents.

Cristina looked in the mirror. Her sallow complexion was in need of some serious care and attention. She looked into her own sad, brown eyes, and the reflection made her uneasy—she immediately looked away. After a moment, she looked up at her image once again and gently ran her hands along her forehead and cheeks, feeling the dryness of her face. In just a few days of not taking care of herself, her skin showed signs of how she felt—tired, dehydrated, and blemished. Cristina had not had a breakout on her face in months, and yet, there it was. She looked at the painful raised red bump on her chin and thought, *Great, my stress acne is back.*

Cristina's skincare routine had always been important to her, but she had abandoned it since arriving at her family home. It didn't matter to her when she had hit the pause button on her life. But now, she was ready to get back to a feeling of normalcy.

The tap water in the sink took a few minutes to warm enough to wash her face. Preferring it a little cool, Cristina kept her hand under the flow of the water until it felt comfortable. She tied her long hair into a ponytail and reached for her skincare products: these were small steps toward finding herself again.

Smelling the cleanser's fresh scent as she applied it in circular motions, sensing the cool water splashing on her face, feeling the slight tingle of the toner on the cotton ball as she covered her face with the solution, and allowing the richness of the day cream to soak into her skin—these were all part of Cristina's familiar, treasured routine. After a week of being checked out from her daily life, this ritual felt cleansing in more ways than one.

She bathed with the fragrant gels and skin-smoothing scrubs Lolita kept in the bathroom. She felt like a new woman. *Taking a hot shower and putting on a clean set of clothes can work wonders,* thought

Cristina. Her youthful complexion did not need much to radiate beauty. She carefully applied her simple makeup products—foundation, blush, mascara, and lip gloss—and the results were subdued and lovely. Cristina knew she needed to start somewhere on her road to recovery and move forward into her new life.

She slowly opened the door to her bedroom and looked around the dimly lit hallway leading to the kitchen. The rich smell of a *cafécito Cubano* brewing—Cuban espresso coffee—filled her senses, bringing back memories of her parents' daily, early-morning routine. They enjoyed sharing this special time and had done so for as long as she could remember. Cristina learned to drink *café con leche*—coffee with milk, when she was a small child, as is customary in Cuban homes. As she grew older, she always started her days with this strong, dark roast coffee, perfectly blended with cane sugar for a frothy shot. It was her reminder each morning of days gone by. This was the first time in more than a week that Cristina felt an almost imperceptible glimmer of hope, despite how she was feeling overall.

The voices in the kitchen grew louder as Cristina got closer. "Of all the places we have visited around the world, the sapphire blue ocean off the coast of Italy is the most beautiful water I have ever seen," said Lolita of their recent trip to Europe.

"It was spectacular. And the time we spent there was magical," added Roberto.

"Yes, it was a dream come true," said Lolita, as her words trailed off and concern crept into the tone of her voice. "You know, I'm worried about Cristina. She said she would be getting up when I went to her room, but that was a while ago." They had been waiting for her to leave her room all week. "Should I go check on her?"

Just as Roberto started to respond, Cristina appeared in the doorway. She quietly pulled the honey stone-washed pine dining chair back, sunk into the seat at the kitchen table, and let out a small sigh. Wishing she could take something to ease the emotional pain and discomfort she was feeling, Cristina knew nothing could help her—the only cure for this kind of pain was the passage of time.

"You look beautiful, my girl," said Roberto. "I'm happy you were able to get up today and join us for lunch. How are you feeling?"

"I'm not feeling great, but I'm better than I've been this past week," said Cristina.

"Your mother is making Monte Cristo sandwiches, and earlier, we cut up some melons and berries to serve as a side."

"That sounds good, but I am not even a little hungry," said Cristina. "I could smell *el cafécito* all the way from my room. Is there any left?"

"I will make a fresh pot for you," said Lolita. She lifted her hand to the top shelf of the pantry and reached for the round metal can of Café Bustelo with its unmistakable bright yellow label. Café Bustelo is the preeminent Latin espresso-style coffee, and every morning, as they enjoyed this tradition, it tasted like a little piece of heaven they so missed—the island home they left behind so many years ago, Cuba.

"Thank you, *Mami*. I have missed it so much—and today, I am looking forward to savoring it once again."

Lolita gently took the etched frosted glass demitasse cups from the kitchen cabinet and placed them into a small round silver frame with a curved handle. They had been a special gift to her from Cristina's travels throughout Latin America. Lolita poured the *café* over the cane sugar in the tiny cups and stirred until they had a light caramel brown foam over the top of the dark, rich, indulgent drink. Lolita placed the three matching silver mini saucers on an ornate pewter tray and carefully set the espresso-filled cups in the center of each one. She tenderly placed Cristina's cup on the table first. She would always be her baby, and it pained Lolita to see her suffering.

"*Gracias, Mami*. This smells so good," said Cristina. "As I think about it, this past week was the first time I remember going for more than a day or two without my *cafécito*."

"Roberto, please prepare a plate with some of the fresh fruit for Cristina as I finish the sandwiches for us," said Lolita.

"Coming right up. Anything for my sweetheart," said Roberto with a slight upturn of his lips. He loved having his children at home but wished Cristina's visit was under different circumstances.

"I am so thankful to have you as my parents," said Cristina, with tears welling at the corners of her eyes. She looked at her father and then at her mother with immense gratitude and love. Her emotions bubbled up. Before she knew it, they spilled out of her eyes onto the starched, white linen napkin she was holding. "You have been the most supportive and caring parents any child could dream of. How did Isabela, Alex, and I get so lucky?"

"Family has always been our number one priority. It was important to us that we raise our children in a loving home—nurturing them emotionally, spiritually, and physically. Our goal was to help them develop into healthy and happy adults," said Lolita.

"We are so pleased with the closeness you, your brother, and your sister share," said Roberto.

"It has been such a wonderful experience to grow up with my best friends and stay that way into adulthood," said Cristina. "They have stood beside me these last few weeks and months and helped me hold my sorrow as if in my hands, supported by their cupped hands around mine. I have appreciated it more than they could ever know," said Cristina.

"When your father and I came to this country, we were in our twenties. We left everything behind in our beautiful Cuba—known as the Pearl of the Antilles—to start our lives over again in the United States. We had big dreams. The courage and perseverance to achieve them came from the strength our family provided for one another."

"Our three children are our biggest joys. We weren't perfect, but we did the best we could. How could we not be here for you during this tumultuous time in your life?" said Roberto, grasping his daughter's hands in his.

"I truly don't know how I could get through this mess without your love and support. Your positive mindset gives me hope that perhaps one day, I will look back at all of the heartache and know that it served to heal and grow me in ways I can't appreciate now," said Cristina.

"When life presents us with circumstances and situations we never imagined encountering, our faith and our family will always get us through," said Lolita. "If I close my eyes and think back to our first day in the U.S., I can still remember the fear and sadness I felt knowing we would never return to our homeland. I had lost hope. And the resilience that had been my trademark quality had quietly faded away," said Lolita.

"My strongest allies were your father, my mother, Angela, and my brother, Emilio. We depended on each other and fully supported one another's hopes and dreams. My outlook began to change, and I realized we had been through so much for this opportunity—the future was ours to design," said Lolita. "Without the love and encouragement of our family, I'm not sure any of us would be where we are today."

"It has been such a gift to us, how the two of you have always put our family above everything else," said Cristina. "I know the decision to leave your home and move to another country—with a newborn baby and without knowing the language—must have been so scary and heart-wrenching."

"We did what we had to do for our future," said Roberto.

"Thank you for the many sacrifices you have both made to give us a charmed childhood and life. I love you very much," said Cristina.

As they were finishing lunch, Cristina glanced over to a round cherrywood table in the living room, and some new framed photos caught her eye. She noticed a sepia picture of a tall older man standing in a marble courtyard with one hand on his hip and the other by his side. Next to it was a pewter frame with a picture of a smiling young woman with several small children seated next to her and a baby boy on her lap.

Cristina didn't remember seeing these photos and asked, "Who are the man and woman in these pictures?" She made her way there and picked up the frame of the mother and her children. Cristina ran her finger along the bottom edge of the frame as if she were trying to feel all of the details from the moment the image was made. Noticing a small amount of dust on the tip of her finger, she lost herself in the photo. Just then, Roberto walked to where Cristina was standing, and with love in his voice, he said, "They are my mother and father. Your grandparents. You never got to meet them, but our family was full of love—despite many challenges and heartbreak. Your mother and I received two very small and damaged photos from a distant cousin a few years ago. We put them away but recently had them restored—I had not seen a picture of my parents in many, many years. It brought joy to my heart to see them again, when they were happy."

"I'm glad you were able to rescue these pictures that mean so much to you," said Cristina. "What were their names?"

"My father was Daniel and my mother was Gabriela."

"My grandfather was so handsome, and my grandmother was beautiful," said Cristina with a slight grin, revealing her charming dimples. "I see where you get your good looks from."

"I would love to see more pictures of our family from long ago and learn about those who came before us in Cuba," said Cristina curiously. She welcomed the distraction from her overwhelming emotions. "Can you tell me more about our family?"

"Well, let's go back to 1936...."

CHAPTER TWO

RÍO BLANCO,
PINAR DEL RÍO, CUBA

1936

The Cuban Royal Palms are one of the more than one hundred varieties of palm trees in Cuba. It is a special palm because it is the national tree of Cuba, and standing between forty to sixty feet tall, it is a majestic sight to behold. The tropical palms stand stately and regal, and the long fronds—the leaves of the tree—sway gently in the wind. The Royal Palms are often used to line grand avenues in large cities or small, winding country roads among Cuba's rolling hills. Daniel Martínez de Osaba was accustomed to seeing the towering trees as they were the centerpiece for the elegant landscape designs of his boyhood home.

Growing up on an expansive ranch in Río Blanco, in the province of Pinar del Río, Cuba, Daniel would later tell his children stories of how he would sit under the emerald green palms as a boy and daydream for hours of how his life would be when he grew up.

"The warm late-afternoon sun would peek through the leaves of the tall palms, and the gentle breeze would beckon me," said Daniel to his children, who listened to him intently. Daniel would sit on the velvety grass and lean against the smooth, flared, gray trunk. He would look up in wonder at the bright green canopy of luxurious leaves.

As he relaxed in the cool shade, he could see himself taking over his family's ranch. He'd have his own big family with a lot of children to run around and play in the wide-open spaces under the bright blue Caribbean sky. He knew that, eventually, they would be old enough to help him with the chores and that the ranch would not only help them make a living but provide fresh produce and dairy for the family year-round due to Cuba's tropical climate.

As a boy, Daniel had a thin frame. But he had grown into a tall and muscular young man. His piercing green eyes appeared to see straight through people. His skin was tanned from years of being outside, under the island sun. He was always either helping his father on the ranch or going to the beach with his friends.

Their favorite beach was Cayo Levisa for its clear, warm, turquoise water and the coral reef snorkeling. They never tired of seeing the black coral and the tropical fish in electric blue, yellow, and orange colors. The thirty-minute boat ride was relaxing, and the salty air energized them for their escapade. They knew that when they could see the white sand and coconut palms of the cay, they were only minutes from having a great time among friends. After spending a glorious day in this tropical paradise, Daniel and his friends always waited for the last scheduled boat to return to the mainland. They wanted to squeeze every last drop of sunshine and fun from their day.

At only nineteen, Daniel was offered the opportunity to have his own farm in La Palma, named La Paloma, and he welcomed the chance to have something of his own. He would miss his friends, but he was thankful for his good fortune to create a successful future.

A few months earlier, Daniel had met a pretty girl with angelic features who had come to visit his home. She was tall for a girl, but she was as graceful as a ballerina on a grand stage when she moved.

Daniel swooned when she walked past him with the fragrant scent of sweet honeysuckle.

He was instantly smitten.

"*Hola* Daniel," said the older woman who was with this beautiful girl. "I've known you since you were a baby, and you have turned into such a handsome young man. I'm so happy to see you all grown up."

"*Gracias*. It is nice to see you too."

"Daniel, this is my granddaughter, Gabriela Azqui," said her grandmother, Juliana.

"*Hola*," said Daniel. Gabriela timidly smiled and tilted her head to one side.

"Would you like a glass of cold lemonade?" Daniel asked. "My mother just made it with the lemons from our yard."

"*Sí, gracias*," said a shy Gabriela—her voice quavering with nerves. She lowered her gaze and clasped her trembling hands behind her back. Daniel could see her enchanting, light brown eyes as she slightly lifted her face to meet his. Daniel invited her into the kitchen, where he glanced at the cobalt blue ceramic pitcher on the counter for an instant before fixing his gaze back on her.

The ice cubes clinked when he placed them in their glasses. As he poured the sweet, fresh-squeezed lemonade, it rushed over the ice until it nearly spilled over the rim. Daniel carefully picked up Gabriela's glass and extended his arm to give her the drink. She delicately placed her long, manicured fingers around it and took a small sip.

"This is very good. Thank you," said Gabriela.

"It's my favorite!" Daniel responded.

A soft smile appeared on her face, and Daniel noticed a hint of a sparkle in her eyes.

Gabriela had taken a bus to the town center today with her grandmother. She had been looking for knitting yarn in yellow and light blue for a baby blanket she was making for her neighbor. She also needed several spools of cross-stitch thread in brighter colors—pink, coral, and turquoise for another project, one she was going to keep for herself. They had stopped by Daniel's home to say hello, but also,

Gabriela's grandmother was coming to pick up several boxes with sewing and crafting supplies that Miriam, Daniel's mother, no longer needed.

"*Muchas gracias.* This means so much to me," said Gabriela's grandmother.

"You are most welcome. I am happy that I could share those with you. I know you will make some wonderful things for your family."

While the women made small talk, Daniel and Gabriela were chatting and had almost finished their refreshing drinks. Daniel liked to make her laugh and didn't want her to leave. Gabriela had opened up a little and was starting to warm up to Daniel. They both secretly hoped they could see each other again, but how?

"It's time for us to leave, Gabriela," said her grandmother. "We need to be at the bus stop right at 3:35, or we will have to wait until 4:15 for the next bus."

"Okay, *Abuela.*"—Grandmother, said Gabriela.

Daniel's mother and Gabriela's grandmother embraced for a moment as she was preparing to leave. They both reached down to pick up the boxes at the same time and bumped their heads. As they stood up, they chuckled.

The boxes weren't heavy, but Gabriela offered to carry one home for her grandmother. They all said their goodbyes, and Gabriela and her grandmother were on their way home.

Daniel had never felt this way before. He wanted to leave with them so he and Gabriela could continue their conversation. He knew he couldn't do that, so he had an idea. He changed out of his cowboy boots and into a comfortable pair of leather sandals and walked the two kilometers to the bus terminal.

"Can I please see a copy of the bus schedule going to San Rafael?"

"Yes, here you are," said the friendly woman behind the counter. "On the left side, you will see the name of the destination. In the center column, the time of departure is listed. The last column on the right has the corresponding bus number you will take. Do you have any questions?"

"How much is the bus fare?" asked Daniel.

"The bus to San Rafael is *cinco centavos*—five cents in each direction."

"Thank you for this information," Daniel said excitedly.

He turned and walked home with a wide grin on his face that he couldn't conceal.

As he approached the house, he saw his mother and a friend talking and laughing while sitting in the new white rocking chairs on the freshly painted white wraparound porch. Miriam liked a crisp, clean look, and everything she had selected for the porch was in shades of white—the planters hanging from the top railing, overflowing with bright fuchsia hibiscus flowers; the large white ceramic pots with dark green cone-shaped topiary trees on either side of the front door; the white wicker set of armchairs with small tables on the far side of the porch; and all of the decorations.

The late afternoon sun was setting, and the golden light bathed the front porch. The bright green freshly cut grass smelled of earth and spring, and the intense colors of the tropical flowers in the yard came alive this time of year. The women were leisurely sipping mojitos in tall, etched crystal glasses and reminiscing about their time as majorettes in middle school.

"I remember the days in sixth grade, spending long hours after school practicing our baton-twirling routines for the grand parades," said Daniel's mother as she smiled with nostalgia. "Time goes by much too quickly."

"Yes, that was such a beautiful time in our lives. I will never forget the uniforms we wore—the navy-blue swing skirt, the crisp, white, short-sleeved button-up shirt, the white cap with navy trim, and the white knee-high boots. We were thrilled to be chosen to lead our school. The selection committee only chose one principal majorette and one backup majorette from each school. How lucky were we to be selected for the two spots? Do you remember the best part of that uniform?" asked Aurora with a sheepish grin.

"I do," said Miriam, smiling at the thought. "It was the amazing white cape that had a single clear button at the neck and navy-blue trim all the way around. I called it *mi capa mágica*—my magical cape. It flowed freely as we marched ahead of the band, keeping them in rhythm with each step and movement of the baton. I can still hear the horns blaring and the snare of the drums playing loudly in the streets as the parade route wound around the main streets of Pinar del Río."

"I can hear it just as clearly as if it had happened yesterday. Here's to the adventures we have shared and the many more that await us," said Aurora, raising her near-empty glass and toasting with joy.

"*Salud*"—cheers, said Miriam and raised her glass to meet Aurora's. Mojitos were Miriam's favorite cocktail, and anytime she had visitors, she would prepare them using the Cuban gold standard for rum: Bacardi. She placed the sugar, lime juice, and mint leaves at the bottom of each glass. Next, she would muddle the ingredients together until the mixture released its fragrant notes. Once combined, she would add the rum and ice and pour the mixture into a shaker, shaking it for a few minutes, making it ice cold. The last step was to pour it back into the glasses and top them with soda water. It was a refreshing mixed drink invented in *La Habana* in the early 1930s and was still incredibly popular.

The sweet aroma of the mint leaves always brought to mind the first time she tasted this delightful elixir. Her husband, Miguel, had raved about a new drink called a mojito after attending a dinner at the Masonic Lodge in Pinar del Río. He had never tasted such an interesting combination of flavors and was excited to share this discovery with his wife. They quickly learned how to prepare them and enjoyed sharing them with each other and their friends. Mojitos were always a crowd-pleaser.

The rocking chairs, moving back and forth rhythmically on the solid wooden boards, had a comforting quality—they were perfect for entertaining friends.

"Daniel, this is my friend Aurora from the Río Blanco Women's Association. We serve on the same volunteer committee for historical preservation. Where have you been?" his mother asked.

She noticed the funny look on his face. She wondered if this had anything to do with Gabriela.

"Well, I like Gabriela and would like to get to know her. I've never met anyone like her," said Daniel.

"Son, I could see from how you behaved when she was here that you were fond of her," said Daniel's mother with a knowing smile. "I can understand why you feel that way. She is a beautiful girl and seems kind and caring."

"Well," said Daniel, "you are right. As soon as Gabriela and her grandmother left this afternoon to go to the bus terminal, I went to get information about the bus schedule to San Rafael to see her. Can you please tell me how to get to the house where Gabriela lives?" Daniel asked his mother.

"Yes, once Aurora finishes her visit, I will go inside and write it down for you."

"¡*Gracias*! I would like to go this weekend," said Daniel as he smiled and walked past them to open the door into the house.

He now knew which bus he needed to take to get to Gabriela's home to see her again, and soon, he would be getting directions to her house. Daniel felt nervous and excited at the same time and knew he needed to do this.

For the next weeks and months, Daniel and Gabriela spent a lot of time together, getting to know each other. Every evening after working long hours on the farm, Daniel looked forward to seeing Gabriela. She would greet him at the door, and they would spend hours talking and laughing late into the night. Today, when the front door swung open, her grandmother was standing there and welcomed him. "*Hola*, Daniel, come in. Gabriela is out back in the garden, gathering a handful of gladioluses for an arrangement."

"*Gracias*," said Daniel. He continued walking without stopping until he reached the door leading to the patio.

Daniel wrapped his hand around the door handle to step outside. As soon as the door cracked open, he could hear a beautiful melody wafting through the air. It was a woman's voice singing *Aquellos Ojos Verdes*—"Those Green Eyes." The song was a beautiful bolero that had recently been released on Cuban radio. It reminded Gabriela of the green eyes she was so enamored with.

"Gabriela," Daniel called out.

The singing stopped, and Gabriela turned around from where she was pruning the leaves of her yellow and lavender flowers.

"*Hola*, I didn't know you were here," said Gabriela. "I am picking flowers for an arrangement that will welcome guests as they come into the house."

"Those are beautiful. Was that you singing?" he asked with a questioning look.

"Yes, I like to sing when no one is around," said a shy Gabriela.

"You have a lovely voice. I had no idea you could sing like that," Daniel said with a surprised look on his face.

"Thank you. I love to sing but am embarrassed for anyone to hear me," said Gabriela with a coy smile and a glance from the corner of her eye. She picked up her basket full of colorful flowers and started walking toward the house. Gabriela turned to glance at Daniel as he followed her inside.

Gabriela's grandmother was a gifted seamstress. She was sitting at her sewing machine in the corner of the living room, weaving her magic. *Zzzzzz . . . zzzzzz . . .* with each tap of her foot on the pedal, the motor buzzed as the needle pierced the silky, midnight-blue fabric. The gown she was making cascaded from the sewing table onto the floor, with the appearance of a rich, dark, metallic liquid spilling out of an antique glass bottle.

The exquisite cloth had been hand-loomed in Andalucía, Spain and had been specially ordered for the first lady of San Rafael, Gloria Castillo de Sandoval. The style she had selected—a cinched waist and an off-the-shoulder neckline—would flatter her hourglass figure.

She would wear a delicate, dove-grey *mantilla*—an intricate lace shawl—over her head that would flow from her light brown, wavy hair onto her smooth porcelain shoulders. Señora Castillo de Sandoval would make her grand entrance on the arm of her husband, *el alcalde*— Mayor Mauricio Sandoval. All eyes would be on her in this stunning, form-fitting gown at next month's charity ball in the neighboring village, benefiting *el Hogar de Niños de San Emiliani*—the San Emiliani Children's Home. It would be the social event of 1936.

Señora Castillo de Sandoval shared with Gabriela's grandmother that the orphanage had been founded by the sitting First Lady of San Rafael in 1904, Elena Vázquez de Moreno. As head of the organizing committee, she had led the fundraising efforts over several years. Once construction was nearing completion, Señora Vázquez de Moreno had the honor of naming the home that would house, feed, educate, and care for eighty abandoned children. After weighing several options, she ultimately chose to honor San Emiliani, the patron saint of orphans.

The mayor's wife had started the orphanage with great enthusiasm and was fortunate to have the unconditional support of her husband. It was a project close to her heart, as she had once been an orphan herself in one of the most notoriously awful orphanages in Cuba. Just the thought of those days sent shivering chills down Señora Vázquez de Moreno's spine, and she would have to choke back tears—though often, a single hot tear would escape and roll down her cheek. No child should ever have to endure such significant trauma upon their already broken hearts.

Deep in thought, Señora Vázquez de Moreno's memories of her time at the orphanage flooded her mind. It was an awful place—sterile, yet filthy—lacking any semblance of care or love.

She scratched the back of her neck as she recalled the stiff collared shirts all the children were forced to wear. The first goal was to strip them of their identities by forcing them to wear generic clothes. There were no sizes, and the children drowned in the oversized clothing, like potato sacks hanging from their skinny frames. The children were made to feel unimportant and ugly.

Señora Vázquez de Moreno was a tenacious woman, determined to turn those terrible years into something good, something that could change children's lives for the better. She worked tirelessly, healing her own deep wounds along the way, and was finally able to see the purpose in her pain and bring the dream of a more nurturing orphanage to fruition.

The opening of the orphanage in February of 1904 was a tremendous success. The San Emiliani Children's Home welcomed thirty-three children to their new home.

When each child arrived, they were assigned two sets of clothing—black pants, white shirts, and simple, two-piece blue pajamas with plain white undergarments. In addition, they received a new last name, Vázquez, to give them a sense of belonging.

Although the children would grow up without their natural families, they would eventually come to embrace the ones they would build at San Emiliani. They readily settled into their daily routines. Most came from unstable and grievous backgrounds and appreciated the structure and attention they received from the caring staff, even if they didn't outwardly show it. The orphanage had been designed to feel like a real home and not an institution.

The dining room had tall ceilings that magnified the low hush of the small voices waiting in line to fill their trays. Each child carried their tray to their assigned seat. Instead of the long tables that were usually found in institutional settings, ten round tables with eight seats each had been placed throughout the room. This layout was more conducive for the children to feel they were dining in a family setting. Every opportunity to break the children into smaller groups was a chance for them to be among friends. She so badly wanted this because she had felt so alone.

Señora Vázquez de Moreno would watch the children quietly talking and laughing as they ate their meals, and it warmed her heart.

The wooden desks and chairs in the classrooms were arranged by size, facing the black chalkboard on the front wall. In the center of the building, at the top of the pine staircase, were the ten bedrooms. The boys' rooms were to the left and the girls' to the right. Each of the bunk beds had one pillow and a white blanket. The linens were washed once a week, as was the laundry. A pile of clean clothes was dropped at the foot of each bed. The children over the age of four were expected to fold and put their clothes away in their assigned drawer in each room's small wooden dresser.

Señora Vázquez de Moreno wanted the home to truly feel comfortable to the children who had already suffered immeasurable loss at such a young age. She knew the sadness of being a child alone in this world. Her parents both died of yellow fever when she was only six years old. With no relatives to take her into their homes, she was relegated to a strict, dark, and depressing children's home on the outskirts of San Rafael. By the time she was eighteen years old, she left the orphanage, hoping for a better life. As she grew older, she dreamed of changing the terrible conditions there for future generations of children, never imagining she would grow up to take on a position of prominence that would enable her to do just that.

Several years later, Señora Vázquez de Moreno suffered a terrible fall down the wooden staircase at the very orphanage she founded. After a few days, the injuries to her brain remained severe. At forty-two years old, she passed away peacefully in her bed, surrounded by her grieving family. Within a few short years, San Emiliani fell into great disrepair without her guidance and oversight. It was once again the awful, lonely place in which she had grown up.

Gabriela's grandmother thought about everything she had learned about the orphanage and was honored to make the gown for the mayor's wife for the upcoming fundraiser.

Gabriela rinsed the flowers with cool water in the kitchen sink and laid them out to dry on a large, light blue cotton dish towel. She reached above the sink to pull down the large, white ceramic pitcher she would use for her arrangement.

"Let me get that for you," said an attentive Daniel.

"*Gracias, mi amor.*" Thank you, my love, said Gabriela.

He placed it on the counter and watched as Gabriela selected the flowers, one by one. She put together a lovely design to display at the entrance to her home. Daniel helped her carry it and gently lowered it onto the small wooden table. They both stepped back to admire it.

"I am so proud of you. You are so creative," Daniel gushed.

"*Gracias.* I've always loved beautiful flowers," said Gabriela.

She put the finishing touches on the arrangement and grabbed Daniel's hand to lead him back to the patio. They stopped for a moment and watched her grandmother work with the breathtaking blue fabric.

Gabriela squeezed Daniel's hand, and they continued outside, where they would sit on the garden swing. The more time they spent together, the more they realized how much they loved being with each other.

Before they knew it, they had fallen deeply in love. Daniel knew she was the one for him, and he couldn't leave her behind. He needed to ask her to be his wife before he moved to the new farm, La Paloma. He never imagined that he would meet the love of his life just a few months before moving away.

When he proposed, she was thrilled. She accepted his proposal with tears of joy. She looked forward to being Daniel's wife and to building a beautiful life together.

They planned a simple wedding in the backyard of Daniel's family home. They both wanted something intimate, so they only invited their closest friends and family. Daniel's mother made all of the arrangements and didn't miss a single detail.

Gabriela wore a white, simple bias-cut wedding gown made of a smooth silk satin with a modest V-neck and a rhinestone belt that cinched her slender waist. Her grandmother had spent long hours at the sewing machine to ensure it would be perfect for Gabriela on her special day. The delicate freshwater-pearl rosary Gabriela's grandmother had given her was gracefully wrapped around her bouquet of coral and white rose blossoms.

When Gabriela appeared at the end of the aisle in the garden, Daniel couldn't take his eyes off her. She was radiant. Gabriela took each step to reach Daniel with elegance and grace and a slight smile parted her rose-tinted lips. He was dashingly handsome in navy blue linen trousers and an untucked traditional white *guayabera*—a casual, short-sleeve cotton or linen Cuban shirt with sections of tiny pleats down the front and back and four patch pockets on the front, two near the chest area and two along the waistline.

The vibrant colors and intense fragrance of the tropical flowers made for a beautiful backdrop. They exchanged their vows and promised to love and cherish each other until the very end.

After a traditional Catholic ceremony, the priest declared, "You are now husband and wife. You may kiss your bride." With anticipation, Daniel lifted the white tulle and lace veil. They embraced and shared a sweet kiss before joining their guests for a wonderful reception. It was an unforgettable evening of music, dancing, and delicious food surrounded by their loved ones.

Gabriela and Daniel had chosen romance classics and island tunes from legendary artists, such as Ignacio Villa, Esther Borja, and Tito Gómez. The music reverberated into the night sky and mingled with the luminescent stars. It was a crystal-clear sky, and there were millions of visible twinkling stars. As Gabriela and Daniel danced to their favorite song, they looked up into the night sky and were drawn to the North Star. It was bright and beautiful, and they realized they had each found their own north star in each other.

As newlyweds, Daniel and Gabriela were excited to start their new life at La Paloma. They made the three-hour move to their new farm and felt on top of the world. They had the freedom to decide which crops to plant and harvest and what kind and how many farm animals they would raise. They were ready to work hard and build the life they imagined.

"I know our home is modest, but I hope to one day build us a big house on this property. We will be happy here, and this is where we will raise our family," said Daniel.

Gabriela felt her heart skip a beat. She could feel the love Daniel had for her, and she loved the anticipation he had for their future together.

CHAPTER THREE

LA PALMA, PINAR DEL RÍO, CUBA
1953

Daniel and Gabriela relished having a large, growing family. Their cozy home was made of concrete cinder blocks with white wooden boards neatly arranged horizontally around the outside and a palm leaf thatched roof. Gabriela loved the togetherness, and although it wasn't big or fancy, there was so much joy in that small home she and Daniel had built together.

Gabriela was lost in thought as she washed the lunchtime dishes, her hands submerged in the warm soapy water. She caught a reflection of herself in the window, dried her hands, and tidied her chestnut brown hair. It had loosened from her bun during a morning full of chores and now framed her beautiful face with soft waves. Gabriela was almost full-term, but one would barely know as she was tall and slender. She was ready to hold her new baby.

Gabriela and Daniel had already chosen a name for this baby. If it were a girl, it would be María de los Angeles, meaning María of the Angels. If they had a boy, his name would be Miguel in memory of Daniel's father.

Gabriela often thought about Miguel's courage to leave his family while he was still a very young man and travel 3,600 miles across the Atlantic Ocean for an opportunity to earn a living and build a life in Cuba. Miguel left his family in the summer of 1914 on the island of La Gomera, one of the Canary Islands belonging to Spain, but just off the coast of Morocco in Western Africa. He boarded a cargo ship as a stowaway to work in a sugarcane field on a plantation close to Havana.

Miguel was a force to be reckoned with. He was a towering man with broad shoulders, big green eyes, and a scruffy beard. His wavy black hair was just past his shoulders, and his long, thick eyelashes curled upward and skimmed his eyelids.

He appeared much older than his sixteen years, but he still had this boyish charm about him.

He embarked on this journey with only a red canvas bag he carried on his shoulder, with some essential things he would need and a large container of fresh water. It was not easy for Miguel to carry it and sneak onto the ship without drawing attention to himself. He knew that he could survive for several days at a time without food, but he couldn't go without water for very long—he would ration it to last him for the entire trip.

The voyage to arrive at *El Puerto de La Habana* took thirty-one days but felt like an eternity. He had to stay out of sight in the damp, dark, and musty bowels of the ship—hiding inside or behind containers, engine rooms, and tanks, or concealed behind fake walls. The stench was not so bad for the first few days of the trip, but each day after that, it grew increasingly putrid. This was where all of the garbage and rotting food was stored. It made his eyes water. Some nights, just as he was trying to get comfortable and fall asleep, the rolling swell of the ocean would create large, angry waves that would batter the sides of the ship, tossing him around. The old wooden vessel's creaking boards felt and sounded like they would come apart every time a new wave would dwarf the ship.

Each time this happened, Miguel was frightened because he was sure no one knew he was there or could help him if he got hurt. He was able to get a few hours of sleep on other nights when the sea was calm—on those nights, there was barely any movement, and he would rest as best he could.

In the middle of the night, he would sneak to the lowest-level open deck, when no one was awake, to get some fresh air. He would stare off in the distance, looking for lights or signs of land but only saw the dark sky and ocean—on clear nights, he was in awe of a sky full of the brightest stars he had ever seen.

The ocean was so peaceful, and the clean salty air filled his lungs with every breath. Somehow, it made him feel it was cleansing away some of the foul odors that had attacked his senses for days.

He would crouch down and look around before sneaking back inside and quietly opening the door to the galley, tiptoeing to see if any leftovers had not been thrown away. He had luck some nights and would find half-eaten ham or pork sandwiches and soups that were now cold. He liked when he would find desserts. Miguel had a sweet tooth, and he knew the sugar would give him the additional energy he needed. His favorite was *la torta de vilana*, a sweet cake that was perfectly dense but not dry—made with raisins, almonds, cinnamon, and lemon zest—a delicious and filling treat.

The rich cakes were cut into smaller rectangles and brought onto the ship in large covered trays. They were stacked in the back of the galley to save space and could last several weeks in airtight containers, making them a good choice for a long trip across the ocean.

It reminded him of the holiday cakes his *abuela* would bake in La Gomera with dried fruits and nuts. He had fond memories of sitting at her small kitchen table and listening to her recount stories of how she and his grandfather met. When Miguel would visit her modest home, the smell of pastries, *bizcochos*—fabulous cakes with homemade meringue icing, and cookies of different flavors—filled the air. His favorites were the lemon and the orange blossom ones. She showed her love by indulging him with a delectable assortment of all his favorites. He treasured the time they spent together. They always laughed, and she enjoyed seeing Miguel unsure when deciding on which he would eat first. Her eyes would crinkle when she smiled. He missed those carefree days.

On the nights he could find some food, it gave him the strength he needed because he didn't know when he would get to eat again.

The days were long, and the nights were longer.

Miguel had brought a small, white pocket calendar with him that had the month and days in August of 1914 printed in red. Every day, he would scribble a big black X to mark the passing of another day.

On the thirty-first day, Miguel was awakened very early by a tremendous jolt and the terrifying sound of crashing into something solid and unforgiving. He wasn't sure what the ship had struck, but he immediately knew he had to get to a higher deck in case it started to take on water, as he was sure he would drown.

He dressed quickly and threw a few things into his red canvas bag. He feared being seen, but he feared drowning even more, so he was very deliberate in trying not to be noticed as he moved toward the staircase leading to the uncovered deck. To his surprise, there were not many people around. He quickly walked to the starboard side of the ship and felt like a fool. He had been keeping track of the days but failed to realize how early the ship would dock on this trip. Today was their last morning.

The ship's crew had dropped the massive anchor by pier number 54 in *el Puerto de la Habana*. It made a terribly loud noise as they started to unwind the anchor line, made of chain, rope, and cable, to lower it into the harbor. They were using immense white ropes to secure the ship, and once they carried out a few safety checks, the crew would be allowed to disembark. Miguel stayed on the deck and did his best to remain inconspicuous. He kept his head down and tried not to look around too much. He waited with great anticipation for the gangway door to open. After three long weeks in hiding, he was in desperate need of a shower and a proper hot meal—not to mention a full night's sleep.

He could see *el Castillo de la Real Fuerza*—the oldest fort in the Americas. It had been built in the harbor in the late sixteenth century, and Miguel was ecstatic to lay eyes on it. It meant he had arrived safely at his new home.

Life on the plantation was more work than he had fathomed. The vast size of the property reached almost a thousand acres—approximately three-fourths of this was taken between the fields used to plant and harvest the sugarcane. This was a labor-intensive process that was done by planting the individual stalks by hand. One acre could yield up to twenty-five tons of sugarcane with each harvest.

The remaining land held the massive *azucarero central*—a sugar mill where all of the crops were processed for distribution as granulated sugar, molasses, and other products, such as paper and cardboard. The sugarcane was loaded onto the waiting ox carts pulled by the mammoth, muscular animals and deposited at the entrance to the mill for processing. Although the planting and harvesting were carried out from sunrise to sunset, the mill operations ran continuously, day and night, to stay ahead of the harvest's perishable nature every day of the year. The crops needed to be processed within seven hours of harvesting, and the plantation had a rigorous plan in place to ensure they maximized each harvest. Unlike other crops, sugarcane could not be planted with seeds and stored for months.

The fertile soil of Cuba's subtropical climate produced a plentiful supply of sugarcane between October and April. The owners brought in thousands of workers and gave them three meals a day and housing on the plantation. The accommodations were rustic, but at least Miguel knew he had a place to lay his head at the end of another long day. This ensured the workers would be close enough to walk to the front entrance within a few minutes. They were also all living together, and by building a community, it encouraged loyalty, as this became more than just a job.

Miguel worked harder than anyone else. He appreciated the opportunity to earn a living and make something of himself. He was assigned to work with one of the groups of men that harvested the sugarcane stalks. He was strong and agile and would consistently complete his rows before anyone else. Miguel would go to the next row without taking a break and continue cutting with the large machete needed to slice through the thick, fibrous stalks.

Within a short time, the owners took notice of his work ethic and gave him more responsibility. Over the next few years, Miguel continued to excel in his roles. He was promoted several times—from field worker to crew manager to assistant manager of the field workers division. After a few months in his new position, the other assistant manager was involved in an accident while showing a new employee how to prepare and add the sugarcane stalks to the processing mill. The rolled-up sleeve of his white shirt got caught on the machinery, and he lost his right arm to his elbow. It had been a gruesome scene. He would not be returning to work for many months.

The owners had to decide on who would best replace him. The group of field workers had grown to four hundred, and although Miguel was only thirty years old, his leadership had guided the company to tremendous growth and profitability. He was promoted to general manager, and they chose another two highly experienced managers to take the assistant manager roles.

A few years had passed, and now Miguel was in his mid-thirties and had gotten married. Within a few years, he and his wife Miriam started a family of their own. Their children, Daniel and Raquel, were the center of their world. After working at the plantation for close to twenty years, Miguel and Miriam decided to raise their family in the country where they could own land. They purchased a seventy-acre ranch in Río Blanco with farmland, pastures, gardens, cattle, and other farm animals. Daniel learned how to plant and harvest crops, raise and take care of animals, and prepare the meats, cheeses, milk, produce, and other products to be sold at the market or wholesale.

Miguel's efforts were richly rewarded, and he built his family the home of their dreams on the property. He lived to the age of seventy-three and was an admirable man who left a remarkable legacy.

He was the bravest man Gabriela had ever known. If her baby were a boy, she would consider it to be an honor for him to carry on his grandfather's name.

Gabriela rubbed her hand across her belly as she stood there in the kitchen, grateful for the new baby that would come into their lives. She knew in her heart this baby was to be a gift from God. All of her children were, but this new life was somehow special. At thirty-six years old, she already had the big family she had dreamed of as a little girl. With six boys and three girls, this new baby would complete their brood, which made her happy. At the same time, her mind drifted to what Dr. Enrique Rodriguez told her the last time she saw him. He had been there to care for all her children, but Gabriela had been very sick during the third trimester of her last pregnancy with Ramon, and the doctor had told her it was best not to carry another pregnancy.

Test results had revealed Gabriela suffered from decreased kidney function. Unfortunately, the symptoms of this condition are sometimes absent until it is too late, and the kidneys are no longer filtering waste out of the body.

Dr. Rodriguez warned Gabriela that it would be dangerous for the baby, as well as for her. Because Gabriela was feeling well overall, it was something that she quickly pushed out of her thoughts, and she went back to her work. Although she didn't always follow the advice Dr. Rodriguez gave her, she was woefully sad knowing this new baby would be the only one of her children he wouldn't care for. Dr. Rodriguez had been Gabriela's doctor since she was a child. He was a middle-aged gentleman then, but many years had passed. He practiced a healthy lifestyle, eating a wholesome diet and staying active. Still, a few months ago, just after turning seventy-three, he suffered a cerebral hemorrhage and died at the very clinic where he had saved so many others.

Though Gabriela was remarkably bright and loved to learn, she had only attended school until the fifth grade, when she left to help raise her three brothers and four sisters. As the eldest in her family, Gabriela helped with the chores from the time she was eight years old. Once she turned ten, she learned how to make simple meals to feed her family while her mother washed clothes, cleaned their home, and made sure all the things required to keep a large family in order were done. Gabriela didn't fully understand the consequences of not taking care of her health and avoiding another pregnancy.

As she finished her morning chores inside their humble but comfortable home, Gabriela loved watching the scene that unfolded as she looked out through the small kitchen window onto the sprawling green fields. Her children were playing in the midday spring sunshine. She smiled as Rolando and Rigoberto took the younger girls, Georgina and Elisa, by their little hands and formed a circle. Skipping around happily, they danced around and around while singing the traditional Cuban nursery rhyme, *A la Rueda Rueda*—Ring Around the Rosie.

A la rueda rueda, de pan y canela; dame un besito y vete pa la escuela
Y si no quieres ir; acuéstate a dormir

Giggling, they dropped to the ground like ragdolls when the song ended. They jumped back up yelling, "Again! Again!" repeating this until they were completely worn out. Gabriela so loved seeing their pink cheeks and hearing their silly laughter bouncing in the air. Their sweet voices made Gabriela's heart happy. Her children were everything to her.

Knowing her outdoor chores awaited her, she gathered the pile of dirty clothes that needed to be washed. As she stepped through the old screen door, the bright noon sun shone down to warm her fair complexion. Gabriela's skin was smooth and luminous. Even after having nine children, she remained youthful. She could pass as her older children's sister.

Daniel helped by carrying and pouring the water she had heated on the old gas stove into the washing vat when he was on his way to the barn.

"I am so lucky to have you, Daniel," Gabriela said as he started down the path to care for Martina, the family pet rabbit, and her new family.

Daniel turned to face her. With contentment in his voice, he said, "No, I am the fortunate one. You and our children are my heart, and I could not ask God for anything more." The sun made his eyes glisten as he lovingly winked at Gabriela and turned around to continue his walk to the barn. Gabriela still felt like a schoolgirl in love when Daniel looked at her with his enchanting green eyes, like she was the only woman in the world.

Gabriela heard Georgina and Elisa's sweet voices in the distance and smiled from ear to ear when she saw her beautiful girls excitedly running toward her. They raced to see who could hug their mother first. The girls wove themselves through Gabriela's legs, and all three started to laugh. Gabriela reached down and cupped the tiny faces of her girls in her hands. Their flushed faces were filled with loving adoration for their mother. It warmed Gabriela's heart to see her two little girls, so full of love and whimsy.

Just when she least expected it, a twinge of sadness crept in as her thoughts turned to their sweet baby boy, Rodobaldo. He had been born between Georgina and Elisa and died at only six months old. Gabriela and Daniel never knew what caused his death, but each child has their unique place, even with a large family.

They would always miss their sweet baby, Rodobaldo.

After a moment, the girls untangled themselves and ran off to find Daniel, who had promised to show them the newborn bunnies in the barn this afternoon. They giggled and brimmed with excitement, knowing the babies were finally here.

They were thrilled because although they loved to see all of the new tiny animals on the farm, the bunnies had always been their favorite. Daniel had just finished setting up a warm and safe place with blankets and straw for Martina, the tired mother, with her litter of four precious little ones when the girls came bouncing into the barn. Daniel motioned with his hand for the girls to slow down and brought his index finger to his lips, tapping them gently.

"Shhh . . . quiet, my girls," he said. "You don't want to wake Mom and her babies."

Elisa carefully stretched out her hand to gently touch the fur on Martina's back. It was bloodied and matted from the birth. But otherwise, Martina was doing well.

Daniel reminded her to be very careful not to wake Martina. "You know the rabbits need their rest, and we need to be very quiet."

"We will not make a sound, *Papi*," whispered Georgina.

Georgina wanted to pick up one of the babies to snuggle it but knew she would not be able to. She slowly moved her face closer and closer until she could feel the warmth of this sweet new little family. She smiled broadly, and her eyes sparkled at the wonder of new life at this moment.

It was perfect.

Georgina was only seven years old but wanted to be obedient and set a good example for four-year-old Elisa, who looked up to her big sister. Georgina's eyes glistened as she asked, "When can we play with the bunnies?"

"In a few weeks they will be hopping around the farm, and you can play with them then. But for now, they have to stay safe in the barn with their mother," said Daniel.

Back at the house, Gabriela was on the back porch where she kept the old, galvanized ribbed metal washing vat, paddle, and scrubbing board. She picked up the soiled clothes, piece by piece, and placed them into the hot water.

Gabriela added the laundry soap that smelled of violets, and as was her ritual, she took a deep breath of the fresh scent. Tide was a product from America that had only been introduced in Cuban stores a few years earlier, and as such, it was a novelty. It had become her favorite brand and one of the few simple pleasures the family could afford.

Once she had placed all of the clothes into the washing vat, she took the scrubbing board and washing paddle from where they were propped against the patio wall. She began to vigorously stir the clothes around until all of the pieces had been soaked, and a thick lather had built up inside the vat. She scrubbed the clothing back and forth against the washing board to remove more prominent stains. It would have been strenuous work for any woman but so much more for Gabriela as she neared her baby's delivery.

The stains on their clothes were mainly of the wild-growing grass and fertile dirt by the creek that lined the back of their property. During long days at La Paloma, Daniel and the children spent hours exploring the creek. It was their special place to escape for an afternoon of fun, away from their farm chores. Sometimes, she would find that the younger boys had stashed sand and smooth pebbles from their adventures in their small pockets.

Gabriela's breathing felt increasingly labored with each movement of the paddle as her growing belly made it harder to stir. She took a step back to catch her breath and, after a moment, leaned over to open the valve, which drained the water. As it spilled out on the ground, Gabriela walked back into the house to fill a large metal container with cold water from the tap to rinse the clothes.

With her pregnancy progressing, it was getting more difficult each week to carry the water outside on washday, as it had become too heavy for her. She walked to the front room of the house to find Manolo and Roberto discussing their plans to help Daniel harvest the fruit from the mango and avocado trees in the next few days.

"Please come help me with the fresh water for the laundry," she asked her sons.

"*Sí, Mami,*" they both said in unison.

Manolo and Roberto were the oldest boys at seventeen and thirteen, and they adored their mother.

They were happy to help her, so they quickly followed her to the kitchen and took the water outside. They poured it into the tub, and while Gabriela rinsed the clothes, they went back inside the house to collect fresh water several more times until they could see it run clear as it came out of the release valve. Gabriela was grateful to have her sons' love and knew that she could always count on them.

Despite her exhaustion, she looked at them with love. "*Gracias, mis amores.*"

She was ready to hang the clothes out to dry in the sun. Gabriela looked forward to the smell of fresh air and sunshine that the clothes would have when dried.

Gabriela hummed to herself as she prepared to drape the clothing on the line. She would wring out each piece and place it gently to dry. After almost an hour, she finally lifted the last piece. Her arms were heavy and sore from the weight of the wet clothes. When all the clothes were hung to dry, she rubbed her tired arms while she slowly made her way back to the house.

Gabriela stopped by *el escusado*—the outhouse, to relieve herself before reaching the house, as she had not taken a break in several hours. Daniel had built this new one out of the remains of a farm cart that had been deteriorating for years. He reinforced it with dried bamboo beams and added a thatched roof, just as he had done with the family home.

As Gabriela was walking back to the house, she looked down at her feet and noticed how swollen they had become from standing all afternoon.

Gabriela's feet had started to retain fluid with this pregnancy more than with the others, and it concerned her that something might be wrong. Once again, her fatigue was overwhelming. She pushed that thought out of her mind as she walked back into the house.

She breathed a sigh of relief as she sat on a small stained wooden bench with faded arms. The bench, located to the right out of the kitchen into the dining area, had a seat with a light blue fabric cover decorated with small white flowers. Gabriela had never been so happy to relax in its comfort.

Whenever Gabriela saw it, a feeling of being loved washed over her.

This bench had belonged to her grandmother, Juliana, and no one cared for Gabriela when she was a child like her grandmother did.

Gabriela's mother, Rosa, was a stern woman with sharp features and piercing brown eyes. She loved her daughter, but she wasn't the type to offer hugs and laughter freely. Her loving grandmother filled that void for Gabriela, and the two were best of friends until her grandmother's passing when Gabriela was twenty-five years old. She was grateful her sweet grandmother was able to meet the oldest of her and Daniel's children. Manolo, Lilia, Roberto, and Rolando, with their curly dark hair and charismatic smiles, were the apples of her grandmother's eye.

While Gabriela rested, someone rhythmically knocked at the front door. She contemplated calling out for one of the children to open the door. She felt exhaustion deep in her bones. It would be time to start making dinner for her large family soon, so she decided this was as good a time as any to get up.

As she placed her still tender and aching hands on the arms of the old bench to lift herself up, whoever was at the door knocked again. This time, harder. "*Un momento,*" she said—one moment—then in a raised voice, added, "I'll be right there."

Gabriela slowly waddled to the door. When she pulled it open, she was pleasantly surprised to see Carlota standing there, the maid for the family who lived on a neighboring farm.

Carlota had a wide, ear-to-ear smile on her soft round face that barely showed her age. Her grandmother had been brought to Cuba on a slave ship in the early 1880s, and Carlota's family had remained there long after slavery had been abolished in 1886.

She stretched out her arms, holding a large serving platter and a small pot that smelled absolutely delightful. Gabriela recognized the pleasant aroma. It was the most delicious meal of *picadillo*—seasoned ground beef on a bed of fresh, hot white rice and a small pot of perfectly seasoned black beans. These authentic Cuban dishes were Carlota's specialty. The family recipes had been handed down from her grandmother, getting tastier as the recipes passed through each of the women's hands.

Today, Carlota had taken great care to make extra servings for Gabriela's family. Carlota remembered how much they all enjoyed this meal when she brought it to them a few months ago. She knew Gabriela would appreciate a break from the kitchen as she grew more tired with each passing day.

"*¡Para ustedes!*"—for you, exclaimed Carlota.

"*¡Muchas gracias*, Carlota! You are an angel."

This kindness—the heart-warming meal—was just what Gabriela needed. She was drained from the day's activities, but despite her tiredness, she knew her family would still need to eat. When Carlota surprised her with a ready-made meal, Gabriela felt relieved and grateful for the graciousness of her friend.

Gabriela's hungry family sat around the dinner table that night, laughing and sharing stories of their day while enjoying this marvelous feast. *What a joy*, Gabriela thought to herself as she sat back, rubbed her belly, and took in this wonderful time among the people whom she loved more than anything.

This was a beautiful end to another ordinary day on the farm.

CHAPTER FOUR

LA PALMA, PINAR DEL RÍO, CUBA
1953

It was early spring now. The days were beginning to get longer. With more daylight, Daniel and his children could work later each day and accomplish more on the farm. As they did every evening, Manolo and Roberto helped Daniel with the end-of-day routines.

They took great care to ensure the animals had clean water to drink and were secured in their pens or stalls for the night. Just as they finished with the last of the boars, they noticed the dark clouds rolling in. The heat and humidity were unseasonably high this early in the year, which could only mean one thing. The islanders could expect strong tropical storms.

"*Mira*—look, it looks like a downpour is coming," Daniel said to his sons. He pointed toward the ominous-looking sky over the *mogotes* in the distance—steep-sided hills, typically formed of limestone or marble, that stand tall in the shape of towers with stunning, lush vegetation.

"Let's get inside before it starts raining," said Roberto. "I think it's going to be bad."

The barn where the animals lived was on the far side of the property, at the bottom of the hill. The clouds moved fast across the sky and quickly turned deep shades of grey and blue. Raindrops started falling lightly, but within seconds, began pelting them. The three of them took off running toward the house. By the time they reached the old metal screen door leading into the kitchen, they were completely soaked. It had been a long time since they had seen rain like this. A wall of water had appeared suddenly, and it would settle in for the night.

They took turns bathing in a small makeshift shower fashioned out of a shallow, galvanized retired horse feeder, located in a corner of the one-story house. Each of them took a pitcher of water they heated in the kitchen to pour over their heads. The family used *Jabon Candado*, an inexpensive Cuban soap brand. It wasn't a quality product as it hardly produced any lather; it also left a slight waxy film on their skin; but it was the best they could afford.

They changed into fresh clothes before joining the family at the dining room table. Gabriela made over-easy fried eggs that were perfectly salted and served them over a bed of fluffy steamed white rice with *maduros*—fried sweet plantains that are served as a side to many Cuban dishes. The family frequently enjoyed this traditional and inexpensive rustic meal.

The torrential rain continued to fall and was now splashing hard against the window on the far wall. The wind was beginning to whip and made a deep howling sound. Just then, a loud thunderclap startled everyone around the table. The younger boys looked up from their dinner plates, their eyes wide with fear. At eleven and nine, Rolando and Rigoberto were still children. They were afraid of things they couldn't control and didn't fully understand, such as bad weather and the dark. Tonight's storm seemed much worse to them than their fear of darkness.

Daniel reassured them that over the years, Cuba had endured many tropical storms and hurricanes. He told them how he and his good friend Armando, with a few other men, had built their house out of solid materials to withstand heavy rain and wind.

Daniel was proud of his simple but comfortable house and liked sharing that it was made of concrete cinder blocks held together with lime mortar and wooden boards secured around the outside. He told them the palm leaf thatched roof would keep them dry and wick all the moisture away from the house. The ancient Egyptians had used a mixture of lime or gypsum, sand, and water to plaster the Pyramids of Giza. For ages, this had been the standard for construction on the island to ensure safety against the inevitable storms, mostly during hurricane season. As the children took comfort in listening to their father, Daniel worried that the rains would bring flooding to the main roads of La Palma. He had plans to attend the agriculture auction in the morning in Pinar del Río. Although the distance was only fifty-seven kilometers, it would take him more than two hours in his old red farm truck. He had been saving his money for six months and hoped to find two baby goats for the farm. The popularity of goat's milk had been growing in recent years, so he needed to replace the two that had run away.

The older children continued to eat, talk, and laugh without concern.

"*¡Qué rico, Mami!*"—this is delicious, said Lilia.

The oldest of the girls and second oldest child in the family after Manolo, Lilia was sixteen and already spending a lot of time with her friends, outside of their home. They liked to go to *el Parque de la Mariposa Blanca*—the White Butterfly Park—named after Cuba's national flower, the white butterfly. The park had beautiful winding paths lined with blooming clusters of the lovely *mariposa blanca* flower on a plant that could grow to seven feet. The smell of the fragrant blossoms had a fruity, floral bouquet with a hint of honey and ginger undertones that was intoxicating. Beautiful wrought iron benches were scattered throughout the lush garden.

The serene lake in the center of the park was a favorite spot for visitors looking for a peaceful getaway. The surrounding walking trail was thoughtfully designed with natural earth and mulch and was well manicured. The trail was flanked by landscaped islands with meticulously trimmed vegetation and vibrantly colored, fragrant flowers, making for a picturesque walk. The glistening sunlight sparkled on the water like silver and golden glitter scattered on the ripples as the lazy hum of bees lingered in the air.

Families of long-necked grey geese and beautiful ducks with deep brown feathers and striking emerald and brilliant blue markings swam gracefully in the lake. The children called to them excitedly and motioned for the birds to come closer. Extending their small hands, the children took the torn pieces of white bread they had brought from home, releasing the tiny treats as soon as the majestic animals were close to the shore.

It was the perfect place for Lilia to sneak a cigarette with her friends or be alone with Pablo, a new boy at her school that year. Gabriela and Daniel had only met Pablo once, but they both got the same impression from him. Pablo wasn't interested in studying and didn't have any plans or dreams for the future.

"*¿Cómo está la escuela*, Lilia?" Daniel asked her about school.

"*Bueno*, it's okay," she responded with a shrug of her shoulders.

Lilia was bored with school and found any excuse to skip classes. She didn't care much about being there for her large family, either. She used to pitch in around the house and on the farm, but that rarely happened anymore.

Lilia had been a big help to Gabriela as each baby was welcomed into the family. It was a busy but happy time for them, and Lilia stepped in to lend a hand where she could. Her mother's focus was primarily on feeding and caring for the new baby, and with Lilia being the oldest of the girls, she enjoyed helping her mother. She would take care of her younger brothers and sisters, feeding, bathing, and teaching them until they were old enough to go to school. Gabriela was proud of her, but in the last year, Lilia had changed. She would find excuses for not taking part in family chores and activities. Now that Gabriela was nearing the end of this difficult pregnancy, she held onto the hope that Lilia would want to help care for her family. There would be so many tasks to be done, and Gabriela would need help as she recuperated from the delivery and took care of this new baby.

Gabriela started to pick up the dinner plates when Daniel stood up and put his hand out, motioning for her to leave them there on the table.

"I know you have had a long day, and I can tell how tired you are," said Daniel.

"I'm fine to clear the table and wash the dishes," Gabriela said with an expression that Daniel had seen before when she didn't really want to do something but felt she should.

"I've noticed how swollen your ankles have been lately, and I want you to get some rest. Our baby will be here in a few weeks. You need to be healthy."

Gabriela looked at Daniel lovingly and said, "*Gracias, mi amor.*"

Daniel and the children quickly took all of the dinner plates into the kitchen and placed them in the sink. The children did not overhear their parents' conversation, so they assumed Gabriela would wash the dishes as she did every night. Instead, she took her pitcher of hot water to the shower and washed the sweat and soreness of the day away. She was ready to get in bed and put her feet up on a pillow. Gabriela hoped the next few weeks would pass quickly so she could feel some relief and meet their new baby.

It wasn't long before Daniel helped the last of the children into their beds.

He put on his white cotton V-neck T-shirt and light green pajama pants before lying down next to Gabriela. She was already dozing off.

Daniel pulled the covers over Gabriela and gently kissed her on the forehead. The storm outside continued to rage, but inside, the house was quiet, warm, and safe.

Daniel was tired from a busy day on the farm that had ended with him and the boys getting soaked in the rain. His eyes felt heavy. With a slow, relaxed exhale, he drifted off to sleep. Tomorrow would be a long day.

It felt like they had only been asleep for a few minutes when, around 3:45 in the morning, a crash of thunder woke Daniel, Gabriela, and everyone in the house, except Roberto. Even if the world were coming unglued just outside his window, Roberto could soundly sleep through it. The loud boom shattered the silence, and it felt like a lightning bolt had struck right outside their front door. Daniel rolled over and tried to go back to sleep, but he had too much on his mind. In recent months, the farm had not been producing as it had in previous years. Sales continued to decline and the bills from suppliers fell further and further behind. Daniel didn't want to worry Gabriela, but it weighed heavily on his mind. His large family depended on him. The fear of failing them grew by the day.

Gabriela threw on her pale blue slippers and yellow floral housecoat before checking in on all of their children. As she was leaving her bed, she glanced out the window. Gabriela saw lightning race across the midnight sky as the heavy rain continued to fall. She checked on her youngest, Ramon, first. He was standing up in his crib crying. Gabriela picked him up and patted him on the back. She whispered, "Shhh . . . it's okay, it's okay," until he fell back asleep, and then she carefully placed him back into his crib and covered him with a small white crocheted blanket before going to check on the other children. She found the older children getting settled as they were trying to go back to sleep. The two younger boys, Rolando and Rigoberto, and the two youngest girls, Georgina and Elisa, were wide awake and scared. Their beds were arranged as close together as possible to fit in their small home—this gave them a sense of comfort. They were not alone.

Gabriela had always loved to sing, and the children loved her lullabies to soothe them when they were tired or afraid. Tonight, they were both. It only took a few minutes for all four children to relax and go back to sleep. Gabriela went back to bed, quietly slipping out of her housecoat and slippers.

She nestled in under the warm covers, and as soon as her head touched the pillow, she was fast asleep. Daniel tossed and turned for the next few hours and never could fall back asleep.

Before daylight, he got up as quietly as he could and got ready to leave for the long drive that awaited him. He left without having breakfast. Today, he decided he would get something to eat from one of the small vendor carts that were just outside the main entrance to the agriculture auction. This was common for some of the farmers, but it was a special treat for Daniel. He had a few extra *pesos* in his pocket, and he was going to spend them. He had earned a little extra money by helping Ricardo, the owner of the only *bodega*—a small market in the neighborhood.

Daniel would always use any money he made to take care of his family's needs, but when he told Gabriela, she said, "I see how hard you have been working, and you never do anything for yourself. Keep this money and use it for something special, just for you."

"Are you sure you want me to do that?"

"Yes, I am sure. It is only a few *pesos*. You deserve this and so much more."

After Daniel had made a delivery of fresh produce a few weeks ago, Ricardo asked him to help unload and set up new shelving he had purchased for the baked goods at the front of the store. His employee, Adan, would have already been there to help Ricardo, but he had fallen from a ladder onto his wrist while changing a light bulb at the store two days ago. He would need a few days until he felt well enough to come back to work. Ricardo offered to pay Daniel, but because they were friends, Daniel declined. Ricardo insisted, "I would have had to pay Adan, and I know you could use it, so please take it."

"Thank you." Daniel smiled and looked down. "You know I'm always happy to help."

This morning, Daniel was extremely cautious as he drove to the auction. The tires on his old truck were bare, and the roads were slick from the rain. After two hours, he finally reached his destination and pulled his vehicle to the far-right corner of the small gravel parking lot. The gates to the auction wouldn't open for another twenty minutes, so it gave him time to eat the breakfast he had been looking forward to all morning.

The rain had stopped now, and as Daniel stepped out of his truck, the different smells of savory and sweet foods were like a magnet pulling him in. Looking around, he could see the other farmers enjoying all sorts of delicious food, and he could hear the conversation and laughter as he waited for the auction to open. Daniel walked around and surveyed the offerings the vendors had on display. They could easily move their small, white carts with the little black rubber wheels to different events in the town. Each had their own special fare, and Daniel wanted to see what his choices were. Some had fresh-cut tropical fruit, others had eggs prepared in a variety of ways, and yet other vendors had *café con leche* with an assortment of sweets, including *churros*—the perfect concoction of fried pastry dough covered in sugar and cinnamon. There were so many choices, and he was overwhelmed by the mixture of delicious smells—all reminders of his favorite childhood memories.

He was hungry, and they all looked appetizing, but one caught his eye. It took him back to the heartwarming breakfasts his family would enjoy growing up in Río Blanco. His mother would shop every day to find the freshest ingredients and prepare delicious meals that the whole family enjoyed while sitting under the kelly-green-and-white-striped awning on their back patio.

The farmland was quite a distance from their home. As they looked past the manicured lawn with the grand palm trees and fragrant blooming flowers, they could hear the creek rushing in the distance. It was a picturesque scene, and Daniel loved to remember the happy times he shared with his parents and sister on the ranch.

He was lost in thought for just a moment but had already decided this was the breakfast he wanted.

"*¿Cuánto cuesta?*" Daniel asked the operator of one of the carts for the price as he pointed to the breakfast plate with two fried eggs and ham on pressed Cuban bread and a side of sliced tomatoes with a dash of salt.

"*Un peso*," replied the man as he lifted one finger.

"*Gracias*. How much would it cost to add a *batido de mamey*—a *mamey* milkshake and four ham *croquetas*?" *Mamey* is a sweet tropical fruit with colors ranging from yellow to orange to ruby red, with a unique flavor profile of apricot, sweet potato, nuts, and spices. *Croquetas* are made of seasoned ground chicken or ham rolled in breadcrumbs and lightly fried until they are a perfect golden color. The texture is heavenly—crispy on the outside, soft and creamy on the inside.

"*Dos pesos por todo*," the man replied. Two *pesos* for everything.

"*Sí, gracias*. I'll take everything. Here you are," said Daniel, and he handed over the money. Daniel was ready to eat. Within a few moments, the man delivered his plate of food, along with the milkshake.

He took his plate and looked around for a good place to sit. He wanted to savor his breakfast on one of the benches to the side of the cart, but they were all wet from the storms.

Daniel walked back to his truck, avoiding the deep rain puddles dotting the parking lot, so he could sit and enjoy this special treat. He took one bite, and the memories of those sunny days with his family all rushed back in an instant. He didn't mean to eat so quickly, but before he knew it, he was finished. It was delicious, and nostalgia washed over him. He could see the farmers starting to gather at the entrance to the auction as the gates would open any moment. He still had half of his milkshake, so he carried it with him to wait with the others.

Not long after Daniel arrived, the gates opened, and the familiar smell of farm animals escaped as the large overhead door lifted. He dashed down the center aisle, passing all sorts of livestock that were to be auctioned. This area, just inside the entrance, was the largest auction in the market. Tall, metal bleachers surrounded the huge, enclosed dirt pen. Behind the auctioneer's podium, colorful advertisements for farm products covered the wall. Hundreds of black, brown, and spotted cows waited in a long row of wooden stalls until it was time for the doors to open. They were classified by groups—steers, heifers, bulls, and Holsteins—and would walk at a brisk pace in a single file line to be brought in front of the audience for inspection, albeit at a distance. Once the bidding started, it was noisy, and the auctioneer moved it along quickly. If you didn't raise your hand at the precise moment, the cow or bull you had an eye on would be going home with someone else.

Daniel was not interested in cattle today. He turned right at the third aisle and took a seat in the front of the section where the goats would be auctioned. This area was much smaller, but the baby goats didn't take up quite the space that the cattle did. There were bales of golden hay on either side of the small, dark, wooden platform where the auctioneer would stand. Reaching the end of his tasty milkshake, Daniel jumped up to throw the empty cup in a garbage can at the entrance before the bidding started. He quickly got back in his seat and looked at the clock on the wall, wondering how long it would be before the auction got underway.

After about ten minutes, Daniel could hear the little hooves of the baby goats prancing on the packed dirt as they made their way to the auction floor. The handlers lined them up, and as soon as he saw the first one, he raised his hand. He outbid two other farmers for the goat and still had money left for the second one. They brought out two more, but those didn't catch his eye. The fourth one was perfect, and again, he raised his hand. This time the bidding started at a higher price, and no one bid against him. He had enough money for both goats and would be taking them home with him. He placed the animals inside metal crates and secured them in the back of his truck. He left knowing he got the best little goats he could afford.

He started his trip back home and noticed the gas gauge was close to empty. He drove a few miles, but he didn't see a gas station and began to worry that he would run out of gas with his new animals. Just then, he turned a corner and saw the sign for Standard Oil—an American petroleum company with gasoline filling stations in Cuba. He didn't have very much money left over from his purchases, so he only filled the tank halfway. This would be enough to get him home.

It was close to noon when he turned onto the highway that would take him through Viñales and into La Palma.

He was only about twenty kilometers from home when he spotted a 1952 Chevrolet Styleline four-door sedan on the side of the road, and he could see it had a flat tire. He recognized the automobile because even though he couldn't afford one, he loved the innovation of cars and kept up to date on the latest models. As he drove past, he felt compassion for the driver and knew he would need help. Daniel looked for a place to turn around where his old truck would not get stuck in the mud from the heavy rains. He made the turn and drove back to the parked car, pulling in behind it.

The man in the front seat lowered the window when he saw Daniel approaching through the rearview mirror.

"*Hola, ¿qué pasó?*" Daniel asked him what had happened.

"I was on my way to *el Policlínico* at *Avenida Rosalía*, where it crosses *la Carretera Central*—the main highway, when I heard a loud explosion and stopped," the man said. "I looked around the outside of the car and noticed that my rear driver-side tire had blown out. *Me llamo* Joaquin Sánchez. I am the new obstetrician-pediatrician at the clinic." He was polished and well-dressed with raven-black hair that had been slicked back.

"*Mucho gusto. Me llamo* Daniel." It's a pleasure to meet you. My name is Daniel. "Do you have a spare tire in the trunk? If you do, I can help you change it." Dr. Sánchez nodded and got out of the car to walk around and open the trunk. Daniel reached in and pulled out the new tire.

Dr. Sánchez was grateful that Daniel stopped to help him. He had never changed a tire before, and without Daniel's help, he didn't know how long he would have had to wait for someone else to come by to help him. The doctor and his wife, Margarita, had recently moved to La Palma and didn't know very many people, so Daniel was a godsend.

"This is a beautiful car," said Daniel. "How long have you had it?"

"I bought it a few months ago in Havana before we moved here to start my new position at the clinic.

They made small talk and shared details about their families and why they were both in La Palma while Daniel worked to get the flat tire off the rim. Daniel told the doctor about his wife and the nine children they were raising on their farm, La Paloma.

"We are expecting a new baby very soon too!" he said excitedly. "It would be fantastic if you could take care of this baby. The obstetrician that took care of all our other children sadly passed away a few months ago.

Dr. Sánchez said, "I would be happy to meet her and help her when she is ready to give birth. My wife and I do not have children and would one day very much like to have a family of our own. You have been blessed with such a large family."

It only took Daniel a few minutes to change the tire and put the flat into the trunk.

He was familiar with the process; he had changed several of the tires on his old truck, even though that had been a very long time ago. Daniel closed the trunk, and as he did, Dr. Sánchez extended his hand. With a smile, he said, "*Muchas gracias*! I appreciate your kindness. Thank you for stopping."

"*De nada*—you are welcome. I'm glad I could help."

With that, they each turned, got into their vehicles, and drove away.

CHAPTER FIVE

LA PALMA, PINAR DEL RÍO, CUBA
1953

The following day, Daniel went to the *bodega* early in the morning to pick up a loaf of bread. When he opened the door, the smell of freshly baked bread wafted through the store. It was terrific, and he couldn't wait to get it home to toast a few slices, add fresh butter from his farm, and have it with *café con leche* for breakfast today. He would prepare the same for Gabriela. By the time he got back home, she would have already prepared the children's meals, and this would be their special time. They knew that once the new baby arrived, everything would change. They wanted to enjoy any small interlude, away from the demands of their lives, even if only for a few minutes.

Ricardo baked the best bread for miles around, and the other bodegas in this area also bought their bread from him. It was fluffy and airy—crispy on the outside, and the inside melted in your mouth.

There's nothing like the slightly sweet and yeasty smell of this simple tradition first thing in the morning. *This is heaven*, thought Daniel.

"*Hola*, Ricardo. *Buenos días*—good morning."

"*¿Cómo estás*—how are you, Daniel?"

"*Muy bien, gracias*—very well, thank you. I like the way your new shelving looks, holding all of the pastries and fresh bread. It's nice that you see them as you walk into the store. It is almost impossible to smell them and not want to buy everything you have," joked Daniel.

"*Gracias*, Daniel, and thank you for helping me put it together a few weeks ago."

"It was my pleasure. You are very welcome."

Daniel made his purchase, turned around, and opened the door to leave. Just as he was about to step outside, Dr. Sánchez was walking into the store.

"*Hola*, nice to see you again, Dr. Sánchez," said Daniel as he smiled at the newcomer.

"Yes, what a pleasure to run into you," said Dr. Sánchez and returned the smile.

"If you are looking for fresh bread, it just came out of the oven—hot and delicious."

"That sounds wonderful, but I am headed to the back, where the butcher keeps the best meats, to select a small steak and ask him to make a *pan con bistec*—a steak sandwich with sautéed onions and placed on a hot press to perfection. I like to add Swiss cheese. He makes the best sandwiches, and I usually stop here a few times a week to pick up my lunch before going into work."

"That sounds great. I know the meat here is fresh because I make deliveries from my farm twice a week," said Daniel. "Also, I thought about what you said yesterday—about meeting my wife before her due date. Would you like to stop by the house after work today? I know she would like to meet you too."

"Yes, I think that would be a good idea," said Dr. Sánchez. "I can be there after five this afternoon."

"Thank you. My farm is about thirty kilometers from *el Policlínico*. Head east on *Calle Salvador Cisneros* and then turn left at the first cross street. You will drive about three kilometers and turn right where you see a small auto repair shop with a big white and red sign that reads *Taller de Reparaciones Blanco*—Blanco Repair Shop. Stay on this road for about another twenty kilometers and then turn left onto *Calle Mesa*. Our farm will be about seven to eight kilometers down the road on the right side with a sign that reads 'La Paloma.' I will see you later today," said Daniel as he waved and got in his truck.

When he got home, Gabriela was finishing cleaning the dishes from feeding the children.

"Please take a seat and rest while I prepare our breakfast," said Daniel.

Gabriela smiled and said, "*Gracias, mi amor.*" She slid into a chair at the dining room table to wait for the breakfast Daniel was making. It was only 10:30 in the morning, and she was already starting to feel tired. She was counting the days until her baby would be here. At the beginning of her pregnancy, Dr. Rodriguez had told her that she would deliver around the first week in April. This was only two weeks away, and then, it could happen any time. Daniel quickly prepared their meal and took it to the table. Gabriela's appetite had grown with her pregnancy, and she was excited at the smell of the freshly brewed coffee in the *café con leche*. It was just what she needed. They spent a few minutes just enjoying their breakfast and being alone, which was a rare occurrence with eight children in the house, soon to be nine. The peace and quiet of the moment were shattered when baby Ramon came in crying because he needed a diaper change. "The joys of parenthood," said Gabriela with a smile. She picked up Ramon and took him to the bedroom to put him into a clean diaper and get him out of his pajamas.

Daniel placed the dishes in the sink and rushed down to the barn. Even though Roberto and Manolo had already milked the cows, as they did every day at sunrise and again in the late afternoon, Daniel liked to start his chores before dawn each morning. The troughs needed to be filled with the animal feed made of grain, hay, and corn, and the fresh water poured into the large containers at each stall. Daniel also had the new baby goats he had brought home yesterday. They were in a separate part of the barn with blankets and hay. Rolando and Rigoberto would help when there were any new baby animals. They were at the barn early this morning to bottle feed the baby goats and ensure they felt safe and cared for since their mother was not there to do this. Daniel went into each of the stalls to ensure all the chores had been completed. He was proud of the family he and Gabriela were raising and, in particular, their boys, who took on the responsibility to help around the farm. They did a great job.

The day went by quickly, and in the late afternoon, as Daniel stood near the garden on the side of the property, he could see the new Chevrolet at a distance. The elegant car was the only one in sight, and it owned the road. Daniel couldn't take his eyes off the stylish automobile as it got closer to the house. He knew he needed to finish his work for the day before he could welcome Dr. Sánchez into their home. He quickly finished spreading the fertilizer on the crops and returned the wheelbarrow to the storage shed behind the barn.

As Daniel briskly walked back to the house, he watched as the doctor approached the entrance to La Paloma. The light seafoam green paint on the new car glimmered in the sunlight. Daniel felt optimistic that he, too, would someday have a fancy car like this one.

He dreamed of driving his wife and children to the seashore for a day of sunshine and waves on a white sandy beach with crystal-clear aquamarine water. He would roll down the windows so they could feel the warm tropical breeze and smell the fresh ocean air. Daniel envisioned Gabriela wearing a white headscarf tied at the nape of her neck to keep her flowing, brown hair in place. She would turn toward him and grin—this would be precisely what she had imagined so many years ago when they committed to building a life together. In this moment, all was right with her world.

The children would be excited to spend a day at the beach together. Their laughter and chatter would fill the car. Wearing their swimsuits with colorful plastic sandals—navy for the boys and red for the girls—each child would carry their own towel under their arm. When Daniel finally parked the car, the children would jump out of the car and excitedly run toward the ocean. Making their way to the beach, they would stop for a moment, taking it all in—the white-crested waves crashing against the beach and the high-pitched calling of the seagulls flying overhead. The instant their feet would touch the warm sand, they would scatter and sprint to the water's edge, flinging their towels behind.

The younger children would sit right on the edge of the tide on the wet sand with their yellow buckets and red shovels, building sandcastles, their favorite beachside activity. The older children would jump in the warm water and swim around to their heart's content—occasionally disappearing—popping in and out of the waves. Daniel would have helped Gabriela prepare and set out a delicious picnic of homemade ham and cheese sandwiches made with ingredients from the farm and *mariquitas*—thinly sliced, fried green plantain chips sprinkled with a bit of salt. He would have thrown in some fresh fruit and refreshing, ice-cold drinks. These were the foods he remembered his mother taking to the seashore in Río Blanco when he was a child. He wanted to recreate the memories of those happy times with his own family.

It would have been a perfect day at the beach.

Daniel cleaned up before the doctor arrived. He washed his calloused hands and changed out of his dirty clothes that showed all the signs of a busy day on his farm. He put on a crisp white cotton shirt and a fresh pair of overalls. Just then, he heard the knock at the door.

"*Bienvenido*—welcome, Dr. Sánchez," said Daniel, inviting the doctor into his home. "Please come inside."

"*Muchas gracias*, Daniel, and thank you for inviting me to meet your wife and family."

"It is my pleasure, doctor."

At that moment, Gabriela walked toward the front door and greeted Dr. Sánchez. She was relieved that he had come to their home to meet her. Gabriela had not seen a doctor for several months since just before Dr. Rodriguez passed away and was anxious to speak with Dr. Sánchez. She extended her arm and shook his surprisingly soft hand.

"*Hola.* Thank you for coming to visit with us. Please, have a seat."

Gabriela immediately noticed his fancy clothes and polished shoes. They rarely had guests that didn't wear simple clothes, like farmer's overalls and heavy boots. Dr. Sánchez couldn't have been older than her and Daniel. It was apparent to her from his clean hands and nails and his pale complexion that he had never worked outside a day in his life and had a very different life from them.

"*Hola. Soy el doctor* Joaquin Sánchez. How have you been feeling? Your husband told me you are less than two weeks away from delivering your baby."

"I am fatigued all of the time and am getting terribly uncomfortable. This is nothing new, as I've experienced these symptoms with all my other children. The one thing I've noticed with this pregnancy that I didn't have with the others, except with Ramon, and then only a little bit, is the swelling in my ankles."

"Let me see. Can you please stretch out your legs so I can take a look?" Dr. Sánchez walked over to where Gabriela was sitting. He bent down and pressed his thumbs into her ankles and feet.

"You definitely have a good bit of swelling," said Dr. Sánchez. "Are you spending more time standing up than you did in the past? Are you eating more salt than usual?"

"I have been doing all of my chores just as I did with my other pregnancies. I also have not been eating more salt than usual," replied Gabriela. "My obstetrician, Dr. Rodriguez, who passed away recently, told me during my last pregnancy the problem I was having with swelling had something to do with my kidneys, but I have not felt anything unusual."

"Let's make sure to keep an eye on this. If you notice it progressing, please call the clinic for an appointment, and we can check your bloodwork," said Dr. Sánchez.

"I will do that and also call if it gets worse."

As the doctor stood up to leave, the younger children ran into the house. They had been playing outside and were covered with mud from the storms of the last few days—on their clothes, shoes, and even some on their faces, arms, and hands.

"Rigoberto, Georgina, Rolando, Elisa, please say hello to Dr. Sánchez," said Gabriela. The children were giggling, and their cheeks were rosy from an afternoon of fun and adventure outdoors. They became timid, all of a sudden, and looked down as they each semi-whispered, "*Hola.*"

"*Mucho gusto*—it's very nice to meet you," Dr. Sánchez said and smiled as he looked at the children and then at Gabriela and Daniel. "They are delightful. You are fortunate to have such a lovely family."

"*Gracias.* We also have three older children. The oldest is seventeen years old, and we have a two-year-old boy. We are also very excited to welcome this new baby in just a few weeks. Our children are our pride and joy, and I wouldn't trade this life at La Paloma for anything in the world," said Daniel with so much love in his heart for his family. "Ours is not an extravagant life. We don't have fancy things, but we have love. That is what matters most to us."

"I must say, you have been privileged to receive the most important things in this life: children to raise and carry on your legacy and the love that you all have for one another," said Dr. Sánchez with admiration for Daniel and his family. "I can only hope that one day, God will see fit to give Margarita and me a family of our own."

With that, Daniel stood up and agreed with the doctor. "I hope that you and your wife will experience the happiness children bring into a home. Thank you for coming to meet our family."

"Thank you, and I will look forward to seeing you both soon. Goodbye." Dr. Sánchez left to walk to his car, and when he was almost there, he stepped into a muddy puddle in the soggy yard. He looked down and lamented, "My expensive shoes are ruined." He remembered he had the bag from his lunch today and used it to cover the floorboard in front of the driver's seat. He drove away as the children watched from the living room window. They were used to visitors, but none wore stylish clothes or drove a magnificent new car like the doctor.

On the drive home, he replayed the visit in his mind and wished that he could experience the warmth of a large family like Daniel's. He was happy that he and Margarita had moved to this small town and hoped to fill their new home with a child's laughter. They had purchased a beautiful, white, brick and wood two-story home in Santa Cruz, an elite neighborhood not far from his new job at the clinic. It had five bedrooms, five bathrooms, and all the luxuries considered standard with this type of home—indoor plumbing, electricity, hot water, a fully appointed kitchen with the latest appliances, and an extraordinary wraparound porch. The porch was his favorite part of the house.

Every day after work, he and Margarita would sit on the white rocking chairs to the side of the front door and talk about their day while enjoying an ice-cold *mojito* or a *Cuba libre*—a rum and coke with a lime wedge on the rim of the glass. They were both very discriminating about the rum they used in their cocktails and only drank Bacardi. The company was founded in Santiago de Cuba in 1862, and mixing a drink with this quality brand was a tradition passed down to Joaquin from his father and his father before him.

Margarita was enjoying the late afternoon sun, planting a row of pink tulip bulbs, when she noticed Joaquin's car turn onto their street. She finished with the last two bulbs and quickly gathered her gardening supplies to take to the greenhouse. She had ordered these bulbs from the Netherlands and looked forward to seeing them bloom—in colors of the most beautiful rainbow—in the next few weeks and then each year after that.

"*Mi amor*, how was your day?" said Margarita with a loving smile and a warm embrace as Joaquin returned home. She looked down at his shoes and said, "Oh my goodness. ¿*Que pasó*—what happened?"

"I went to visit the home of the man I mentioned to you yesterday—the one that helped me change the flat tire on the car. He told me his wife was about two weeks away from delivering her baby, and he invited me to meet her. I was only there for a few minutes, and she seemed fine, but I am concerned with the swelling in her ankles. Her previous doctor told her it was from some type of kidney issue, and that worries me."

"It sounds dangerous," said Margarita. "I hope that the rest of her pregnancy and delivery will go well."

"I hope so too. I was so taken with this family. They live in a very humble home on a farm not far from here. The man's name is Daniel, and his wife's name is Gabriela. They have eight surviving children ranging in ages from two to seventeen years old, and this new baby will make it nine children."

"That is a huge family. With the addition of this new baby, I can't imagine how she will be able to take care of the whole family."

"I know, it sounds like it would be chaotic, but . . . there is so much unity and love there. I got to meet four of the younger children, and they were adorable. All the children help out on the farm. I know they will help with this new baby, too. Daniel's family may not have the material things we have, but they have something money can't buy—a beautiful family and the love they share with one another."

"I wish we could have our own big family," said Margarita. "I pray to Santa Ana, the patron saint of women who want to become pregnant, first thing every morning and last thing every night before I fall asleep. I know we have talked about this so often, and even though we agreed not to continue bringing it up until it happens naturally, I long to have at least one child. I know they would fill our lives with such joy."

"Yes, darling, you know I feel the same way. But in the last year, we have had so many disappointments, month after month, that I believe we shouldn't focus so much on this. It will be a wonderful surprise when it does happen. Don't you think so?"

"Yes, but the heartache of waiting is so painful," sighed Margarita. Joaquin reached for her tender hand. He desperately wanted to comfort her and make this dream a reality. "I will also pray to Santa Ana and ask for a miracle," he said.

CHAPTER SIX

LA PALMA, PINAR DEL RÍO, CUBA
1953

Gabriela stood in front of the wall calendar in the kitchen. She wiped her hands on her apron and gently removed the single tack holding it in its place. She flipped the page from March to April with excitement in her heart. Two cherubs were the image for April. *How appropriate*, she thought to herself. There was a star on the first day of the month and several doodles that the children had drawn in orange and green crayons. Everyone had been anticipating the arrival of the new baby. The date was finally here, and she wished she could deliver the baby on this very day. Dr. Rodriguez told Gabriela her approximate due date was to be the first week of April, and she knew it could be any time now. *So, why not today?* she thought. Her belly felt tight, and from the pressure in her hips, she knew she was getting close to delivering the baby.

To take her mind off her discomfort, she decided to go to *el Parque de la Mariposa Blanca* and take a long walk around the lake. The tranquility would be good for her, and the exercise could hasten the baby's arrival.

Before she could head out this morning, she needed to prepare breakfast for her family. Today, she would only use ingredients from the farm as they were low on money. She could still serve a delicious meal, and they would be none the wiser. Gabriela prepared *una tortilla Española*—a Spanish-style omelet with eggs, sliced potatoes, onions, and seasonings that she would make in a large round pan and cut into triangles. The texture was creamy and dense, and there were never any leftovers when she made it for her family. Gabriela learned how to cook this savory and filling dish from her grandmother Juliana. Although it was easy to prepare with simple ingredients, it was one of her family's favorite meals.

The fruit trees at La Paloma were beginning to bloom, and some of the fruit was starting to ripen. She opened the window, and the breeze filled the kitchen with citrus and the sweet scent of tropical fruit—mangos, guavas, and bananas. She sliced and arranged them all on a large plate. The wonderful aromas coming from the kitchen were starting to bring the children around. "When will the breakfast be ready, *Mami*? It smells so good," said Roberto.

"Give me another five minutes to set the table, and we can sit down to eat. Please let your brothers and sisters know so they can wash their hands," said Gabriela.

"*Esta bien, Mami*—sounds good," replied Roberto and went to round up the rest of the children. Gabriela opened the kitchen door to let Daniel know breakfast would be ready in a few minutes. Before she could say anything, he was already almost to the door.

"I was going to call you to come eat. You beat me to it," smiled Gabriela.

"I knew when I saw Roberto rounding up the children, you were ready to serve breakfast," chuckled Daniel as he gently took Gabriela's hand, walking her back inside.

As they stepped into the kitchen, they could see that the children were all seated in the dining room. Roberto loved to help his mother, and making sure all the family was at the table for meals was an easy chore. Gabriela had already set the table, so the only thing left to do was sit down with her family and enjoy their company. She loved cooking for her family, especially whenever she could use the recipes her grandmother had handed down to her. She missed her terribly, and this made her feel closer to her. Gabriela started by serving the younger children their smaller portions, and she let Daniel and the older ones help themselves.

"I love that you can take the fruits, vegetables, and dairy from our farm and prepare such a delicious meal," said Daniel.

"I'm happy you like it," said Gabriela with a smile. The children chimed in with their appreciation. "You are all very welcome."

Daniel was still finishing his breakfast, but the children were all done and starting to get up from the table.

"Roberto, Manolo, Rolando, and Rigoberto, I know you will be going back down to the barn to help your father. I am going for a walk in the park. I need a few minutes to myself, and I think this walk could hasten my labor. I will take the number 13 bus and drop off Georgina, Elisa, and Ramon with my friend Clara, and then pick them up on my way back."

"I want to go to the park," said Georgina. "Can I please go?"

"Me too," cried Elisa. "I don't want to go to Clara's house. I want to go to the park with you."

"No, girls. I have to take Ramon to Clara's house so you can stay there and play for a little while. I will be back to get you very soon."

"*Por favor*, please, please, please take us with you," Elisa whined in drawn-out tones.

Gabriela felt sorry for them and decided they could come along with her.

"Okay, I'm going to take you with me, but I need you to be on your best behavior. I cannot be running around after you. We will walk around the lake a few times, and then we will head home. Do you promise to be good?" asked Gabriela.

"Yes, *Mami*, we will behave. We promise," said Georgina, answering for both.

"Please put your shoes and socks on while I clear the table and change out of my housecoat into anything that still fits me," said Gabriela.

The girls scampered to get ready and were finished before Gabriela had washed all the dishes. She rinsed the last two and put them on the wooden drying rack that Daniel had made for her. Gabriela dried her hands on a bare thread dish towel and quickly changed into a maternity dress her neighbor and kind friend Señora Consuelo Lopez had loaned her.

Gabriela had a thin frame, so it was still a little loose, but she needed to be comfortable for her walk. She put on her old tan leather flats. These were still comfortable for her, even though her feet were puffy and her ankles swollen.

She opened her small, colorful cloth handbag to make sure she had enough money for the bus fare.

Gabriela took both younger girls and the baby, so she calculated the cost for the trip to and from the park and ensured she had the necessary change. They walked to the bus stop, and after about ten minutes, they boarded the brightly colored bus with the teal and red stripe going all the way around it, placed about halfway between the windows and the tires en route to *el Parque de la Mariposa Blanca*. They would stop on the way at Clara's house to leave Ramon while Gabriela and the girls enjoyed some time in nature. It was a short walk from the bus stop to Clara's house—only two blocks. This was convenient for Gabriela, and Clara loved it anytime she could take care of Ramon. He was a sweet and well-behaved boy.

After giving him a quick kiss on the top of his head and saying goodbye to Clara, Gabriela took the girls by the hand and rushed back to the bus stop to finally get to their destination. The girls were ready to be there, and the eight minutes it took to arrive at the park seemed like forever.

The driver pulled up to the bus stop located at the main entrance to the park. Gabriela and the girls were the first ones off the bus. It was a beautiful spring day, and there was not a cloud in the sky. The weather was warm but not too hot. It was the perfect day to visit the park. There were thousands of colorful blooming flowers everywhere. The sweet smell of the gardenias and gorgeous colors of the *campanillas*—yellow morning glories—enraptured the senses. Gabriela was taking it all in when she noticed the girls started to get ahead of her.

She called out to them. "Georgina, Elisa—please come back here and walk with me. You promised to behave, and I need you to stay close to me."

"*Sí, Mami,*" they said in unison and ran to her side.

"I have a surprise for you."

"You do?" said Elisa. "What is it?"

"I packed a small bag with leftover bread so you can feed the geese and ducks in the lake. Let's go there first, and then we will walk around the path, where we can see the turtle families, frogs, and other animals."

The girls started jumping up and down and screaming with excitement.

"*Gracias! Gracias, Mami,*" said Georgina.

"*Sí, gracias,*" chimed in Elisa.

Gabriela took the bag with the bread out of her purse. The girls were clapping their hands in double time. They couldn't contain their excitement.

"Here is some for you and for you," Gabriela said, handing some to each girl.

"*Gracias,*" they said as they crept closer to the water, hoping to reach a large white goose that was nearby. "Come here, come here," they shrieked with excitement in the hopes that the goose would swim in their direction. It started to turn toward them, and both girls threw some pieces of the bread into the water, just by the shoreline. They could hear the honking noises the goose was making getting louder and louder as it got closer. It glided toward them, and when they could almost reach out and touch it, the goose scooped up the bread the girls had thrown its way. Before long, six baby geese with yellow and grey feathers were swimming toward them.

"Look at the babies!" exclaimed Georgina.

"Those are called *ansarinos*—goslings," said Gabriela.

As the tiny geese got closer, the girls threw more bread into the water until their little bags were empty.

"I wish we had more," said Elisa with a sad look on her face.

"I know. That was fun. But we can bring more the next time we visit," said Gabriela. "We will even be able to bring the new baby with us."

"Yes, we would love that. Thank you for surprising us with the bread to feed the geese. Weren't those babies so sweet?" asked Georgina.

"Yes, they were," said Gabriela. She had begun to feel a bit short of breath. Even so, she was glad to be spending this time outdoors with her girls as she awaited the arrival of her new baby.

"I am glad you both enjoyed seeing and feeding the geese. Now, let's sit down for a few minutes before we take our walk."

The girls skipped ahead to one of the wrought-iron benches. Gabriela took her time getting there and steadied herself before deliberately taking a seat. She immediately felt a reprieve from the pressure of the weight she was carrying and slowly exhaled a sigh of relief. As Gabriela rested for a few moments, she looked around to see other families laughing and playing with their children while enjoying the glorious weather. In the shade of some tall palm trees, four older men sat laughing and enjoying a game of dominoes. It brought back wonderful memories from her childhood—watching her grandfather and his friends play for hours. Growing impatient, the girls began chasing one another in circles around the bench. Gabriela didn't mind because they stayed close to her.

"When can we go walk around the lake?" asked Elisa.

"Do you feel better now?" asked Georgina.

"In a moment," said Gabriela as she slipped off her flats. The cool grass felt refreshing on her puffy feet. Recently she began having a burning sensation on the soles of her feet near the end of each day, and her ankles were more swollen than in previous days. This gave Gabriela pause, and she wondered when her delivery day would be. She knew everything would return to normal once the baby was born. Gabriela was ready to have this baby. *Maybe today will be the day,* she thought.

"Yes, I'm feeling a little better, so let's go now," said Gabriela.

As they circled the lake, Gabriela and the girls chatted and laughed. They saw some beautiful ducks in green, red, and brown colors gliding around. They could hear them quack from the other side of the lake. The girls spotted the turtles first.

"Look! There on the rocks. A family of six turtles in different sizes," said Georgina.

Gabriela was only a few steps behind, but when she saw the turtles sunning themselves, she said, "Turtles like to sit on the rocks at the edge of the lake and warm themselves in the sun. Did you know that?"

"No, I didn't know that," said Elisa.

"Me neither," said Georgina.

After a few moments of watching the turtles, one by one, they dropped into the water and paddled away into the center of the lake.

Gabriela and the girls continued their walk, and a short while later, they noticed a rare hummingbird with an iridescent green body, a yellow crown over its beak, and stunning bright blue tail feathers with red at the ends. They stopped to watch as it diligently worked to draw the nectar from a brightly colored *azucena* flower—a daylily. The girls were mesmerized to see how fast its wings were moving.

"Did you know that a hummingbird's wings can flap at up to eighty beats per second?" asked Gabriela.

Georgina and Elisa were fascinated with this magical bird. They couldn't take their eyes off it long enough to even hear their mother's question.

It finally had enough of the sweet liquid and flew away, but not before Gabriela and the girls looked at each other in awe. They had never seen such an enchanting bird.

Gabriela stooped down and placed her swollen hands on her aching knees. She moved her face close to the girls' faces and said, "Isn't it amazing to see how it hovers long enough to sip on the nectar, and when it is finished, it flies away in a flash?"

As they finally came back around the lake to where they had started, Gabriela and the girls were ready to go home. They were happy to spend this time together and to see all the animals. Gabriela and Daniel's children loved animals and being raised on their farm allowed them the opportunity to take care of them.

They walked back to the park's front entrance and took the bus back the way they came. After a few minutes, they stopped at Clara's house to pick up Ramon. He was so happy to see Gabriela and came running to her as soon as he heard her voice. She picked him up but immediately put him down when she felt a stabbing pain in her back.

She let out a loud cry. Ramon looked at her with confusion in his eyes. He didn't know what was happening.

"What is wrong, Gabriela?" said Clara with concern in her voice. "Here, please sit down here on the sofa."

"I'm not sure what is wrong with my back, but it is killing me," said Gabriela.

"Just rest here for a few minutes, and I'm sure you will feel better."

Ramon sensed something was wrong, and he started to cry. Georgina tried to pick him up, but he only wanted to go with his mother. She was in too much pain to do anything but take deep breaths and try to get into a better position. Hoping to find some relief from the pain, she slowly leaned back onto the sofa. Nothing was working. The pain was still unbearable.

"Can you turn on your side?" asked Clara. "I will rub your back to see if this relieves some of the pressure." Clara carefully helped Gabriela roll over.

"I need a favor, Georgina," said Clara. "Can you please reach in the cabinet to the left of the sink, where you will see a small jar of Numotizine, and bring it to me?"

Georgina and Elisa had been silent since seeing their mother unable to move without tremendous pain.

"Yes. I will go and get it," said Georgina.

When she handed the salve to Clara, she unscrewed the lid, and the most pungent medicinal odor immediately escaped. It was a mauve pink color and had the consistency of wet clay. Georgina quickly wanted to get away from the awful smell, so she sat down next to Elisa and didn't say a word. They were frightened and sat motionless, staring at their mother.

"This will help you. Our family has been using this for many years, and it has always alleviated any muscle soreness," said Clara.

She massaged the thick pasty ointment on Gabriela's back for a few minutes. Gabriela could feel the cool menthol from the healing balm on her skin. It seemed to relieve her pain a little, but she wanted to wait a few minutes before attempting to get up. She needed to get home, but it would be impossible for her to take the bus, carry Ramon, and keep an eye on the girls. Gabriela lay there for about twenty minutes, but when she tried to sit up, the pain was excruciating.

They heard keys jangling at the front door. When it opened, it was *el Padre* Diego García —Father Diego García, Clara's older brother. He walked in to find this unexpected scene and was immediately drawn into the situation. He had come home to pick up his notes for Sunday Mass but was now concerned that he should stay and be of assistance.

"Clara, what happened to Gabriela?" asked Padre García.

"She felt a terrible pain in her back and had to lie down. I rubbed her back with Numotizine, but I'm not sure it is helping," said Clara.

"Gabriela, how are you feeling now? Any better since Clara put the medicine on your back?" asked Padre García.

"Just a little. But I tried to sit up a few moments ago, and it was too painful, so I lay back down. I need to get home with the children but cannot take the bus back. Do you think you could go and let my husband know?" asked Gabriela.

Padre García had a car that originally belonged to the church, but it was given to him when he began to pastor the parish. "I can let him know, but I believe it would be better if I drive you and the children home," said Padre García.

"I am so sorry to change your plans, but I think that is a better idea. I am not sure if I can get up, but I will try again in a few minutes," said Gabriela.

"What if Clara and I each stand on either side of you and try to lift you up?" asked Padre García.

"We can try that," said Gabriela.

Clara and her brother got into position and gently placed their forearms under Gabriela's arms to help her up from the sofa. They hoped this would relieve some of the soreness she was experiencing. Gabriela still felt tremendous pain but thought she could tolerate it for a few minutes—enough to get into the car. Now, if she could just get home to lie down, she knew she would feel more comfortable.

Padre García opened the passenger side door. "Gabriela, take a seat first, and Clara and I will bring your legs around." After carefully backing up as close to the seat as she could, Gabriela slowly sat down and leaned back so Padre García and Clara could help her get settled. Once Padre García closed the door, Clara turned and gathered the children. She helped them into the backseat and got in behind them.

"Are you comfortable? Am I driving too fast? How is your pain?" asked Padre García nervously.

"I am fine, just ready to be home. Thank you," said Gabriela.

The drive to La Paloma was only a few kilometers away, so in less than ten minutes, Padre García pulled into the driveway leading back to the farm. Gabriela felt every movement of the car as the tires crunched the gravel. Daniel was in the front yard when he saw Padre García's car, and he wondered why he would be visiting. As the car got closer, he noticed that Gabriela was in the front seat with a pained look on her face, her head tilted back. He rushed to see what was happening and opened the door before the car came to a complete stop.

"What happened to Gabriela?" he asked in a panicked tone.

"She was at the house with the children, and when she picked up Ramon, she must have pulled something in her back because she immediately let out a scream and put him down. She sat down and then lay down, but nothing really helped her," said Clara.

"We brought Gabriela and the children home so she could get into her own bed, where she could be more comfortable," said Padre García. "Let me go around to help you get her out."

Daniel and Padre García saw the anguished look on Gabriela's face and tried to be as careful as possible. They each put one hand on her shoulder and one hand behind her lower back, carefully pulling her closer to the edge of the seat. Once her feet were on the ground, they repositioned their hands, preparing to pull her to her feet.

"Okay, let's be very careful, but we will go on three. One ... two ... three ... slowly pull up," said Daniel.

As they did this, Gabriela cried from the pain. They were supporting her the best they could, and as she took the first step, she felt a rush of fluid escape down her legs. At that moment, Gabriela felt her back pain intensify.

Clara ran ahead and yelled out, "Gabriela's water just broke. She needs help getting into the house."

Lilia was familiar with the preparations for childbirth, so she ran to get the towels and hot water.

They helped her into the house and placed some towels on the bed to try to get her to relax. They carefully lowered her onto the bed, placing pillows behind her back. Her contractions were coming quickly and were more intense than with her previous deliveries. She tried to practice her breathing exercises but was overwhelmed by the pain.

CHAPTER SEVEN

LA PALMA, PINAR DEL RÍO, CUBA
1953

Gabriela could no longer lie motionless in the bed. She needed to get up and move but couldn't find the strength to pull herself up.

"Daniel, Clara, Lilia . . ." Gabriela called out. "Please help me get up. I need to walk around a bit."

Daniel had been just outside the room. Listening. Worrying. When he heard Gabriela yell out for help, he jumped to his feet and ran into the room.

"I can't lie still anymore. I need to get up and move," groaned Gabriela.

"Okay, I'll help you up. Just take it easy, *mi amor*." Daniel carefully lifted her from the bed, now soaked with sweat, being sure she was steady on her feet.

"There you go. Has your back pain gotten any better?" asked Daniel hoping she was feeling better. He hated to see her in pain.

Gabriela began pacing. The floorboards creaked and cracked below her feet, and she dug her fists into her lower back. The contractions were gripping every muscle in her body, but the worst of it was in her lower back. She felt like her body was being torn in two. Rocking back and forth, shifting her weight from one swollen foot to the other, Gabriela was now in the throes of full-blown labor.

Though she had been through childbirth nine times before, each time was different, and she never knew what to expect. The contractions were intensifying, coming in insufferable waves about two to three minutes apart. Gabriela knew it wouldn't be long before it was time to push.

"Daniel, get Adela now," she uttered in between deep guttural moans. Adela had been Gabriela's midwife for each delivery. She couldn't imagine doing this without Adela by her side. There are just some things men do not understand—she needed another woman who knew exactly how she was feeling at every stage of the delivery.

"I am going now, *mi amor*," answered Daniel, his voice shaking and cracking with nerves. He, too, had been through this nine times, but seeing Gabriela in such pain made him feel powerless every single time.

"I can drive you there to pick my sister up if you would like," said Padre García with a slight quaver in his voice.

"Thank you, but it is just two blocks from here, and it will be faster if I run," said Daniel. He sprinted down the driveway kicking up plumes of dust and gravel. Adela was Padre García's youngest sister and lived just a few houses past the *bodega*—the corner store. As he was rounding the turn onto the main road, Manolo, Roberto, and Rigoberto met him in the street. He screeched to a halt, bending over to catch his breath.

"The baby is coming," Daniel said between gasps.

"Is *Mami* okay? What's happening?" Manolo asked with fear welling up inside him. The boys knew nothing of childbirth. Seeing their father in such a panic was enough to strike fear in all their hearts.

Rigoberto was just nine years old. His already-big brown eyes widened even more with worry.

"Go! Make sure your mother is okay. I will be back with the midwife." He took off again into a full sprint toward Adela's house.

"Is *Mami* going to be okay?" Rigoberto searched his older brothers' faces for any sign of fear. Manolo and Roberto looked just as panicked as their father, and they all turned and ran toward home.

When the boys ran into the house, they immediately heard the painful cries of their mother. They had been there for the births of their siblings but couldn't remember hearing this type of agony. They all rushed to her side.

"Are you okay, *Mami*?" asked a frightened Rigoberto. Gabriela was still pacing; the floorboards were still creaking underneath her feet.

"I will be just fine," she managed to say in between contractions. "Go now. Your baby brother or sister will be here before you know it." She bit hard into her bottom lip, waiting for the boys to leave the room before she let out a low primal moan. *Something feels very wrong,* she thought. She had been in unbearable pain with each delivery, but this time felt so different. Stabbing pain filled her belly and wrapped around her lower back and pelvis, making her dizzy and nauseous. Dropping to her knees on the bed, she vomited onto the freshly washed sheets.

Gabriela cried out for Daniel and fell onto her back, wiping sweat from her forehead and cleaning her mouth with the back of her hand.

"*Mami!*" yelled Georgina, running into the room. She saw the bunched-up, soiled sheets and began gathering them to be washed.

"I will clean this and get you some water. Just lie there, *Mami*. Don't try to get up."

Gabriela barely managed a pained, "Thank you, Georgina."

Georgina rushed out of the room, now smelling of sweat and vomit. She was not accustomed to seeing her mother this way. She was always so in control—graceful—a far cry from the woman she just saw lying across the sweat-stained bed. The whole scene scared her. At that moment, she thought to herself that she would never have children.

Her hands shook as she reached for a glass. Her fingers slipped, and the glass crashed to the floor, breaking into a million tiny pieces. It startled her, and she began to cry.

Manolo ran into the kitchen. "It's okay, Georgina. I'll clean this up." Manolo grabbed the water pitcher and filled a glass with water. Handing it to Georgina, he said, "Take this to *Mami*. I'll send someone in to help."

"Please have them come quickly," Georgina implored, her voice cracking with fear.

Georgina walked out of the kitchen just as Daniel and Adela came through the front door.

"Thank God you're here," Clara said with a sigh and leaned against the wall, feeling like she could faint.

"*Papi*, I think something is wrong! *Mami* vomited all over the sheets, and she was dripping with sweat. She can barely talk," said Georgina.

"It's okay, Georgina," Adela jumped in and took the glass of water from Georgina. "This is all very normal. This means the baby is very close to arriving. Don't you worry. I am here now, and I am going to take great care of your *Mami*."

Adela placed a firm hand on Daniel's arm. "Stay here. I want to check on her first."

Daniel, still out of breath, fell back into the nearby chair. He was exhausted, but his only concern at this moment was Gabriela and their new baby. The children gathered around him, all looking terrified. The sounds from the bedroom continued to intensify. At this point, it sounded like a dying animal more than their beloved mother.

Daniel tried to ease their obvious fear. "Don't worry," he said. "The midwife is with her. It shouldn't be much longer."

Adela approached Gabriela.

"I'm here now, Gabriela. We are going to get you all taken care of. Don't you worry."

The stench in the room was overwhelming. When Adela got close, she realized that Gabriela had vomited again, and this time it had not landed in the sheets. She was covered. Adela quickly opened a nearby window, hoping a fresh breeze would make its way through the room, cleansing the putrid air.

"Gabriela, let me help you out of your clothes." She could see Gabriela was in unbearable pain. Adela had delivered hundreds of babies, but she felt in her gut that this was not going to be an easy delivery. This was Gabriela's tenth delivery, and Adela thought she should not be laboring with such extreme intensity. *Her body should know what to do,* Adela thought as she rolled up her sleeves and prepared to help Gabriela out of her clothes.

Just as Adela pulled Gabriela's dress over her head, a contraction took hold. Gabriela writhed and wailed—her voice hoarse from all the screaming. Adela threw the soiled dress to the ground and grabbed Gabriela's hand. Gabriela squeezed back. Adela winced. Gabriela's slender hand gripped hers and nearly crushed it with a combination of fear and strength.

"Gabriela, listen to me . . ." Gabriela looked at her in a daze. "You have to tell me what you're feeling so I can help you."

Gabriela muttered, "Water . . . I am so thirsty." Adela had forgotten about the water. She gently brought the glass to Gabriela's cracked lips, and she managed a few sips before falling back onto the bed.

Adela knew she needed to examine Gabriela. She placed a few pillows behind her upper back.

"I am going to check you now, Gabriela. Please open your legs as wide as you can and try to relax." The contractions were right on top of each other, and Gabriela howled and bore down. She was ready for this baby to be outside of her body.

"Not yet, Gabriela. Try to breathe. Short breaths . . . remember . . . *whoosh, whoosh, whoosh.*" Adela tried to keep her from pushing. She needed more time to check on the baby. "Come on now, short breaths," she repeated, making the sounds again, hoping Gabriela would follow her lead.

Adela grabbed her medical bag, doused her hands with alcohol, and hurried back to Gabriela's side. She steadied Gabriela's leg with one hand and checked her cervix with the other. She was fully dilated and effaced. The baby had dropped and was in position. *There must be something else*, Adela thought. She lowered herself onto her knees beside the bed and looked carefully. The baby should have been crowning by now.

Adela finally saw and felt the issue causing the delayed delivery. The baby's head was not tucked at the chin, ready for delivery. The head was craned backward—chin up. There was no way she could deliver this way without causing serious damage to the baby.

Adela had seen this on many occasions in her time as a midwife. She knew what needed to be done, but she worried about Gabriela as she was already in so much pain.

"Gabriela . . . Gabriela . . . look at me." She was worn out past the point of being able to make eye contact with Adela. With each contraction, she was becoming less and less responsive. She could hear Adela speaking to her, but she could not move herself to respond.

Adela cupped Gabriela's face with her hands. "Gabriela, I need you to turn onto all fours. Can you do that for me? All fours . . ." Gabriela was barely able to nod. All she wanted was to lie back on the pillow.

"Okay, on the count of three, I am going to help you onto all fours. Are you ready?" Adela didn't wait for a response.

She grabbed Gabriela under her right armpit and heaved her over with the force of her entire body. Gabriela was a tall woman, so this was no small feat. Gabriela tried to steady herself on her hands but fell onto her elbows. Sweat ran off her face in a pool onto the bed.

Another contraction came on, and Gabriela was so emotionally and physically spent all she could do was whimper and cry.

"I can't do it. I can't do it anymore . . ." she sobbed.

"Yes. Yes, you can. You're already doing it," Adela encouraged her. "I am going to try to reposition the baby. You are going to feel a lot of pressure. I will wait for this contraction to pass."

Adela felt Gabriela's belly and could feel it soften a bit after the contraction. She wasted no time. Adela reached inside with four fingers and tried to maneuver the baby's head. She was able to move it slightly, but before she knew it, another contraction bore down on Gabriela's body. She swayed and moaned and wanted so badly to push. The pressure was insufferable.

"Not yet, Gabriela." Adela massaged her lower back and continued making the *whoosh, whoosh, whoosh* sound, encouraging Gabriela to join her.

"I want to push!" Gabriela screamed. "Why can't I push? What's wrong?"

"The baby is not quite ready to come yet, Gabriela. I will need to try to reposition the baby's head again."

"Is the baby okay?" she cried. "Tell me ... is there something wrong with the baby?" She was beginning to panic. "Where's Daniel? Please get him. I am frightened."

Again, Daniel was right outside the door and came in at Gabriela's request.

He slowly approached Gabriela, not knowing what to say or do in this moment. She fell back onto the bed, reached out and gripped his hands, and stared into his eyes with a look of terror. Daniel's heart raced, beads of sweat ran down his face, and he suddenly felt light-headed.

Adela, no stranger to a father-to-be fainting, encouraged Daniel to have a seat in a nearby chair.

"We don't have a lot of time. I need you to get back on all fours, Gabriela." Adela, though she knew she could handle this, was beginning to feel the panic in the room.

Gabriela wailed as she landed again on her elbows. Adela wasted no time. Again, she attempted to gently tilt the baby's head. She could feel that this time had been more effective than the last and sighed in relief. She sat back on the bed and waited for her next chance.

"You're doing great, Gabriela," she assured her.

"Get it out," Gabriela implored. "Just get it out!"

Another contraction. Gabriela bit down on her lower lip, drawing blood to the surface.

"Get it out!" Gabriela screamed.

"Short breaths, Gabriela . . . don't push yet . . . *whoosh, whoosh, whoosh . . .*"

"I can't! I can't! I can't!" cried Gabriela, panting.

Gabriela could no longer keep from pushing. The pain was gnawing—splitting her apart.

She groaned and bore down hard.

The baby's head tore through. Gabriela whimpered and whined—a mixture of relief and searing pain. Bright red blood poured out onto the towels, soaking straight through to the mattress. Gabriela would need many stitches. The forceful delivery had torn her in many places that would take weeks to heal.

Adela cradled the baby's misshapen head in her bloody hands waiting for the next contraction. She knew it would startle the parents to see the baby's head this way, but she also knew it would return to its normal shape after a few hours. She had a small, yellow crocheted hat in her bag that she used for this exact reason.

"Okay, Gabriela, the baby's head is out," Adela said with a deep sigh of relief. She hadn't realized she had been holding her breath.

Adela quickly cleared the baby's mouth and nose and the small bedroom filled with the howl of the baby's first cry.

Hot tears ran down Gabriela's flushed cheeks onto the bed. *Gracias a Dios*, she thought. Thank God.

Another cry reverberated through the house. The children, Padre García, and Clara all broke out into loud grateful sighs and cheers. Daniel smiled and wiped tears from his worried eyes. He braced himself and stood slowly from the chair. He walked to Gabriela's side, placing his worn hand on her back, rubbing it gently.

"Our baby is almost here, *mi amor*," Daniel said. He had never felt more pride for his wife than in this moment. She had endured pain that he could not even begin to fathom. He was grateful that it was almost over, and they could finally meet the newest addition to their ever-growing family.

The next contraction came, and with a final long, low, desperate groan, Gabriela delivered her baby. She felt immediate relief and fell onto her back, completely spent.

"You've done it, Gabriela," said Adela. "You've done it. You have a beautiful baby girl."

Adela clamped and cut the umbilical cord. "She's a healthy girl with a powerful set of lungs," Adela said over the loud cries of the new baby. She carefully placed the yellow crocheted hat onto the baby girl's head, wrapped her in a small linen blanket, and gently laid her on Gabriela's chest.

"She's beautiful. Perfect," Daniel said, staring into their baby's honey-colored eyes. He was filled to overflowing with love. He didn't know it was possible to feel this deeply. Each of their children brought a new layer of love—he felt like the luckiest man alive.

Gabriela cradled her baby girl.

"Hello, my sweet girl."

The baby's cries immediately quieted at Gabriela's soft voice, staring back into her mother's loving eyes. They knew each other and were already in love. They stayed this way for a long time, taking every ounce of each other in. Gabriela could see all the possibilities that lie ahead for her new daughter. She imagined all that they would do together and smiled, a single tear running down her cheek.

The children gathered outside the bedroom door, excited to meet their new baby sister. Gabriela and Daniel could hear the giggles and taps of eight sets of feet on the wooden floorboards.

"Come on in," Daniel shouted toward the door.

The heavy door swung open—all eight of them falling through. They gathered themselves, still giggling, and crowded around their mother.

"*Mami*, a boy or girl?" asked Rigoberto.

"A girl . . . a precious baby girl." Gabriela beamed.

They all took turns touching the baby's tender cheeks, oohing and ahhing at how adorable she was.

"Be gentle," Daniel reminded the younger children. "There will be plenty of time for each of you to hold her soon."

After the family welcomed their newest addition, Adela began cleaning Gabriela's ragged tears. She stitched up a few to quicken their healing.

This precious baby came into the world on April 5, just as Dr. Rodriguez had said—around the beginning of April.

"Adela, could you take the baby?" Gabriela asked, sounding sleepy. "I need to rest a bit."

CHAPTER EIGHT

LA PALMA, PINAR DEL RÍO, CUBA

1953

Hours passed and Gabriela was still in a deep sleep. She needed to rest after laboring for many grueling hours to deliver her baby girl. Adela stayed with the family to ensure Gabriela was feeling better and would be able to take care of her baby when she awakened.

"It was a very difficult delivery. Your mother needs this time to rest," said Adela. "Her body must begin healing, and sleep will help her recover," she explained to Daniel and the children as they were all seated around the living room.

"Have you and Gabriela decided on a name for your baby?"

"Yes, her name is María de los Angeles—María of the Angels," announced Daniel sweetly, with an expression as though he had just uttered the name of the most beautiful flower.

"I like that name, *Papi*," said Manolo. "She will be our little angel."

"Yes, her name is so pretty," said Georgina.

Daniel sat on one end of the sofa and lovingly held his new daughter in the crook of his left arm as she slept peacefully. The side of her tiny head rested on his chest. *How precious*, thought Daniel. *This baby already knows she has my heart.* He loved that new baby smell—a mixture of vanilla extract and a fresh ocean breeze. Each time he breathed, he felt he was breathing it in for the very first time. Daniel looked at her perfect features and was already so in love. She had a headful of dark hair and little lips that looked like she was blowing a kiss. Just like with all his other children, he had loved her before he met her. Daniel didn't want anything to disturb her sleep, so he did not move. He just sat still and stared at her, taking in every moment.

Adela was waiting for Gabriela to awaken. She needed to see how she was doing before going home for the evening. Adela would return in the morning to check on Gabriela and the baby, but Adela was exhausted too. It had been a very long day. She looked forward to lighting a candle, drawing a warm bath, and relaxing for a few minutes before heading to sleep. Tomorrow, she would start her routine again—house visits to check in on her patients and their new bundles of joy.

"How much longer should we wait to check on Gabriela?" asked Daniel.

"We need to give her ample time to—"

Adela was interrupted when the baby started to rustle. She began moving her delicate little hand and then lifted the other until she stretched both arms out wide.

Daniel looked at Adela. "Look. She's waking up."

The children approached Daniel and the baby with cautious excitement. They couldn't wait to hold her, but she was still too brand new. Daniel wanted to keep her swaddled and close to him until she could lie on Gabriela's chest and feel her warmth. He knew how special that bonding time was to both mother and daughter and didn't want to take that away from them. María de los Angeles was one day old. She owned their hearts and completed their little world.

The baby was mid-stretch when she opened her tiny, almond-shaped eyes. Daniel then turned to the children with a smile and said, "She is finally awake. Meet your new baby sister." They were all in awe, as they were every time a new baby was born into the family.

Roberto gazed at her fair complexion and long, dark brown eyelashes with adoration.

He was very protective of his mother and of the girls in the family. Now he had one more girl to look after and love. María de los Angeles was starting to get fussy, and this could only mean one thing. She was ready to have her first feeding. Her cries were faint to begin with, but within minutes, they got louder and louder, prompting Adela to check on Gabriela and rouse her from her deep sleep.

Adela softly opened the door to Gabriela's bedroom. "How are you feeling?" she asked. "Your baby girl is awake and wants to see you. She seems to be pretty hungry."

Gabriela took a few shallow breaths and tried to look in Adela's direction. She couldn't. The very center of her head was throbbing, and the room was spinning. Adela could see she was in pain.

"I have a splitting headache," murmured Gabriela, unable to open her eyes.

"Your labor and the delivery of this baby were far more demanding and complicated than that of your other children," said Adela.

"Can you please give me some water? My mouth is parched," asked Gabriela.

"Yes, I will be right back with your water," said Adela. Gabriela had drifted back to sleep and didn't hear Adela.

"Let me help you sit up. Gently . . . gently . . ." Adela urged her as Gabriela tried to awaken. In a semi-sleep, Gabriela leaned slightly forward and took a sip of water. The pain was excruciating.

"Adela, my head is killing me. This has never happened before. What do you think could be wrong?" asked Gabriela as she slid back onto her pillow.

"I'll be right back. I'm going to get you aspirin for your headache. I also need to take your vital signs," Adela said. She went back to the living room to retrieve her medical bag. Daniel was pacing and gently tapping on the baby's back with his open hand as she cried to be fed. "Can I take her in now? She is ready to nurse."

"Give me a few minutes. Gabriela has a terrible headache. I want to give her something to start alleviating the pain. I will come back and take the baby in as soon as she takes the medicine and uses the restroom. I also need to check her vitals, so once I'm finished, I'll be out," said Adela and turned to walk back to Gabriela's room.

Gabriela had fallen asleep once again. "I have your medicine here," said Adela as she realized Gabriela was having a hard time staying awake. She walked to the edge of the bed and gently placed her hand on her shoulder.

"Can you hear me? I need you to sit up so I can give you this aspirin that will help with your headache. I also need to take your blood pressure and temperature."

Gabriela knew she needed to take the medicine to relieve her pain, so with a tremendous amount of effort, she sat up; Adela propped her up with some pillows on the bed. Adela extended one hand with the two white pills and the other with the glass of water. "Please, take these."

Gabriela drowsily plucked the aspirin from Adela's hand and placed them on her tongue. She swallowed them with a few sips of water.

"Now, let's get you up and moving so you don't form any blood clots. I am going to help you to the bathroom." Adela stood by Gabriela and with great care brought her legs around so she could stand up. Gabriela leaned into her, feeling incredible pain throughout her body. She realized that the headache had only been the focus of her pain. Adela steadied herself to support Gabriela's weight but was alarmed when, out of the corner of her eye, she noticed a huge red stain on the bed where Gabriela had been lying. She turned her head to see the extent of it—this was not normal and was very concerning to Adela.

Adela didn't say anything but asked her, "How do you feel now?"

"I feel terrible. I'm hurting everywhere," she said while trying to remember to breathe. Lightheaded and dizzy, Gabriela slowly shuffled to the bathroom. The experience was so much worse than she remembered from every other delivery. The burning. The searing pain. The fatigue. Gabriela prayed for some relief from the all-encompassing misery—a misery like she had never known. What Gabriela didn't expect was the amount of blood loss. With great fear in the pit of her stomach, she looked up at Adela.

"You have lost a lot of blood. Let's get you back in the bed," said Adela, trying not to worry her.

The women slowly made their way toward the bed. Gabriela had no energy and kept her head down. As they got closer, she looked up to see the blood-soaked sheets and felt faint. Adela sat her on the end of the bed so she could remove the soiled linens and spread out clean sheets and towels for her to lie on. The more bed coverings Adela pulled off, the more she realized they were in trouble. Everything was soaked with dark red blood: her gown, the sheets, the towels . . . even the mattress was soaked.

She helped Gabriela back into the bed and slightly elevated her head with additional pillows. Adela quickly took the blood pressure cuff from her black bag and wrapped it around Gabriela's arm. She squeezed the bulb several times, expecting to release the valve within a few seconds to get the reading. Instead, she had released more than half of the air from the bulb before she heard Gabriela's faint heartbeat. The meter barely registered 90/45, causing Adela increased anxiety. Adela's blood pressure began to rise. She wanted to see if her numbers were accurate. Adela removed the cuff and placed it on Gabriela's other arm—this time, the reading was 85/40. She quickly evaluated the situation and determined Gabriela needed immediate medical attention beyond what she could provide. She began to mentally go through her checklist of what needed to happen. She placed the glass thermometer under Gabriela's tongue. It only took seconds for the mercury to rise to 38.8 degrees Celsius—101.8 degrees Fahrenheit. Gabriela was approaching critical condition with myriad symptoms, and Adela knew she needed more advanced medical care.

"Daniel! Daniel!" Adela yelled. "I need help!" her hands trembling as she put the thermometer on the wooden nightstand. Daniel came running with the baby still screaming and ready to be fed.

"What is happening? Is Gabriela okay?" Daniel blurted out.

"Is something wrong with *Mami*?" asked a worried Manolo as he ran in behind his father. The other children followed him, trying to see what all the commotion was about.

"Manolo, I need you to take the children outside and keep them there for now. I will let you know when you can come back in," said Adela between nervous breaths. He turned and did as Adela had asked but was scared by what he'd just witnessed.

With the children out of the room and amid the baby's cries, Adela said, "Gabriela has developed some extremely dangerous symptoms, and I do not have the equipment or training to diagnose or treat her. You stay here with the baby—I will make a milk formula for her to drink. Can you send the older boys to get Dr. Sánchez and tell him we have an emergency? He needs to come here immediately."

Daniel felt the blood rush from his head as he tried to understand the words Adela was saying. Gabriela had always been a healthy woman. Her pregnancies and deliveries had all gone smoothly, except for the last one with Ramon a few years earlier. And even then, the doctor had treated her at home.

"Manolo . . . Roberto . . . I need you to take the horses and ride to Dr. Sánchez's house. Please ask him to come here at once. Tell him it's an emergency," yelled a panicked Daniel through short, ragged breaths.

Confused, Roberto asked, "Is she going to be okay?"

"We won't know until the doctor can see her. Just go already!"

"We will go now," said Manolo. They turned and ran toward the stable. Quickly throwing the saddles on the fastest horses they had, they took off. They galloped up the hill and past the house, turning onto the main road within minutes. They leaned forward and kicked their heels into the sides of the horses, pushing them into a full sprint.

Dr. Sánchez's home was only about eight kilometers or five miles away on horseback, but it seemed like forever to them. Their mother was very sick, and Dr. Sánchez was the only one who could help her.

They jumped off in front of the doctor's home and raced to the door. With trembling hands, they knocked repeatedly. "Dr. Sánchez! Help! Please help us!"

Dr. Sánchez's wife opened the door with a puzzled look on her face. Manolo and Roberto didn't even give her a chance to speak.

"Our mother had a baby this afternoon, but now something is very wrong. Adela, the midwife, asked us to come to get Dr. Sánchez right away. It's an emergency. Can you please get him? We need him to go see her right now," begged a desperate Manolo.

"Boys, what do you need?" asked Dr. Sánchez as he approached the door. He had not heard their impassioned pleas for help, only their distressed voices.

"Please come with us. Our mother needs your help. She had the baby this afternoon and is now very sick," said Roberto with tears welling in his eyes. Hearing this boy of only thirteen years old delivering this terrible news was heartbreaking.

"Give me a few minutes to get my medical bag. I will meet you there. You can head back home, and I will be right behind you," said Dr. Sánchez. Then he turned and ran to get ready.

Manolo and Roberto leaped back onto their horses and pushed them once again to race toward home. The wind dried their tears almost as soon as they ran down their cheeks. The clopping of the horse's hooves on the dirt road echoed in their ears. Within minutes, they were back at the house. Manolo was first to jump off his horse. He threw the front door open and between heavy breaths, uttered, "Dr. Sánchez will be here in a few minutes."

CHAPTER NINE

LA PALMA, PINAR DEL RÍO, CUBA

1953

After Dr. Sánchez rushed to Gabriela's side, he saw she was in critical condition. He knew right away that there was nothing he could do for her here.

"I will drive to *el Policlínico* and send an emergency vehicle right away," said Dr. Sánchez as he ran out of the house. He swung the car door open, stepped on the clutch, and shifted into high gear as he swerved down the dusty driveway, tires screeching as he turned onto the main road.

"Daniel, please take a seat on the sofa," said Adela. "I need you to help me with María de los Angeles." Adela hurried to the kitchen to prepare a homemade baby formula mixture. She used simple ingredients from the kitchen—evaporated milk, water, and a touch of corn syrup. She sterilized a feeding nipple, and when it had cooled, she poured the mixture into a small glass bottle and secured the top before handing it to Daniel.

"Here, take this. Feed your daughter—she must be hungry," said Adela, knowing this would calm Daniel's nerves as he waited. He was gripped with fear and Adela wanted to distract him.

All the children were inside the house, but no one would've known it. They sat or walked around quietly, waiting to see why the adults were so panicked.

The faint warning siren of the emergency vehicle at a distance grew louder and louder as it got closer to Daniel and Gabriela's home. The soundless room filled with whispers, and the echoes of the siren quickly flooded the space, frightening the small children. The hospital medics blared up the gravel driveway, blowing the horn repeatedly, as they left white clouds of gravel and smoke in their wake. Within minutes, they had carefully placed an ailing Gabriela onto a burlap blanket wrapped around a solid wooden stretcher and secured her with three wide cloth belts. They moved quickly and didn't delay in pushing the stretcher carefully into the waiting car. They shut all the doors before stepping on the gas and charging back down the driveway, heading to *el Policlínico*.

Manolo knew that their father had to stay at the house to take care of María de los Angeles and could not be at Gabriela's side. Manolo motioned to Roberto by swiftly moving his head and eyes back and forth toward the front door. They both knew what they needed to do.

"We are going to stay with *Mami* so she is not alone," said Manolo.

Before Daniel could say anything, the boys ran outside and untied the dusty horses from the front porch. They jumped into their saddles and pushed their spurs into the horses' sides—at first gently—but with increasing pressure until they raced down the long gravel driveway, kicking up dust and gravel and galloping onto the road that would lead them to *el Policlínico*.

Everything happened within minutes. By the time Daniel and the children realized it, it was over. Daniel continued feeding his beautiful newborn daughter, but a burning uneasiness began to smolder deep inside his chest. It grew into a ball of anxious feelings.

"My heart feels as if it is beating outside my body," said Daniel, turning to Adela with fear in his eyes.

"I understand how you feel. I've gotten to know Dr. Sánchez, and I can tell you he will take very good care of her. He is an excellent doctor and a kind man."

Adela's words gave him some comfort, but they weren't enough to stop his hands from shaking.

In the old car, Gabriela was disoriented and weak as it bounced over muddy potholes and around sharp corners. With every vibration, she felt like she was losing a little bit more of herself.

Lying in the back of the vehicle, Gabriela prayed. "God, please help me. I want to stay here for my children and my husband and my precious newborn, María de los Angeles—she needs me most right now. I beg for your mercy and . . ." Her voice trailed off.

In the crowded living room, Daniel and the children sat in stunned silence, praying for Gabriela.

"I hope they can help *Mami* feel better," said Georgina through stinging hot tears.

"They will take good care of her," said Adela, concealing her panic at seeing Gabriela's rapid spiral into a life-or-death situation.

Daniel's thoughts raced wildly. He knew he couldn't stay here—he had to be by Gabriela's side.

"Adela," Daniel said with a trembling voice. "I have to leave." Daniel knew Gabriela could be in danger. He stood up and immediately felt lightheaded. His legs felt as if they could buckle under him at any moment.

"Could you please stay here with the baby and the younger children so I can go to the clinic? Gabriela can't be alone right now," said Daniel. He extended his arms to carefully give María de los Angeles to Adela.

She took the newborn and pulled the little pink blanket around her. Daniel rushed to change his shirt, stained with baby formula over the left pocket.

"Gabriela is my everything and was just taken out of here in an alarming state. I cannot let her feel alone," said Daniel. He hurried to the front door and sprinted to the barn where he flung open the door to the stall of his favorite horse, Mantequilla. He threw the saddle on her back and jumped into the seat, pushing her to full speed within seconds.

The emergency attendants who transported Gabriela to *el Policlínico* took great care to move her from the back of the emergency vehicle to a small bed in one of the two rooms that were used for critical patients. They slowly laid her on the thin mattress atop a worn steel bed frame. The white-walled room was barren, with only one brown folding chair and a small wooden countertop to hold the medical supplies. The attendants noticed her teeth chattering and her body shivering and draped a cotton blanket over her.

At that moment, two nurses rushed into the room to take her vital signs.

"I noticed a large amount of blood on the bed sheets when we were moving Señora Martínez de Osaba onto the stretcher," said the concerned medic.

"*Gracias,* I will let Dr. Sánchez know," said the nurse as she turned to speak to Gabriela.

"Señora Martínez de Osaba, we are here to help you." Gabriela couldn't muster the energy to speak or even look their way. As the nurses began taking her blood pressure, temperature, and pulse, they realized why Gabriela felt very cold and was nearly unresponsive.

Dr. Sánchez was anxiously awaiting news that Gabriela had finally arrived at *el Policlínico.* "The moment Señora Martínez de Osaba gets here, I need a nurse to alert me," he announced loudly so everyone on the floor could hear him.

No sooner did the words come out of his mouth, than a nurse rounded the corner and breathlessly yelled, "Dr. Sánchez, Señora

Martínez de Osaba is here and appears to be in serious condition. Her breathing is labored, and the color has drained from her face. The staff are taking her vital signs now."

"Please come with me, Josefina," he said to the nurse. "It sounds like she is getting worse by the minute. I saw her less than an hour ago and she was very sick, but what you are describing concerns me greatly."

They took off toward the emergency department down the long white tile hallway—it seemed to go on forever. Their steps echoed as they moved with increasing urgency, halting only when Dr. Sánchez grabbed the door frame to Gabriela's room. Swinging around, he demanded, "What are her vital signs?"

"Readings two minutes ago: blood pressure 78/38, and temperature 38.8 degrees Celsius—101.9 Fahrenheit. Her heart is pounding, and her pulse is 125 beats per minute," said the dreadfully concerned nurse. "The medic alerted us to substantial blood loss, which he observed when moving Señora Martínez de Osaba onto the stretcher." The nurses were used to the chaos of the emergency department, but this situation was dire.

"Let's address the bleeding first. She also appears to be severely dehydrated. I need you to administer IV fluids immediately," said Dr. Sánchez, addressing the head nurse. He knew they needed to act swiftly. He was growing increasingly alarmed.

"Gabriela . . . Gabriela," said Dr. Sánchez nervously. Gabriela lay listless and unable to respond.

"Let's move quickly before her symptoms continue to deteriorate." The doctor's usually calm demeanor had given way to a look of distress on his face, and he was giving orders faster and more loudly than usual.

"We need to run laboratory tests and draw a crossmatch to get her blood type for a potential transfusion at once," said Dr. Sánchez.

The results for the crossmatch would not be available for at least one hour while precious minutes ticked away. The remaining laboratory tests would take several days. Josefina stood beside Gabriela's bed with a stethoscope and listened to her heart and lungs again. She was concerned to hear Gabriela's quick, shallow breaths and racing heart. The other nurses frantically applied a tourniquet to her right arm and drew several vials of blood. Gabriela appeared to be in agony—her skin felt clammy and her hairline was beaded with drops of sweat. They were all working diligently to determine the best course of action. Even though the medical team was doing everything in their power to stabilize Gabriela, they knew from her symptoms that she was fighting for her life.

Fully aware that they were in a race against the clock, Dr. Sánchez discovered the source of the bleeding. Gabriela was in a perilous situation: she had massive postpartum hemorrhaging, the most serious of all her symptoms.

With all the commotion in the room, no one noticed that Roberto and Manolo had snuck in and stood quietly in a corner, partially covered by a white cloth curtain that served as a partition.

Despite Gabriela's condition, the fluids were starting to bring the slightest bit of life back into her achy body. She slowly opened her eyes and mumbled in a hushed tone, "Can I please have some water?"

"*Sí*, Señora Martínez de Osaba," said a surprised Josefina. "I'll be back with your water in just a moment." She turned to go find Dr. Sánchez and let him know Gabriela was semi-conscious and asking for water.

With the doctor and nurses out of the room, the boys felt safe to come out from behind the curtain and approach their mother's bed. "Are you feeling better, *Mami*?" asked Manolo.

Gabriela was still dazed about where she was but would always recognize her children's voices. "*Hola, mis amores*," she said with a faint breath, feeling exhausted and drained. "I am praying that the doctors will help me feel better."

"*Mami*, we love you so much and want you to get better so you can come home soon," said Roberto.

Gabriela tried to smile but only the slightest upward curve appeared on her lips. "I love you both so much. I am . . . very tired . . . but please stay . . ." Her voice gradually faded away, and her eyelids became heavy.

"We love you too," said Manolo. The boys exchanged glances—they couldn't tell if their mother had heard them.

"Can you hear us, *Mami*?" asked Roberto. Gabriela didn't answer and struggled to open her eyes. She only managed to slightly lift her eyelids, but her gaze was somehow different now. Her eyes were hazy, and she had a faraway look.

"*Mami, Mami*," said Roberto, needing reassurance that she would be okay. Desperately, he tried to get his mother to stay with them.

But Gabriela couldn't focus. Once again, sleep overtook her.

Her face and body began to loosen and relax. She started whispering as if she were having a conversation with someone.

Daniel arrived at the clinic. He jumped down from the saddle and tied his horse to the tree closest to the entrance of the building. He ran inside and appeared breathlessly in the doorframe of Gabriela's room. "How is your mother doing?"

"We don't know. She has mostly been sleeping but has tried to wake up," said a frightened Manolo.

"*Mami*, can you hear me?" asked Roberto, with more urgency this time and a puzzled look on his face. Only moments earlier, his mother had been writhing in pain—now, she seemed content and as if in a dream.

"We are here with you, *Mami*," said Manolo. "Can you hear us?"

Gabriela didn't respond. She appeared to be in her own world.

Her dream came to her as if in a fog. In it, she could see her grandmother Juliana motioning for her to come and take a seat next to her.

"Gabriela, *ven acá*—come here," said Juliana to her beloved six-year-old granddaughter with a tender smile.

Gabriela was shy but slid into a small brown wicker chair by her grandmother on the balcony of her grandparents' summer home near Playa Mayabeque. It overlooked a small but perfect rose garden with fragrant yellow, pink, lavender, and white roses. This garden had been a labor of love for Gabriela's grandfather Vicente, and it was Juliana's favorite place to be. The fragrant aromas from the blooms floated through the air on a breeze that swirled around and came to rest on their noses, leaving them with a most delightful and nostalgic sense of wonderment.

Juliana adored Gabriela and the two of them liked to play dress-up. Anytime she got to wear makeup, Gabriela felt special.

"I'll be right back." Juliana walked into the main bedroom and stretched her arm to reach inside the armoire where she kept her faded black leather purse—it contained her brightly colored cosmetics. As she returned to the balcony, she opened the handbag and said, "Gabriela, why don't you pick a color for your lipstick."

She quickly chose a ruby red shade.

"That is the perfect color for you," said her grandmother with excitement in her voice.

Juliana glided it across Gabriela's tiny lips. With her fingertips, she gently rubbed the color onto her cheeks until only a rosy glow remained. Juliana took a cotton pillowcase from the bed and used a black ribbon to tie it around Gabriela's waist. Now, she felt like a princess. She was wearing a pretty skirt and having makeup on her face made her feel all grown up. But Juliana wasn't finished with the costume.

"Vicente, can you please bring me one of the empty round cardboard buckets from the shed?"

"Yes," said Vicente. "I'll be right back."

Juliana turned to Gabriela with a grin on her face that showed a surprise was on its way. Gabriela, knowing her grandmother was up to something, couldn't contain her excitement. Moments later, her grandfather appeared at the door with two buckets.

"I brought one for each of you. I am not sure what you are planning to make with these, but both of my girls should have one."

The dream was so bright and vivid, and Gabriela fought to stay within its comfort.

Juliana looked at Gabriela as they both smiled, and she said, "*Gracias.*"

Vicente smiled and his gray eyes lit up. He turned to finish washing and drying the glass bottles that the milkman would take in the morning when he delivered fresh milk.

Juliana took her navy-blue seamstress tracing pencil and drew a line around the bottom third of the bucket. With great care, she placed her fingers around the black handle of the sharp stainless-steel scissors and lifted them from the drawer of her sewing machine. She began cutting along the traced line and within minutes had fashioned a crown adorned with bright pink satin ribbons.

As Juliana placed the crown gently on Gabriela's head, the dream abruptly faded. Gabriela opened her eyes and looked around. She was alert and lucid.

"Daniel . . . Roberto, Manolo, what are you doing here?"

All three ran to her side. "I'm so glad you are awake," exclaimed Daniel.

"*Mami, Mami*," said the boys repeatedly. "Do you feel better?"

"I'm okay but I feel weak and need something to drink. I'm so hungry, too," said Gabriela.

Roberto hurried to find Josefina and tell her the good news. "*Mami* is awake and I think she's feeling better. She wants something to eat and drink."

Josefina quickly prepared a cup of hot *manzanilla* tea—chamomile tea, known for its healing herbal qualities. She placed it on a tray and added a few crackers, to help settle Gabriela's stomach.

"That smells so good," said a feeble yet hopeful Gabriela.

Josefina gently helped her sit up by interlocking her right arm with Gabriela's left and bracing her back for support with her other hand.

"*Gracias*. This is just what I needed," said Gabriela. "It's been a rough day."

"I'm glad to see that you are feeling better," said Josefina. "You gave us a big scare."

Dr. Sánchez was in the hallway and heard Gabriela speaking clearly. He was hopeful but feared this sudden burst of energy could be a bad sign. He had seen this with other gravely ill patients. He called out for Josefina and the other nurses to help take vital signs and said he would be there in a few moments.

The boys hid behind the curtain again before Josefina could notice them. They were terrified but didn't want to be seen as children were not allowed.

After having some tea, Gabriela appeared to be feeling better.

"Where is María de los Angeles?" asked Gabriela.

"She is at home, waiting for you," said Daniel.

As time passed, Gabriela became sleepy again. Her breathing had started to become ragged, and her heart had started beating rapidly again. She began moving around on the bed as if trying to get comfortable.

Although Dr. Sánchez had not made an official diagnosis, Josefina began thinking that she may have a systemic blood infection. Dr. Sánchez was alerted to Gabriela's sudden decline. He interrupted his consultation with two other doctors about a different case, sprinting from his office to her room. Upon arriving at Gabriela's room, Josefina told him of her strange set of symptoms.

"Señora Martínez de Osaba has gone from having overwhelming pain, no urine output for hours, a fever, and a rapid heart rate to being alert and having an appetite for a few moments now, to restless—and her heart rate has shot up again. Her respirations have been slowing for the last ten minutes."

"We also received the results of the crossmatch to prepare a blood transfusion for her. She is O positive, and as soon as you place the order, we can administer it."

Dr. Sánchez suspected what the combination of symptoms represented, and he feared he may not be able to do much more to help her. But he couldn't give up. "Let's get the transfusion ordered right away," he said.

He stayed by her bedside for close to an hour as he observed the decline in respirations per minute. The stark reality was grim. Although the blood transfusion had been started, her vital signs all appeared to be past the point of no return.

"She has taken a turn for the worse," said Dr. Sánchez. "Her vital signs are plummeting, and we are running out of options."

Daniel was wringing his sweaty hands repeatedly. His mind was unable to focus or process the things the medical staff was blurting out—worsening news with each word—just when he thought she was getting better. He looked up to the small, brown wooden crucifix that hung on the wall, and his heart offered a prayer his words could not express.

Desperate to know how their mother was doing, Roberto and Manolo ran out from behind the curtain and startled Dr. Sánchez.

"What is happening to our mother?" asked a weeping and agitated Manolo. His hands were shaking, and the knot that had started in his stomach was now in his chest and throat.

"Please wait in the hallway, boys," said Dr. Sánchez in a stern tone.

"No. Is she going to die?" asked Roberto.

"Please, Josefina, take these boys outside," said Dr. Sánchez.

"No. We want to stay with her," said a distraught Roberto, pleading with the doctor.

Seeing Gabriela in this condition saddened Dr. Sánchez, yet he needed to concentrate only on taking care of her at this moment. "You can sit in the chairs in the corner of the room behind the partition, but I don't want to hear anything from you."

They could barely contain their absolute fear at seeing their mother this way but didn't make a sound.

"We need to make her as comfortable as we can. Bring me the morphine. There is nothing else we can do," said a downcast Dr. Sánchez.

Daniel jumped to his feet with an outburst of great pain and suffering that could be heard outside the room and down the hallway upon hearing Dr. Sánchez's orders.

"*Ay Dios mio*—oh my God. This can't be! What about my other children?" cried a distraught Daniel. "They need to say goodbye to their mother if what you are saying is true."

Dr. Sánchez gave him a look of despair and said, "Sadly, it is true. I'm not sure how long she has. If you want to send one of the boys to bring the other children, he should leave right now."

"Manolo, please hurry and tell Lilia what is happening," begged Daniel. "Your mother is in grave condition and Lilia needs to be here. I think it may be better if the younger children stay at home with Adela. Seeing this would be a trauma they would carry their whole lives."

Dr. Sánchez took the long stainless-steel syringe from the metal tray on the counter and filled it with the sedating medicine before pushing it into her arm.

The boys were in tears but still held onto the hope that their mother would get better and come back to them. Within a short time, she became eerily still, and her breathing was relaxed. Gabriela appeared to be sleeping soundly. After a while, Dr. Sánchez began to count her respirations per minute ... 15 ... 11 ... 10 ...

It felt as if time stood still, but the hours continued their onward march. Just then, Josefina led Lilia quietly into the room. She slowly walked to stand by her mother's bed and burst into tears at seeing her lie motionless.

Dr. Sánchez felt helpless and knew Gabriela's suffering would be over soon ... 8 ... 5 ... 4 ... the last fifty minutes of Gabriela's life were tranquil ... 3 ... 2 ... 1 ...

Dr. Sánchez stood beside her as she began to drift away. Daniel sobbed and held Gabriela's hand as she took her final breath and peacefully walked into the arms of her waiting grandmother.

Dr. Sánchez couldn't help but feel the lump in his throat give way to hot tears filling his eyes. He closed his eyes, raised his arm, and made the sign of the cross. He whispered this blessing on Gabriela: "In the name of the Father, and of the Son, and of the Holy Spirit."

He opened his eyes and looked at the clock on the wall. "Josefina, please record the time of death as 2:40 p.m."

★

"Roberto . . . Manolo . . . Lilia . . . you can come be with your mother now," said a saddened Dr. Sánchez. "She has gone . . . to be with the angels and . . . she is . . . she is no longer suffering."

Manolo looked at the doctor, then at his mother, and back at the doctor. He couldn't process what he was hearing. It only took him a few seconds to realize the finality of what had just happened in this room. He let out an anguished cry. His beloved mother had been ripped away from them. He couldn't make sense of it.

Dr. Sánchez and Josefina did their best to comfort Daniel and the other children, but this was a wound so deep that not even a lifetime would be enough to erase the immeasurable pain they would feel.

"We are going to step outside and let you stay here and say your goodbyes to your mother until it is time to take her to be prepared for burial," said Dr. Sánchez. "The attendants will then transport her to your home for the viewing this evening."

Roberto gazed down at his mother and didn't want to believe his eyes; there were no signs of life within her once-thriving body. Roberto's vision was blurry, but he couldn't make the tears stop.

"I love you so so much, *Mami*," cried an inconsolable Roberto.

With his large hands, Manolo softly moved her hair to the side and between sobs, quietly said, "We all love you so much, *Mami*."

Roberto gently took his mother's worn hands in his. Her color slowly drained, and a pale-yellow hue now replaced the warmth he had always known. It was gone. His beloved *Mami* was gone, forever.

A few days passed before the results from the laboratory tests came back. Just as Dr. Sánchez had suspected, Gabriela had several things happening at the same time, and it was difficult to tell which of her conditions he should have treated first—the colossal post-partum hemorrhaging, the greatly reduced kidney function, or the sepsis that overtook her ravaged body. Dr. Sánchez concluded the official diagnosis that led to Gabriela's death was primarily hypovolemic shock—she had lost more than twenty percent of her total blood volume. The transfusion could not have replaced the tremendous amount of blood she was losing fast enough to save her life.

Dr. Sánchez had been a practicing obstetrician-pediatrician for more than ten years. Losing a patient was always tragic. This time was different. This time, he felt he had lost someone special. She was the wife of a good man and the mother of their large, loving family. Gabriela's sudden death made him feel intense grief, in an unexpected way.

CHAPTER TEN

LA PALMA, PINAR DEL RÍO, CUBA

1953

The hot sun set on this somber day and the darkness of night had swallowed every point of light in the black midnight sky. Daniel sat alone on the edge of the worn sofa in their dimly lit living room with his face buried in his hands. He wept—not a soft, sad cry, but a guttural wailing coming from deep within him. The anguish of Gabriela's death engulfed his entire being and the soul-crushing pain suffocated him.

"No, no, no ..." Daniel cried.

He felt as if he had been punched in the gut. He struggled to find the words that would make any sense of it.

He couldn't.

He could only beg God for an answer to his most simple question: "Why did this have to happen, *Dios mio*?"

Daniel could not accept the sudden loss of his beautiful Gabriela—his first love and best friend. She was the center of his universe, and without her, he didn't know how he could go on living.

Earlier that afternoon, Daniel, Manolo, Lilia, and Roberto were utterly devastated when they had to leave *el Policlínico* without their wife and mother. The emotions welling up in their chests were somewhere between shock, disbelief, and overwhelming sadness. Dr. Sánchez wanted the family to stay together at this difficult time and suggested they ride the bus home. He gave his word that he would have the attendants deliver the horses later in the afternoon.

They boarded the bus just outside the clinic and each took a window seat. They rode all the way home, staring at the passing scenery in complete silence, tears flowing and dampening their cheeks.

When Daniel opened the front door, the other children came running—Rolando, Rigoberto, Georgina, and Elisa.

"When will *Mami* be home?" asked Georgina excitedly. Slowly the children realized that their father and siblings had been crying.

"What's the matter?" asked Rolando, as he started to sense something was very wrong. Elisa and Rigoberto were now afraid to know what the answer to those questions would be.

Daniel had no idea how to say the words that would break his children's hearts forever—this was the hardest thing he would ever do. He had held onto his great sadness as best he could. He wanted to be strong for them, but when his heart could no longer separate his emotional pain from his physical pain, he finally let the rush of emotions overtake him.

Daniel sobbed for what felt like forever. His breathing eventually slowed, and he felt he could tell them the terrible news. "Your mother was very sick, and the doctor couldn't make her better." His voice shook as he uttered the words he never imagined saying to his children. "She is . . . she is in heaven . . . watching over us now. She is our . . . angel," he lamented with unbearable pain. In the corner of the room, Adela stood, holding María de los Angeles. She couldn't help but think, *Hearing the sound of the cracking in someone's voice when they can't hold back the tears is the saddest sound in the whole world.*

The children were inconsolable.

"How could *Mami* be gone?" uttered Ramon.

"Is she coming back?" asked Elisa, on the verge of tears but unsure why. At four years old, she could feel the pain in her heart. That she understood. It ached. Her mind hadn't caught up yet—she was unable to fathom the idea that her mother wouldn't be coming home.

"Come here," sobbed Manolo as he bent down to pick her up and wrap her in his strong arms. "No, *Mami* is not coming back." His voice trembled as he said the words out loud for the first time.

The tears began welling in Elisa's big brown eyes. "Why? Where did she go?"

Roberto walked over to where Manolo was standing with Elisa and threw his arms around Manolo's neck. His heart ached with a pain he never could have imagined possible. He stood there sobbing, his chest heaving. Manolo pulled him closer until their foreheads touched. He reached his hand around and pressed it to the back of Roberto's head. They both let the raw grief they were feeling engulf them, and they cried what felt like a never-ending river of tears.

Time stood still. Gabriela's bright light had been extinguished unexpectedly. She was taken from them in an instant, and their family would never be the same. This was the saddest moment of their young lives, and it held an image that would be seared in their memory forever.

"Why is *Mami* not coming back?" cried Elisa with tears running down her flushed cheeks.

Just then, Daniel looked down to see baby Ramon running toward him with teary eyes, his bottom lip curled under. He had awakened from his nap and wanted his mother. Ramon looked around but didn't see her. He ran to his father, arms outstretched, begging him to pick him up and hold him. Daniel pulled him into a tight hug as Ramon lay his tiny head on Daniel's tear-stained shirt.

Sitting in her mother's favorite blue upholstered chair, Lilia was softly weeping, wiping her tears with her mother's tattered handkerchief. She couldn't believe what she was hearing. How could her mother be gone? She immediately regretted not spending more time with her or being there for the family more in the last few years. *Now, I will never get the opportunity to tell her how much I loved her and what she meant to me*, thought a sorrowful Lilia. Her salty tears stung her face—she would forever wish that she could turn back the clock and make things right.

Preparations for Gabriela's final farewell started within hours of her passing. Daniel and the older boys were in a daze as they cleared the area by the back wall of the living room to make room for Gabriela's viewing. This moment was surreal—Gabriela had been in this very room only days ago, talking and laughing just as she had before the birth of each of their children.

Why was this time different? What happened to our beloved wife and mother? thought Daniel as he stood at the open living room window and looked out. Daniel put his calloused hands in his pockets, waiting for the funeral car that would bring Gabriela home for the last time. He wondered how he and the children would survive the next few days, weeks, and forever without her. Minutes later, the black station wagon turned onto the gravel driveway to make the slow drive to La Paloma. The crunching of the small rocks under the tires was all Daniel could hear as his mind reeled in confusion and agony.

The car slowly rolled to a stop by the front door. Four men got out and walked to the back of the vehicle. The long door opened, and they steadied themselves to pull out the dark-stained wooden casket with the white cotton lining that carried Gabriela's body. Daniel opened the front door to their home and guided them to the corner of the living room where he instructed them to place the casket. They carefully situated it as Daniel had asked and lifted the lid into place for the visitation this evening. Daniel glimpsed at Gabriela lying there, and his eyes widened for just a moment. His mind wanted to believe that his beautiful Gabriela was peacefully sleeping. Reality crashed down on him and he realized that after tomorrow, he would never see his beloved wife again.

"Thank you," Daniel whispered with sorrowful eyes as he walked them out. He slowly closed the door behind them and turned to stand by the casket. He ran his fingers along Gabriela's smooth cheek and wished that love could bring her back. He reached for Gabriela's small hand and took it in his. As he did, so many beautiful memories they had shared rushed in. His heart was filled with joy for an instant. Just as quickly as the memories came, they disappeared when the fact that she was gone brought him to despair.

The sad news of Gabriela's sudden passing quickly spread throughout their small village of La Palma. Family and friends were in disbelief as they began readying themselves to pay their respects that evening.

The older children were in shock and couldn't accept that their mother was gone forever. Manolo, Lilia, and Roberto sat around the kitchen table in silence. Their heads were held low—their cheeks were flushed and tear-stained.

The weight of their hearts was unbearable. They understood the finality of death in an abstract sort of way, but their minds couldn't reconcile that their devoted mother would never again be there to love them as only she knew how. Who would take care of them when they were sick? Who would comfort them when they were sad? Who would hold this family together in the good times and the bad the way she did? All these questions rolled around in their heads. In this defining moment and without uttering a word, the siblings were bonded in their grief. The very real pain of losing their mother ached in the center of their chests in a way they had never felt before.

"I feel a hole in my heart," said Roberto, acknowledging this new bitter feeling. At thirteen years old, he could not have known then that the void he felt that day would last his entire life. Time would pass and smooth the jagged edges of his pain, and through the years, thoughts of his mother with her gentle spirit and open heart would bring him peace, but the pain would never completely go away.

The younger children played in silence in their rooms, coming and going throughout the day, checking on their now lifeless mother. Their young minds couldn't understand the tragedy the family was facing but could see the sadness in the adults' eyes. The sorrow hung heavy in the room. The children were all feeling the loss in different ways, but the true depth of their grief would not yet set in for weeks to come.

Beautiful floral arrangements arrived throughout the afternoon from loved ones expressing their sympathy. The *coronas*—floral sprays and vases were filled with mostly pure white stargazer lilies, carnations, gladioluses, deep red roses, and pale-yellow irises. Others sent bright green plants with waxy, shiny leaves—a peace lily and a *mata de malanga*—a taro plant, overflowing from a white ceramic pot. Daniel found solace as he read the messages of condolences on the attached cards. Each card lovingly expressed the admiration and love they felt for Gabriela with thoughtful, caring words.

Gabriela was so loved by so many, thought a tearful Daniel as he paused, reading each one. At the same time, the stabbing pain he felt in his chest was dreadful. How would he learn to live with this aching in his heart? Daniel's hands trembled as he placed the cards to the side of the casket with great care. This was his last opportunity to take care of Gabriela, and he was going to honor her as best he could.

Lilia watched silently as her father, with his head hung low, went to the door to accept each delivery. She reluctantly moved closer to her mother's casket. A single tear slowly rolled down her cheek and onto her mother's folded hands. Lilia gently wiped it away and caressed her mother's cold hands. Out of the corner of her eye, she could see Georgina and Elisa walking toward her. Lilia blotted her hot cheeks with her mother's white handkerchief and turned around. Kneeling to bring the younger girls into a tight embrace, Lilia mourned her own tremendous loss, but even more so that of her sweet little sisters. She knew the passing of time would fade Gabriela's precious memory from their minds, compounding the sting of losing her at such a young age.

Lilia composed herself and asked the girls, "Can you help me place the flowers near *Mami*?"

"Yes, we can do that," said a sullen Georgina. Daniel and Gabriela's three daughters took the arrangements and plants and one by one, carefully placed them on the floor to the sides and in front of the casket, from the tallest sprays to the smallest plants, ensuring each could be seen.

Aromatic flowers filled the small living room and represented the love so many had for this special wife and mother. The candles placed around the casket gave the room a warm glow, but their real purpose was to mask the odor of death.

"Daniel," said Adela. "Here, please take María de los Angeles. I will return a little later with my brother, Padre García."

In the late afternoon, people from the village began gathering at the family home—mourning her with tremendous sorrow and grieving for the family. The first to arrive was Señora Lopez from the home next door. Roberto and Manolo silently stood by Daniel as he opened the door. No words were needed—only a long and tearful embrace. Gabriela and Daniel were only nineteen when they moved to La Paloma, and Señor and Señora Lopez had taken the young couple under their wing. Gabriela had been like a daughter to them; Señora Lopez felt immense pain at losing her.

"Please come inside, Señora Lopez. I want you to see my beautiful Gabriela. She looks so tranquil—almost like she is sleeping," said Daniel and took her by the hand. Señora Lopez hesitantly walked with him. She didn't want to see her like this. Señora Lopez wanted to remember Gabriela as the delightful girl with the sweet smile of her youth. Daniel put his arm around Señora Lopez, and they stood there in their sadness for a moment until others began to arrive. Then, Daniel excused himself and greeted the sorrowful visitors.

Adela arrived wearing a black lace veil covering her face as she entered the house with her brother. Adela, like all of the visitors, came dressed in black and was distraught at the unexpected loss of this tender-hearted and gentle soul. Gabriela had always found time to help a friend or speak an encouraging word to someone in need. Daniel loved to hear the stories of how she had touched their lives in the most thoughtful ways. Their kind words and lovely gestures were all of great comfort to Daniel. Padre García spoke for a few moments about the life of this wonderful wife and mother they had lost.

"Although we don't understand why this has happened, we are reminded that through our hope of eternal life found in Jesus Christ, we will be reunited with her in heaven someday." In closing, he offered a prayer, "God, I ask you to be with this loving family in their time of sorrow. Comfort them and bring them peace as they face the difficult days ahead. May your light shine on them as they traverse this dark time, knowing that you will be there to guide and sustain them. Amen."

The mourners embraced each other and quietly expressed their sadness at her tragic death, as tears streamed down their cheeks. Gabriela was a young mother and wife of only thirty-six years of age and had now left a large, loving family, including her newborn baby girl. She needed her mother. They all needed her.

Several family members and friends offered to help take care of the children in the coming days or weeks so Daniel could settle the details of Gabriela's passing. Daniel couldn't even begin to think of that at this moment. The idea of not having all his children under his roof at a time like this would be another profound loss that he couldn't conceive.

As the visitors began to leave, the sky opened up with an unexpected rainstorm, and Daniel thought, *Even the heavens are grieving with us in our great suffering*. Gabriela was Daniel's rock. Her children were her joy. And now they were left to navigate this life without her. None of the children could fully comprehend that their world would never be the same again.

The family could not give Gabriela an elaborate burial, but she would be at rest in *el Cementerio de Consolación del Norte* in La Palma, and they could visit her. She would always be close to them.

CHAPTER ELEVEN

LA PALMA,
PINAR DEL RÍO, CUBA
1953

The days following Gabriela's burial were shrouded in a hazy fog of sorrow, turmoil, shock, confusion, and disbelief. It descended on Daniel and his children like an all-encompassing dark cloak of grief. The minutes crept by from the moment Daniel opened his eyes at daybreak until he laid his head on the pillow late into the night. When he would awaken from endless nights of restless sleep, his first thought of the day was always of Gabriela and the abyss her absence had left in their home.

I cannot imagine a lifetime without my Gabriela when I don't even remember how to take the next breath, thought Daniel. The aching and emptiness he felt settled into the hollow place in his chest—slowly evolving into numbness. He didn't feel a thing—only a yearning for the love and connection that had been ripped away when Gabriela died.

Daniel's crumbling emotional state and the demands at La Paloma were overwhelming, on top of taking care of his grieving family.

Gabriela had always taken care of the children and the household responsibilities while Daniel worked on the farm and provided for them.

Now, he was forced to do both.

Daniel and his nine children were completely lost—with no compass to guide their path. Gabriela's death was so sudden and unexpected, and their minds were trying to catch up to their raw and jagged emotions. Gabriela was the rock that had steadied her family, but it had now been pulled out from under them in what felt like a free-fall with no place to land.

Lilia stepped up to take Gabriela's place in caring for María de Los Angeles. The precious newborn had only been in the world one day when she lost the mother she would never know. Lilia tended to every need María de Los Angeles had with the tenderness she had learned from her mother. Lilia had been at Gabriela's side to help after the birth of each of her younger siblings. This time, things were dramatically different.

She had to manage the day-to-day care of the new baby and did her best to feed and look after the younger children. She fell more in love with this perfect tiny baby every day that passed. Lilia could feel her mother's presence as she cared for her family and for María de Los Angeles. The heartbreak of losing her mother was alleviated for just a moment when she envisioned her smiling with pride at her daughter's dedication to their family.

It was an enormous responsibility for a girl of sixteen, but she had no other choice. Teenage rebellion had kept her away from the family the last few years, but having her mother ripped away from them brought everything into a different light.

Lilia had to be here for her family in a way none of her siblings could be.

Rolando and Rigoberto couldn't fully understand everything that was happening around them. Gabriela had a special bond with her sons and although they couldn't articulate their loss, they knew they missed their mother terribly.

The youngest of the girls, Georgina and Elisa, would sit on the dusty floorboards of the small front porch every day with their arms crossed over their knees, waiting for their mother. In the early evening, when she had not returned home, their spirits would be crushed. They would join the family for dinner but wouldn't touch their food. Dinner around the table was no longer a joyful time. Mostly the family sat in silence, just picking at their food.

Two-year-old Rolando wandered around the house alone, looking for his *Mami*—his prolonged crying had left his face crusty with snot and tears. His tiny voice was hoarse and weak. He was covered with stains—collected dried bits of food and drink down the front of his small denim overalls. Gabriela had always helped him as he was learning to eat on his own.

Adela stopped by early each morning to see María de Los Angeles for the first few weeks after Gabriela's death. She would check in to ensure the baby was healthy and that Lilia was able to care for her in the midst of this storm. Their lives had been turned inside out and Adela knew that a young girl taking care of a newborn would require support and help from so many that loved them. Adela's visits were a welcome distraction for Daniel. They were also a momentary respite of the constant awareness of his staggering aloneness. He didn't know how he would face the monumental tasks of life ahead of him without Gabriela.

"You are a godsend, Adela," said Daniel. "Thank you for your help and concern as we start to find our way without Gabriela's love and care."

"She was a very special woman, and no one could ever take her place," said Adela. "I feel comforted to see that Lilia is taking care of María de Los Angeles in such a sweet way at her young age."

"I don't know how I would be able to do this without her," said Daniel.

Although Manolo and Roberto continued helping Daniel with the work around the farm, he was overwhelmed and exhausted as chaos swirled around them.

Daniel longed for the day when some of the special moments and lovely memories he shared with Gabriela and their children would trickle into his broken heart. For now, only immense sadness filled every crevice—crowding out all other emotions.

As the days turned into weeks, Daniel tried his best to hide the emotional shrapnel expanding within him. He was paralyzed and couldn't see life past Gabriela's death. Daniel and his family were slowly drowning—all air seeping from their lungs. They were suffocating under the burden of their loss.

The children grew fearful as they watched their father becoming closed off, withdrawn, and despondent. Every interaction was made worse by his swelling anger and irritability at the slightest things. Their once simple but clean home was now disheveled. Piles of dirty laundry were everywhere and unwashed dishes with crusted remnants of food were piled high and overflowed onto the sticky countertops. Roberto and Manolo tried their best to help with the chores around the house but were busy caring for the animals and harvesting the crops to sell before the prime picking season had passed.

Lilia couldn't keep up with the demands of caring for a newborn along with taking care of everyone and handling the many chores required for such a large family. Although María de Los Angeles was a sweet baby girl with a calm temperament, she still craved the attention and love that only a mother could provide. The nights were the most difficult—she would cry for hours. There was nothing Lilia could do to soothe her.

Our mother was taken within hours of her birth, and the vast void she must feel breaks my heart, thought Lilia. She had tremendous empathy for the suffering her newborn sister and family were going through, but the constant pressure of this new family dynamic was taking its toll on her. She was bone-tired. Attempting to balance it all, she began to struggle more and more. She was running out of solutions.

With Daniel's growing inability to cope, he began disappearing from La Paloma for long periods of time. The children didn't know where he had gone and had to fend for themselves. They were confused and had nowhere to turn for help.

It started in the early morning hours when the children were fast asleep. Daniel would wait until his family couldn't hear him and then would quietly sneak out of the house. He stepped softly into the coolness of the dark night and made his way to the barn with only moonbeams to guide his path. The barn had always been a safe place where he could think, pray—and in the good times, dream. He found peace there while the animals and the rest of the world slept.

Since he recently discovered the *aguardiente* in the barn—a homemade moonshine made from sugarcane—he could think of nothing else. This elixir was the only balm that had taken the sharp edges off the blades slicing through Daniel's heart. He found the dusty, unopened bottle behind the large leather saddles stored at the far end of the barn and didn't know how it had gotten there. Daniel had never been a drinking man, so he knew it had not been him.

Who else could have placed this here, and how did no one notice it for so long? thought Daniel. The thick layer of dust revealed that many years had passed since whoever brought this to the barn had concealed it in the perfect spot. The storage area stayed packed with hay, supplies, and equipment, and some of the things in the very back had never seen the light of day. Daniel racked his brain thinking about who this could have been. After a few days, some out-of-focus memories began to come in fits and starts. Daniel vaguely remembered a friend visiting him there a long time ago, after the birth of one of his children. He came to celebrate the new baby. Daniel had a hazy memory and thought it was possibly after the birth of Roberto, thirteen years ago. He gifted him a heavy old glass bottle, dotted with air bubbles and filled with cheap alcohol. This had been a happy time when life was good. It seemed as if only a few years had passed since then, but Daniel's world was a different place now. He started drinking earlier and earlier each day—not to get drunk, but to forget. Shortly after finding the old bottle, most of it was gone. He needed to find a way to get his hands on more. In a state of stupor, he traded a mule—a tool of his livelihood—for equipment to make the *aguardiente* himself. This would enable him to keep his suffering under control, or so he thought.

Daniel couldn't accept the awful hand he'd been dealt. Although he had never before found comfort in alcohol, he needed something to make him forget when his feelings became heavier than his heart could bear.

Thinking back on his life, Daniel knew that although arduous, it had been a happy one surrounded by his family. His work had been back-breaking but he did it with contentment. Now, all he wanted to do was disappear.

Daniel's spiraling descent into addiction became a monster he couldn't tame. The only relief from the suffering Daniel felt when he drank was the soothing and warm feeling that washed over him. It became his great escape and best friend—choosing it over his responsibilities and commitments—unaware that this new habit wasn't doing away with his grief or sadness like he thought. It was only stealing from his future happiness.

Daniel was losing touch with his new reality bit by bit. His emotions overwhelmed him and drove him to seek solace in the bottle. It offered him a place to hide from the love and the suffering he couldn't contain. The liquor burned for the first few swigs then slowly eased him into a deceptively peaceful oblivion.

Daniel's life had begun to feel like an old ragged rope with a heavy anvil on the end, unraveling faster than he could have ever imagined. His erratic behavior had far-reaching effects, outside of his own inner destruction. Lilia was at her wit's end. She was drained and her resentment and bitterness were reaching a boiling point. She was far too young to deal with all that life had thrown at her. Lilia had done everything she could for her family, and her anger had turned to blinding rage—at God for abandoning her family, at her mother for leaving them, and at her father for disappearing and not taking care of them in this, the most difficult of times.

Her crying had gone from one of sadness to frustration and anger to a burning in her chest with each fast and heavy breath. Lilia decided she had to escape from this seemingly hopeless situation. But first, she needed to find her father and let him know María de Los Angeles's care would now be in his hands. She tore through the house looking for him. There were no signs of Daniel anywhere. She knew he would probably be hiding out in the barn. Lilia stomped through the large open gate and then straight through the barn door. In the corner of one of the empty stalls, her father was passed out on a bale of hay. She was infuriated. *How can he expect me to handle all the responsibilities for our family?*

"Wake up. Wake up!" yelled Lilia.

"*¿Qué pasa?*" asked a dazed Daniel, slurring his words.

"The pressure to keep our home and family together and fed, clothed, and clean has fallen on my shoulders after *Mami*'s death. It has become unbearable and I can't do it anymore. I am leaving," she said through a mess of tears, barely able to catch her breath.

"Wait . . . . don't leave. I need you. Our family needs you," said Daniel, as he tried his best to sit up.

"I just came to tell you that María de Los Angeles will need to be fed soon, so you better clean yourself up and get back to the house," said Lilia, turning to run and gather some things to take with her. She raced into her parent's room and went straight to Gabriela's armoire, frantically searching for a large bag in which to throw her things. Between the drawers and the side panel, she found a large blue and white burlap bag her mother used to bring groceries home from the market.

Through stinging hot tears, Lilia threw her few worldly possessions into the bag amid a frenzy of emotions—her brown, worn sandals, a few dresses, her one pair of white pants, several cotton shirts, and a few undergarments. She grabbed her pink lipstick and compact, along with her hairbrush and a small bottle of her mother's rose perfume. She wanted to always feel Gabriela's presence. Her scent would bring her comfort. Lilia knew her mother would be so very disappointed with her but not even that could make her stay. Speaking in a loud and angry voice, she blurted out to her brothers and sisters that she was leaving and would not be coming back. The younger children started to cry, but Roberto and Manolo instantly became angry. They couldn't believe she was abandoning them. They knew the devastation that awaited their already fragile family.

"How could you do this? Why would you do this to our family?" asked Manolo with a look of disgust on his face.

She ignored his questions and hugged each of the children, torn between knowing how much they needed her and her desire to run as far away as she could from this dismal situation. Her mind was made up. Her family would have to deal with this tragedy on their own. Lilia quickly took her bag and ran down the gravel driveway as the sun started to rise behind the trees.

Daniel felt frozen—paralyzed—by the realization that Lilia was gone, and he no longer had any help with his children. He couldn't delay. As he staggered out of the barn he thought, *The older children can help me keep an eye on the younger ones, but María de Los Angeles is only a few weeks old.* I will have to take care of her myself. Unsure of how he would do this, Daniel managed to get himself back to the house after a few minutes. He knew everything now rested on his shoulders. He was determined he would do his best to run the household. But day after day, he failed miserably.

At times, the food in the pantry and icebox wasn't enough for all the children to eat. The crops Manolo and Roberto harvested needed to be sold to pay suppliers, so very little remained for the family. The older children would take smaller portions so the younger ones wouldn't go hungry. The children were confused and had nowhere to turn.

I need to find some help and food for my brothers and sisters, thought Rolando.

Early one morning, he set out on the path to Señora Lopez's home. She had always been a guiding presence in his mother's life, and he knew she would help their family. Rolando knocked on the door and waited for a few moments. No answer. He knocked again and waited.

After a few moments, Señora Lopez finally came to the door wearing a maroon, polyester housecoat and cream-colored slippers. Her silver hair was wrapped around pink foam rollers and covered with a white kerchief.

"*Hola*, Rolando, what is the matter?" she said sleepily, squinting her eyes to shield them from the morning light.

"Señora Lopez, I'm sorry I woke you," said an embarrassed Rolando.

"Please don't worry. Are you okay?" asked Señora Lopez.

"Yes, but ever since our mom died, we can't find our dad when we look for him on the farm. We don't know where he goes but when he comes back home, he doesn't act like he used to and doesn't take care of us. He stays mad all of the time," said Rolando.

This is alarming. I must reach out to Padre García to get some assistance for Daniel and his family, thought Señora Lopez.

"Let me see what I can do. I will stop by your house later today," said Señora Lopez.

"Yes, thank you. We need help and we desperately need food. My dad doesn't bring home milk and eggs from our farm like he used to," said Rolando.

"Don't worry. I will make sure you and your family get the things you need," said Señora Lopez with tremendous concern in her voice.

"*Gracias*," said a dispirited Rolando as he turned to walk down the dusty path back to their house. This was not a burden an eleven-year-old boy should be carrying. Rolando did the only thing he knew to do—beg for help. His family needed someone to take control.

The ensuing chaos in their home and the collapsing structure of their family led the older children to become resentful, while the younger children felt alone and abandoned. The house was falling apart at the seams, but more importantly, the children needed comfort and reassurance that they wouldn't lose another parent.

Daniel couldn't even offer that.

In the early afternoon, Señora Lopez boarded bus number 78 to go to speak with Padre García regarding the visit from Rolando.

"*Hola*, Señora Lopez, please give me a few minutes to finish up a document for the Catholic Diocese of Pinar del Río," said Padre García.

"Of course, I'll wait. Please take your time."

After Señora Lopez shared the shocking developments about Daniel and his family, they agreed to set up a meeting at 6:00 that evening with some of the families in the parish to decide how to best help Daniel.

CHAPTER TWELVE

LA PALMA, PINAR DEL RÍO, CUBA
1953

Before the scheduled time, several women and couples arrived for the meeting being held in the bottom floor of the old church building. Padre García welcomed them as they filed into the earthy-smelling room. They each found a seat near the front. While they waited for the meeting to start, some of the women began whispering among themselves.

"Who could have ever imagined the desperate situation that Gabriela's family has found themselves in?" asked one of them.

"I hope we can find some good homes for the children so they can be cared for until Daniel can get back on his feet," said another.

"I am terribly sad for her family. The children have been lost without their mother," said Señora Lopez.

Padre García began the meeting with a prayer for Daniel, his family, and their community who would need to rise up to help.

"Thank you all for coming tonight. I am so pleased to see so many of you here. As you know, Daniel has had a most difficult time after the unexpected passing of his beloved wife, Gabriela. We are hoping to come together as a community and bring him the help he needs at this time," said Padre García.

He explained that the most dire situation was that of the care and well-being of the children. Since Gabriela's death, they had felt abandoned by a father who was drowning in his own grief.

"The older boys, Manolo and Roberto, will stay with Daniel for now," said Padre García. "The younger children range in ages from newborn María de los Angeles to eleven-year-old Rolando. Ramon is two. Elisa is four. Georgina is seven and Rigoberto is nine. We hope to find a home for each of them where they will feel safe and cared for until Daniel is strong enough to bring his family back together," explained Padre García.

Several people in the crowd offered suggestions for the children.

"My daughter's children are right around the ages of the young girls," said Señora Lopez. "We can take Georgina and Elisa and care for them as long as Daniel needs." The girls knew Señora Lopez's grandchildren. They had always gotten along and liked to play outside together when they visited their grandmother.

This would be the distraction the girls needed. They missed their mother terribly, but they could no longer sit on the front porch waiting for her to return. The disappointment at the end of each day was more than two small children should have to bear.

"We could use a hand on the ranch," said one of the men. "We will take in Rolando until Daniel is in a better state." Although he was only eleven years old, Rolando liked to help his father with the chores on the farm. He embraced all the aspects of country living. Being on a ranch and busy with daily chores would be a good fit for Rolando.

"I will take Rigoberto and Ramon," said Jose Antonio Martínez de Osaba. Daniel's brother was also a farmer, but his crops and livestock were thriving. He didn't need help on the farm from the small children, but he knew he and his wife could take care of them. Their thirteen-year-old daughter, Carolina, loved her cousins and would be a big help in caring for and playing with them.

Each of the younger children had been spoken for with the exception of the precious newborn baby.

"María de los Angeles is only a few weeks old, so she will need more attention," said Adela. "I don't know if Dr. and Señora Sánchez would be willing to take her in, but I believe they would be the best choice."

"Can you go to their home with me after we finish here and ask them if they are interested in helping to care for her until Daniel is able to take her back home?" asked Padre García.

"Yes, we can speak with them. And if they agree, I will help Daniel prepare her things and be there when they arrive to take her," said Adela. "I don't want Daniel to be alone. He has suffered so much, and I believe this will be very difficult for him."

After discussing some additional details regarding the best way to prepare to take the children to their homes, they felt they had come up with a good plan to alleviate the stress and hardships Daniel was facing. The families in La Palma were mostly simple *campesinos*—farmers, but they valued family above all. When one of them was going through such a desperate time, they rallied around them and pitched in to help them in whatever ways they could.

Padre García was certain the children would be well taken care of. This would give Daniel the opportunity to get to a better place. He could then reclaim them and be the family man he aspired to be once again.

"I would like to thank you for your generosity in attending this meeting on such short notice and even more so for opening your hearts and homes to these children who have lost so much," said Padre García. "Daniel has always been there to help anyone in need. Gabriela was a kind soul that went out of her way to brighten someone's day with a smile, a hug, or a kind word. I am grateful we can pull together to ensure their children feel supported during this tumultuous time."

Padre García offered a blessing to those present and each went their own way. They went home to prepare the rooms that each of the children would be staying in until they were able to go back home.

"Adela, can you please wait here for a few minutes?" asked Padre García. "I need to take care of a couple of things in my office but will meet you back here, and we can take the bus to see Dr. and Señora Sánchez."

"*Sí*, I will wait here for you," said Adela to her brother.

"*Gracias*," said Padre García.

He walked up to his second-floor office and turned the key on the brass lock of the faded brown wooden door. He took a seat at his desk to review the details for the following morning's 9 a.m. Mass. After ensuring his notes were in order and opening a few pieces of mail, he gathered his briefcase and hat and he made the short walk with Adela to the bus stop to pay the Sánchezes a visit. They would share the plan with them and discuss the details for the following day.

The sun was starting to set as Padre García and Adela arrived at Dr. and Señora Sánchez's house. They had no idea what their reaction would be but felt this was the best option for María de los Angeles. They climbed the stairs onto the porch and Adela knocked on the door.

Señora Sánchez opened the door with a look of surprise and worry.

"Is everything okay?" she asked nervously.

"Yes . . . yes . . . we did not mean to startle you, Señora Sánchez. "Everything is just fine. We are here to discuss the new baby that was recently born to the Martínez de Osaba family."

"Oh yes, come in and let me ask Joaquin to join us," she said as she made her way to the living room.

"Joaquin, Padre García and Adela are here. They want to talk with us about Daniel's new baby girl," said Señora Sánchez.

"Is something the matter with her?" asked Dr. Sánchez.

"No, she is fine, but they would like to speak with us," said Señora Sánchez as she led Dr. Sánchez to the foyer by the hand.

"Hello, Padre García and Adela," said Dr. Sánchez. "What can I do for you?"

"The parishioners have come to me with concerns about Daniel and have agreed to help him with his children until he can get back on his feet," said Padre García.

"We discussed María de los Angeles and thought you may be interested in caring for her temporarily," said Adela. "Is this something you would consider?"

Dr. and Señora Sánchez were stunned. They stared at the floor and then at one another as this request began to sink in. They had always wanted children, but this was never the route they thought they would take to making a family. Though temporary, they knew this would be a huge change and adjustment for them.

They stood quietly for quite some time.

"Is this going to be okay with her father . . . with Daniel?" asked Dr. Sánchez.

"We certainly hope so. He has expressed that he is overwhelmed and needs the help. If you agree to care for her, we will visit him and finalize the plans. We believe he will be most grateful for your willingness to help.

"Can you please wait for just a moment, while Margarita and I talk in the kitchen?" asked Dr. Sánchez.

"Yes, take your time," said Adela. "We realize this is a big commitment and we want to make sure we do the right thing for everyone."

"We will be back in a few minutes," said Dr. Sánchez as he and Señora Sánchez pushed the swinging door that led to the kitchen.

It only took them a few minutes to come back and let them know they would be happy to take María de los Angeles for however long was needed.

"That is great news, thank you," said Padre García.

"We are going to Daniel's home after we leave here to share the plans with him," said Adela. "He will be happy to know that you both will be caring for María de los Angeles. Please be at La Paloma to pick her up tomorrow afternoon. I will be there to help Daniel gather her things and have her ready for you."

They exchanged goodbyes and Padre García and Adela walked back to the bus stop to visit Daniel.

Dr. Sánchez slowly closed the door. They were both in disbelief at the visit from Padre García and Adela. It was so unexpected that they needed a few minutes to process their thoughts. They knew they wanted to help but even more than that, they were filled with joy at the idea of having a baby in the house. Their stoic faces quickly turned to smiles as they embraced one another. They wouldn't sleep that night. Their excitement was beyond measure.

By now the sun had set. Padre García and Adela walked up the long gravel driveway to La Paloma. They looked around. Even though it was dark, they could see that the grass was overgrown, and it appeared as if it had not been cut in many weeks. Daniel's old truck was in the yard and the front driver's side tire was flat. Padre García looked in the distance and the barn was dark and quiet. He realized the animals were no longer there. They looked at each other with pained looks on their faces, knowing this would be a difficult conversation for Daniel. They stepped onto the porch, and as they did, Adela looked down and noticed the paint was dull and weathered—there were more chips than paint. Daniel had always taken pride in his family's farm, so Padre García and Adela were saddened to see it in this condition. Padre García knocked on the door and after a brief moment, Daniel slowly pulled the door open.

"*Hola*, Daniel," said Padre García. "Can we speak with you for a moment?"

"*Sí*, please come in," said Daniel. "Let's have a seat."

Padre García was somewhat surprised to see the extent of the mess in the home. He was even more surprised to see how quickly everything had fallen apart following Gabriela's passing. The family, the home. It had been less than a month since Adela had been here, and now, there were piles of dirty laundry and dishes everywhere. The trash had not been taken out in who-knew-how-long and the terrible odor reached the living room.

"Daniel, how have you been?" asked Padre García.

Daniel sat on the edge of the sofa with his elbows resting on his knees and his hands folded, looking at the floor. His despair hung over him like a heavy coat and stalled him from taking even one step forward toward healing.

"Gabriela's death has turned my life upside down in ways I never would have thought possible," said Daniel. "I am trying to get my life back. I want to be able to take care of my family and my responsibilities, but every day is a struggle."

"I am truly sorry, Daniel. I know the last few weeks have been extremely difficult for you and your children. Gabriela was a wonderful mother and wife, and her absence has left a gaping wound," said Padre García.

"If I am honest with myself, I don't know how I am going to be able to move past this loss. My wife. My soulmate. My best friend," said Daniel.

"You are not alone. God is always with you, and our community is going to help you. Fellow parishioners have stepped forward to help with the children and will come by La Paloma tomorrow afternoon to take them to their temporary homes. Each is welcome to stay as long as is needed for you to gather your strength."

"Thank you, Padre," said Daniel. "It shouldn't be more than a few weeks. I am committed to getting better and reuniting my family."

"I am here if you need a listening ear. Please don't keep your grief bottled up, Daniel," said Padre García.

"*Gracias* to you both. Your kindness means the world to me. I am also so appreciative for the families that are willing to help us during this time,' said Daniel. The older children will all be fine. My biggest concern was María de los Angeles. Being left to care for a large family, including a newborn, is the most challenging thing I've ever done."

"I understand," said Adela. "That is why I suggested Dr. and Señora Sánchez. They don't have children of their own, and he is a pediatrician."

Daniel agreed that the Sánchezes were the best people to care for María de los Angeles. The doctor had been so kind, and he knew this would be a safe and loving place for María de los Angeles.

"May I visit her?" asked Daniel.

"Yes, of course," replied Padre García. "You can work out a visitation schedule when they come tomorrow afternoon to pick up María de los Angeles."

"I am sure they would be happy for you to see her as often as you would like," assured Adela.

"Although it is difficult for my children to be separated, it gives me the time I need to truly grieve and recover so I can be the father they need," said Daniel.

"I am glad you feel this is a good plan. Adela will be here to help you tomorrow as the families arrive to pick up the children they have agreed to care for," said Padre García.

They made their way to the door as it was getting very late. Daniel put María de los Angeles to bed and he fell into a deep peaceful sleep. He dreamed of Gabriela and all the children. He dreamed of happier times when his family was together and thriving.

This last bit of hope allowed Daniel the respite he needed—he had not slept this soundly since the last night Gabriela lay by his side. He awoke in the night to the faint cries of María de los Angeles. He sat in a chair near the window as he fed her a warm bottle. Daniel stared at her moonlit face. She was content. And he felt all the glimmers of possibility.

They fell back into a peaceful sleep until the early morning sun streamed through the bedroom window. Daniel rubbed his eyes and suddenly remembered the conversation with Padre García and Adela from last night. It all happened so quickly but for the first time in a long time, he felt hopeful for his family's future. The morning passed by in a flash as Daniel tried to clean up and remove the clutter before the families arrived. Adela came to the house, as promised, and helped Daniel prepare for the visitors. She helped Daniel pack a bag for each of the children and placed them by the front door.

Although he would miss his children terribly, Daniel felt this was the beginning of his healing on the path to a full and happy life with his family.

Just after noon, there was a knock on the door. Dr. and Señora Sánchez were the first family to arrive to pick up María de Los Angeles.

"*Hola*, please come in," said Daniel, relieved to see them.

"*Gracias*, Daniel," they said in unison.

Just behind Daniel's right shoulder stood Adela, holding María de los Angeles. Dr. and Señora Sánchez were happy to see the baby and he commented, "She has grown so much since the last time I saw her."

"She is just beautiful," said Señora Sánchez.

They were both thrilled to take María de los Angeles home, even if she would not stay with them forever. In the hours since they had agreed to care for her, they talked. And hoped. And dreamed.

Daniel took a few steps back and watched the scene unfold.

"May I?" said Señora Sánchez, with outstretched arms.

"Yes," said Adela and placed María de los Angeles in her arms.

Señora Sánchez smiled as she looked at the sweet baby girl she was holding. She smelled of baby powder and violets, her dark curly hair combed to the side. Señora Sánchez looked at Dr. Sánchez and he couldn't help but smile back. He had never experienced these feelings before and instantly knew he wanted to do everything in his power to protect and care for this baby.

"I can help you out to your car if you would like," said Adela.

"We can manage, but thank you, Adela," said Dr. Sánchez. "I can take the baby's bag and Margarita can carry her in her arms."

They all looked at Daniel, expecting an emotional goodbye. A small smile crossed Daniel's lips and he let out a sigh. It was a sigh of relief—an expression of the gratitude he felt inside, even surprising himself.

"I don't know how I could ever repay your kindness," said Daniel. "Thank you for agreeing to take care of my baby girl until I can bring her back home."

"Daniel, we want to help you bring your family back together," said Dr. Sánchez.

"Please let us know whenever you want to see her and we will make sure to have her ready to spend time with her father," said Señora Sánchez.

"I appreciate your graciousness in the face of so much change," said Daniel.

"You are welcome. Don't hesitate to let us know if you need any help," said Dr. Sánchez. He and Señora Sánchez turned and took the bag holding her diapers and clothing by the door.

Daniel walked them to the door. He kissed María de los Angeles on the top of her head and smoothed her fine caramel-colored hair. His emotions collided, thankful that she would be safe and cared for with the trusted doctor and his wife and at the same time, he felt utter sadness to see María de los Angeles, the last memory he created with Gabriela, go home with someone else—no matter how temporary it was.

Dr. Sánchez opened the front passenger door of his automobile and helped Señora Sánchez sit comfortably with María de los Angeles on her lap. He waved to Daniel and Adela as he walked around to the driver's side. Dr. Sánchez slid into the car, closed the door, and slowly drove away, not wanting to disturb the sleeping baby.

Daniel stood at the living room window, watching them leave La Paloma. He felt a sense of peace, hoping this would be the start of his recovery.

As the Sánchezes rolled down the gravel driveway, Señora Lopez and her daughter were arriving to pick up Georgina and Elisa. The girls were excited to go somewhere different and play with their friends. There had been no other children to play with since their mother died. Their lives were entirely out of sorts. The structure of living with another family would be healing for them as well as for all the other children.

The afternoon was a steady stream of families committed to helping Daniel and his children. His brother, Jose Antonio, was also tall and thin but with big blue eyes that lit up when he smiled. He was happy to see Daniel and pulled him into a bear hug. The brothers stood around and talked for a few minutes until Rigoberto and Ramon had gathered their things and were ready to go. Daniel opened his arms wide and took both boys into a tight embrace. They would not be far away, and Daniel could go see them anytime. He said another silent prayer of gratitude.

Rolando was the only one of the younger children remaining. He was looking forward to living on a big ranch. He had been sitting by the living room window for at least an hour, waiting for Señor Alvarez's truck to come up the driveway. After what seemed like forever to him, Señor Alvarez finally arrived. He ran to tell Daniel and Adela, who were in the kitchen preparing toasted ham and cheese sandwiches for the three of them to eat.

"He's here! He's here!" said Rolando, with excitement in his voice.

Daniel dried his hands before walking to the family room to welcome Señor Alvarez. Daniel opened the door and squinted as he felt the tropical sun on his face. He stood on the porch as Señor Alvarez circled around the front of the house and parked his black pickup truck. He jumped out, his cowboy boots faded and dusty. The straw *campesino* hat he wore, a farmer's hat, framed his rugged face. In only a few minutes, Rolando had thrown his belongings in the truck and was ready to start his adventure on Señor Alvarez's ranch. Before Rolando stepped up into the seat, Daniel pulled him in close for a hug and a kiss on the top of his head.

"*Gracias*, Señor Alvarez," said Daniel. "I appreciate your generosity in agreeing to care for Rolando. He will be a big help to you. He is very good with the animals—feeding them and keeping the stalls clean—even milking the cows."

"I am glad I can help you during this time," said Señor Alvarez. "He can stay with us as long as you need."

Daniel smiled and lowered his gaze. He could feel the emotions bubbling up in his throat. Rolando was the last of the younger children to leave. He was grateful for all the help and hopeful that better things were ahead for all of them. He was also immensely sad at the thought of a quiet house when he'd lay his head on the pillow at the end of the day. He lifted his face and thanked Señor Alvarez. Daniel closed the passenger door and waved goodbye as they drove away.

One single tear rolled down his cheek—it was filled with all the gratitude, fear, hope, and sadness it could hold.

The days and weeks passed quickly. Daniel was giving himself the space and grace to prepare his mind, heart, and home to welcome his family back. Daniel had stopped drinking. He knew his sobriety was the only way to get his life back.

He and the older boys, Roberto and Manolo, worked on the farm from sunup to sundown. They tended to the crops and brought them back to their previous healthy condition, selling them for a nice profit. Manolo made a list of some of the repairs the home needed and bartered for the supplies with store owners in the community.

Daniel was starting to feel his life had meaning and purpose again. The hope in his heart and the long days on the farm were all he needed.

By now, many in the surrounding towns had heard of how other families were standing by Daniel's side and caring for his younger children until he could reunite with them. The mayor of Pinar del Río, the province in which the village of La Palma was located, began asking around to see how he could help. He wanted to know more about the situation. Juan Navarro and his wife Luisa were known to be generous and caring members of the community. He was an attorney who would regularly provide pro bono legal services for those who couldn't afford to hire him. They had two beautiful girls—Sara was fourteen and Marina was eight. They were the apples of their father's eye.

The family lived on *Rancho Santa Catalina*, one of the two ranches they owned. It was a sprawling twelve-hundred-acre farm situated close to the center of San Cayetano, not far from La Palma.

Their large chalet-style home stood at the entrance to the ranch. It was an extraordinary forty-seven-hundred square foot modular house with massive windows that revealed spectacular views of the endless fields and dark green mountains behind them—perfect for the vast ranch. Juan ordered it from the Sears Roebuck Company in 1949 for $11,000 through a dealer-builder in Miami. The company placed it on a cargo ship, and ten-and-a-half hours later, it arrived in Puerto Cabanas, near Havana. Two-thirds of the acres on the farm were dedicated to raising cattle—cows, goats, sheep, hens, and pigs. The meat from the animals was taken to a processing plant to be distributed to wholesale and retail customers. The girls' favorite animals were the llamas, which are part of the camel family. Their cute faces and soft wool reminded them of their favorite stuffed animals. The llamas served an important role on the farm—protecting the other animals from foxes, coyotes, and dogs. Juan also kept twelve horses to work in the fields and for roaming around the rambling property. The girls learned how to ride from a young age and participated in yearly equestrian competitions, winning awards regularly. An orchard of tropical fruit trees comprised the other third of the acreage, with mango, avocado, mamey, papaya, *níspero*, and anon trees planted in neat rows. Each Wednesday, the farmhands responsible for selling the fruit would prepare and pack bushels of each type and set up in one of the largest booths at the Pinar del Río Farmers Market. After a few hours, they would completely sell out—week in and week out.

The other ranch the Navarro's owned, *Hacienda del Sol*, was a bustling dairy farm with thirty-seven Holstein cows on seventy-five acres a few miles away. Each cow could produce up to twenty-four liters of milk a day—more than three-hundred-thousand liters a year. Additionally, there were hundreds of hens that could each lay eggs daily or every other day, yielding more than eighty thousand eggs per year. The milk and eggs were also taken to the market each week, but the majority would go to stores—from neighborhood *bodegas* to grocery store chains like Minimax, an American company importing many American products onto the island.

The Navarros learned that the two older boys, Manolo and Roberto, were the only ones still living with Daniel. At seventeen, Manolo would have his own life soon, so they discussed taking thirteen-year-old Roberto in until he was able to go back home. Juan and Luisa agreed that Daniel was struggling, and they could help him. They decided to extend the offer to have Roberto live at *Rancho Santa Catalina* temporarily. Juan got up early the following day to visit Daniel. He took his 1951 Willys CJ-3A Jeep—a post-WWII civilian model—to make the forty-mile drive to La Paloma. At 8 a.m. sharp, he knocked on the front door of Daniel's home. Daniel and his sons had been out in the fields since daybreak. When no one came to the door, Juan jumped back into the Jeep and drove around the side of the property, where he found the three of them tilling the vegetable gardens.

Daniel heard the sound of the engine getting closer and turned to see who could be driving onto his property this early in the morning. He didn't recognize the vehicle and asked his sons to give him a few minutes to see what this person wanted.

As Juan got closer, Daniel recognized him. They had met once, years ago, and Daniel was puzzled as to what this visit could be about. Juan stepped out of his vehicle and walked toward Daniel.

"*Hola, buenos días*," said Juan as he extended his hand to Daniel.

"*Buenos días*," replied Daniel, smelling of sweat and hard work. He quickly brushed the palm of his right hand on the side of his overalls to wipe off some of the dirt and shook Juan's hand.

"My apologies for interrupting your work, but I would like to talk with you for just a moment," said Juan.

"Sure, I have a few minutes now," said Daniel.

"I have spoken with several people, including members of the Pinar del Río city council, in the past week and they have mentioned to me the difficult situation you have been going through since your wife's death," said Juan.

"Yes, thank you," said Daniel. "It has been a very tough few months since my wife, Gabriela, suddenly passed away. I have been blessed to receive a tremendous amount of support and care from various families in La Palma and from nearby towns."

"That is precisely what I wanted to speak with you about," said Juan. "My wife and I would like to invite Roberto to live with us until you are ready to bring him back home. If you agree, I can take him today."

"He is currently helping me on the farm, but ever since his mother died, he has not gone back to his studies. Our days here are very long and the three of us are the only ones working the land. He could help you on the ranch part of the day and whenever he's not working, he can dedicate his time to studying. I can bring someone in to take his place."

"Roberto, can you please come here?" asked Daniel.

"*Sí, Papi*," said Roberto. "I will be right there."

Roberto walked over to the pond and dipped his hand in the cool water to rinse away the dirt and grime of tilling the land with the ox cart. He made his way to where his father and Juan were standing.

"*Hola*, Roberto," said Juan.

"*Hola*," said Roberto, not recognizing him.

"Señor Navarro and I have been talking about the possibility of having you go live with him and his family for the time being. What do you think of this?" said Daniel.

"But I help you here," said Roberto, glancing at Daniel with a confused look on his face.

"Roberto, you can help Señor Navarro on his ranch as well as continue your studies," said Daniel. "We are working very long hours here, and it leaves you no time to prepare to go back to school."

"I would like to continue my studies but don't want to leave you," said Roberto.

"I will be alright, *hijo*—son," said Daniel. "It is important for you to continue your education. It's what your mother would have wanted. I will manage here. This is a good opportunity for you."

"Okay," said Roberto, with apprehension in his voice.

"Señor Navarro can take you with him today, so please gather your things and he will wait for you here."

"It will take me a few minutes to clean up and throw my things into a bag," said Roberto. "When will I be able to come back home?"

He looked at his father and then at Señor Navarro.

"It shouldn't be too long," said Daniel with hope in his heart. "My dream is to have everyone back home again soon."

Juan and Daniel made small talk while Roberto ran to wash up and pack his bag. He took a quick shower, and when he had dried off, he tied the towel around his waist and went to the closet to pick the clothes he would wear today. His day-to-day wardrobe had been the overalls and T-shirts he wore each day to work on the farm. He wanted to wear something nicer today. He had two shirts hanging in his closet, a white short-sleeve button-down, and a light blue *guayabera* that his cousin Pepe had given him. He placed the guayabera on his bed along with the only pair of khaki pants he owned. Pepe had also given him several pairs of shoes, including some light brown loafers he had outgrown—he would wear those.

Roberto hastily got dressed and immediately realized that his shirt was too small, and the pants were too short. He was tall for thirteen, but he had no other choice than to wear the ill-fitting clothes. He didn't want to make Señor Navarro wait any longer than necessary.

Roberto threw a few things into a large burlap bag: a comb, some T-shirts and overalls, his prized cowboy boots, and the books Adela had given him. He had also kept a small picture of his mother on the dresser. This would be the most important possession Roberto would take with him. He tossed the bag over his shoulder and hurried out the door.

"It looks like you are ready to go," said Juan.

"Yes, I have everything I need in my bag," said Roberto.

Daniel gave Roberto a tight hug and didn't want to let go. Although Daniel knew this would be for his benefit, it didn't make it any easier. This goodbye would be no different from the others. Daniel loved each of his children equally. Being separated from them for even a day gave him the motivation he needed to work day and night and bring his family back together as soon as he could.

"*Gracias*, Señor Navarro," said Daniel.

"I am happy that we could help you with Roberto, and he is welcome to stay for however long you need," said Juan.

"I really appreciate your kindness and I hope to have my children back home as soon as I am feeling stronger," said Daniel.

They shook hands and Juan settled into the driver's seat. Roberto jumped in and closed the door.

"*Te quiero, Papi*—I love you, Dad," said Roberto as the Jeep started to roll toward the gravel driveway.

Juan and Roberto both waved at Daniel, but he was lost in thought and hesitated before raising his hand to wave goodbye. By then, they had already turned onto the main road and didn't see him. Daniel stood there for a while in the midday heat, thinking about everything that had happened in the last few months. His world had been turned upside down, but he was determined to keep moving forward, one step at a time.

Roberto liked riding in the open Jeep and as it picked up speed, the hot air blowing in his face felt freeing.

"It looks like you've grown a lot recently," said Juan.

"Yes, last year, I grew four inches and have put on about twenty pounds," said Roberto.

"You need some new clothes," said Juan. "We have some time before we have to get back. I am going to take you to a clothing store near the ranch where my wife and I buy clothes for ourselves and our daughters. We can get you some work clothes and some shirts and pants that will fit you."

"*Gracias*," said Roberto.

"*De nada*—you're welcome," said Juan.

Roberto was embarrassed to be wearing clothes that were too small for him but felt relieved that he would soon have something new to wear. After trying on a few things, Juan and Roberto left the store with several casual shirts and pants, overalls, white cotton T-shirts, a pair of brown leather cowboy boots to work on the ranch, and black leather shoes to wear when he had somewhere special to go. Roberto even got new dark blue swim trunks to use at the lake on the ranch. He had never had new clothes or shoes. Everything he owned had been handed down from his older brother, Manolo. Roberto was happy to have something that was just for him. He was shy, but the gratitude he felt for this stranger was huge.

"*Muchas gracias*, Señor Navarro," said Roberto.

"You can call me Juan. I'm glad you are happy with the things we got for you," said Juan. "We will be at the ranch in a few minutes. Are you hungry? Dinner will be at six, so we have time to take a look around the ranch and get cleaned up before we join the family at the dining room table."

"Okay, thank you. Yes, I am getting hungry," said Roberto.

He was a growing boy and was always ready to eat.

Roberto was dumbfounded by this new experience. No one had ever taken him to a store to pick out new clothes for himself. Only a few hours ago, he was tilling the soil at his family's farm. Now, everything had changed.

They drove for close to an hour when they finally made the turn onto the long driveway leading to the entrance of *Rancho Santa Catalina*. Roberto was speechless. They rode through the tall wrought-iron gates, and as Roberto looked around, he was in awe of the endless fields of crops and the huge, sprawling house.

"Welcome to our home, Roberto," said Juan.

"*Gracias*," said an overwhelmed Roberto.

The ranch was unlike anything Roberto had ever seen but he was excited to be here. They drove around the property for the next few hours, jumping in and out of the Jeep to see the livestock, the crops, the barn, the outbuildings, and the lake with several surrounding *mogotes*. Roberto was amazed at the sheer size of the ranch. La Paloma could have fit in a small corner of this expansive acreage. After a tour of the ranch, they got back in the Jeep and drove to the house. Juan parked around the back and jumped out. Roberto did the same.

"I will introduce you to my family and show you around—then, you can get ready for dinner," said Juan as he opened the glass door into the living room.

"Luisa, I'm home. And I've brought Roberto with me," said Juan.

"I'm here, in the kitchen," said Luisa.

"*Hola*," said Juan as he leaned down to give his beloved wife, Luisa, a quick kiss. "I would like for you to meet Roberto."

"*Mucho gusto*—pleased to meet you," said Luisa.

"*Gracias*," said Roberto with a smile. "It's very nice to meet you too."

"Juan, why don't you show Roberto to his room so he can take a shower before dinner?" asked Luisa.

"Sure, I will do it now," said Juan. "Come with me, Roberto."

Juan carried the large bag Roberto had brought from home and Roberto carried his new purchases. He followed Juan up the stairs and into his room. Roberto had never been inside a two-story house. His room was a comfortable size with a double bed that had soft linens, one wooden nightstand with a lamp, and a small desk and chair. He was glad to have his own room.

After dinner with Juan, Luisa, and the girls, Roberto slept soundly. The day had been filled with so many new things for him. He was looking forward to what tomorrow would hold.

Roberto settled into his new life and the many chores made for long, hard days on the ranch. He would regularly ride a horse to town by himself to pick up supplies for the ranch or for their home. As the weeks passed, he learned more and more and took on increasing responsibility. He also saw some things he wished he never had—a young man that worked with him on the ranch was mowing the grass with a tractor and started to go up a *mogote* when the tractor flipped over and landed on him, killing him instantly. Another man was responsible for blasting rock on the *mogotes*. He had been doing this for years. This time, he didn't place the dynamite correctly and the rocks that were blasted rained down on him, killing him. Roberto was distressed when he saw the man's right leg had almost been severed and his tibia was completely outside his skin. Roberto matured quickly as the weeks and months passed. He was able to make time for his studies and knew that his mother would be proud of him. Roberto learned discipline from Juan and his loyal team of workers.

Back at La Paloma, Daniel, Manolo, and Leo, the new farmhand Daniel had brought on after Roberto left, kept the farm going. The crops were plentiful, and Daniel was feeling hopeful for his future and that of his family. He wanted to discuss bringing animals back onto the farm with Manolo and Leo. He invited them to meet him at the house for a lunch of rice, grilled chicken, and steamed fresh vegetables they had picked that morning. They were all looking forward to a hot lunch. Daniel had saved some money from the sale of the crops and had been thinking about purchasing several cows, goats, and pigs at the auction. It had been a long time since he had been there and was looking forward to taking one more step toward feeling like himself again. The three sat down and started to eat their meal. Daniel began sharing his plans and asked for their help in the next week to pick out the best animals to bring to the farm.

"I am always available to help you, Señor Daniel," said Leo.

Manolo hesitated and lowered his eyes.

"Manolo, what do you think?" said Daniel

"I have to tell you something," said Manolo.

"What is going on?" asked Daniel with concern in his voice.

"I have met a beautiful girl named Olivia," said Manolo with a quaver in his voice. "She is the daughter of the man from Spain who we sell corn to in Cantalete. I have been fearful of telling you. We met a few months ago and I have asked for her hand in marriage. Her father has asked me to work with him and help him grow his business. I will be leaving next week."

Daniel could not have been more stunned with the news Manolo shared. He sat back in his chair and stared at the floor. When the full weight of Manolo's news sank in, it only took a few moments for

Daniel's world to crumble around him once again. Everything he was working so hard to bring back—including himself—would now be gone. He excused himself from the table without saying another word.

Daniel went to his bedroom and locked the door. In a daze, he sat on the side of the bed and leaned forward, putting his face in his hands. *I can't continue making progress on the farm without Manolo's help,* he thought. *We have been a team for a long time, and I cannot afford to bring on anyone else to take care of all the responsibilities Manolo handles.* He felt himself slipping back into the dark place of sadness and grief that he had worked so hard to crawl out of. He didn't know if he would be able to come back for a second time. Daniel laid back on the bed and closed his eyes. His body and his soul were exhausted. He needed to rest.

At the end of the following week, Manolo left—just as he said he would. No matter how much he loved his father and his family, he was ready to start his own life with the girl he loved.

Daniel tried his best to keep things on the farm running with Leo, but when they couldn't produce and sell enough crops to pay him, Leo had to find work elsewhere. Daniel had been left utterly and completely alone. The alcohol, once again, became his best friend.

CHAPTER THIRTEEN

LA PALMA, PINAR DEL RÍO, CUBA
1953 — 1959

The children had disappeared one by one ... little by little, he could see that his family was fading away. After a few weeks, he mustered the will to quit the alcohol in the hopes of bringing his family back together, but he still craved the alcohol to ease his pain. One evening, he drove to the home of Dr. and Señora Sánchez. He parked his rusted, old red truck across the street and stood outside, looking at the golden glow of the soft lights inside the windows. The Sánchezes had a beautiful, large white home with a wraparound porch. It reminded him of his childhood home—when life was easy, and happiness encircled him.

He stood for what seemed like forever, memories and lost dreams flooding his mind. He finally brought himself to take a few steps forward, feeling more weary with each one. His hand reached for the railing leading up the steps to the porch. He steadied himself and with each step he climbed, his feet became heavier and heavier. His sober mind could not easily process the barrage of emotions he was feeling. He raised his hand to knock on the door but hesitated. After a few seconds, he knocked weakly. No one answered so he tried again, more forcefully this time. Señora Sánchez pulled open the tall wooden door and let out a small sigh. She hoped Daniel did not notice her disappointment. Señora Sánchez wondered why he was there unannounced. She had already grown attached to María de los Angeles, and seeing him reminded her that the baby was not hers to keep.

"May I see my baby?" asked Daniel.

She shuffled from foot to foot, searching for words when a simple yes would have been enough. Her mind was swirling.

"Oh, yes . . . yes, Daniel," she finally sputtered. "She is just now finishing her bath. Please have a seat, and I will bring her down in a few minutes. Please make yourself comfortable."

Daniel looked around the home and was overwhelmed by the fancy surroundings. The furniture was all fine wood with detailed carvings. He had not seen such ornate furnishings since his childhood. He ran his calloused hand over the soft leather couch before taking a seat. He thought this to be such a perfect place to raise a child and was grateful the Sánchezes had agreed to care for María de los Angeles while he became strong enough to bring his whole family back home to La Paloma. He imagined making their small home just as comfortable and welcoming in the coming weeks before bringing his family home.

Deep in thought, Daniel was roused back to reality by the sweet coos of his baby girl.

"Here is your daughter, sir," said the nanny.

Señora Sánchez stayed upstairs listening but could not bring herself to go back down and face Daniel again.

"Ah, *sí*, she is just as beautiful as I remember," said a doting Daniel.

A few tears escaped his exhausted eyes as the nanny handed a bundled-up María de los Angeles to Daniel. She was warm and smelled of violets—a scent he was accustomed to from his newborns before her.

He stared into her eyes and she stared back at him. He was completely overtaken by his love for her.

"Dr. Sánchez should be home shortly, sir," the nanny said.

"*Gracias, Señora*," Daniel replied without taking his eyes off María de los Angeles.

She left them alone for a while. Daniel sang sweet songs to her and played with her fingers and toes. She was perfect.

"Daniel, it's good to see you," said Dr. Sánchez as he entered the room.

Daniel stood to his feet with the baby in his arms.

"Doctor, it's good to see you too. You have a lovely home and I can see that María de los Angeles is very well cared for here. I can't thank you and Señora Sánchez enough for all that you have done to help my family," said Daniel as he shook the hand of Dr. Sánchez.

"We are more than happy to help, Daniel. She is a pleasant baby. She only cries when she is hungry. Otherwise, she is playful and very curious and has begun smiling and laughing a bit, too," Dr. Sánchez said as he massaged María de los Angeles's tiny toes.

"How are you doing, Daniel?" asked Dr. Sánchez, hoping to hear good news.

"I am doing better, thank you. There are still moments when I can't believe all that has happened, but I am determined to get better and bring my family back home," said a hopeful Daniel.

"That is wonderful," said Dr. Sánchez.

In the recesses of his mind, Dr. Sánchez knew he too had become attached to María de los Angeles. He wanted nothing more than for Daniel to get better but the thought of having to give up the baby broke his heart.

The nanny returned to the room, "It's María de los Angeles's bedtime."

"Yes, of course," said Daniel.

He handed the baby to her with one final loving gaze into her tiny hazel eyes.

Daniel turned to Dr. Sánchez and said, "It was wonderful to see my daughter. Thank you for letting me spend a few minutes with her before she goes to sleep."

"It is good to see you, Daniel. Keep taking care of yourself and let us know if you need anything," said Dr. Sánchez.

Daniel walked out into the humid night. The stars were visible, and he took a moment to say a silent prayer that he could do what was needed to become the father he needed to be.

Señora Sánchez heard Daniel's truck pulling away and came downstairs to speak to her husband.

"He is gone?" She knew he was but was again struggling to find words.

"Yes, my dear, he is gone," replied Dr. Sánchez.

"I was so shocked by how I felt when I saw Daniel," she shyly admitted.

"I was too," agreed Dr. Sánchez.

"I pray he finds the strength to get better, but a part of me wants María de los Angeles to be ours," she said.

Dr. Sánchez took her into a tight embrace. He did not say the words she was willing to say, but he was feeling the same emotions.

★

Before Daniel knew it, he was pulling into the gravel driveway of La Paloma. He didn't remember driving there. His thoughts had taken over and his drive had been automatic. He parked his old truck but didn't get out right away. All the dark feelings he thought were starting to lift came back to him in a rush of emotions he could not contain.

He felt like a failure and knew that the only way he could quell his emotions was the comfort he found at the bottom of a glass of *aguardiente*. He would only have one.

With the first sip, he felt the familiar warmth in his chest. With each sip, the dream of bringing his children back to him became a distant possibility. The alcohol had such a hold on him by this time that he could not see past his next drink. He thought he had it conquered—but it was conquering him.

The next few weeks were a blur. Daniel was drinking from the time he awoke to the time he passed out in the barn each night. His hopes of seeing his children were drowned each day as he lost more and more control of his drinking. Along with his endless drinking, his depression grew. There were no signs of life left at La Paloma. A once fruitful farm was now overgrown, and the animals had long since escaped to find food and water. The home was a shell of its former self—as was Daniel.

People from the village would try to visit Daniel, but as soon as he heard the crunch of gravel outside, he would hide himself away in the back of the barn. Eventually, people stopped checking in on him. They all knew he was there and had lost control of his life, but there was nothing they could do to save him if he did not want to save himself. The news of Daniel's decline spread quickly. Everyone in the village thought he had completely given up on himself and his family.

The younger children and their caregivers tried to visit Daniel and La Paloma often in the weeks and months and even years after Gabriela's death. Each time they would come to visit, they would find the farm in worse condition than the last. On some visits, they found him in the barn, passed out from a day of drinking. When the caregivers would find him in this condition, they would rush the kids away. Their hearts broke for their father and they wondered why he was not trying to get better for them. They so badly wanted to come home, but not to this home. They longed for the home of the past.

The years passed and Daniel found himself barely surviving. He found enough odd jobs to keep up his drinking—all the while, his mental state had become an endless downward spiral.

He stopped eating, and sleep only came after a long day of heavy drinking.

Once in town buying ingredients for his homemade alcohol, he passed a park and caught a glimpse of Dr. Sánchez and María de los Angeles. Through hazy eyes, Daniel could see that María de los Angeles was growing into a beautiful young girl. Seeing her there with Dr. Sánchez made him sad for the time he had missed with her and for the realization that he may never be able to bring his family back together, the way he had always dreamed.

He parked his car behind a large hedge of bushes and slowly approached, hoping to get a better look. Though he thought he was being careful, he tripped and fell onto the street, causing all the people in the park to stare in his direction.

He stood up and fell over once again.

Dr. Sánchez ran out of the park onto the street.

"Daniel, what is wrong?" he asked.

Daniel looked up at him from the ground. The world was spinning, and he couldn't comprehend what the doctor was saying to him. He scuffled back and somehow made it onto his feet. "I'm so sorry," mumbled Daniel as he staggered back to his truck and quickly drove off.

Dr. Sánchez watched him drive away in a panic and was mortified at the condition Daniel had fallen into. It had only been a few years and the thought of turning María de los Angeles back over to this man made him fear for her safety.

One's capacity for good versus evil is universal when it comes to our children or loved ones. Dr. Sánchez decided at that moment that he would do anything to protect and care for María de los Angeles, even if it meant going beyond what he swore he would never do.

Roberto and Manolo had grown into young men and would periodically check in on Daniel. They knew their family would never be back together again, but they so desperately wanted him to get better. They would bring their father groceries and supplies when they visited but knew it wouldn't be long before the cupboards were bare, and Daniel's only sustenance was once again the booze. Nothing changed in Daniel's life over the next few years. His cycle of drinking and sleeping prevented him from living. He just existed.

In a moment of despair, Daniel decided to try to see María de los Angeles once again. He had no idea where his other children were, but he knew exactly where his baby girl was. He took the familiar drive to the Sánchez's home and was dumbfounded when he arrived.

The sprawling house was completely empty. The wraparound porch was bare—the furniture and lush plants that once decorated the house were gone. Nothing remained.

He peered inside the dusty windows hoping against hope that they would be there. He was crushed. All the furnishings were gone, and the light fixtures were covered in large dust covers. It looked as though the Sánchez family had been gone for some time.

The last few bits of his heart shattered.

His final hope of having a family was gone.

María de los Angeles was gone.

Daniel had completely forgotten the conversation he had with Dr. Sánchez a few months earlier about their plans to move to Havana and then on to the United States. Cuba was changing rapidly, and the doctor had the forethought to plan his family's departure. Daniel, in his stupor, was not fully aware of the changing political climate. Though he heard the words coming from the mouth of Dr. Sánchez, he didn't completely understand what was taking place and he was too embarrassed to let his naiveté show. He only understood that they were taking his daughter to Havana temporarily, but he didn't piece together the fact that they were never to return to La Palma. Had he known the finality of this conversation, he would have tried to fight for his daughter.

Now she was gone.

Our family will never again be together, thought an inconsolable Daniel.

María de los Angeles's new family was cemented when they made the move to Havana. The move was a complete break—Daniel would never be able to locate her in his condition. He had no resources, his mental state was continuing to deteriorate, and his drinking was all-consuming.

The Sánchez family settled into a nice community in Havana while they awaited their visas. María de los Angeles attended the International School of Havana, the most prestigious school in the city. She was growing into a smart, loving, and beautiful young girl. Joaquin and Margarita loved María de los Angeles as their own. Their dream was to create a beautiful life for their family and give her the best of everything. Each evening, Margarita would lay out her navy-blue pre-school uniform skirt, starched white button-down shirt, and white ruffle lace socks next to her classic black and white saddle oxford shoes. Her light brown hair was always parted down the middle with two neat little braids. She had bangs that skimmed her forehead just above her eyebrows and framed her adorable face. After a healthy breakfast of eggs, toast, and fruit, María de los Angeles would gather her lunch bag and a navy-blue sweater before kissing Margarita goodbye. It was a sweet exchange and a scene that Joaquin never tired of.

"Are you ready to go, *muñeca*—doll?" asked Joaquin with a smile.

"*Sí, Papi*," I am all ready," said María de los Angeles.

"*Vámonos*—let's go," said Joaquin as he walked to the front door and opened it for her to pass through. They walked to the car and went around to the passenger side so María de los Angeles could climb in. When she was comfortably settled in the front seat, he walked to the driver's side of his new turquoise 1959 Chevrolet Bel Air and slid into his seat before driving away. María de los Angeles loved to talk. She especially loved to talk with her father and tell him stories of things that happened during her school day. He loved listening to her many adventures. This was their special time every day, and he wouldn't trade it for the world.

There was never a day when María de los Angeles was not treated like the princess she was to her new parents. Her life was privileged. She was the only one of Gabriela and Daniel's children to have this great fortune—it was a world apart from the rest. Joaquin and Margarita's decision to take her in was the best thing that happened to her, after losing her mother so suddenly and not long after, her father, for very different reasons.

She knew nothing about her true family back in La Palma. Joaquin and Margarita, thinking they were protecting her, decided to keep the secret of her birth family. They couldn't bear the thought of ever losing her and they feared the worst if she were ever to know the truth.

María de los Angeles and her father were extremely close—she felt as though he understood her and they both shared a heart of compassion for others. As María de los Angeles became older, she tried hard to connect with her mother, but they never could see eye to eye. They were like oil and water—they loved each other, but there was never a close mother-daughter bond. She wondered many times about this disconnect and wished she had a mother to whom she could tell her most precious hopes and dreams.

The Sanchez family was falling into a daily routine in Havana, but the political climate had become even more unsettled and they were anxious to receive their visas.

Dr. Sánchez was working at *la Clinica Latina de la Habana*, but he had a connection in Chicago for a position at a large pediatric practice. As soon as their visas arrived, they would be ready to leave. After waiting eighteen months, the letter they had been looking forward to finally arrived. The documents contained all the details of their departure. Three seats were reserved for the Sánchez family on a *Cubana de Aviación* flight into Chicago's O'Hare International Airport the following week. They were leaving Cuba—never to return.

CHAPTER FOURTEEN

HAVANA, CUBA
1959 — 1967

Cuba was a bustling country in 1959. The capital city of Havana had a busy city center and Cuban residents lived on par with other industrialized nations. The architecture was stunning with beautiful mixtures of bright colors and textures. The streets were narrow with tall buildings filled with shops, cafes, and hotels on either side. Bright lights were strung above the streets. It felt very modern but also had a uniqueness and charm that was unlike anywhere else in the world. The sounds and smells were undeniably Cuban. Traditional salsa music filled restaurants and shops, spilling into the streets. Food vendors lined the sidewalks—the savory smells of hot Cuban sandwiches filled the air as a combination of meats and cheeses were pressed in a piping hot sandwich press. People would line up all throughout the day for this distinctly Cuban treat. They were wrapped in simple brown paper and people would snack on their sandwiches while shopping and sightseeing. Cafes served *cafécito* all day long and people would pop in for a quick pick-me-up and a guava *pastelito*—pastry.

The city was alive all through the day and late into the night. American influences had begun to appear all throughout Havana. The intersection of Galiano and San Rafael was filled with shops like Woolworth's—affectionately known as "Ten Cent"—meaning "five and dime," which carried a large variety of American goods that the Cuban people flocked to and loved. *El Encanto* was a massive four-story department store filled with luxury goods and merchandise that would rival any upscale American department store. It had everything one could imagine.

El Gran Teatro de la Habana—The Grand Theatre of Havana, was home to the Cuban National Ballet. It was designed by Belgian engineers in 1914 and still stands in all its splendor today, having been restored solely by private donations. The exterior of the theatre was lined with intricately carved statues, inspired by ancient Greek architecture. The arched entryway opened to a foyer, flanked by massive marble columns. It had high ornate ceilings, shimmering crystal chandeliers, and plush velvet seats. The outside of the elegant entryway was lined with huge rounded windows that would fill the theatre's lobby with gorgeous filtered sunlight.

Located on the harbor, the smells of ocean air mixed with the smells of the city created a delightful ambiance. Beautiful lush palm trees lined the perimeter of the city. Tourists filled the beaches and downtown Havana. The Havana Hilton Hotel was the desired place to stay. It opened to great fanfare in 1958. The large thirty-story high building offered 630 luxuriously appointed rooms and suites with private balconies. The hotel's amenities were unmatched. It was fully air conditioned and included a fine dining restaurant, a large outdoor swimming pool, and a trendy and fashionable rooftop bar.

Havana and its beaches were vacation and honeymoon destinations for wealthy Americans as it was just a short plane trip away from most U.S. cities on the East Coast. People loved the warm, tropical climate during the day, and the spectacular nightlife by night. The clubs were filled wall to wall with people dancing, drinking, and enjoying life. The Copacabana and The Tropicana were well-known nightclubs with beautiful showgirls dressed to the nines with elaborate costumes and headdresses covered in sequins and feathers. Quintessential Cuban cigars, such as Montecristos and Cohibas, were everywhere and accessible to all. Thick smoky curls of cigar smoke wafted through the air of the clubs out onto the cobblestone streets. It felt like a never-ending tropical dream. There wasn't a care in the world when Americans and Cubans alike filled the streets, cafes, and clubs.

★

The early part of the twentieth century saw Cuba's economy grow tremendously from the sale of sugar to the United States. The sugar economy led to Cuba being among the most successful and advanced countries in all of Latin America. The economy in the 1950s was booming and the numbers were impressive. Cuba, despite being a small country with just a few large cities and many rural areas, was a leading country in per capita income. Ownership of automobiles and telephones secured Cuba's ranking as the third-largest country per capita. Televisions were unbelievably popular, and per capita, Cuba ranked first in the southern hemisphere for number of TVs. Incredibly, the literacy rate was above 75%, and for the number of doctors per capita, Cuba ranked eleventh in the world. For its size, Cuba maintained pace with the United States in education, socioeconomics, and cultural and societal traditions that were being admired by the rest of the world.

Havana remained insulated as the rest of Cuba began to feel the impacts of the continued reduction of the robust sugar exports to the United States in the 1940s and 1950s. Many American companies that depended on Cuba and had invested in the sugarcane industry began taking over the production facilities after the Cuban producers' loans defaulted. The United States had its own processes in place and began exporting sugarcane to the U.S. on its own, having a devastating impact on the farmers, the workers, and Cuban companies that relied on the sugarcane economy. Cuba's national economy began to suffer and soon spiraled after the loss of its share in the global sugar market.

In addition to the loss of the sugarcane industry, the political situation in Cuba had been simmering under the corrupt administration of dictator Fulgencio Batista. The Cuban people began to see their beloved country turning into a police state—all their personal freedoms and human rights were slowly being stripped away.

A fresh group of young rebels emerged with revolutionary ideas to bring back a thriving democratic Cuba. They began staging their attempts at a coup in the densely forested Sierra Maestra mountain range. After several failed attempts to overtake Batista's government throughout the 1950s, they finally succeeded on January 1, 1959.

After so much upheaval and corruption under Batista's rule, the revolution forced him to flee Cuba for the Dominican Republic, and tens of thousands of Cubans and Cuban Americans in the United States celebrated the end of Batista's regime.

Fidel Castro along with his brother, Raul Castro, and Argentinian-born Ernesto "Che" Guevara quickly established their power. The Cuban people were elated to support this new government under Fidel Castro, which promised to bring back the tenets of the Cuban Constitution.

"The revolution is as green as the palms," Fidel Castro declared, giving the populace confidence in what he promised to be a democratic government and a thriving economy.

Before long, the United States government became suspicious of Castro's leftist ideologies, in spite of his democratic rally cry toward the people. The students that had been in support of Castro from the very beginning began questioning some of the newly enacted policies. It became clear that Castro's vision for Cuba was aligning with a socialist ideology, not what they had been promised.

Within a few months, more than six hundred Batista supporters had been put to death by the revolutionary regime. Anyone, including civilians, who disagreed with Castro's ideology was subject to brutal beatings, disappearances, and even murder by firing squads.

Almost immediately, Castro's government began confiscating guns from people named on lists that had been compiled by the previous regime. At first, they started with rival revolutionaries and expanded to civilians. A totalitarian government must disarm its citizens to remove the possibility that they could revolt and overthrow the tyrannical regime.

The government also began implementing private agricultural industry reform—forcing local farmers out of business and stripping them of ownership of their land and supplies. All small business and corporate entities were seized and became property of the Cuban government, as allowed by Law 890, passed in 1960.

Cuban banks were taken by force under Law 891 and the national currency was devalued. They printed a new currency and stripped all Cubans of their savings and livelihood. Their money was now merely meaningless paper—it had zero value.

The urban reform law of 1960 forced large landlords to abandon their rental homes and hand them over to their tenants as property. The state now owned every part of the Cuban economy along with personal property and wealth.

In December 1961, Castro addressed the Cuban people in English in a televised speech and solidified what the United States government already knew. "I am a Marxist-Leninist and shall be one until the end of my life. Marxism or scientific socialism has become the revolutionary movement of the working class."

The nationalization of all private assets on which the foundation of the health care, housing, and educational systems were built still remains. A thriving country full of promise had been turned into the abject failure that it is today. The human rights violations and the scarcity of food, medicine, and consumer goods turned this picturesque tropical paradise into an island prison for seven million Cuban citizens overnight.

The Cuban people were deceived from the beginning. And the foothold Castro got by disarming, starving, oppressing, and beating the Cuban people into submission is still in place, more than six decades later.

★

Daniel's family was still separated, and he remained at La Paloma, alone and isolated. Seven years had passed in what at times seemed like the blink of an eye and at others, the torturous ticking of a clock, marking each movement with a loud tick ... tick ... tick. His children had settled into their new lives and Daniel had not seen most of them in years. He missed his children terribly and he thought about them every day. He wished so much that he could turn back time to when he, Gabriela, and their children were happy at La Paloma.

Daniel had always wondered where Lilia was but had no way to locate her. He asked everyone he came into contact with in Pinar del Río if they had seen her. With sadness in their eyes, they always said, "No, I'm so sorry." For many years, no one knew what had happened to her, but one day, word got back to Daniel that Lilia had died. He was distraught once again, blaming himself for pushing her to walk out on them so many years ago. No one knew of her deception as she was, in fact, alive. She had asked a friend to relay that message. Lilia never wanted to be found by her family again.

Everything changed one ordinary day. An old friend of Daniel's told him that he had seen Lilia with her two children visiting a friend in Santa Clara. He told him how he had recognized her and greeted her saying, "Lilia, how have you been?"

"My name is not Lilia. It is Belkis now, and I don't want to be reminded of my past," she responded.

Daniel's initial reaction to his daughter being alive was one of tremendous happiness and relief. But almost immediately, his thoughts turned to disgust as he remembered how she had left her younger brothers and sisters at a time when they desperately needed her.

★

Roberto had grown into a tall and handsome young man and was the only one of his children who kept in touch with him. Daniel was grateful that even though Roberto was busy, he still made the time to visit him at the farm occasionally and bring him groceries and supplies. Roberto loved his father, but at nineteen, he was ready to explore life on his own and start his studies at the University of Havana. After much discussion with Juan and Luisa, he decided to leave *Rancho Santa Catalina* for the possibility to work and study in Havana. Because he had always been drawn to numbers, his dream was to pursue an accounting degree.

Luisa gave him the contact information for a man of Chinese descent she and Juan knew who owned a grocery business in central Havana. His name was Francisco Chan. He had married a Cuban woman, and together, they ran a successful business, Bodega Chan. They carried a large selection of pantry staples and fresh meats and dairy.

Roberto needed a job, so he decided he would make the two-hour drive from Pinar del Río to visit Francisco and see if he would hire him. This was an important step toward independence. He didn't know anyone in Havana and didn't have a place to live.

Francisco liked him and offered him the job the same day. Francisco knew Roberto didn't know anyone else in Havana, so he offered him a place to stay in the back of the warehouse. Francisco had set up a room in a corner of the building with a small bed, a round wooden table he used as a nightstand, and an old dresser with chipped white paint. Roberto was grateful for a place to live and the opportunity to make a living as he learned the grocery business.

Roberto worked behind the counter gathering items for customers from the large bins that lined the back wall. All the groceries were kept behind the counter; Roberto would take the customer's order then retrieve all the items on their list. Many of the products came in bulk and had to be weighed and put into individual bags or containers.

When Roberto was interviewing for this job, the owner had asked him, "How many ounces are in a pound?"

"Sixteen," Roberto had quickly answered.

But Francisco "corrected" him, saying, "No, that would be 'fourteen' ounces." So although Roberto knew otherwise, a pound was now fourteen ounces each time he weighed anything for a customer.

He spent his time working during the day and studying and attending classes at night. On his days off, he would make the drive to Pinar del Río to pick up his father for medical treatment in Havana. Daniel's addiction and mental condition had been deteriorating for years, but it was now to the point where he needed electroshock therapy. Roberto would leave very early in the morning and be back in time to take him to his midday appointment at *el Hospital de la Caridad*—Charity Hospital in Havana. They would have a Cuban sandwich and a mamey milkshake before making the drive back to La Paloma. Eventually, the electroshock therapy treatment stopped working. Roberto found a new doctor for Daniel who prescribed several different medications for him. They improved his depression and made him feel better than any of the other treatments and medications he had used in the past.

After living in the warehouse of Francisco's store for several years, Roberto was now twenty-one years old. He moved into a hostel and continued his studies with a close eye on the deteriorating political climate.

On April 17, 1961, the United States sent 1,400 CIA-trained civilians who had fled Cuba for the U.S., in an attempt to take back the Cuban government with an advance on the Bay of Pigs and establish a beachhead on the southeastern coast of the island. The plan for the civilians, code-named Brigade 2506, included an airstrike to take out Castro's air force. A series of terrible decisions, leaks of information, and failures by the United States government led to one of the most devastating operations in American history. The four-day-long attempt failed and ended with some of the brigade members escaping out to sea, another 1,200 surrendering, and more than 100 dead. The 1,200 prisoners were kept captive for eight months while Castro and Attorney General Robert F. Kennedy negotiated. They agreed to exchange the prisoners for 53 million dollars' worth of medicine and baby food.

Later in the year, the United States government officially cut ties with the Cuban government. The Soviets were increasing their support of Castro and his policies, and the American government recognized Cuba's descent into communism was gaining strength.

★

Roberto thrived at the university and soon met a lovely young girl named Lolita Herrera. She was only eighteen years old but was mature and had dreams for her life. Roberto's cousin Berti introduced them. She had been friends with Lolita since middle school and asked her to her home for lunch. Berti told her she had a handsome cousin that she wanted her to meet. Lolita dressed up and asked her brother, Emilio, to drive her to Berti's home. Emilio was a student at the University of Havana and took classes in the evenings. During the day, he worked as a laboratory technician at the *Clinica Bautista*—the Baptist Clinic. His dream was to be a doctor one day.

When Lolita arrived at Berti's house, before she could knock on the door, Roberto swung it open with a huge smile on his face. He had been waiting for this girl that Berti described as "so beautiful" and he could hardly believe how stunning she was as she made her way to the front door.

As they enjoyed lunch and lively conversation, Roberto couldn't take his eyes off of her. It had been the perfect meeting. Roberto wanted to see her again.

"May I see you again soon?" asked Roberto.

"Yes," replied Lolita.

"Where would you like to meet?" asked Roberto excitedly.

"We can see one another Sunday at church," said Lolita.

"Yes, perhaps we can go for lunch afterward," suggested Roberto.

"That would be very nice," replied Lolita with a shy grin.

After their first date following the church service, they began attending church together each week.

"May I call you?" asked Roberto.

"Yes, my phone number is 30-29-81," Lolita replied." You could even stop by if you'd like."

"I would love to," said Roberto. "What is your address?"

"We live at Calle 8, #259 Alto, between Calles 11 and 15, Vedado, Havana," said Lolita.

As the courtship progressed, he would go to Lolita's house for dinner a few times a week, and afterward, they would take frequent strolls at *el Parque de Jose Marti*. They enjoyed watching the spirited chess games being played by university students and local elderly men.

Although they didn't have much in common, they greatly enjoyed spending time with each other. They were a handsome couple—both very attractive on their own—but together they were stunning. Their relationship grew, and Roberto became like one of the family. Roberto admired Lolita's brother Emilio immensely. They became fast friends—more like brothers than friends—taking in the occasional baseball game or grabbing a Cristal beer and engaging in a spirited conversation among friends.

Roberto and Lolita enjoyed taking the scenic drive along *la Avenida de Maceo* toward *el Malecón*—a four-mile esplanade or seawall wrapping around Havana Bay—from Old Havana to El Vedado. Although it was built to protect the island's capital city from rough seas and unusually high tides, Cubans enjoyed meeting their friends or sweethearts there as well as fishing and even selling things to earn a few extra *pesos*. Walking hand in hand, Roberto and Lolita would stroll up and down the boardwalk, taking in traditional Cuban sights, sounds, and smells. It was their favorite place in the whole world. Couples in bright colorful clothing danced to the upbeat rhythms of *Guantanamera*, little children ran and giggled, and the sweet smell of cinnamon-covered *churros* wafted in the air. It was joy, excitement, wonder, intrigue, and the promise of dreams coming true all rolled into one.

They would sit for hours looking out into the ocean of possibilities, watching the white-capped waves crash against the seawall. At times, the waves were so big, Lolita and Roberto would feel the spray of saltwater on their skin. Time passed in moments as they fell more and more in love.

Lolita was working part-time as a receptionist at the same clinic as Emilio. It was only a block away from home, but as she was unable to make very much money, Lolita took interest in becoming a hairdresser. She had always enjoyed making beautiful updos for her friends and family, so she approached a woman that owned a small salon. The woman agreed to help her and wrote a letter to the academy where Lolita wanted to attend. Lolita was thrilled when they notified her that she had been accepted into the class.

Lolita was invited to an interview and asked to bring a hair model. The owner of the academy was highly impressed with her abilities and told her she could take the four-month course for free if she would be willing to teach a class each Wednesday. Lolita agreed—and in just a few months, she graduated at the top of her class. Lolita started working with the woman that wrote her letter of recommendation. She put Lolita's certificate in a picture frame and hung it on the wall in the beauty shop.

Emilio progressed in his studies as the government continued its socialist march toward communism. One day, by chance, he didn't attend classes, and later found out the government forced the University to expel five of his friends. They were arrested for disagreeing with the government, but they were soon released. Emilio did not go back to the university for fear that he too would be expelled and arrested.

The economic conditions deteriorated to the point of affecting everyday citizens and their businesses. Lolita's father, Oscar, owned an auto repair shop near their home.

He had started his business, *El Rápido, Taller de Mecánica*—Speedy Auto Repair, fifteen years earlier and had been proud of being able to support his family. As the years had passed since communism had infiltrated every part of society, it became more difficult to run his business.

One day, Oscar stepped out for lunch. When he returned, out of nowhere, he found armed militia soldiers taking his equipment and loading it into a large military vehicle.

"What are you doing? Why are you taking my machinery and tools? I need these for my business!" shouted Oscar.

"We are only here to do as we have been ordered—to confiscate private enterprise assets. If you don't like it, you can go to city hall and argue with them."

Oscar ran toward the truck to take back his property. A broad-shouldered, young soldier reared back his rifle and used the end to punch Oscar in the stomach, knocking him out. Everything he owned was confiscated, and he was arrested. The family didn't know where they had taken him. When Oscar came to, he was alone on the ground in a jail cell and realized that all the equipment that had taken him years and large financial investments to buy were gone. He was thirsty, but even after repeated requests for water, he was denied. When he was released later that night, he walked home, four miles—arriving bruised and in tears. He had been humiliated and left with nothing. They had stolen everything from him.

Roberto realized that there was no future for him and Lolita in this oppressive regime. He started making preparations to leave Cuba, but although he applied for an exit visa, they never contacted him. He soon lost his job with Francisco. Once a visa was applied for, the government no longer allowed one to work. He and Emilio hatched a plan to make money by taxiing people around the city in Oscar's 1959 Opel. It was a reliable car and was known as the German Chevrolet.

They each would take shifts, driving around the clock. This allowed them to continue making an income in hopes of soon leaving Cuba. The oppressive political situation increasingly made life more difficult for the average citizen.

While they waited, Roberto knew he had found the love of his life and asked Lolita to marry him after only six months. He proposed with a beautiful diamond ring that Juan and his wife, Luisa, helped him select from the finest jewelry store in Havana. They loved Lolita and wanted her to have a gorgeous symbol of her and Roberto's love.

Roberto couldn't wait to propose to Lolita. He picked her up on a Saturday afternoon and they drove hand in hand to their favorite place in the world—*el Malecón.*

They made their way to their favorite bench overlooking the sea and sat while the sun began to set. Pink and orange colors filled the sky and reflected on the water.

Roberto reached into his pocket with a shaking hand and pulled out the ring. Lolita turned and gasped as she saw the beautiful diamond shimmering in the last bits of daylight.

"I love you more than words can say, Lolita. I want to spend the rest of my days with you and only you. I can't promise you much right now, but I know I can give you a life full of love and adventure," said Roberto with tears filling his eyes.

He held out the ring toward Lolita. She reached out gingerly and placed it on her slender ring finger.

"Yes, my love. Yes! I want to experience all of my life with you. You make my life most interesting and beautiful and I can't wait for a lifetime full of memories," replied Lolita.

They were so excited to share the news of their engagement with friends and family. Everyone was overjoyed—especially Emilio, who would now be able to call Roberto his brother.

Lolita started planning their wedding with tremendous joy and continued working at the beauty salon. The money she made was pooled with her family to pay for living expenses and to purchase items on the black market. Cuba had gone to a rationing system early on in Castro's communist regime, and each person received monthly food and supplies by exchanging a coupon from their *libreta*—a government-assigned coupon booklet, for their allotment.

Lolita and Roberto continued trying to get exit visas out of Cuba as they wanted to have their wedding in the United States. After repeatedly applying in vain, they set the date for their wedding, October 30, 1965, at William Carey Baptist Church in downtown Havana.

The government had a special program for brides and grooms. They would receive two sets of white undergarments, a pair of dress shoes for each, and a white shirt for the groom. When Lolita went to get her order, they were out of female undergarments. They were also out of Roberto's size in the shoes and the shirt. He only received one pair of underwear. This was a one-time coupon and they could not go back. They would have to make do with what they had. The storefronts in once-thriving downtown Havana were empty now. Most shops were closed and the few that remained open had a very limited selection of very few products.

The church offered each bride the opportunity to borrow a beautiful wedding gown and veil with a rhinestone tiara. There wasn't a selection of several gowns. It was only one gown that each bride took turns using for their wedding.

The greatly anticipated day had arrived, and Lolita was full of a mixture of wonderful emotions. She wanted everything to be perfect. As she stood at the entrance of the church, she began feeling nervous. She had been afraid that her father wouldn't live to see this day. His health had begun to decline due to heart disease caused by heavy smoking. As soon as she took his arm to walk down the aisle, her nerves immediately calmed, and she knew they were exactly where they were supposed to be.

She was a vision in white. The bridal dress was an off-the-shoulder design with a lace bodice and a flowing A-line satin skirt adorned with pearls and rhinestones. It was gorgeous and flattered Lolita perfectly. She wore an antique silver cross on a short chain that her mother, Angela, had gifted her. It sat perfectly on her chest and accented the delicate neckline of the dress. The thin veil fell gently to her perfectly manicured fingertips, and the rhinestone tiara framed her gorgeous face and exquisite olive complexion, highlighted by her jet-black hair. She was absolutely stunning.

Roberto waited for her in a black tuxedo he had borrowed from Juan, at the front of the church, with Emilio at his side. Roberto looked like a movie star.

Lolita had one bridesmaid, her best friend, also named Lolita. Her father, Reverend Fernando Fuentes, performed the simple but meaningful ceremony. They lit the unity candle, exchanged their vows, and finally were able to share their first kiss as husband and wife. They turned and the minister introduced them for the first time as *Señor y Señora* Roberto Martínez de Osaba. They walked down the aisle with huge smiles on their faces and tenderly embraced once they reached the back of the church. They made their way to the reception hall and after a few photos, their guests began arriving to join in the celebration.

Juan and Luisa wanted to give Roberto and Lolita a beautiful wedding and reception they would always remember. It was a most generous gift, but he had always been like a son to them.

The centerpiece of the reception was a gorgeous cake with two tiers and cherubs made of meringue holding up the second tier. It was exquisite. It was made by the award-winning *Pasteleria Francesa Sylvania*—Sylvania French Bakery. The cake was such a luxury for them. Their friends and family had pooled their egg rations to give the bakery so they could make the perfect cake to commemorate this special day. Everyone wanted this to be an amazing day for Lolita and Roberto. They also collected the empty *SON* brand soda bottles so Lolita could take them to the store to be refilled. It was the only way to get soft drinks if they weren't part of your monthly allotment. They all sacrificed to be a part of this most perfect day. They all needed a reason to celebrate.

Each guest received a cute little box with macaroni salad, tea sandwiches with cream cheese and ham filling, and some butter mints. Juan had a friend that had many connections and made the boxes for the special day. After greeting their friends and family and enjoying a few bites, the new couple was ready to embark upon their new lives together.

Angela sewed fabric rose petals from her sewing scraps and asked her friends to give her any extra rice they had to throw when Lolita and Roberto left the reception for their honeymoon. They were showered with rice and colorful petals as they made their way to the waiting car. Emilio's boss, Dr. Ulasias, gifted Lolita and Roberto the getaway limousine that was decorated with flowers and illuminated from the inside. Everywhere they drove, people cheered and clapped as they passed. The driver took them to the Hotel Riviera where they spent three nights. It had been a gift from another of Emilio's friends from the clinic. Juan had taken his dark green Oldsmobile and left it in the parking lot of the hotel. He dropped off the key at the front desk so Roberto could drive him and Lolita the three hours to Tierra Azul in *el Valle de Viñales*. It was a resort known as a romantic honeymoon destination with charming cabins in a lush tropical wooded property.

In days past, people had gathered by the pool and the palapa hut to enjoy sandwiches and drinks—but the pool was empty, and all that was long gone. Now the restaurant didn't have much, if any, food. They met three other couples that had gotten married recently and enjoyed talking with them. Lolita and Roberto looked for places where they could buy something to eat as most restaurants were either closed or had been taken over by the government and had very little to offer other than *café con leche*, bread, and some simple fruit. They were so disappointed at the selection as they actually had money that friends and family had saved for them to spend during their honeymoon. They had to be resourceful and enjoy the activities offered by the resort. They went horseback riding and spent the days exploring the vast property with creeks, and beautiful trails around the *mogotes*. In the late afternoon, they would sit in the shade of the giant Cuban Royal Palm trees and enjoy the island breeze.

They returned home sun kissed and blissful. The next few months in their own small rental apartment were wonderful as newlyweds.

They still awaited news of their exit visas but made the best of each day. Before they knew it, they found out they would need to add one more exit visa to their petition—they were expecting a baby. They were absolutely thrilled, but Lolita had hoped they would welcome their first child in the United States. She was enjoying her pregnancy, and each month, during her visit to the obstetrician, he would tell her that she and the baby were healthy and doing well. Lolita and Roberto loved watching her belly grow and dreamed of the family they would have. They finally received word that they had been approved for entry visas to another country—Lebanon. This was not where they wanted to build their new life but were desperate to leave. They decided they would pursue their exit visas to start a new life in Lebanon, but the Cuban government denied them the exit visas. They were back to square one. Just before Lolita and Roberto's wedding, Castro and other members of his government had organized *el Partido Comunista de Cuba*—the Cuban Communist Party—and the family's urgency to leave the island grew stronger.

Right before the start of the new year, the family decided it would be best to have Lolita and Roberto move in with her parents, Angela and Oscar, and her brother, Emilio. They could pool all their resources to save for the new baby and their living expenses until they could leave for the U.S. Throughout the next few months, Oscar's health continued to deteriorate, leaving his heart in a weakened condition. There was no surgery or treatment available for him. He was no longer able to help Roberto and Emilio drive their Opel around the city to make extra money. He grew weaker by the day and prayed he would live long enough to leave his homeland behind and find the liberty he so much desired. This was not to be. In the midst of so much uncertainty, Oscar died of heart failure in the late afternoon of August 31, 1966, at the age of fifty. Some would say of a broken heart, never to take another breath as a free man. Lolita sat at the foot of the hospital bed, her anguished tears spilling out uncontrollably. She adored her father, and his death brought pain worse than anything she had ever felt. Emilio put his arm around her.

"Don't cry. Everything will be fine," he said, through the tears he couldn't contain himself. "*Papi* is no longer suffering."

Lolita didn't reply. All she could do was weep for her tremendous loss.

Angela couldn't contain her emotions at seeing her two children mourn their father. She began sobbing. Roberto put his hand on her shoulder to comfort her.

Dark and heavy were the days that followed. Their beloved father was gone, but Emilio and Lolita knew they had to push forward and persevere as a family. It is what their father would have wanted for them.

Lolita's pregnancy continued to progress wonderfully, but the political unrest had become unsettling. She needed to help bring in more money for the layette, and although she was eight months pregnant, she knew she could make additional income styling her clients' hair on New Year's Eve. She called all her clients and asked them if they wanted to schedule an appointment to have their hair fixed. They would need to put their rollers in their hair themselves since she didn't have a blow dryer, and Lolita would then be ready to style their hair when they arrived. She started at 8 a.m. and worked until 9 p.m. She saw fifteen clients and made 200 *pesos*. Each of the ladies wanted a small accessory to put in their updo, so weeks before, Lolita had taken an old pair of Roberto's black pants and cut them into cute bows with stones and anything she could find to decorate them. She placed them in a wooden cigar box and stored them under her bed for just an occasion like this. That day, she sold all the ones she had made. At the end of the night, she was exhausted—her back was aching, and her feet were sore and swollen. Even so, she loved being a hairdresser and it felt wonderful to be able to help the family.

Just after the new year, they all applied for exit visas to Spain, where they could process paperwork to legally enter the United States. The following month, on Saturday, February 25 at 11 p.m., Lolita was walking back to bed after getting a glass of water, and as soon as she took the first step, her water broke. She called the doctor, but her contractions weren't strong, so he asked her to call him every thirty minutes to let him know how she was doing. Finally, at 10 a.m. the following morning, her contractions were five minutes apart. The doctor asked Lolita to meet him at *el Hospital del Sagrado Corazon*—Sacred Heart Hospital. Emilio ran to meet her in the operating room. The anesthesiologist was his friend, so he let him attend the birth. The doctor administered the sedative and in less than two hours, Cristina was born. She was a beautiful baby girl with black hair and thick eyelashes. Her olive skin was smooth and soft, and she had the tiniest dimples on her little face. She was perfect. The nurse quickly took Cristina to get cleaned up and Lolita was moved to a different room to recover. Lolita had wished so much that Cristina would have been born in the United States, but there was nothing she or anyone could have done.

Lolita slept for a while, and when she opened her eyes, Emilio was sitting in a chair next to the bed, holding Cristina. He was the first to hold her in his arms and was enamored with this precious baby.

Just a few months after Cristina's birth, they finally heard back on the status of the visas to Spain. They celebrated the wonderful news that they had been granted entry visas into the country. Several days passed before a boy on a bicycle brought them a telegram, telling them they had been approved for exit visas out of Cuba and they would all be leaving for Madrid in a few short weeks. This was the most amazing news of all—the one they had been waiting on for years. Their scheduled flight to freedom was on May 21, 1967, with *Cubana de Aviación* to Madrid, Spain. The weight limit for personal items was twenty pounds per person. How do you decide which things will make up the twenty pounds that you each take to start a new life at twenty-two and twenty-seven years of age?

While the family waited to leave the country, the state sent government officials to do a complete inventory of everything that was in the house (furniture, housewares, linens). Every single item was accounted for and expected to be left in the house when the family departed. Not only were their home and all their belongings going to be seized by the Cuban government, but everything would now belong to this corrupt regime—including their car.

In the early evening on the day before their scheduled departure, Emilio had a small automobile accident as he was leaving from his last stop on his last shift, which damaged the front left fender of their Opel. Only blocks from his destination, a small boy ran out into the street, chasing a ball. Emilio had been taken in watching a group of boys playing baseball in an old field, just as he had done when he was a child. He steered the car into a hibiscus shrub to avoid the boy. Emilio was grateful that the boy was not hurt. He immediately became distraught when he realized the consequences he would face if there were any damage to the car. He had been on his way to turn it in to the authorities, as scheduled, but when they noticed the torn fender, they told him that if it was not fixed and returned by the next day, he would not be allowed out of the country. It was getting late; the family began to panic. Who would they find to fix it at this hour when the flight was scheduled for 4:30 p.m. the next day? Roberto and Emilio found an automobile body repair man who worked through the night to fix the damage so the car could be taken in and not delay their departure. The next morning, Emilio turned the repaired car over to the Cuban government without any problems and made his way back to the house for the final time. He breathed a sigh of relief as he knew they could have detained him for any small infraction and deny his exit visa.

As he approached the house, he saw the government officials ready to seal the home after conducting their final inventory inspection and finding everything to be in its place. Lolita, Roberto, Angela, and baby Cristina were ready to leave for the airport as soon as Emilio arrived. Loaded into a white taxi were a modest bag for each person, and a large Chinese thermos for Cristina's feedings that Lolita had been able to buy on the black market. They all got in and closed the doors. The day they had all been praying for was here. It didn't seem real.

CHAPTER FIFTEEN

HAVANA, CUBA
TO MADRID, SPAIN

MAY 21, 1967

As the car rounded the corner onto the long, palm tree–lined road leading to the José Martí International Airport, everyone sat quietly, staring out the windows that were rolled halfway down. There were no words anyone could say to make this moment feel any different as they were being forced out of their homeland in search of freedom.

Words just don't exist for these kinds of feelings.

Angela was the first to exit the taxi when the driver parked in front of the terminal. At forty-eight years old, she had only been widowed a few months and felt out of sorts leaving her island home. With her dark hair pulled back into a tight bun, she looked around and knew that she would probably never again set foot on Cuban soil. Her sadness was compounded as she thought of Oscar's excitement and anticipation when he talked about being able to live in a free country. He started dreaming of moving to the United States as soon as Fidel Castro's revolution turned from a campaign to remove dictator Fulgencio Batista from power to establishing a Marxist-Leninist government. The suffering of the Cuban people under communism became more evident with each passing day, and Oscar wanted to live far away from here.

In theory, communism makes sense. In reality, it destroys everything it touches.

Oscar knew this, and as his health deteriorated, he feared he would never enjoy life as a free man again. Angela and her children mourned the life that he so deeply wanted and would never have. Amid their grief, they knew they had to keep moving forward. There could be no looking back.

Emilio was next to step out of the taxi. As he did, he turned back around to face Lolita. With his arms outstretched and his hands open, he said, "Give me Cristina so you can get out of the car."

Lolita wrapped Cristina tightly in a pale pink cotton blanket. It had a white, hand-embroidered border and a silky white ribbon woven into the embroidery. Cristina's initials were stitched in the bottom-right-hand corner and were surrounded by three tiny buttercup flowers in a bright yellow thread with green leaves. The blanket had been a gift from her favorite elementary school teacher, Señora Rivas. They had kept in touch over the years, and when Lolita wrote to announce she had given birth to a beautiful baby girl, Señora Rivas wasted no time in gathering what she could find to start working on making something very special to give Lolita for Cristina. The scarcity of all materials and supplies in the country made this gift even more special to Lolita.

Emilio reached out and took Cristina in his arms so Lolita and Roberto could get out of the taxi.

"*Ay, Dios mío. Gracias*, Emilio," sighed Lolita.

Once Roberto was out of the car, he extended his hand to help Lolita slide out of her seat. At twenty-seven years old, Roberto was a doting husband and father. He was a solid provider for his family and took his responsibilities seriously. He had learned this from his father growing up on the farm. He loved his father and ever since he could remember, he wanted to be just like him. Roberto often said his father was the greatest man he had ever known.

"*Gracias, mi amor*," said Lolita.

"Of course. Let's go, *cariño*—sweetie." Roberto could feel his heart pounding, and his hands were now sweating. His anxiety was escalating, but he kept a calm demeanor for his wife and the others.

They joined Emilio, Angela, and Cristina and with all their belongings in their hands. The family was prepared to sacrifice everything for the opportunity to live in a free country. Walking into the airport, they felt the humid tropical air inside the open building, and it felt thick. They walked past the boys selling trinkets and shells and waited in line at the *Cubana de Aviación* check-in counter behind another family to get their boarding passes. When it was their turn, the agent took her time filling out each of the paper boarding passes. She was in no rush to help them make it to their flight on time.

Emilio asked, "Could you please write a little faster, so we don't miss our flight?"

She didn't bother with a reply. She looked up only long enough to give him a condescending look out of the side of her eye and then continued writing.

No one wanted to say anything that could jeopardize this trip, so their eyes darted around as they looked at each other and stood there silently. When the agent finally handed the boarding passes to them, they quickly gathered their things and rushed down a long hallway to the security inspection point.

As they prepared to pass through, a large government official looked at Lolita then at the thermos she was carrying. He looked at her once again and said, "Give me that thermos."

Lolita began to cry hysterically and begged him to let her keep it as it held the four feedings needed for her three-month-old baby girl. Emilio and Angela pleaded with her to calm down and reminded her that she could be denied permission to leave Cuba for anything the officials deemed worthy.

Angela urged her daughter to be quiet. "*Por favor*, Lolita."

Emilio was becoming more concerned with each second that passed. He cupped his hand to his mouth as he told Lolita, "If we are forced to turn back now and we miss this opportunity to escape the misery that our lives have become, we may never have this chance again."

A flight attendant saw what was happening and whispered in Lolita's ear that she would help her once they boarded the plane. She assured her that she would place the bottles of baby formula in the airplane's refrigerator but to please stop crying, as they could deny her from leaving the country.

Lolita composed herself and with trembling hands, removed the baby's bottles and surrendered the thermos. The family was permitted to pass through to board the plane.

★

They arrived at the gate and saw that the boarding process had already begun. Roberto stayed back with Lolita as she took a few minutes to give Cristina a final feeding before boarding the plane for the long night ahead.

Emilio and Angela shuffled into the line. They nervously waited in the jetway for the passengers ahead of them to make their way to the boarding door. Lolita, Roberto, and Cristina joined the line as it was starting to dwindle. Once the family walked into the main cabin of the aircraft, they were greeted by three flight attendants.

Each was wearing a crisp, white short-sleeve shirt, a royal blue knee-length skirt, and a red short scarf tied around their neck. These are the colors of Cuba's flagship airline, which had been established in 1929. Their hair was pulled back, braided, and tucked under to ensure it would not interfere with their duties. Lolita recognized the kind flight attendant from the security checkpoint and smiled at her.

"*¿Cómo te llamas?*" Lolita asked to know her name.

"*Soy* Nancy. You can give me your baby's bottles, and I will place them in the refrigerator in the galley until you need them. I will warm them for you when you are ready."

This gesture touched Lolita's heart as she knew that without being fed, Cristina would not be able to endure the flight.

As each passenger boarded, the flight attendants helped to direct them to their seats.

"*Por aquí*, Señor," motioned another of the flight attendants after reviewing the boarding passes for the family. She handed them back to Roberto and he started down the aisle. Lolita, with Cristina wrapped in her pink blanket, followed him. Emilio and Angela had already found their seats.

While Lolita and Roberto got settled for the flight, they saw the same look of uncertainty on the face of every Cuban citizen that boarded the plane as they walked to their seats. Lolita looked around at the other passengers. No one spoke. Everyone sat in nervous silence, wondering what would await them once they landed, as there was no turning back now. They had no way to know if they would ever again see the family and friends they left behind. In this very instant, the life they knew would remain in the past, but their hope for the future propelled them to pursue the freedom they so desired. All the years of frustration and waiting to be granted permission to leave Cuba had brought them to this moment.

Once everyone was in their seats, the flight attendants closed the boarding door and the pilot dimmed the cabin lights in preparation for departure. The family had never been on an airplane before and didn't know what to expect. All the sights, sounds, and smells were part of a new experience for them.

The pilot announced over the loudspeaker, "Ladies and gentlemen, welcome to *Cubana de Aviación* flight number 825 to Madrid, Spain. My name is Alberto Perez-García and I will be your captain this evening. Assisting me is first officer Teodoro Dominguez, and our Havana-based flight crew are here for your comfort and safety. We are now ready to push back from the gate. At this time, all passengers must be in their seats with their seat belts securely fastened. Our flying time from Havana to Madrid, with a layover for refueling on the island of São Miguel, in the Portuguese archipelago of the Azores, will be approximately ten hours and twenty-five minutes. Flight attendants, please prepare for departure." He then taxied onto the main runway.

The pilot steered the aircraft into position for an immediate departure. Once the plane started its slow and steady roar down the runway for take-off, Lolita and Roberto exchanged glances and Roberto pulled her closer. He kissed her forehead and whispered, "Everything will be fine." She touched his cheek and felt comforted by his words as tears streamed down her face. They gripped each other's hands tightly as Lolita cradled Cristina. They felt as if they were waiting to breathe until they knew no one could take this away from them. The emotions were so intense; they were almost more than either of them could stand. *How could the grief of leaving your life behind be mixed with so much relief and joy?* thought Lolita. Their hope at the possibility of what could be was greater than any doubts they had.

Lolita looked over at Emilio and Angela and saw they had both bowed their heads in prayer.

"Lord," Angela whispered, "we thank you for your mercy in bringing us to this moment, and we pray for a safe trip to our new home. Amen."

Once they finished, they lifted their heads and could feel the increasing pressure pushing them back into their seats.

Just then, the aircraft had picked up enough speed for the wheels to lift from the tarmac and the airplane took off into the early evening sky. As the airplane climbed, Emilio looked out the window with mixed emotions. He knew in his heart that he was seeing the lush mountains and turquoise waters surrounding his home for the last time.

When the plane was finally in the air and everyone on board knew this was actually happening, the passengers erupted into applause, cheers, laughter, and tears all at once.

They could all now breathe.

★

It took a while for everyone to settle down from the elation of take-off. The sounds of whispers, conversations, some cautious laughter, and hopefulness began to fill the cabin.

After twenty minutes, the pilot once again addressed the passengers. "We have now reached thirty thousand feet. If you need to visit the facilities or move around the cabin, please use caution. While at your seat, please keep your seat belt fastened at all times."

Angela had been waiting until it was safe to leave her seat so she could go to the restroom. As she walked up one aisle and down the other, she passed Lolita and Roberto with the baby.

Angela stopped to ask, "How has everything been so far? I could hear Cristina crying once the airplane took off. Is she okay?"

"Yes, she is fine now. She cried herself to sleep."

"I'm glad to see she is resting now."

The next few hours were unremarkable. The weather was clear, and because they had boarded in the late afternoon, some people were starting to unwind while others were getting sleepy. The flight was a little bumpy, but nothing that would make most people fear for their safety.

During this time, the flight attendants began their in-flight service at the front of the plane. They served the meals and snacks based on their destination's time zone. Madrid is six hours ahead of Havana, so the first meal was a late dinner. It consisted of buttered new potatoes, a ground beef patty with brown gravy, and a garden salad along with a hard bread roll and a cup of dulce de leche pudding.

The quality of the food was lacking, but it was what they had come to expect since the U.S. placed an embargo on Cuba in October of 1960. Many ingredients and some prepared foods from the USSR had flooded the market, and regrettably, they were mass-produced with cheap by-products and had become their only choices.

The soft drinks they offered on board were not the Cuban ones Lolita and Roberto loved from their youth—Malta, Jupiña, Ironbeer, and Materva. The airline served the Soviet ones that were less carbonated and with flavors such as licorice, rye, and herbs. Most Cubans had not developed a taste for them. These, however, were now the only soft drinks available on the island.

Emilio was ready to eat as the flight attendants approached the row where he and Angela were sitting. Although he was hungry, he was also concerned because he heard the man behind him say that the aircraft was only operating on three of the four engines. As soon as the flight attendant placed his meal and drink on his tray, he asked her about the engine.

"Yes . . . that is, in fact, true. But we don't announce it as we don't want anyone to panic. Although we have flown it in this condition for seven months, we will be retiring this aircraft once we return to José Martí International Airport because the parts to repair the engine are not available," said the flight attendant.

Emilio couldn't hide his concern for their safety but thanked her for letting him know that what he heard was actually true.

Others on the flight were also mentioning it, so it began to spread among the passengers in hushed tones. They were calling the airplane *el Gallo Ronco*—the Raspy Rooster—because of the strange noises coming from the engines. There was nothing anyone could do now but hope and pray they would arrive safely in Madrid.

Lolita, unnerved at hearing the woman across the aisle from them repeat, in horror, the news of the critical situation with the engine, barely touched her dinner. Cristina started to stretch, move around, and open her eyes. It was time for a feeding and her cries quickly went from a low, fussy cry to a loud hunger cry.

"Please hold Cristina so I can put away my dinner plates and stand up," she asked Roberto.

Lolita got out of her seat, lifted Cristina from Roberto's lap, and tossed the oversized bag over her shoulder. It had Cristina's supplies along with some of their belongings necessary for the move to a new country. She started walking toward the back of the plane, looking for Nancy, who had kindly offered to help her.

Nancy saw Lolita as she approached the galley and pulled the bottle from the refrigerator. She stood it inside a large container filled with hot water and said, "I am the mother of three children. I have two boys and a girl. I know how it is to feel helpless when you need to take care of your child and the circumstances are against you."

Lolita felt so much gratitude for her kindness. After a few minutes and with tears forming in her eyes, she took the bottle that Nancy extended to her.

"¡*Gracias*! ¡*Gracias*! I can't tell you how much I appreciate what you have done."

"My pleasure," replied Nancy. Lolita was able to use a small cushioned bench in the galley to change Cristina's diaper before returning to her seat. She thanked Nancy once again and turned to walk back up the aisle.

Cristina's cries were now loud enough to hear over the engine noise, and several passengers turned to look as Lolita hurried back to her seat to give Cristina her bottle.

Once she was seated comfortably, Lolita quickly placed the baby on her lap and started to feed her. Cristina was contentedly drinking her bottle when the flight attendants began the after-dinner coffee service. Once again, they started at the front of the airplane. The aroma filled the cabin and Lolita wanted something to keep her awake so she could care for Cristina. When the flight attendants stopped at Lolita and Roberto's row, they saw the watered-down coffee from the USSR the airline was serving and not the strong Cuban coffee they had hoped to taste again. They both asked for sugar and milk for their coffee, which made it tolerable.

The cabin lights were dimmed to allow the passengers to continue to acclimate to the new time zone in which they would be arriving.

With only a little more than a couple of hours left on the flight, their exhaustion grew and the caffeine in the Soviet coffee was not enough to keep them awake. Cristina was now wrapped in her warm blanket again and had fallen asleep on Lolita's lap. Lolita hoped she would stay that way for the rest of the flight and gently put her head on Roberto's shoulder. He leaned into her and rested his head on hers. Within moments, all three were asleep.

★

They were abruptly awakened by Cristina's screaming and immediately felt the airplane losing altitude. Lolita knew her daughter's ears were hurting. She placed her pinky finger in the baby's mouth with the hope that Cristina would latch on, releasing the pressure in her ears. This calmed Cristina, and she was able to fall back asleep.

"Ladies and gentlemen, we will be making our initial descent into the Aeroporto de Santa María on the island of São Miguel, Azores shortly for refueling. At this time, please return to your seat and securely fasten your seatbelt. Ensure your seat back and tray table are in their full upright and locked positions. The flight attendants will be passing through the cabin to collect any remaining cups and any items you wish to dispose of."

Angela and Emilio gathered their things as they prepared for landing. Roberto reached under the seat in front of him to collect Cristina's belongings. Lolita held Cristina while telling Roberto all the things that needed to be placed back in the bag.

"This is your captain once again. We have been cleared for landing and are making our final approach into the São Miguel airport. We will be arriving at the airport service area, where the ground crews will service and refuel the aircraft for an estimated time on the ground of one hour and five minutes before an on-time departure of 4:10 a.m. Once the aircraft is safely parked, you will be free to move around the cabin and use the facilities, or you may choose to deplane. Please do not leave the airport service area as we will begin our reboarding process thirty minutes prior to departure. Flight attendants, please take your seats."

This was the pilot's final message before the wheels touched down with a thud. Lolita and Roberto were not sure what to expect and were frightened when they experienced the rough landing. The passengers were all thrust forward in their seats as the airplane continued to roll down the runway while the pilot decelerated to a taxiing speed.

After their initial distress, Lolita and Roberto exhaled and felt a tremendous sense of relief to have finally arrived safely in a different country. Roberto looked at Lolita with tired eyes and said, "I can't believe it. We are here." Lolita smiled and said, "Only one more flight and a few hours before we arrive in Madrid."

"Ladies and gentlemen, please remain in your seats with your seat belts securely fastened until we are parked at the airport service area and the seat belt sign is turned off. This will indicate it is safe to move about the cabin. Please check around your seat for any personal belongings. If you need assistance, please let a member of our flight crew know. Thank you for flying *Cubana de Aviación*, and we will see you shortly."

Angela and Emilio were ready to get some fresh air and to walk around for a few minutes, so they were among the first to exit the airplane. Roberto and Lolita were undecided if they should awaken Cristina, but knew they had another three hours of flying time and decided it was best to follow Angela and Emilio.

When they stepped off the plane onto the tarmac, a gentle rain was falling. The airport gate would have been a good place to spend this time, but the airplane was parked far away, and as it was in the middle of the night, the airport was closed. The only option was to walk around on the tarmac, near the airplane. Lolita and Roberto, who was now carrying Cristina, walked toward Angela and Emilio to stand under the wing of the airplane for shelter from the rain.

"I am so tired and sleepy," said Angela.

"I am as well. I think I'm going to reboard the airplane," said Emilio.

They were all exhausted. After a few minutes, they decided to return to their seats.

The flight attendants were busy preparing the cabin for the last leg of the trip. Shortly after the family boarded, the flight attendants started the reboarding process for all passengers. This time, everyone went directly to their seats, so it was much faster than when they boarded in Havana.

The news about the critical situation with the engine that had been quietly passed around the main cabin had been terrifying to the passengers. Even so, it wasn't enough to dissuade a single soul from reboarding the airplane for the flight to Madrid. The unknown steps forward would be better than any steps turning back.

Once everyone had reboarded the airplane and the boarding door had been closed, the pilot again took to the loudspeaker. "Please take your seats and fasten your seatbelts." He repeated the preflight instructions from the earlier flight and before the airplane full of Cuban refugees realized it, the airplane picked up sufficient speed to take off into the night sky.

The next time the boarding door opened, the passengers knew they would step out and inhale the sweet smell of freedom.

For Lolita, the last three hours of the trip seemed to go by slowly. She wanted to fall back asleep, but after all the commotion around the refueling stop, she wasn't able to relax enough to take even a short nap. Roberto had an easier time falling asleep—he dozed off for over an hour and a half.

Because this flight was only a little more than three hours, there would be no formal meal service. Shortly before descending into Madrid, the flight attendants served a light, traditional, Spanish-style breakfast of *café con leche*, orange juice, ham and cheese toast, and a slice of *tortilla Española*—a Spanish omelet in the shape of a small triangle. Emilio and Angela were excited to try the new Spanish cuisine but were disappointed with the diluted consistency of the *café con leche* and the orange juice. The ham and cheese toast was cut into two small rectangles. The presentation on the white plastic plate, including the *tortilla Española*, looked appetizing but was not enough for Emilio to consider it breakfast—only a small snack.

Just as quickly as the flight attendants served the passengers breakfast, they moved back through the main cabin to collect the trash and prepare for landing. Nancy quickly checked in with Lolita to see if she needed anything before taking her seat.

The captain, once again, gave his landing announcement and asked the flight attendants to take their seats.

Angela looked out the window as they were approaching Madrid. The sun was starting to rise against the horizon. She gazed at this beautiful city with many tall buildings, much larger than in Havana, and wondered, *How can I begin a new life at forty-eight years old?*

Within a few minutes, the wheels touched down gently for a smooth landing, and this time, the passengers clapped and cheered with gusto. They were beyond the reach of the Cuban government. Each person was now free to make their own decisions, choices, and plans. They could design the life of their dreams.

As each Cuban refugee passed through the open boarding door into their new life, the possibilities felt endless.

CHAPTER SIXTEEN

MADRID, SPAIN

MAY 22, 1967

In what felt like a blur of emotions, the family arrived at the Madrid-Barajas International Airport just after 7 a.m. As they walked down the jetway and into the terminal, the excitement they felt for this new life was palpable.

"Can you believe this? We are finally in Madrid after waiting for so many years!" said Emilio, as they walked through the airport.

"I am so happy! I truly can't believe we are finally here," said Lolita.

Roberto and Angela agreed with Emilio's and Lolita's sentiments as they made their way to the baggage claim area. Once the family retrieved their small, personal bags, they walked to the end of the next terminal to be inspected by the immigration and customs officials.

They approached a long and wide staircase with a large yellow overhead sign that read *INSPECCIONES* and a black arrow pointing down. At the base of the stairs, they could see the tables where passengers were placing their suitcases for inspection. Emilio and Angela started to walk down the stairs. Roberto was behind Lolita as she was preparing to follow them. Lolita wrapped Cristina tightly in her pink blanket and then in another blanket that the flight attendant had given her as she was leaving the airplane. Lolita took one step and then another. She carefully placed her feet on each step until she was about halfway down. When she took the next step, she felt the baby slipping through the blanket and screamed out, "*¡Auxilio!*—Help!"

Cristina was falling fast and was about to hit the concrete steps.

Emilio was already at the bottom of the stairs and watched in terror as Cristina slipped through the bundle of blankets toward Lolita's feet. He leaped up the stairs and caught Cristina one second before she would have landed on the step. At that very moment, Lolita lost her footing, and the three of them tumbled until they landed on the floor with a thud.

Roberto lost control of the suitcases, which flipped end over end until they reached the floor below as he rushed to help his family. Fortunately, Cristina was well protected and was not hurt as Emilio had grasped her and the blankets just before they all fell.

Lolita and Emilio were sore and bruised, but they collected themselves and got in line with Roberto and Angela to have their bags inspected.

The process was time-consuming as all family members traveling together had to be presented with their documents at the same time. The lines were long, but with several officials working each line, the family made it to the end and were ready to leave the airport in under an hour.

Lolita, Roberto, Emilio, and Angela looked at each other curiously and wondered what would happen next. They had no contacts in Madrid or plans to have anyone pick them up from the airport. They didn't know if they would have to sleep there or if they would be able to find someone to help them. As they stepped outside of the immigration and customs area, they noticed a tall, older black man with a sign that read, *"Familia Emilio Herrera."* They were surprised but relieved that someone knew they had arrived in this new country.

The Spanish government had set up a process for Cuban immigrants to help them transition with temporary housing and assistance with employment.

"*Hola, yo soy Dagoberto,*" said the stranger. "I am here representing *la Iglesia Católica de la Virgen María* and Church World Services. I am here to take your family to the hostel where you can stay until you can find your own boarding house. The church will pay for you to stay at the hostel for three days. After that, you will be responsible for the boarding fees or for finding another place to live. You will also have access to the church resources, should you need them."

"*Sí, gracias,*" said the group—they were just happy to know they had a place to sleep after a long and exhausting trip. The car ride to the hostel was silent. Everyone was staring out the windows, taking in this new country that was so very different from Cuba. Large buildings surrounded them, and the traffic was back to back—horns honking—and people filling the sidewalks. The heat inside the car was stifling. They could barely breathe. They had never before experienced the heat and smog of a big city.

They finally arrived at the hostel, a ramshackle building with an entrance below street level, and the room was sparse with very little ventilation.

They looked around, feeling all sorts of emotions. They were happy to be there, but these were not the conditions they were used to even though they were accustomed to simple living. After unpacking a few things and feeding Cristina, exhaustion took over and they all fell into a deep sleep. Though the room was bare, they did have mattresses to sleep on and lightweight blankets to cover them.

Lolita used cotton blankets to line a small, white, rectangular laundry basket, to use as a crib for Cristina. Even she fell fast asleep after the long journey.

They were told of a nearby soup kitchen frequented by other immigrants and ate most of their meals there. The soup was brothy with just a few meager pieces of carrot and potato. Some meals consisted of meat and bread, but it couldn't be counted on. Mostly they stayed hungry.

On one of their trips to the soup kitchen, they happened to run into a friend from Havana who was leaving Madrid and offered her family's room at the boarding house. Their residency request had been approved and they were preparing to leave for the United States. Lolita, Roberto, Angela, Emilio, and Cristina moved out of the hostel after a few days and into the room at the boarding house.

Roberto looked up at the sign on the building reading Jaime el Conquistador, #11 Madrid 5, España. This would be their home until their U.S. residency was approved.

They carried their bags up four flights of stairs to a one-room flat on a floor that would be shared by several other immigrant families. There was no kitchen—no refrigerator or stove—only one shared hot plate burner for all the residents. A few Spanish students offered the use of their blender so Lolita could make baby food for Cristina. Perishable items were kept on the outside porch once the weather turned cool at night. There was only one simple bathroom for over a dozen people.

While they waited for the paperwork for their U.S. residency, Roberto found a job at *Fabrica de Plasticos*—a plastics factory, earning one hundred *pesetas* a month—just enough to cover their rent. It was one hundred and thirty degrees inside the factory. He worked alternating shifts—switching back and forth weekly from the day shift to the night shift. The schedule and conditions were grueling. He had to quickly learn the train system. His stop was the very last stop in the morning and in the evening. Once he exited the train, he had to walk a mile and a half at the end of his daily trips. The commute was exhausting—the trains were overcrowded, and the heat of the summer months was overwhelming. But he didn't complain. The job was good, and he just hoped they would not be there long.

Through a connection in Cuba, Emilio began working as a lab technician. He also earned one hundred *pesetas* a month. This would be the only spending money they would have month to month for the five of them. It was barely enough to survive on, but somehow they made it work. They lived very simply, keeping only a few staple food items and formula on hand.

While the men were working, Lolita and Angela took care of Cristina, tidied their family's area in the boarding house, and ventured out to gather what they could on such limited income. They frequented a thrift shop for immigrants and bought what few things were left at the end of the day. The women quickly learned if they went first thing in the morning, they had many more choices. Lolita's twenty-third birthday was approaching. She wanted to buy a beautiful outfit to wear for her special day. They spent every extra penny they had on a navy-blue dress and white kitten heels. Her birthday arrived and she was excited to have a night out with Roberto. He wore the light tan suit and navy-blue tie he had left Havana with. They looked dashing and like any other young couple out for a nice dinner.

Lolita had been hearing about *tapas*—small plates of traditional Spanish finger foods—and *sangria*—a sweet and fruity wine drink. Lolita couldn't wait to experience this new and exciting type of meal. The evening of her birthday finally arrived, and they got dressed up and ready for the town. They rode a train into downtown Madrid, taking in all the sights, smells, and stunning architecture. The city and the people were so vibrant. There were people dancing in the streets, and they could hear singing coming from the inside of cafes as the train passed by.

The train finally came to a stop at the Madrid Atocha station. Lolita was giddy with excitement at the opportunity to celebrate her birthday with Roberto in the city. He took Lolita by the hand and they stepped onto the train platform. They walked a short distance and took the steps up to the street level. They stopped for a moment at the top and looked around to see which direction they should go. They weren't sure, so they asked a passing young man, selling newspapers.

"*Hola*, can you tell us how to get to *el restaurante Sol y Luna*—Sun and Moon restaurant?" asked Roberto.

"*Sí*, walk to the end of the street and go left. You will see the restaurant two blocks down on the right-hand side."

"*Muchas gracias*," said Roberto as Lolita now took him by the hand in her anticipation.

The outside of the modern building was made of smooth concrete with cut-out shapes of stars, moons, and suns. Behind the shapes, light poured through cobalt blue-colored glass onto the street. A large wrought iron lantern with thin brass chains attached to each corner hung over the entrance. Lolita and Roberto looked into the glass frame holding the menu and with dismay, realized they did not have enough *pesetas* to even share one dish. They couldn't even afford a glass of *sangria*. Lolita looked at Roberto and back at the menu. She didn't say a word and lowered her head. Tears fell from her eyes onto her beautiful new dress. Roberto placed his hand on her back and pulled her close. He was disappointed in himself that he had let her down. They stood there for a moment and allowed themselves to feel the sadness. They quietly walked back to the train station for the ride home. Roberto didn't know what he could do to make her feel special on this day. He knew all their sacrifices would soon be worth it but for now, he felt the sting of not being able to treat Lolita to a lovely night of celebration.

Tonight represented a milestone for them, and it had not turned out the way they envisioned—it felt like a failure.

Once home, they started feeling ill. They noticed that Cristina was especially fussy. As Lolita changed her diaper she noticed a blotchy red rash on her belly. She called for Emilio. He came right away and knew immediately what he was observing. He had seen the beginning stages of chickenpox before in one of his medical journals.

"It's *varicela*—chickenpox, Lolita. I'm sure you've seen it before. It is a virus that causes little blisters on the skin that itch terribly and usually come with a mild fever and fatigue. We need to check ourselves, as it is very contagious."

Angela and Lolita went into the bathroom to check each other. When they came back into the room the color had drained from their faces.

"Lolita has a large red patch on her back, and I have a small patch on my stomach," said Angela.

Emilio and Roberto both found red patchy splotches on their arms and chests. The first night went by with just Cristina feeling the brunt of it. She cried all through the night and eventually developed a high fever. Lolita did everything she knew to bring down the fever, but she was now beginning to feel very ill herself. The crying continued for days. Everyone was miserable. Emilio and Roberto couldn't go to work, meaning no money came into the household. They had no idea how long this would last and no one to reach out to for help. They spoke to an elderly neighbor through the window and she told them about her experience with chickenpox. She asked if they laundered the sheets after the last family moved out.

"No," Angela and Lolita said. "We have no laundry soap, and they appeared clean when we arrived."

"I am sure it is from the sheets and bedding," the elderly neighbor shared. "Please strip the beds and bag up the linens and leave them on the curb. I will call to have someone come pick them up to be laundered. In the meantime, my daughter will bring freshly washed sheets and blankets you can borrow. She will leave them at the base of the stairs."

"Thank you so much," said Lolita.

She also recommended a doctor come see Cristina as she was able to hear what misery she was in from her apartment across the street. She told Lolita she would send a note to the doctor. The wailing was a clear sign that something else might be very wrong. The doctor came by the next morning to see Cristina. After examining her, he realized that she had a ruptured eardrum from built-up fluid behind her ears combined with the force of her crying.

He left them with ear drops to help with Cristina's ear pain and a medicinal salve that they could all use on their itchy patches.

"It'll just be a few more days. Try not to scratch. And rest as much as possible," the doctor said. "Please send a note or call if your symptoms get worse."

The doctor was impressed that Emilio was able to diagnose the issue and as he was leaving, took his name down for a possible job once he recovered.

They all were feeling much better in a few days just as the doctor had told them they would. Emilio and Roberto went back to work—trying to make up for lost time, they both took double shifts. And life in Madrid continued. They fell into a steady pace of life as they waited for the day they could finally leave for the U.S.

Soon the hot weather turned frigid. They had never experienced cold weather like this before. It was brutally cold. Lolita and Angela stood in line at the thrift store before it opened, hoping to find four coats, something warm for Cristina, scarves, gloves, and hats. They were able to afford a coat for each person and a small wool bodysuit for the baby. There were no hats left by the time they reached the store.

"We are in desperate need of hats," Lolita said to the store clerk. "My husband's ears are blistering from the cold."

The store clerk recommended using scarves that Emilio and Roberto could wrap around their heads as they commuted to and from work. Lolita and Angela had to dig through a mountain of gloves on a large wooden table. After a few minutes, they were able to find two matching sets of men's gloves and one matching set of lady's gloves, which they would share. They never expected they would need to buy such heavy winter clothing to weather the season.

They all agreed they needed to have a bit more income to make it through the winter. Emilio contacted the doctor who had come to help when they had fallen ill with chickenpox. The man was happy to hear from Emilio, and after a few brief interviews, he offered him a job as a pharmaceutical sales representative with *Farmacias Brelia*, which was growing and expanding into new territories.

The position was perfect for Emilio. He was charismatic and eager to learn. He was excited to use the knowledge he had gained during the two years he had attended medical school in Havana. As Madrid became increasingly crowded with more and more immigrants throughout the winter months, the additional income from the new job would help the family with food and additional expenses. The lines at the soup kitchen were longer than in previous months, and despite the cold temperatures, people stood for hours just waiting for a hot meal. The weather and long lines kept the family from using this as a free resource. They used much of Emilio's paycheck to purchase a few groceries and they cooked the best they could on the shared hotplate.

The thrift store also became overcrowded and bare by early morning. Angela and Lolita had to purchase more expensive items from a local store. On one of their shopping outings, they had planned to go to a new store that one of the ladies at the boarding house had told them about. It carried Cuban products and they were excited to find anything that would remind them of the comforts of home. They bundled up with their coats and scarves before leaving. Lolita used the one pair of gloves they shared, and Angela used her pockets to keep her hands as warm as possible. They walked past the beautifully decorated boutique storefronts and admired the fashion they knew they couldn't afford. When they reached the end of the street, they turned the corner and saw a large, magnificent department store straight ahead. The building was at least ten stories tall with gorgeous window displays and a sign over the top floor that read *El Corte Inglés*.

During their entire time in Madrid, they had never been in a store like this.

"Let's just step inside for a few minutes," said Lolita, her eyes wide with wonder at the sights she was seeing for the first time. Angela smiled, knowing there would probably be nothing inside they would be able to buy.

"Yes, let's take a look," said Angela.

Lolita pushed Cristina in her stroller through the heavy doors, into the cosmetics department. Many different lines were represented, and it brought back memories for Angela of the decadent beauty products at the fancy department stores in Havana before the revolution. They only wandered for a few minutes before feeling completely out of place. They hurried to the door but turned to take one last glance at the life that was unattainable to them now.

"Someday, I will be back, and I will buy to my heart's content," said Lolita.

Angela nodded in agreement. They left the store, but that dream never left Lolita.

A few blocks down they finally found the Cuban store they had set out to find. Inside, they were overtaken by the sounds and smells of a home they desperately missed. They scanned the shelves and quickly found a tin of Café Bustelo. They also picked up a few items to make Cristina's baby food. It was a tiny respite from the bustling streets of Madrid. Just as they were leaving they saw the bottles of *Agua de Violeta*—violet water—and knew they couldn't leave without taking one of the most well-loved scents for Cuban children. It transported them back to the warmth of their island home. This had made their entire trip worth it.

Life in Madrid was becoming more strenuous and Roberto checked daily on the status of their residency paperwork. They were all eager to finally be settled in America. Their daily routines kept them busy as a few more months passed. But on one of the coldest days yet, they received a letter indicating that their paperwork had been fully processed and approved, which overjoyed them. They would be leaving Spain in just one week's time and arriving in their new home, Atlanta, Georgia, after a brief layover in New York City. Once Emilio and Roberto notified their employers, they began packing their belongings for another long trip. When the day was finally here, they woke to soft, white snow covering the streets.

A car arrived to take them to the airport—another resource offered by *la Iglesia Católica de la Virgen María* and Church World Services. They all sat in silence as they had when they arrived, taking in the city one last time as they headed northeast to the airport. They thought about all that they had been through while in Madrid. Each felt a mixture of emotions, but mostly they all felt a deep sense of hope and longing for the life that was awaiting them in America.

CHAPTER SEVENTEEN

NEW YORK CITY, NEW YORK AND ATLANTA, GEORGIA
JANUARY 31, 1968

Thick, heavy clouds were scattered above New York City and the cold rain pelted the small windows of the large Pan Am Airlines jet as it approached JFK International Airport. Roberto was seated next to the window and positioned his face as close as he could to catch his first glimpse of the big city below. He and the entire family had dreamed of this day—the day they would finally arrive in America. He moved his eyes from left to right and back again. He looked off in the distance and thought, *This city is immense.*

The steady fog and rain were not letting up as the airplane continued its descent. He noticed something in the distance and squinted his eyes to focus on the tall structure. For just a moment, there was a clearing in the fog, and he knew what he was looking at—the symbol for freedom known around the world. The Statue of Liberty.

Roberto felt an indescribable sense of relief and happiness he couldn't contain. He nudged Lolita's arm. "Look! Look!" he said. "It's the Statue of Liberty. Right there." He pointed to the spot where he had seen it only seconds before. Lolita leaned over and squinted her eyes as she tried to focus on the famous monument. It was now shrouded in fog once again, and she and Roberto could no longer see it.

"I am so sorry you missed it, but I am overjoyed that I saw it with my own eyes," said Roberto. "It represents the freedom we have so desperately pursued, and I can't believe we are truly here now," said Roberto with eyes wide open.

"I'm very happy too, but I am just exhausted. All I want is to sleep for three straight days when we get to our new home," said Lolita.

"You will be able to rest once we get there," said Roberto, as he nodded his head. Lolita had not been able to sleep more than a few minutes all night. Angela and Emilio were seated across the aisle from them, and although they looked out the window, they weren't able to see anything from their side of the airplane. They were also ready to be at their new home. The long flight from Madrid was only minutes away from landing.

Lolita turned to Roberto and said, "I'm so thankful Cristina slept most of the flight. I had been so worried about her during this nine-hour flight. The pressure in her ears had built up and hurt her most of the flight from Havana to Madrid, but I learned from that experience that giving her a bottle on take-off and now, on landing, helps to reduce the pressure in her ears."

The airplane touched down gently and within a few minutes they were taxiing to their gate. Angela and Emilio had slept most of the flight, so they felt refreshed and ready to board their flight to Atlanta.

"Ladies and gentlemen, this is your captain speaking. Welcome to John F. Kennedy International Airport. The local time is 5 p.m. Please remain seated with your seatbelts securely fastened until we come to a complete stop at the gate and it is safe to unfasten your seatbelts."

The passengers were restless and anxious to deplane after being in the air for such a long time. Although many of them were staying in New York City, others were taking connecting flights to their final destinations. The family knew that once they exited the airplane, Church World Service would have a car waiting to take them to their next flight, departing at 6:45 p.m. for Atlanta, Georgia—their new home.

"Ladies and gentlemen, we are parked at gate B-13. It is now safe to unfasten your seatbelts," said a flight attendant. "Please gather all of your belongings before exiting the aircraft through the boarding door at the front of the airplane and use caution as you walk down the steps onto the tarmac. The entrance to the gate area is straight ahead, through the blue door marked with the gate number, B-13."

The hard rain continued to fall and none of the passengers had umbrellas. They gripped the handrail as they filed out so as to not slip on the stainless steel steps. Lolita bundled up Cristina tightly and Roberto situated the diaper bag on her shoulder. He picked up their two carry-on bags, which were filled with a few belongings and the essentials they had brought for the trip. Roberto carried one in his hand and slung the other over his shoulder. To support and steady Lolita, he placed his hand on the back of her arm.

Angela and Emilio were already in line to exit the airplane. A few passengers stood behind them before Roberto and Lolita took their place in the line. After only a few minutes, Emilio and Angela were standing on the tarmac, wet and cold. They could see their breath as they looked around to find which car was waiting for them. Emilio noticed a tall, thin man under a tan umbrella, standing by a black Chevrolet Impala station wagon. He was near the tail of the airplane and held a sign that read "Herrera and Martínez de Osaba families."

"Hello," said Emilio as he waved and walked toward the man. Emilio motioned for Angela to walk behind him. Although the man didn't speak Spanish and they didn't speak much English, they all knew why they were there. The man greeted them with a warm smile and a handshake. He quickly unlatched the rear-facing back door of the car and placed their bags inside. Emilio opened the rear passenger side door for Angela to get in the car while he kept an eye on the steps for Lolita, Roberto, and Cristina. As they neared the bottom of the steps, Emilio rushed to help with their bags.

"Follow me," said Emilio. "The man from the church is here to pick us up."

"Thank God," said Lolita with a deep sigh.

Once they were all by the car, the man greeted them and took their bags. He placed them in the back with the others and drove them to the airplane for their next flight. They were all soaking wet from the storm, but that didn't matter to them—all that mattered was that they were almost home.

It was a quick drive to the gate where the Delta Airlines jet was parked. The man pulled the car alongside the airplane and parked as close to the steps as he could for them to board. They retrieved their belongings, thanked the man with smiles, head nods, and handshakes, and boarded the airplane. As Lolita walked through the boarding door, she noticed it was a new jet with a beautiful interior. The flight crew welcomed everyone with a smile and Lolita immediately felt comfortable and ready for the flight home.

"It is getting late—and we have had a *very* long day—but the excitement of finally arriving at our new home is overwhelming," said Angela as she found her seat.

"Yes," said Emilio, following his mother. "We are so close to being home."

The family settled in for the two-and-a-half-hour flight, and shortly thereafter, departed JFK on time. The flight was uneventful, and Roberto and Lolita were past the point of exhaustion. They couldn't wait to take a hot shower and sleep in a real bed. At 9:17 p.m., they landed at the Atlanta Municipal Airport and were parked at gate D27. Emilio, Angela, and Roberto gathered their belongings and followed Lolita with Cristina as they carefully walked down the steps onto the tarmac, through the terminal and into the baggage claim area.

After waiting for about fifteen minutes, they retrieved their suitcases and walked to the arrivals area at the front of the airport.

"We need to find the church members from West End Baptist Church that will take us to our new home," said Emilio. "The woman from Church World Service told me they would be meeting us here."

"It is too cold outside," said Lolita. "Let's wait for them here."

She took a seat and Roberto stood next to her. Angela and Emilio were only a few feet away and looked around for anyone holding up a sign with the family's name. Emilio noticed a couple holding a small white sign with black letters. He couldn't make out what it said, but there weren't too many other people in the terminal. When he made eye contact, they started to walk toward him. They were there to pick up four adults and a baby, and this appeared to be the family they were looking for.

"Hi, are you Roberto and Lolita Martínez de Osaba? And Emilio Herrera and Angela Herrera?" asked the lovely woman with fair skin and shoulder-length silver hair.

Although no one in the family understood much English, they knew these were the people there to meet them.

"Hello," said Emilio with a smile. That was only one of a handful of words he could say in the English language.

"Hi, we are Luke and Eleanor Stone," said Luke.

Roberto, Emilio, Lolita, and Angela each pointed to themselves, placed their hand over their chest, and stated their name.

They all smiled because they knew they had found each other. Luke helped Roberto with one of the bags, and the family followed Luke and his wife out of the airport and to the parking lot. The temperature had dropped even more from the time they left the airplane. It was a cold and rainy night in Georgia and everyone in the family was drained. But they would not trade this day for anything—the day they would start the new life they had been dreaming about.

They didn't walk far before Luke pointed to his white, two-door 1964 Ford Galaxie. He opened the trunk and helped Emilio and Roberto place their bags inside. The family looked at each other, wondering who would sit in the backseat. They decided that Emilio and Roberto would climb into the backseat first. Lolita stretched out her arms and placed Cristina in Roberto's lap. She took her seat next to Roberto as Eleanor and Angela got into the front seat.

The church had rented a small, two-bedroom, one-bath home for them a few miles away. The outside of the house was wrapped in wide, white shingle siding and was positioned on a wooded lot with a level backyard.

The kitchen, dining room, and family room were set up as one open area with the bedrooms and bathroom at the back of the house. Being so close to the church ensured that church members could take turns assisting the family as they assimilated into this new culture. In the driveway, a light blue, 1961 Ford Falcon was parked to the side. The church knew Emilio and the family would need to get around the city soon, so they took care of the first two months' payments. They made arrangements with Emilio and financed the car for him.

It was 10:30 p.m. when Luke turned the key and opened the door to their new home. Emilio stepped in first. Lolita, Roberto, and Angela followed him. Eleanor and Luke stayed back to allow the family to go into their new home.

Once they were all inside, Eleanor walked them around. The home was cozy, and no tour was really needed, but Eleanor was happy to show them the love and care with which the church members had filled it with used furniture, bedding, clothing, toiletries, and food. The church members had packed two refrigerators full of meat, chicken, milk, yogurt, cheese, fruits, and vegetables. They had stocked the pantry with baby food, cereal, oatmeal, grits, canned beans, and other vegetables along with rice and potatoes. The family looked at each other in disbelief. They had experienced food shortages in Cuba and in Spain. Now, their home was filled with everything imaginable. They were incredibly grateful for the kindness of these strangers.

Lolita turned to walk out of the kitchen and was surprised to see the black rotary dial phone on the wall. She had no one to call but knew it would be their lifeline. Eleanor reached into her brown handbag and pulled out a small, creased piece of paper with the number 243-0456 scrawled on it in blue ink.

"Here is your new telephone number," said Eleanor, as she stretched out her hand to Lolita.

"Thank you," said Lolita timidly. She was unsure how her English words would sound to an American.

"You are very welcome," said Eleanor with a smile.

Angela and the others just looked around and couldn't believe the generosity of the people that had worked so hard to make them feel welcome.

"Thank you. Thank you," said Emilio.

The family could not stop smiling, knowing they were finally home. After Luke and Eleanor showed them everything, Luke held his hand out with the key and put it in Emilio's hand.

"Welcome to Atlanta," said Luke with a smile.

"Thank you. Thank you," said Emilio once again.

Luke and Eleanor waved goodbye and turned to leave. Lolita, Roberto, Emilio, and Angela waved back with smiles and hearts full of gratitude for this new start.

They were all exhausted following a long day of travel. After a quick shower, Roberto and Emilio were the first to fall asleep. Angela helped Lolita feed and bathe Cristina. Lolita placed the baby in her first real cradle ever, and within seconds, she was sound asleep. Lolita and Angela each took showers and collapsed into their beds.

This day, January 31, 1968, would separate the life they left behind from their new life. It was their first night sleeping in the freedom they had dreamed about for so long.

★

During the first few weeks, various church members took turns checking in on them. They would often bring the family prepared meals, such as casseroles, roasted vegetables, pot roast with mashed potatoes and desserts—pecan and apple pies were their favorites. These were all new foods for them and they all immediately loved the unique flavors and textures.

Roberto and Emilio were ready to find a job after just a few days. They needed to start working quickly to support the family. They both had big dreams, and this was the first step toward achieving them. Luke had plans to teach Emilio and Roberto how to drive and then take them to get their driver's licenses. They would need a few weeks to prepare.

For now, Luke would take them to look for new jobs. He arrived the following Tuesday, just after four in the afternoon, to pick them up. Luke drove them to the local Church World Service offices in Atlanta, where a Spanish-speaking man would help them apply for jobs.

After reviewing a half-dozen positions, Roberto applied to the Sweetheart Cup Company as a forklift operator. He didn't have any previous experience for this role but was told that if he were selected, the company would enroll him in intensive training once he started. Roberto was elated when they called him a few days later to offer him the job—he would report for work the following Monday at 8 a.m.

Emilio was ready to use his medical training, and there was an opening for a laboratory technician at Georgia Baptist Hospital. The day after he applied, he received a call asking him to come in for an interview. He asked the bilingual man from Church World Service to accompany him. The interview went better than Emilio expected, and they extended an offer for him to start the next day.

Luke was happy to help them secure their new jobs but would not be able to take either of them to work or pick them up. He was an accountant and worked about twelve miles away. Roberto and Emilio would need to take the bus for the time being until they had their driver's licenses.

Emilio quickly developed a good rapport with his colleagues, except for one physician named Dr. Frederick Moore who insisted on putting him in his place. Dr. Moore didn't like the fact that so many responded to Emilio's warm personality and caring demeanor. He was intimidated by Emilio's intelligence and didn't like that he spoke with an accent. Late one night, Emilio was overcome with exhaustion and decided to lie down on the cot in the back of the lab. He needed to rest his eyes for a few minutes. Dr. Moore found him there and kicked the cot with full force using the heel of his shoe. It startled Emilio and he shot up. After a few terse words from Dr. Moore, Emilio quietly returned to his work, feeling humiliated and guilty.

Despite some challenges, Emilio and Roberto settled into a steady routine of working during the day and practicing their driving and parking skills with Luke in the evening. Lolita and Angela took care of Cristina and kept up the home. Eleanor would sometimes visit with Lolita and Angela; although their conversations were limited to a few words, hand motions, and facial expressions, this did not stop the women from trying to communicate.

"How do you like Atlanta so far, Lolita?" asked Eleanor.

I only understand the word Atlanta, but it sounds like she is asking me a question. Lolita smiled and said, "Yes."

Angela excused herself to use the restroom. She would check on Cristina when she returned.

"Tell me about your father," said Eleanor. "Will he be coming to Atlanta too?"

I understand the words "father" and "Atlanta." Maybe she is asking me if my father will be moving to Atlanta. I have to tell her my father passed away two years ago, but how? I know. I will show her he is "sleeping," thought Lolita.

Lolita lay down on her back on the living room floor. She put her hands together in a praying pose over her chest and closed her eyes.

"He is sleeping . . . sleeping forever," said Lolita.

At that very moment, Angela returned from the restroom and started screaming when she saw Lolita, motionless on the floor.

"What happened?" asked Angela, who was now hyperventilating.

"It's okay, *Mami*," said Lolita. "I am alright. I was just trying to explain to Eleanor that *Papi* had died, but I didn't know which words to use."

"Oh my," said Angela. "I almost had a heart attack."

"I'm sorry to scare you, but I had no other way to explain to her about my father," said Lolita.

"Here, take my hand," said Angela, helping Lolita to stand up.

"*Gracias, Mami*," said Lolita and sat back into her chair.

Eleanor understood what was happening and the three women had a chuckle.

Just then, the men walked through the door and Roberto triumphantly announced, "We are ready to take our driving test."

"Luke has agreed to take us on Saturday morning," said Emilio.

"That is wonderful," said Lolita as she smiled and clapped her hands. "I want to be next." Lolita was anxious to start working and wanted to be prepared, even though the family only had one car for now.

"Yes, Lolita," said Luke. "I am happy to help you as soon as Emilio and Roberto pass their tests. I also want to get everyone set up with checking accounts to make it easier to pay your bills. I will take the men to the bank after their driving tests on Saturday.

Eleanor offered to take her to see the same bilingual man at the Church World Service office so he could help her find a job. Lolita had been a licensed hairdresser in Havana since the age of eighteen but did not have the credentials to apply for this type of position in the United States. Of the few job openings available, the one that interested her most was assembling undergarments at the Lovable Bra Company. She had learned how to sew from Angela, who had been a professional seamstress since she was a young woman. Two days later, they called to offer her the position and asked if she could start on Monday at 7 a.m.

"Yes, yes," said Lolita with great excitement, knowing her income would help the family move one step closer to achieving their dreams.

The timing could not have been more perfect. If Roberto and Emilio passed their tests on Saturday, they could drop her off on their way to work on Monday and she could take the bus home.

Saturdays were for cleaning the house and for getting everything ready for the week. Lolita was scrubbing the side of the bathtub and

Angela was sweeping the kitchen when Roberto and Emilio burst through the front door and exclaimed, "We passed!"

Lolita and Angela dropped everything and ran to congratulate them.

"I'm so proud of you both," said Lolita as they all hugged.

"I am too," said Angela, beaming with pride.

"Thank you," said Roberto.

"*Muchas gracias*," said Emilio.

Roberto and Emilio were thrilled to come home and flash their new temporary paper licenses.

"The laminated ones will arrive in the mail in the next few weeks," said Emilio.

This gave them the mobility they needed. They purchased a map from the local gas station and studied the area so they could get around.

On Sundays, the family attended the morning service at West End Baptist Church. Although they didn't understand the minister, it felt good to worship in a church once again. Each week after the service, they were invited into the homes of different families for lunch. It was a wonderful experience to feel so welcomed and included.

Angela soon learned that a new group of Hispanic immigrants had formed and was meeting in the basement of the church for services on Tuesday evenings with Pastor Adam Silva.

The family started attending the services and enjoyed gathering to hear Pastor Silva's message in their own language. They felt fortunate to find new friendships there as well. The group also held English classes in one of the classrooms with a volunteer professor from Georgia State University on Thursday evenings. Lolita, Roberto, and Emilio attended each week, and their pronunciation and vocabulary continued to improve.

Lolita, Roberto, and Emilio diligently worked at their jobs and took any available overtime. They had discussed something that was very important to them—to repay Church World Service for their sponsorship. The organization had generously taken care of them and met all of their needs when they arrived in Atlanta with nothing.

Although the organization had told the family there were no expectations of being reimbursed, if they could, one day, return some of the money, it would be used to help others.

Lolita, Roberto, and Emilio decided this debt would need to be paid first—before they could buy furniture, take Cristina to the beach, or spend money on any other nonessential items.

Each week after payday, Roberto and Emilio went to their office and gave them a small envelope with cash toward their balance. Within ten months, they had paid off the full amount. The woman who took their last payment was pleasantly surprised.

"We rarely have anyone who repays our organization, and even more commendable is that you and your family did this in less than a year," said the woman. "I want to thank you. Now we can help another family."

"No. Thank you," said Roberto. "We are grateful for the benevolence of Church World Service and appreciate the many wonderful opportunities that are available to us in America." With the extra money they now had each month, the family began thinking about moving to a bigger home. Their first holidays in America were around the corner, so they decided to wait until the beginning of the year to look for their new home.

They had never before heard of a holiday named Thanksgiving and were unsure of what to expect. They were looking forward to celebrating at the home of Luke and Eleanor with their children and extended family.

When Lolita, Roberto, Emilio, and Angela arrived, Eleanor greeted them warmly at the door. The family smelled the delicious scents wafting in the air and were excited to taste what Eleanor had prepared. She was a wonderful homemaker and hostess and had decorated everything so beautifully for this special day. The family had a marvelous time and loved all the new foods and flavor combinations Eleanor served at this traditional Thanksgiving table.

"We need to learn how to make some of these dishes," said Lolita to Angela. "I think we should start with something simple, like the green bean casserole."

The next few weeks flew by, and before they knew it, Christmas was here. Lolita and Roberto bought and decorated a perfect, fragrant pine tree for the first Christmas in their new home. They couldn't wait to see Cristina's face light up when she saw the twinkling multicolored lights, ornaments, and shiny tinsel. This was Lolita's favorite holiday growing up. She anticipated the *Noche Buena* festivities all year long. Traditional Cuban Christmas is celebrated on *Noche Buena*—the literal translation is Good Night, but it represents Christmas Eve. On this night, Cuban families all over the island gathered to enjoy family, friends, food, and fun.

Christmas Day and Santa Claus were not the focus of the celebrations; instead, children looked forward to small gifts and treats from *Mami* and *Papi* and their extended family and friends. They would run with great excitement to place them by the nativity scene, under a brightly decorated tree.

The *Noche Buena* dinner was a feast everyone looked forward to, highlighted by the *lechon asado*—tender roast pork, fluffy white rice, black beans, *tostones*—crispy fried green plantains, and *yuca con mojo*—baked yuca with mashed garlic, olive oil, and sautéed onions, all served with salad and toasted bread.

Dessert was a creamy, rich *flan*—a custard dessert made with a clear glaze of caramelized sugar and a tray of *turrones*—nougat style candy, with or without nuts, some chewy and some crispy—not easy to describe but a delicious, long-standing tradition when celebrating Cuban holidays. Dinner was served late, around 8 or 9 p.m. so they could eat and then open the gifts as soon as the clock struck midnight and it was officially Christmas Day. The kids loved staying up late, and the adults loved watching the joy on their faces as they unwrapped their presents. The next day, the families would visit friends and wish them happy holidays.

Since these traditions were close to Lolita's heart, she wanted to include them as they integrated into American life. Lolita and Angela bought some colorful decorations and prepared the house for an intimate *Noche Buena* with the family. After dinner, they all piled into the car and drove around the neighborhood to see the sparkling lights—no one enjoyed them more than baby Cristina. She clapped her little hands and her baby giggles filled the car with happiness.

The holidays in Cuba were filled with many wonderful traditions. Here, Lolita had a few more that she would keep. She picked up a large bag of green grapes the following week at the grocery store in preparation for a quiet New Year's Eve at home. Just before ringing in the new year, Lolita gave Roberto, Emilio, and Angela each a small bowl with a dozen grapes. They started the countdown until the clock struck midnight... ten... nine... eight... seven... six... five... four... three... two... one. They all cheered and ate one grape with each of the twelve chimes of the clock, representing each of the next twelve months and ushering in a year of good luck and prosperity.

"*Feliz Año Nuevo*—Happy New Year!" said Emilio, and the others echoed his good wishes.

"1969 is going to be a good year for this family," said Angela as they all took turns hugging each other.

Indeed, the new year was off to a great start. One final Cuban holiday tradition that was celebrated on January 6 was *el Dia de Los Tres Reyes Magos*—Three Kings Day. It marked the twelfth day after Jesus' birth, which was when the three wise men arrived bearing gifts for baby Jesus. The night before, children and some adults would leave their polished shoes, awaiting small presents and treats from the kings. Sweet wine and small cookies were left in anticipation of the visit from the three kings and their camels. With this, the holiday season came to a close.

After the wonderful celebrations of their first holidays in America, Roberto, Lolita, and Emilio continued to do well at their jobs and to save money each month. It was time to start looking for a larger home, and Luke and Eleanor offered their help to find a good house for them.

On one of their trips, Lolita found a four-bedroom house off Westmont Road, not far from their jobs. They were able to make the move before the end of the month and commemorated the one-year anniversary of their arrival to the United States in January of 1968, celebrating around the dinner table in their new home.

CHAPTER EIGHTEEN

ATLANTA, GEORGIA
1968 — 1970

Cristina was growing and had started talking. Before she turned one, she was walking and getting into everything within her reach. Angela spent the days playing dolls and dress-up with her. Cristina loved when her grandmother would read her books. She was so animated, changing her voice to fit each character.

Lolita and Roberto loved being parents and enjoyed taking Cristina to playgrounds and parks where they could spend time with their baby girl. There were so many other places they wanted to take her. One evening after work, Roberto had an idea.

"I would love to take Cristina to the beach one day," said Roberto. "Maybe we can plan a trip to visit my great aunt Carmen in Miami when we save up a little money."

"Yes, it would be wonderful to get away," said Lolita. "Let's see if it's possible to make plans for this summer. We haven't been to the shore since we left Havana almost two years ago. If I close my eyes, I can smell the salty air and feel the warm sunshine on my skin."

"It sounds like you are ready to leave the cold weather here for the tropical climate of Miami," said Roberto with a grin. "Let's see if we can make this happen."

"That would make me very happy. And I know Cristina would be mesmerized by the motion of the tide coming in and out and the sand between her toes," said Lolita with a look of excitement.

"We still have time to save before the hot summer weather gets here, so perhaps we can think about going in July," said Roberto. "What do you think?"

"I think that would be terrific," said Lolita. "I know Emilio will probably not be able to join us because of his busy work schedule, but my mother would love to come with us and see some of her relatives too."

"We'll take her with us," said Roberto.

He loved Angela, and ever since Oscar had died, he felt the need to look after her.

For the next few months, Lolita and Roberto saved every penny and thought about how amazing it would feel to take their first vacation in America. Their excitement grew by the day. Lolita began asking some of her friends that lived in Miami for hotel recommendations near the beach—she could hardly contain her joy.

Although Lolita was grateful to have a job, she wished she could bring in a bigger paycheck. Planning for this trip made her realize that they would need more money for the things they wanted to do.

One Tuesday evening after the church service, several women were discussing their jobs and how they would like to find better positions.

"I have been thinking about looking for something where I can make more money," said Lolita.

"I'm in the same boat. I would like to find another job taking care of children but with a family that can afford to pay me more," said another woman.

"I don't know anyone hiring for child care," said Pastor Silva, who overheard the women talking. "But I work at First National Bank, and they have some open positions in proof and coding—processing checks using a number keypad for the totals. Would you be interested, Lolita?"

"Yes, I can type very fast. How do I apply?" said Lolita.

"I will get the contact information for you tomorrow and call you at home," said Pastor Silva.

"Thank you," said Lolita.

"You are welcome," said Pastor Silva.

In less than a week, Lolita had passed the hiring requirements at the bank and turned in her resignation notice at her factory job. She was excited that she would be earning $.50 more an hour. Her English skills were improving, so she was looking forward to working in an office environment. They asked her to start the following week and she was ready for this new opportunity.

Although the timing may not have been the best, Roberto had been thinking about growing their family. Roberto thought about the love his brothers and sisters shared and wanted that for his own children. He and Lolita had decided early on that they wanted a big family. Cristina was a little more than two years old, and it would be nice to have them be close in age.

"*Mi amor*, what do you think about giving Cristina a little brother or sister?" asked Roberto. "I don't want to wait too long between our children, so they can play and be close to one other as they grow."

"I know that you and I are both looking forward to the day we can bring more children into our family, but I think we should wait until our financial situation is a little more stable before getting pregnant again." said Lolita.

"I agree with you. But I don't want to wait too long," said Roberto.

"Okay," said Lolita. "Why don't we talk about this in a few months and see how we feel?"

"I think that's a good plan," said Roberto.

Their long-awaited trip to the beach was now only a few days away. Angela had packed her suitcase last week and was now helping Lolita with her bags. They gathered the things they would need for Cristina and started placing everything that was ready to be put into the car in a corner of the living room. The day for their vacation was finally here. The family would take their first road trip from Atlanta to Miami. Roberto was looking forward to driving the six hundred and fifty miles but knew that it would take them a full day of travel with his mother-in-law and baby Cristina. He was happy to take his family to the beach and to visit their relatives, and although it was a long drive for only a few days, he didn't mind at all.

They decided to spend the first day seeing family. Angela's cousin, Federico, and his wife had invited the family to their house for breakfast. They had prepared a simple Cuban meal of *café con leche*, toasted and buttered Cuban bread and some *pastelitos*—pastries with flaky dough and delicious fillings like guava, guava with cream cheese, and coconut that he had picked up at their favorite bakery, La Rosa. Angela was happy to see her cousin. It felt like no time had passed, even though it had been many years since she had seen him.

Roberto's great aunt Carmen had been living in Miami since 1960, and she and her husband had a lovely home. She invited the family for dinner and served them a delicious traditional Cuban meal of *arroz con pollo*—yellow rice and chicken with *maduros*—sweet fried plantains along with a tomato and avocado salad. Carmen was a wonderful cook and a gracious hostess. They talked and laughed for hours. It was heartwarming for Roberto to see Carmen and her husband after all these years.

"I had such a wonderful time," said Roberto as they got in the car and headed to their hotel.

The next few days were filled with sunshine, laughter, and a chance to catch their breath after two years of sacrificing everything for their future. Cristina loved the ocean and played in the sand while Lolita, Roberto, and Angela enjoyed the sounds of the waves and the feeling of nostalgia for the beautiful turquoise waters of their island home—only ninety miles from the Florida Keys—but worlds away. Lolita had bought Cristina a tiny navy swimsuit with a white peplum ruffle and a little red polka-dot ribbon in the center of the scoop neck.

"She looks like an adorable little sailor," said Roberto.

"Yes," said Lolita. "She is so precious."

The temperatures had reached into the mid-nineties, and Roberto was ready to cool off with a dip in the ocean. The shimmering blue water looked inviting. He took Lolita by the hand, scooped up Cristina, and started walking toward the water's edge. They took only a few steps before they glanced at each other with a panicked look on their faces.

"This sand is on fire," said Lolita.

"Let's hurry and dip our feet in the water," said Roberto as they took off running.

The ocean water felt refreshing after lying under the hot midday sun. Roberto placed his hands around Cristina's sides and playfully dunked her up and down in the water. She laughed and squealed, "Again, again!" It was so much fun for Roberto and Lolita to see their little girl soaking up every last minute of this summertime adventure.

The days went by much too fast. They returned home sun-kissed and relaxed, having enjoyed their time at the beach. They were happy to have spent time with family.

"This vacation was just what we needed," said Lolita.

"It was wonderful," said Roberto. I want to explore more of this big country—there are many beautiful places to see."

"I always like having something to look forward to," said Lolita.

While Lolita, Roberto, and Angela were away, Emilio worked long hours at the hospital and took as much overtime as he could. He didn't have time for much else, other than sleeping, but he did carve out a little time for some detective work. He had fallen in love with baby Cristina and had started thinking of one day having a family of his own. Emilio remembered a captivating girl with stunning green eyes he knew from years ago in Havana. He had always had a soft spot in his heart for her and wondered where she was. When he asked around in their group of friends, one of the men that was close friends with her father told Emilio that the family had moved to Buena Park, California.

California is all the way on the west coast of the United States, thought Emilio. *I know it is far, but I would love to find that girl again.*

He could not stop thinking of this girl who had stolen his heart in Havana. Emilio asked Lolita if she had any information about Ana Ortiz. He imagined she had grown more beautiful and wondered if she was still single.

"Do you happen to know if she has married?" asked Emilio.

"No, I am not sure, but if we can get her phone number I'd be happy to call her. I would love to catch up with her and see how she is doing in California," replied Lolita.

"That would be great," said Emilio with a twinkle in his eye. He was smitten.

Emilio went back to the man who told them they were in California and asked for her family's phone number. He tried to hide his interest in Ana and told the man Lolita was looking forward to catching up with her old friend from Havana.

The man offered the phone number, and Emilio rushed home so Lolita could make the phone call that very evening.

"I have the number . . . can we call her right now?" asked an anxious Emilio.

Lolita was finishing the dinner dishes. "Yes, let me dry my hands and we can give her a call. I hope she will be home," said Lolita.

"Me too," said Emilio.

Lolita stood at the phone and Emilio sat near her at the kitchen table. He was so nervous that he was tapping his feet on the linoleum floor.

"Calm down," Lolita said. "It's ringing," Lolita covered the phone and whispered to Emilio.

After just a few rings, a man answered the phone, and Lolita spoke.

"*Hola*, my name is Lolita. I am a friend of Ana's. I am hoping she lives at this number, said Lolita.

"*Sí*, she is here," he replied.

"May I please speak with her?"

Let me see if she can come to the phone," he replied.

Ana said *hola* with curiosity in her voice. But as soon as Lolita said hello, she recognized her voice. She was so excited to hear from her friend. They talked for hours, catching up on the years that had passed.

Lolita wanted to get rid of Emilio, so she asked if she was married very early on in the conversation. When she said "no," Lolita gave Emilio a thumbs up and shooed him out of the kitchen so she and Ana could continue to catch up.

As he made his way out of the kitchen, he motioned to Lolita and put his hand to his ear and mouthed the words, "Ask her if I can call her."

Lolita mouthed back, "I will . . . now go!"

The following day after work, Emilio rushed home to call Ana. He didn't have a clue what he would say. He just wanted to hear her voice and hoped she felt the same after all these years.

Ana picked up the phone after a few rings. He melted at the sound of her voice and didn't know if he was going to be able to get words out.

"*Hola*, Ana. This is Emilio," he uttered between shallow breaths.

"*Hola*, Emilio," she replied sweetly.

They bonded immediately as if no time had passed. They talked excitedly about the wonderful times they had shared in Havana and all that they had been through since.

"I would love to come see you in California," said Emilio after hours of conversation.

"I would love that too," Ana replied shyly.

They talked every day in the weeks to come and planned for Emilio to visit in late July. As the trip approached, they were getting to know one another more and more and the attraction continued to grow between them.

The day came and he was sitting across a small round table from Ana. She felt the same excitement that Emilio did. They could barely talk at first, but once the nerves passed they couldn't stop talking and laughing at each other's jokes. They spent their days walking in the park, visiting local shops, and in the evenings eating Ana's homemade meals. She was naturally an amazing cook. Emilio loved everything she made, and her cooking transported him back to those sunny days together in Havana.

They were falling in love. Emilio did not want to leave her side. Before making the trip back home, he wanted to ask Ana if she would like to be his girlfriend.

"I have loved our time together here. I would love to spend many more days with you, Ana," Emilio said with a shaking voice. "Would you like to be my girlfriend?"

Ana replied in an instant. "Yes! Yes, I would love to be your girlfriend, Emilio."

They both took a deep breath and sighed. They stared into each other's eyes and began dreaming of their future together.

When Emilio returned to Atlanta they spoke every single night on the phone. They wrote love letters to one another and began making plans for her to visit Atlanta for the holidays.

The hot, humid summer weather began to turn crisp and cool. As Emilio and Ana were making their plans, Lolita found out she would be having another baby next summer.

Life was beautiful. They all had so much to be grateful for. This new life was becoming all that they had dreamed of. The holidays arrived and Lolita learned to prepare her first American Thanksgiving. This pregnancy reminded her of when she was expecting Cristina. She felt great and spent the days leading up to Thanksgiving in the kitchen making recipes from the holiday edition of *LIFE* magazine.

Emilio and Roberto loved the warm, sweet smells and would sneak into the kitchen to steal bites of the savory dishes. Emilio wished Ana was here now to enjoy Thanksgiving with him. He was counting the days until her visit at Christmas. Seeing Lolita in the kitchen and the nostalgia of the holidays made him wishful that someday he and Ana would have a home and family of their own.

★

Emilio could hardly concentrate on his duties at the hospital knowing he would be picking up Ana at the airport today. The minutes ticked by slowly until it was time for him to leave at 4:30 p.m. He cleaned up his work area, and on his way out, his co-worker, who knew today was a special day for him, wished him good luck.

Emilio left with enough time to stop by the market and pick up a beautiful bouquet of colorful and fragrant flowers. He parked at the airport and made the long walk to the gate where Ana's airplane would be arriving. He stood at the tall glass windows, looking for any sign of an airplane turning toward this gate. When he saw the big jet turn his way, his heart started beating faster.

His mind was racing. His only thought was of seeing her walk down the jetway toward him. He couldn't wait to wrap his arms around her in a tight embrace. The moment he saw her, the hairs on his skin stood straight up and his whole body was filled with butterflies. She was just as stunning as he remembered—if not more. Her emerald green eyes were shining and made him feel like he could faint, like a young schoolboy.

After a long embrace, Emilio took her delicate hands in his and lightly kissed her. She leaned in and kissed him back. They felt like the only two people in the whole world. It was a moment they had both been waiting for—it was clear they would have many more moments like this together in the years and decades to come.

Ana fit in with Lolita, Roberto, and Angela perfectly. It was as though she were already family. Angela could see that Ana was a perfect fit for her beloved son and she was so pleased they had found each other again.

Ana and Lolita loved their time together in the kitchen with Cristina making cookies and special dishes for Christmas. Emilio and Roberto would join them in the evenings, sharing stories and laughing long into the night.

Emilio and Ana enjoyed shopping for Christmas gifts—especially for young Cristina. She was beginning to understand Christmas traditions, and they both wanted to give her wonderful memories of the holiday.

They had a beautifully decorated tree in the corner of the living room. It was full of charming ornaments and golden tinsel. The top was donned with a shining golden star. Underneath the tree, they had the most unique wooden nativity scene with delicately carved figures. The manger and baby Jesus were the centerpiece surrounded by Mary, Joseph, the wise men, and various barn animals. Cristina loved to play with the figures, rearranging them and making pretend conversations between them.

Ana already felt the warmth among them as though this were already her family. It was a special time of celebration, and Emilio and Ana continued to fall more and more in love. The whole family fell in love with her too—Ana was the missing piece. She was so easy to love.

Noche Buena and Christmas morning were magical. After a night of celebration, they gathered early in the morning to exchange small Christmas gifts. They all delighted as they watched Cristina unwrap her gifts—there were dolls and toys and candies all over the floor. Cristina was in heaven. Ana and Emilio gave one another small mementos of their time together, reminding them of their love when they would be apart. Roberto gifted Lolita a small, simple gold necklace with her initial—a delicate cursive "L." This was something she had been wanting for a long time. Roberto unwrapped a cozy sweater and scarf that would make his morning commute more comfortable. They had a huge surprise for Angela. They had all pitched in to purchase a Singer sewing machine so she could start making and selling her elegant designs. She was so overwhelmed with gratitude and joy. She had to leave her beloved sewing machine back in Cuba—this gift transported her to that place and time and gave her hope that she could reconnect to her first love, sewing beautiful designs.

Ana and Lolita made *café con leche* and served an assortment of breakfast pastries. They enjoyed their time together, soaking in every moment before Ana had to return to California. The days had gone by far too quickly. With hope in their eyes, Emilio and Ana talked eagerly about the next time they would see each other.

The next morning came too soon and Emilio packed Ana's bags into his car. They held hands as they drove through the city to the airport. He walked Ana to the gate and stayed with her until she boarded the plane. This goodbye felt different—they had a deeper connection now, and each couldn't imagine being away from the other.

★

The Christmas season wrapped up and everyday life resumed. Lolita's belly was growing by the day. She loved being pregnant and enjoyed the times when she could feel her baby kick and move. Angela immediately began using the sewing machine. She made gorgeous maternity dresses for Lolita. The ladies at the church all marveled at her designs and began placing special orders for their own unique dresses.

Emilio was working day and night. He had a plan. He had seen the most exquisite ring at a local jewelry shop. It was simple, but the small circular diamond reminded him of the sparkling stars he and Ana would sit under in Havana. He spent every last bit of his savings on this ring. He wanted Ana to be his wife and to feel as special as she made him feel. He could not wait until he would see her again. Valentine's Day was approaching, and he thought this would be the perfect time for her to receive the ring. The jewelry store helped Emilio prepare the ring for shipping. They carefully secured the ring in a blue velvet box, wrapping it in layers of fine cotton cloth.

Emilio enclosed a small handwritten love letter inside the package and sealed it. He went straight to the post office and addressed the package to Ana. Emilio slipped the small box into the mailbox and hoped it would arrive in time for Valentine's day.

He was on pins and needles waiting for Ana to receive the package. He knew she would immediately call him. He didn't want to spoil the surprise, but he let her know to be expecting a package from him. He anticipated her reaction when she opened the box and saw the perfect ring—a symbol of their love and future together.

Each time the phone rang, Emilio felt the same butterflies he had felt every time he was at her side. A few days passed and Emilio knew it would be any day now that she would call with news that she had received the package.

"Emilio, the package just arrived," said an ecstatic Ana.

"Did you open it?" asked Emilio excitedly.

"No, I wanted to be on the phone so we could open it together," said Ana with a quaver in her voice.

"Go ahead. Open it," said a nervous Emilio.

Ana carefully peeled back the layers of brown cardboard and cotton cloth until she saw the delicate blue velvet box. Her heart began racing.

"Emilio . . . what have you done?" said Ana with a big smile on her face that he could hear through the phone.

With shaking hands, Ana slowly pulled open the box revealing the diamond engagement ring. Tears instantly filled her eyes. All of her dreams were coming true—she was speechless.

"Ana, are you there?" asked Emilio.

"Yes . . . I am here," said Ana through shallow breaths.

"I know you can't see me, but I am down on one knee," said Emilio. "Ana, you are the light of my life and the joy of my heart. I can't imagine living another day separated from you. Your love has changed me, and I will love you for all of my days. Would you do me the honor of becoming my wife?"

"Yes! I love you. I want to spend the rest of my life with you," said Ana.

"You have made me a very happy man, and I can't wait to start our new life together," said Emilio. "How does the ring look on your hand?"

Ana carefully took the ring from the box and slipped it on her finger. She lifted her hand into the light and admired the radiant shimmer of the diamond.

"It is breathtaking," said Ana. "It's absolutely perfect."

Emilio sighed in relief. He had found the woman of his dreams.

CHAPTER NINETEEN

ATLANTA, GEORGIA

1970 — 1973

As spring approached, Roberto and Emilio decided they would like to start their own business. Emilio knew he would not have much time to dedicate to this, but he wanted to do anything he could to help Roberto get the business off the ground. They approached a man named Charles Wells at church who was an attorney and had a reputation for being good with business. He helped them research various opportunities and eventually advised them to get involved with Union Oil Company—a major petroleum exporter.

Charles agreed to loan Emilio and Roberto six thousand dollars to get started, on the condition they pay him back within twelve months. They shook hands, and with tremendous excitement, they started planning their new business. In March of that year, Emilio and Roberto rented an existing gas station with the perfect location from Union Oil. Emilio and Roberto quickly turned the business into a bustling full-service gas station with three bays for auto repair, enabling them to increase their income. Emilio and Roberto worked day and night. Emilio worked at the hospital overnight and attended classes during the day. He would sleep a few hours and spend the rest of his time helping Roberto. Within six months, Roberto and Emilio had paid Charles back his full investment.

As Emilio and Roberto were doing everything they could to create a lucrative business, Ana and Lolita had begun long-distance preparations for Ana and Emilio's July wedding. It was a busy time for everyone, and Lolita continued to make preparations for the new baby's arrival in mid-June. Angela created the loveliest embroidered blankets in colors of green and yellow. She also knitted tiny precious booties and miniature sweaters for the new baby.

Before the new baby was to arrive, Lolita had started looking for a preschool where Cristina could attend a few days a week. She wanted to find a place close to their home and decided to stop in at a beautiful nursery she passed every day on her way to and from work. When she stepped out of her car, she inhaled the magnificent scent of magnolias and fresh green leaves. *This seems like a lovely place for Cristina to make new friends and spend time outside*, thought Lolita.

"Hi, can I help you?" said a young man in a kelly-green apron embroidered with the words "Hastings Nursery" in bright yellow letters.

"Yes. I have a three-and-a-half-year-old little girl, and I would like to get information about your programs," said Lolita in broken English.

"What type of programs are you asking about?"

"I am expecting another baby very soon and it would help me if she could attend preschool a few days a week," said Lolita.

"I'm not sure I understand," said the confused young man. "This is a plant nursery. We have seeds and plants for gardeners to purchase."

"Yes, she 'sits' down," said Lolita, who had misunderstood "seeds" for "sits"—sometimes that happens when you are learning a new language.

"I'm sorry, ma'am," he said. "We do not have anything for children here."

Lolita thanked him and left, embarrassed, but also amused, thinking of this young man's reaction as he tried to make sense of what she was saying. She went home and shared her story with Roberto and Emilio, and they all had a good laugh.

The business at the gas station was growing at a rapid pace and Roberto and Emilio were staying busy ensuring the weekly orders for gasoline, tires, and parts for the auto repairs were submitted on time and within budget. Roberto, Lolita, and Emilio continued learning English, but it seemed as if every day brought them a new lesson.

"Hey, man, how are you?" asked Roberto when a customer pulled around to a gasoline pump.

"I'm alright. Can I get a couple of bucks of unleaded gas?" replied the man.

"Sure, I'll be right back," said Roberto.

After a few minutes, Roberto returned to collect the money for the gasoline.

"That will be five dollars," said Roberto.

"No, I said a couple of bucks. That means two," said the man as he held the two dollar bills out the window and drove off.

It cost Roberto three dollars to learn that lesson, but he never forgot that a couple means "two" and not "a few."

One afternoon while visiting Roberto at the gas station, Lolita began feeling intense contractions and knew she needed to call her doctor. He told her once the contractions were five minutes apart to head to the hospital to be admitted. Emilio took over at the station and Roberto drove Lolita to the house to rest and count her contractions. In a few hours, the contractions were five minutes apart. Lolita was in a great deal of pain at this point. Roberto gathered the packed suitcase and made her as comfortable as possible in the front seat of the car and they headed to the hospital.

Lolita's contractions continued to intensify as they were getting her settled into her room at the hospital. The doctors and nurses continued to check on her regularly, keeping her as comfortable as possible, until she was fully dilated. Once the labor pains became unbearable for Lolita, they wheeled her hospital bed into the operating room. The nurses quickly placed an IV in her hand and administered a sedative. Lolita felt herself relaxing but could still feel immense pressure. The doctor asked her to begin counting backward from ten ... and within seconds, she was completely out.

She awoke feeling very groggy. The immense pressure and tightness in her belly were now gone but replaced with searing pelvic pain. She begged the nurses for something to relieve her pain. Once she was comfortable, she was able to focus her eyes on the tiny bassinet beside her. She could see that her new baby was wearing a tiny pink hat. She and Roberto had another baby girl. She couldn't wait to tell him the news. They had decided on the name Isabela Marie if they had a girl. She had thick black hair, adorable brown eyes, and olive skin. She was absolutely perfect in every way.

When they arrived home, Angela and Cristina were over the moon. This new small bundle of joy brought so much more love into the home. Cristina had been waiting to take care of her new baby and she was finally here.

The baby's first month passed quickly and before everyone knew it was time for Ana and Emilio's wedding. Ana had been preparing for months. With only two weeks before the wedding, Ana packed her most precious belongings and said goodbye to her family in California. She arrived in Atlanta and was greeted by Emilio's whole family. They all cheered as she got off the plane. She was finally home.

The day of the wedding was unseasonably warm, even for Atlanta in July. They all raced around making last-minute preparations. The church was decorated with the most delicate white and pink flowers. The altar was filled with fragrant fresh greenery and white candles.

Cristina had been so excited to be a flower girl. She looked adorable in a long, pink voile dress with matching ballet flats and a white headband sprinkled with gold glitter. She walked with Ana's nephew as they smiled at everyone and scattered white and pink rose petals down the aisle of the church.

Ana was a gorgeous bride dressed in a white lace gown that flattered her porcelain skin. Her golden hair was perfectly coiffed underneath a pearl crown holding her long tulle veil in place. Her bouquet was overflowing with the most brilliant white and pink roses. She was a sight to behold.

Emilio was dashing in a black tuxedo and crisp white shirt. He wore a black bowtie and a white rose boutonniere on his lapel, his thick black hair slicked back. Ana's family traveled from California for the big day. Her mother was dressed in topaz blue and her father in a black tuxedo with a satin lapel. The rest of the families were dressed in their Sunday best.

The wedding ceremony was enchanting. The music was lovely, and the pastor spoke beautiful prayers over their marriage. Finally, the pastor declared them husband and wife, and Emilio gave Ana the most tender and loving kiss. They turned and greeted their families as Mr. and Mrs. Emilio Herrera. There wasn't a dry eye in the house.

The reception was simple. They enjoyed finger foods, cake, and punch and enjoyed seeing friends and family they had not seen in a long while. They made their way through the room greeting everyone with hugs and kisses. They were a striking couple and didn't leave one another's side. Only when it was time to change did they separate. Ana changed into a form-fitting dress with an ivory lace bodice and sapphire blue knee-length pleated skirt and off-white kitten heels. Emilio wore a new camel-colored suit with a sapphire-colored tie to match Ana's dress.

Friends and family created a path on either side of Ana and Emilio. They showered the new bride and groom with rice and hugs and kisses as they made their getaway to Emilio's new black car. It had been decorated with ribbons and bows, the words "just married" scrawled on the back window.

Lolita and Roberto's gift to the new couple was a one-night's stay at the Hyatt Regency in downtown Atlanta. It was a tremendous luxury—the tallest high-rise hotel in the Atlanta skyline at the time. The room was perfectly appointed, and the bed had been scattered with red rose petals. It was a magical night that they would always remember.

The morning light streamed into the room and the newlyweds were excited about the ten-day honeymoon they had planned to New York City and New Jersey. They had a long drive ahead of them and wanted to get an early start. After a wonderful breakfast in the hotel's rooftop restaurant, the Polaris, they embarked on their new life.

Ana and Emilio returned home to Atlanta after a whirlwind honeymoon trip. Emilio continued his daily routines of going to school, working at the hospital, and helping Roberto at the gas station. They had rented an apartment nearby and Ana took a job at the bank where Lolita worked. Lolita knew she would be leaving soon to work with Roberto at the gas station, and the bank manager was happy to bring Ana on to take over some of Lolita's responsibilities.

Angela was busy at home taking care of Cristina and Isabela and making dresses for the women at the church. Everyone in the family was working hard to contribute as much as they could. They all dreamed of the time when they would be able to purchase a house of their own. If they all chipped in, they knew it would not be long before they could.

The holidays were a very special time of year for Roberto and Lolita—and now that they had the two girls, it would be a joyous time of celebration for the whole family. Lolita planned a family dinner for *Noche Buena* and invited Emilio and Ana. She would help with the preparations and the food. This time, as Emilio's wife.

Early into the new year, Ana wasn't feeling well. While working at the bank one day she felt so ill she had to go home early to rest. She talked with Lolita that night on the phone and she told her based on her symptoms she thought she may be pregnant. Ana went to the doctor the following day and sure enough, Lolita was right. Ana and Emilio would be expecting a baby in November. They were overjoyed by this news. The family was growing, and everyone was so excited to welcome another new baby.

After talking with Ana, Lolita and Angela made a simple dinner. It had been a long day, and everyone was exhausted. After dinner, Lolita bathed the girls and prepared them for bedtime. It was her usual routine to sing them songs, read them books, and recite their favorite poem, *"Los Zapaticos de Rosa*—The Little Pink Shoes."

"*Mami*, I am ready for the special poem about the pink shoes," said Cristina. It was her favorite part of bedtime. Though she didn't understand the depths and complexity of this poem, she loved the vivid language, imagining this young girl offering her shoes to another young girl in need.

"Snuggle in," said Lolita as she prepared to recite the poem.

Cristina eagerly pulled the blankets up to her chin with a smile.

"I'm ready," she said.

Lolita couldn't imagine being anywhere else. She loved sharing this poignant poem written by Cuban patriot José Martí with Cristina and couldn't wait until Isabela could also enjoy the story.

Lolita began with a hushed but engaging tone that Cristina loved.

"Los Zapaticos de Rosa"	**"The Little Pink Shoes"**
Hay sol bueno y mar de espuma	There is good sun and a foamy sea,
Y arena fina, y Pilar	And fine sand, and Pilar
Quiere salir a estrenar	Wants to go out to wear for the first time
Su sombrerito de pluma.	Her small feathered hat.
"¡Vaya la niña Divina!"	"Go, my divine girl!"
Dice el pae, y le da un beso:	The father says, and gives her a kiss,
"Vaya mi pájaro preso	"Go, my caged bird
A buscarme arena fina."	Go look for fine sand for me."
"Yo voy con mi niña hermosa,"	"I'm going with my beautiful girl,"
Le dijo la mae buena . . .	The good mother said . . .

Cristina had drifted off and Lolita's eyes were heavy from the long day. She laid her head down, thinking she would just rest her tired eyes for a moment, and she fell fast asleep next to Cristina.

Ana's pregnancy progressed and her early morning sickness had resolved. She was back working full time at the bank. Emilio was about halfway through earning his Bachelor of Science degree from Georgia State University. He was now working days at the hospital, and a few nights a week, he would attend classes. Ana and Emilio were enjoying being newly married and spending time together dreaming about the family they were becoming.

Emilio was so good with children. He adored Cristina. They had a special game they would play where Emilio would surprise Cristina with life-sized treats and gifts that he would leave at her front door. Cristina would fondly remember these gifts long into adulthood. One of the most special was a large Bundt cake inside a pale pink box from the local bakery. Emilio rang the doorbell and hid. Cristina opened the door and saw the beautiful box. She knelt down and cracked it open to see what was inside. She could smell the sugar and knew it was a sweet treat. Just as she was reaching into the box, he jumped out.

"How do you like that little donut?" he shouted happily.

"That's not a little donut, *Tio*—uncle, that's a cake!" laughed Cristina.

"No, that's a little donut," he repeated, laughing.

"*Tio* ... you're so silly ..."

They both were laughing hysterically. Emilio picked up the box and swooped up Cristina and headed to the kitchen where everyone would enjoy a slice of "the little donut."

The most meaningful gift of all was a life-sized doll that Emilio left outside the door. He once again rang the doorbell and hid. Cristina came to the door, and standing before her was a doll that was almost as tall as her. The doll had piercing green eyes and long straight blonde hair. She wore a smocked dress with orange, navy blue, and white squares. She was magnificent. Cristina couldn't believe her eyes. She had never seen such a beautiful doll and surely had never seen a doll this big! As she was admiring her new friend, Emilio jumped out.

"How do you like your little baby doll?" he joked.

"Little ... ? She's almost bigger than me," said Cristina with a look on her face somewhere between surprise and pure glee.

"What should we name your new little doll?" asked Emilio.

Cristina didn't have to think. Her name would be Ana. Her aunt was one of the most beautiful women she had ever seen, and she adored her. The doll's green eyes and blonde hair instantly reminded Cristina of her favorite aunt. When Emilio shared this story with Ana, it melted her heart to know Cristina loved her so dearly. It made her even more excited to welcome their own baby into their family. Emilio and Cristina had a special bond, and Ana couldn't wait to see him as a father to their child.

Lolita and Roberto continued to save money in hopes of building their own house. They met with a home builder who had emigrated from Cuba and worked with other Cuban families who were hoping to build their dream homes. He explained the process and what they would need to get started. They agreed to connect after Lolita and Roberto had discussed everything.

They went home to go over the details and they knew that if they continued to save at the rate they were, they would be able to sign a contract and break ground on their new home after just six months. They were elated at the possibility of designing every element of their new home. They knew they wanted a large basement for the girls to play and for Angela to set up her sewing studio. They wanted five bedrooms and four full baths plus a large kitchen. They dreamed of a big backyard with lush green grass where the girls could safely play to their hearts' content.

They had hoped to take another summer vacation to the beach but decided to save every penny they could and put it toward the building of their dream home. Lolita dreamed of how she would decorate the new house, looking through magazines and clipping ideas for decorations and furnishings. She was excited by all the choices. She had no idea what was involved in building and designing a home. This was a whole new world to her, but she loved every minute of it. Just a few years ago they had nothing and were fleeing a country that used to be their home. She couldn't believe how far they had come in just a short time. The possibilities truly felt endless—she was elated.

The business was doing well, and life was good. Summer turned to fall, and Ana began planning for the new baby's arrival. Lolita helped her design the nursery. They chose pale colors in yellow and green, not knowing if the baby was a boy or girl. They chose a white crib with soft yellow bedding. Above the crib hung a mobile with various baby animals. It would spin and play soft lullabies to ease the new baby to sleep. It was beautiful and serene, and Ana couldn't wait to rock her baby to sleep in the rocking chair she had been gifted by their friends at church.

Once everything was in its place, Ana began helping Lolita to prepare for Thanksgiving. They had a huge meal planned and Ana spent hours on her feet each day. Two nights before Thanksgiving, she began to feel painful contractions at just eight months. She knew it was much too early, and she was frightened. She thought that perhaps she had spent too much time standing, and rest would resolve the contractions. She called her doctor, who advised her to immediately check in to the labor and delivery floor at Georgia Baptist Hospital. Emilio raced home from the lab and helped her pack a small bag before heading to the hospital. They held hands and prayed as Emilio drove as quickly as he could. Ana checked in and the nurses started to do all that they could to stop her contractions. Nothing was working. This baby was ready to arrive.

After a full day of labor, Ana and Emilio said their first hello to their new baby girl just after midnight. Without being able to hold her, the nurses whisked her away and checked that all was well due to her early arrival. Ana and Emilio watched from afar and continued to pray that all would be well with their baby. They both longed to touch and hold her. After an hour or so, the doctor and nurses informed the new parents that the baby would need special care due to her early arrival.

They would be able to see her through the nursery window in a clear incubator but would not be able to hold or touch her until she became more stable.

Ana broke down in tears.

"I just want to hold my baby. How will she know that I am her mother?" pleaded Ana.

Emilio tried to comfort her, but he was feeling just as scared and heartbroken by this news. They had waited so long to meet their baby. The doctor assured them they could visit her every day and just as soon as possible they would be able to touch and hold her.

Before Ana was discharged from the hospital, she and Emilio stood for a long while and watched their tiny baby girl. She was precious but so little. She was wrapped in a pink blanket and wore a tiny white hat. She looked so small inside the plastic incubator.

"What should we name her?" asked Emilio.

The birth had come so quickly they hadn't decided on a name.

"I think she looks like a Lily Amalia," said Ana through tears.

"That's it," replied Emilio. "Our perfect little flower."

Going home without Lily was unbearable. They would have to celebrate the holidays without her. Each night Ana would sit in the nursery and cry for her baby. She was heartbroken and longed to hold Lily. Every morning she would visit Lily at the hospital. She and Emilio would meet outside the nursery window, hold hands, and stare silently through the window at their baby girl.

The hospital allowed Emilio inside the nursery to hold baby Lily. Ana pleaded with the nurses to let her in, but it was hospital policy that only employees could enter the nursery.

Emilio would stand right next to the widow and hold Lily's small hand near the glass. Ana would place her hand over hers and for a few moments, she would feel the love between them.

This lasted for five heart-wrenching weeks. Just days after they rang in the new year, they were finally able to bring baby Lily home. Angela, Lolita, Cristina, and Isabela were there to welcome them with open arms. They were all anxious to hold Lily, but Ana was not ready to let her go after so many weeks of not holding her. She sat and stared into her adorable brown eyes for hours, soaking her in. She couldn't believe how much love she could feel for another human being. This was different from her love for Emilio. She was bonded to Lily in a way only a mother can understand. Lily grew stronger by the day and Ana loved being a mother.

Right around the time Lily came home, Lolita and Roberto were ready to break ground on their new home. After just three years, they had worked hard enough to afford a fifty-five-thousand-dollar custom home on a beautiful one-acre wooded lot at the end of a quiet cul-de-sac. The ranch-style light brown brick house would sit atop a hill, nestled among the dense foliage. Following months of construction, their new home was finally completed in June. This was just in time for the family to enjoy the large backyard and time together with the other Cuban families on Moonlight Court.

On the day that Lolita and Roberto were moving into the house, a cute little girl with a brown pixie haircut knocked on the door and said, "Hi, my name is Luli and I live next door. Do you have a little girl I can play with?"

"Hi," said Lolita with a smile. "Yes, we have two little girls. Cristina is five years old and Isabela is three. Which one is your house?"

"I live right there," said Luli, pointing to the house on their right.

"Who lives there with you?" asked Lolita.

"I live with my mom and dad, my grandmother, and my older brother, Luis," said Luli.

"That is wonderful," said Lolita. I will look forward to meeting them. How old are you?"

"I am six years old," said Luli.

"You are adorable," said Lolita. "I know that Cristina will be happy to meet you. I will let you know when she is here."

"Thank you," said Luli. "I better get back home now."

"Okay," said Lolita. "It was very nice to meet you."

"Bye," said Luli, and she skipped home.

Lolita told Roberto of her visit from the little girl next door and they were both happy to know Cristina already had a friend waiting to play with her before they had even moved into their new home. Cristina and Luli became fast friends and maintained their friendship into adulthood. After so many decades together—sharing playdates as children and later as mothers with their own children, meals, shopping excursions, trips to the beach, and so many secrets—they were family.

Lolita had chosen the most unique elements for the house. She included many Spanish-themed items for the outside of the home. The time they spent in Spain inspired large arched doorways with intricate wrought-iron gates leading to a courtyard with a Moorish feel. The courtyard's flooring was made up of large white marble pieces in many shapes and sizes grouted together to form a beautiful mosaic. The front doors were made of heavy, dark stained wood, intricately carved with a detailed design, also inspired by Lolita's memories of Madrid.

Lolita selected all the interior decorations and furnishings. The large galley style kitchen was exactly as Lolita imagined, complete with a Harvest Gold side-by-side refrigerator. The wall-to-wall cabinets were stained oak and the linoleum flooring was a diamond pattern in shades of brown and gold.

The living room, bedrooms, and hallways were covered in tan lush carpeting. Lolita loved spending time looking through the many sample books and selecting the beautiful patterns and colors for their new home. Everything was complementary and it was a warm and inviting space to raise their family.

Lolita's favorite room to design in the whole house was the master suite. This would be her and Roberto's oasis, so she wanted it to be special. She selected a black marble for the bathroom countertop and matching tiny white tile, marbled with grey veins for the flooring. It was stunning. Lolita wanted to bring a Spanish flair into the decor of the master bedroom. She had a bedspread custom-made in a pale ivory damask with gold and bright red crimson threads running throughout the ornate patterns. She specially ordered pillows from Madrid along with a large flamenco dancer doll with a black *mantilla* as the centerpiece of the bed.

The girls's rooms were perfectly girly. Angela's bedroom was painted a pale green with soft white sheer curtains. It was a cozy space just for Angela. She loved being close to the girls but also having her privacy. When the girls were a little bit older and Angela was downstairs sewing, they loved to sneak into her room and play with her perfumes and jewelry. Isabela would stand in front of the mirror holding a pink bottle of rose-scented lotion while she reenacted commercials from the Lawrence Welk Show. This charade would send the girls into hysterics, giggling and rolling around on the carpet until they were in tears.

The basement was massive with so much room to play. As the girls grew, they even had space to roller skate in the basement. The house was Lolita's pride and joy. She couldn't fathom how far they had come from those most difficult days in Madrid. She was so proud of Roberto and how all their hard work had produced such a beautiful life. Home ownership was a lifelong dream come true. This was the American dream they had always heard about.

The leaves on the trees around the house began to change to the most brilliant shades of fall. Cristina was so excited to start kindergarten at a small private Christian school not far from their home. On the first day, Cristina arrived and found she couldn't understand anyone. She was heartbroken.

At the end of the day, she promptly announced, "I am never going back to school!"

To which Lolita promptly replied, "Okay!"

She smiled and knew that with some rest, Cristina would awake ready to go back and give school a second chance.

Sure enough, Cristina was ready to go back the second day and soon was loving her time in school, learning so much. She loved learning to read and would practice with Lolita and Roberto in the evenings. Another dream of Lolita's was for Cristina to play the piano. They purchased a brand new black upright Yamaha piano and found a lovely woman at church to give her lessons. Soon, she realized that although Cristina was learning how to read music and understand the timing of each of the notes, she had a talent for playing by ear. She could listen to a tune and run to the piano and play it. Lolita and Roberto loved listening to her. They would sit in the living room for hours when she played.

Lolita and Roberto were overwhelmed and overjoyed at how their lives were coming together in such amazing ways.

They celebrated Thanksgiving as a family and prepared to have their first huge gathering at their new home for *Noche Buena*. Lolita invited everyone they knew to come and celebrate with delicious food, uplifting holiday music, and fellowship. It was always a wonderful celebration that lasted into the night. The first Christmas morning and New Year in their new home were a wonderful time for the growing family. Ana was six months pregnant with their second baby, and all the girls were so excited to have another baby to play with and take care of.

As spring approached, Emilio was working to complete his Bachelor of Science degree with his sights set on attending medical school. It was an exciting time for Ana and Emilio as they also were preparing to welcome their new baby. Ana's second pregnancy went much smoother and the delivery was easy and uneventful. They hadn't experienced holding a baby after birth, and when the nurses placed this new baby girl in their arms, they were swept off their feet. She was a strikingly beautiful baby with her mother's porcelain skin and beaming sapphire blue eyes. She also had a head full of jet-black hair that made her eyes even more piercing. They named her Marisol Sofia.

Lolita and all the girls helped with Marisol when Ana and Emilio arrived home. Angela would take Isabela with her and help Ana during the day while Lolita was at the service station helping Roberto. Their business continued to thrive. Roberto was working incredibly long hours to provide for his family. Lolita was there every step of the way to support him. Most evenings she would cook a full dinner for the girls and Angela, clean the whole kitchen, then pack a dinner plate for Roberto and drive it to the service station while her mother was bathing and preparing the girls for bedtime. Lolita would rush home to put the girls to bed as Cristina still loved to hear the special poem about the girl with the pink shoes.

Meanwhile, Emilio continued to work at the lab while applying to dozens of medical schools around the country. He was more than qualified for every one of the programs, but he would receive rejection letter after rejection letter, as he was now thirty-six years old and the average age for admittance to an MD program in the United States was twenty-four. One of Emilio's colleagues at the lab had recently gone through the same experience and was eventually accepted into an MD program in the Dominican Republic. Emilio began considering programs outside of the United States, although the last thing he wanted to do was move away from their family and the home they had established.

CHAPTER TWENTY

ATLANTA, GEORIA

NOVEMBER 1973 — FEBRUARY 1974

In mid-November of 1973, Lolita was six months pregnant with her last child. She was nearing the end of her second trimester and her pregnancy had been a healthy and uneventful one thus far. She and Roberto were looking forward to giving Cristina and Isabela a little brother or sister. She got up early on a Friday morning for a routine visit to see her obstetrician, Dr. David Simpson. Lolita left Cristina and Isabela with Angela and had promised the girls the night before, "If you are on your best behavior with your grandmother while I am away, I will take you to the Terrace Shopping Center this afternoon."

They were ecstatic. "We promise we will be good, *Mami*," said Cristina.

The girls had been begging for new ponytail holders with colorful beads, ones they had seen advertised the last few Saturday mornings while watching the Flintstones, the Jetsons, Bugs Bunny, and their other favorite cartoons. Cristina wanted the light blue ones, and

Isabela wanted the pink ones. Lolita was sure they would behave. She loved seeing her girls happy—though this gift was small, it would be something they could enjoy wearing to school every day.

Lolita made the drive in just under thirty minutes. She pulled her light blue 1968 Buick LeSabre into a parking space on the far end of the parking lot. Although Lolita would have liked to have had a new car, she was thankful she had a reliable form of transportation. They had moved into their dream home a year and a half ago, so she was content to wait before upgrading her car.

As Lolita got out of the car and walked toward the white four-story building, she was out of breath. Lolita was excited because today, they would discuss the date they would schedule her hospital admission for the planned cesarean section in February. The hospital where Dr. Simpson and his colleagues had admission privileges, Georgia Baptist Hospital, was also where her older brother Emilio had been working as a lab technician for the last eighteen months. At the same time, he had been studying to complete his undergraduate degree in biology at Georgia State University.

Lolita stepped into the empty elevator and pressed the button for the third floor. As she exited, she turned to the right and only had to walk a few steps to suite 313, and to the black door marked Colorado, Romero, and Simpson OB/GYN. She arrived for her appointment at 8:30 a.m. sharp, and after checking in, she waited to be called.

As Lolita looked around the waiting room, she noticed that only three other pregnant women and two younger women also had early morning appointments. One of the expectant mothers looked as if she had been up all night. She had dark circles under her eyes and appeared exhausted. One of the younger women was wearing a burgundy T-shirt and jeans. Likely here for a yearly check-up with her doctor, she seemed neither tired nor stressed.

The wooden chairs in the waiting room were made of dark stained oak, upholstered with an orange fabric that felt like burlap on the back of Lolita's legs. It made her even more uncomfortable than she already was.

The glass-top coffee tables in the waiting room were smudged with fingerprints, but Lolita noticed the design of the table, as she was in the habit of making a mental note of the styles she liked and might add to her home in the future. She did her best to get settled in her chair and at about that time, she remembered that she had dropped the new Avon weekly catalog in her purse.

This will entertain me for a few minutes, thought Lolita.

As she turned the pages, she saw some things that caught her eye. The Avon catalog had a nice assortment of products: cosmetics, bath products, collectible figurines, children's toys, and costume jewelry. Her favorite was the Sweet Honesty fragrance she had been wearing for the last few years. She also enjoyed that each week, new things were offered, and she could always find something she liked for herself or her family. Additionally, she knew her purchases helped her friend Gloria bring in a little money. She had lost her job as a cashier at the Food Giant grocery store as soon as her boss found out she was pregnant. On top of that, her husband then abandoned her. Now, she needed to find a way to support herself and her four-month-old baby girl.

Just as Lolita was reaching for a pen to mark the things she wanted to buy, the nurse announced to the now-full room, "Mrs. Martínez de Osaba, please come on back." It took a moment for Lolita to gather her things and follow the nurse.

On the way to the examination room, the nurse stopped to take her weight and her temperature. "Everything looks great," said the nurse.

Once inside the room, the nurse grabbed a folded gown from the cabinet and turned to face Lolita. She extended her hand and said, "Please remove all of your clothes and slip on this gown. Wait for the doctor here. He should be in soon."

Lolita undressed and could still get the gown to close once she pulled it around her belly. She sat on the exam table, and after a moment, Dr. Simpson opened the door.

"*Hola, ¿cómo estás*, Lolita?" he said with his usual dry demeanor.

"*Todo bien*, doctor," said Lolita.

Even though Dr. Simpson's bedside manner was lacking, and she would have preferred one of the other two Spanish-speaking doctors in the group, she was glad Dr. Simpson could speak a bit of Spanish since the other doctors were not taking new patients. He had learned it in college, and although his ability was limited, he tried to communicate with her. In the five years she had been in the U.S., she had worked hard to learn English but still felt more comfortable asking him questions in Spanish than with other doctors she had seen in the past.

He listened to her heart and her lungs and said, "Everything sounds good. Please lie back on the table so I can check your cervix and listen to the baby."

Lolita was thankful that she had been feeling well overall. The exam was going as planned. But when Dr. Simpson placed the stethoscope on her belly to listen to the baby's heartbeat, his face grew sober and seemed distressed.

"What is happening? Is there a problem?"

"Wait here one moment," he said as he quickly left the room.

Dr. Simpson could not detect a heartbeat and was gravely concerned. He immediately asked his nurse to locate doctors Colorado and Romero. They were both in examination rooms with their patients, but the nurse let them know of the situation, and the three doctors huddled in the empty conference room to discuss what they should do. Lolita was three months from her due date, but this discovery had turned everything upside down.

Lolita was in tears when the three doctors stepped into her room. Her heart was pounding in her chest and the room was spinning. Waves of nausea washed over her when she saw the grim look on their faces. She knew something was very wrong but didn't know what it could be. Although she had not felt any different today from the other visits, she was scared to death to hear what Dr. Simpson was about to tell her.

"I cannot find a heartbeat. Your baby is dead. Get dressed and go home to rest. If within one month, you have not miscarried, we will admit you to the hospital and schedule you for a D&C. This is a procedure where the cervix is dilated, and the lining of the uterus is removed along with any contents."

Terrified, Lolita could not believe what she was hearing. "How could this be happening? Am I misunderstanding what you are saying? I am feeling this baby moving at this very moment!" Lolita cried out. Between sobs, she said, "Please, let me call my brother who works in the laboratory at the hospital so you can speak with him."

Dr. Simpson agreed and gave Emilio the same news: "The baby is dead."

The next thirty days were the worst of Lolita's life. She had never experienced anxiety like this before. Lolita was carrying this baby that she and Roberto already loved so much, not knowing what would happen when she went back for her visit.

Waiting for a whole month to pass was agonizingly painful for Lolita. At last, the day Lolita and Roberto had dreaded was here. Her eyes were swollen, and she was light-headed from weeping throughout the night when she arrived at the doctor's office.

Once she was taken to an exam room, Dr. Simpson quickly arrived. As he was performing Lolita's follow-up exam, his conclusion was the same as the previous month. "I am still not hearing the baby's heartbeat. After thirty days in this condition, it is certainly dead."

Lolita tried to say the words but could not get anything to come out. She was gasping for air, but finally, she cried, "Dr. Simpson, I don't understand! How can my baby be dead? I can feel my baby moving and you're telling me it's dead!" In exasperation, she raised her voice, "My baby has been moving all during this past month!" Lolita grabbed his hand and placed it on her belly. "Feel it! My baby is moving! How can you tell me there is no heartbeat?"

He pulled his hand away quickly. "What you are feeling are the contractions of the uterus and the tissue dying."

Dr. Simpson showed no emotion in his voice, "Do not eat anything after midnight and be at the hospital tomorrow morning at 7:00 for the procedure."

Everything about him was cold and sterile.

★

Lolita knew in her heart that the doctor's diagnosis was wrong. She absolutely felt her baby moving inside of her. There was no way she would be able to sleep for even one second tonight, knowing what was going to happen in the morning. Lolita couldn't help but lament in anguished silence as she was preparing to give Cristina and Isabela a bath and put them to bed that evening. The girls knew something was wrong with their mother. The sadness they felt at seeing her this way was evident on their sweet faces.

"*¿Qué pasa, Mami?* Are you okay?" Cristina asked in a hushed voice. At almost seven years old, she wondered what could be making her mother so sad.

"*Sí, mi amor*. I am tired and I have to see the doctor very early tomorrow morning. Remember when we went to see Dr. Duarte for your check-up before school started last fall? You and Isabela were afraid to see the doctor and worried that he would give you shots. I am afraid of seeing my doctor in the morning too."

The girls took a quick bath and used the shampoo they had used all their lives, Johnson's No More Tears. The bottle was filled with a yellow gel that felt like sunshine to them and smelled like a summer day.

After they dried off, Cristina and Isabela put on their flannel Winnie the Pooh, Tigger, and Piglet pajamas that they so loved. Lolita had saved for weeks to buy these special pajamas for her girls. She loved to give them matching items so they both felt they were equally loved. The pajamas had a cream-colored background with the colorful characters—in reds, yellows, blues, and greens—walking together through the forest.

The girls shared a bedroom, and each had a twin bed. The walls were painted a soft baby pink, while the coordinating curtains and bedspreads were made of a voile fabric in Wedgewood blue with small white, yellow, and pink flowers. Lolita and Roberto wanted to give the girls everything they didn't have; setting up this princess bedroom for her girls had been a joy for Lolita.

It was the girls' bedtime. But beforehand, they knelt by their beds, bowed their heads, folded their small hands, and closed their eyes to say their nighttime prayers.

"Dear God, thank you for *Mami* and for the new baby that will be here soon," said Cristina. "We can't wait to play with it and help take care of this new, tiny baby. Amen." At seven years old, she loved playing with her baby dolls more than anything. She was excited to be a big sister again and to have a real, live baby doll to play with.

"Dear God," said Isabela. "Thank you for today and for the awesome cupcakes that Johnny's mom brought to our class for his birthday. I liked the chocolate one. It was delicious. Please make *Mami* not be sad. I don't like it when she cries. Amen." Isabela's prayers were always so innocent.

The girls pulled back the covers and crawled into their cozy beds. They put their heads on their pillows and were ready to drift off to sleep after a busy day. Cristina attended school, and Isabela went to the Mother's Morning Out program at the church nursery. In the afternoon, Angela watched them for hours as they played outside in the cool fall weather. Sleep would come easy for them. They were children, after all, and didn't know the weight of the world was bearing down on their home.

Lolita wiped the tears from her cheeks before leaning down to give them each a kiss on the forehead. "I love you both very much. Sweet dreams, my girls." The gratitude she felt for her girls and the desperation in the depths of her being for her baby were an unimaginable swirl of emotions. It was the first time in her life she'd ever experienced a feeling like this.

Lolita had never known such immense grief and hopelessness as she did at this moment. The burden on her heart felt as if it were impossible for it to ever lift. She lay down next to Roberto close to midnight, but after only a few minutes, she felt the need to get up. Roberto did not stir after the eighteen hours he had worked today, so he remained in a deep, deep sleep.

Lolita, pacing around the house with nervous energy, felt a despair so heavy that her tears flowed uncontrollably. Lolita had been through a lot in her twenty-nine years, but this was a dark night of the soul from which she wasn't sure she could come back.

Lolita remembered that ever since she was a little girl, she would watch Angela boil water to make a cup of *manzanilla* tea each evening before bed.

Angela would steep the tea bag for a few minutes and then add a generous pour of local honey to her beautiful burgundy and white porcelain teacup. She treasured the delicate gift that her own mother had given to her—it was her nightly companion. She would sit in the small living room of their home to enjoy a few moments alone before turning in for the night.

Angela and her family valued the honey for its many health benefits, and she was grateful that Oscar had a customer who would use it to pay for minor car repairs. The tea had many healing properties and helped calm Angela's anxiety so she could relax and get a good night's sleep. It worked like a charm, and when Lolita was in her late teens, she would join her mother for a lovely nighttime routine of winding down the day.

Lolita knew she needed to make some tea for herself tonight because her body was past the point of exhaustion. She needed to sleep at least a few hours before the alarm would sound. Lolita didn't want to think of what was going to happen to her and her family once the morning light appeared.

As she prepared her tea, Lolita wondered if Dr. Simpson would try to find her baby's heartbeat again before the procedure.

I felt my baby moving today, so why can't the doctor hear its heartbeat? Lolita contemplated sorrowfully. *I just don't understand this.*

She carefully lifted her hot cup of tea from the countertop and turned to walk to the living room window. As she pulled back the curtain and looked out into the darkness, she wondered how everyone could be asleep when her world was crumbling around her. At the same time, Lolita turned her gaze upward and discovered a splendidly small sliver of a crescent moon in the deep blue nighttime sky, revealing a new lunar cycle. She thought about how more of the moon would be visible as the month progressed until it culminated in a full moon, only to start its unfaltering journey again. The moon's rhythm of birth, death, and rebirth was a somber reminder that as a brand-new moon was rising, the very life inside of her would be gone forever in a few hours.

Ever since she was a child, Lolita had been fascinated by the moon. Seeing the full moon comforted her; she always hoped she would once again see the "biggest moon ever." She loved the mystery and incomparable beauty of the moon—especially a full moon. She would imagine what life up there would be like. It was a constant source of wonder and security. Despite what was going on in her life, she could always count on the moon's presence. Lolita had only seen a supermoon a few times as she was growing up, and each time had been an immense thrill for her. As an adult, she would look at the Moon Phase Calendar in her yearly copy of the Farmer's Almanac so she could make plans to see the supermoons that were scheduled for the following twelve months.

The turmoil of the last month had not inspired Lolita to think about anything other than her baby and her family—certainly not the moon. And although she could feel the tea's calming effect, it did nothing to ease her immense sadness.

Just as Lolita finished her tea and was about to put the cup on the small wooden table by the plaid sofa, she was startled when Roberto sleepily walked into the living room.

"*¿Qué pasa, mi amor?*" asked Lolita. She knew that after a long day at work like he had today, nothing would normally wake him.

"I had a nightmare, and when I reached for you, the bed was empty. I jumped up immediately to make sure nothing was wrong with you or the baby," explained Roberto.

He enveloped Lolita in a hug that felt as if it were coming from the very center of his soul. They stood there for what seemed like forever. They didn't want to let go. As long as they stayed this way, nothing bad could happen to them.

When they finally released their embrace, Roberto took Lolita by the hand and led her to the sofa. He could feel the trembling—she was exhausted and anxious. Her body couldn't contain all that she was feeling. She took a seat next to him, not knowing why he had asked her there.

"I want you to sit back so I can put my head on your belly."

Roberto positioned his ear as close as he possibly could to their baby. Lolita gently placed her slender hand on Roberto's head. He was perfectly still for a few moments when, without warning, the baby started moving and kicked just below his ear.

"Did you feel that? Tell me, did you feel that?" implored Lolita.

"Yes! I did feel it. This baby is strong and just kicked me!"

Lolita and Roberto were more confused and downhearted than ever. Their weariness was overwhelming, so he coaxed her back into the bed as she was visibly exhausted. They both were overtaken by sleep.

In what felt like only a few minutes, it was early morning.

Lolita awakened in a panic and wondered if this all had been a terrible nightmare. She reached for her belly and once again felt the baby moving. None of this made any sense. She reluctantly gathered her things to take to the hospital. She began to get dressed and splashed cold water on her face to ease some of the swelling from a night of sorrow.

Lolita and Roberto arrived at the hospital at 7 a.m. as ordered and were shown to her room before she knew it. Everything was a blur that morning, and her pain at the thought of losing this child that was showing signs of life inside of her was unbearable. Lolita and Roberto sat in wistful silence for close to thirty minutes before a breakfast tray was delivered to her room. They brought her a meal of bland scrambled eggs, plain toast, and orange juice.

Roberto looked at the nurse and then at Lolita, "Wait a minute. The doctor said for her not to eat anything past midnight."

Lolita was puzzled and turned to the nurse, "Why am I being served breakfast? I am supposed to be fasting for my procedure."

At that moment, there was a knock at the door. Dr. Simpson arrived. He made a startling announcement.

"*Hola*, we would like to have you go down to the X-ray department for one last test."

"What does this mean, doctor? Is this standard for this procedure?" asked Lolita.

"We need to ensure one last time that there are no signs of life before we can proceed," he said matter-of-factly, turning before walking out of the room.

Lolita looked at him with disbelief. Not at this latest request but at how emotionally detached he was at this life-or-death moment.

How could anyone in his position not show emotion, or at the very least, some sympathy? thought Lolita.

An orderly arrived fifteen minutes later and took care to gently help her into the wheelchair. He was an older man with kind eyes and a soft demeanor. She was grateful for this because as her world was falling apart, these simple acts of kindness from a stranger made her at least feel seen.

"Please stand at the blue line on the floor and face the X-ray machine," said the technician.

Lolita felt weak in the knees but was able to pull herself out of the wheelchair with the orderly's assistance. She slowly walked to where she had been instructed to stand. After a few minutes, the necessary X-rays were taken. As she turned to walk back to the wheelchair, she felt anxious, lightheaded, and faint—she had not eaten anything since dinner the night before, more than twelve hours earlier—but she got back to her room and waited for the doctor to confirm his diagnosis. Roberto walked over from the uncomfortable, plastic, mustard yellow chair where he had been waiting for her to return. He reached out for her and placed his hand underneath the inside of her arm to help lift her up.

"*Gracias, mi amor,*" she said gently.

Lolita crawled into the bed and wondered how much longer she would have to wait for this nightmare to be over.

★

Emilio worked the third shift at this hospital. Throughout the night, he secretly researched and read through any material he could find, searching for the possibility that the doctors could be wrong. He couldn't imagine what his sister was going through, but the thought of Dr. Simpson wanting to terminate her pregnancy when she was feeling her baby kick forced him into a panic, looking for answers.

Emilio had always maintained a cool sense about him. He kept his emotions in check, even when things were tense or difficult. He would say, "Procrastinate your anxiety. This will give you time to think about your next move."

On this day, Emilio could not procrastinate his anxiety.

Before dawn, Emilio reached out to Dr. Simpson's office, but the answering service said he would not be in until 7:30 a.m. He left a message for the doctor to call him. The anticipation of sharing the results he had obtained with the doctor had his body trembling, his palms sweating.

Emilio's desperation to speak to him grew by the minute. As soon as he placed the phone in its cradle, he collected the manila file folder that held the results for the research he had conducted.

He knew he had to get to Dr. Simpson so he could explain his findings before he proceeded with the D&C. He took the elevator to the third floor and hurriedly walked up to the door of Colorado, Romero, and Simpson OB/GYN at 7:30 a.m. sharp. When he tried to turn the doorknob, it was locked. He immediately realized they wouldn't be open until 8 a.m. Emilio knocked on the door, but no one answered. He knocked again. This time he knocked with such force that it echoed down the marble hallway.

The receptionist nervously approached the door and cracked it open, as she stood behind it.

"We are not open until 8 a.m. Is there something I can help you with?" she asked.

"Hello, my name is Emilio Herrera. I would like to speak with Dr. David Simpson."

"Do you have an appointment, sir?" asked the receptionist.

"No, I do not. I work in this hospital and my sister is his patient. He has admitted her and is scheduled to terminate her pregnancy this morning because he told her he couldn't hear the baby's heartbeat. I need to show him some research I found that shows what has most likely happened, and that Lolita's baby is still alive," pleaded Emilio.

"Please take a seat, sir. I will let Dr. Simpson know you are here to see him," said the receptionist with a shocked look on her face.

Emilio couldn't take a seat. He was pacing back and forth and was ready to share the news of what he had found with the doctor. He was glad that there was no one else in the waiting room at this hour. The lights were only partially on, since the office wasn't open for patients yet.

Moments later, a nurse opened the door to the empty waiting room and looked at Emilio. "Please follow me."

She led him to a large corner office, where Dr. Simpson was sitting behind his desk. The doctor was puzzled as to why a laboratory technician was coming to speak with him and contradicting his findings.

As Emilio stepped into the office, Dr. Simpson asked in a condescending tone, "Can I help you?"

"Yes, my sister is Lolita Martínez de Osaba and she was admitted this morning for a D&C to terminate her pregnancy based on your diagnosis of her baby being dead," Emilio blurted out.

"I believe the nurse told you that I work downstairs in the hospital laboratory. I spent hours researching overnight and reading various articles in medical journals for possible causes that would explain the inability to hear a fetal heartbeat when the mother claims the baby continues to move and the measurements show fetal growth. I believe the reason you are not detecting a heartbeat is because she has anterior placenta!" he frantically explained.

"As you know, with this condition, the placenta is on the front side of the belly rather than behind, as is more common, thus making it harder to hear the heartbeat."

The expression on Dr. Simpson's face was one of disbelief. Disbelief that a lab technician would question his ability to confidently arrive at a diagnosis and determine a plan to move forward—a plan solely based on the best interest of his patients. He could feel his anger growing.

"Who is the doctor here? You or me?" he finally asked.

With a confident yet respectful demeanor, Emilio looked at Dr. Simpson square in the eye. "You are the doctor, but she is my sister—you have made a mistake. I don't know what you plan to do, but I am most certain that Lolita's baby is alive!"

At that moment, he placed the file with the results of his findings on the doctor's desk. Dr. Simpson leafed through the papers in the folder, looked up at Emilio, and back to the papers with an ever-growing look of concern on his face.

The doctor had no choice now but to pay attention to what Emilio was saying.

"I will send orders for your sister to have X-rays right away and see if what you are saying and showing me has any validity," said Dr. Simpson, but this time, with an uneasy tone in his voice.

"Thank you for listening to me and helping to save her baby's life," Emilio said and turned to walk out of the doctor's office.

Dr. Simpson was perplexed—he had never been in this situation before. When he or his colleagues couldn't hear a fetal heartbeat, the standard procedure in their practice was to send the expectant mother home, and if she did not have a miscarriage during the following thirty days, they would check for the heartbeat again. If they still couldn't hear it, they would schedule her for a D&C. This was the process they had always followed.

This case was different.

What Dr. Simpson did not know was that Emilio had already completed two years of medical school at the University of Havana when Castro's revolution wreaked havoc on the island nation, and one of the many casualties to its citizens was the invalidation of all university credits at foreign universities.

Emilio had to start his medical education from scratch.

Something else Dr. Simpson didn't know was that only one year after arriving in the U.S., at the age of thirty, he began to work on an undergraduate degree in biology—for a second time. Not only did Emilio embark on a university major of study that was difficult for native English speakers, he had also only started learning English the previous year. During the day, he was studying to learn a new language and all new medical terminology at the same time. At night, he worked in the hospital laboratory from 11 p.m. to 7 a.m. Sleep was a precious commodity for Emilio during this time, but he had a dream of one day becoming a physician and nothing was going to stand in his way.

Emilio returned to the laboratory to wrap up a few things that needed his attention. He was determined to get to Lolita before the doctor could ignore his findings and proceed with his original plan.

Emilio opened the door to Lolita's room without knocking and was visibly shaking.

"*Hola*, Lolita. How are you feeling? Roberto, how is everything going?"

They were both feeling emotionally and physically drained. "We hardly slept last night," said Lolita.

"Dr. Simpson sent me for X-rays this morning and waiting to hear the results has been tormenting. Do you have any idea why they are delaying moving forward with the procedure?"

"Has Dr. Simpson spoken with you regarding the results of the X-rays?" asked Emilio, ignoring Lolita's question.

"No, not yet. Why do you ask?"

Emilio didn't want to get Lolita's hopes up in case the doctor didn't confirm his findings.

"I just want to know what he found. I will wait here with you," said an anxious Emilio.

After two long hours, Dr. Simpson pushed the door open and said, "We have received the results of the X-rays, and your baby is alive. We made a mistake. You can get dressed and go home."

Lolita had been on a roller coaster of emotions, but this latest news was too much for her to process. She burst into tears. "Are you sure?" she asked. "Are you sure?" She couldn't believe her ears. She knew in her heart her baby was alive, and now the doctor had confirmed it!

Emilio carefully leaned over the bed to hug Lolita. Roberto's eyes welled up with tears as he was overcome with emotion. They had all just gone through one of the most traumatic and life-altering moments of their lives. They needed some time to let this surreal news sink in and become reality.

Dr. Simpson added, "Please call the office to make an appointment for one month from today." With that, he turned and walked out of the room.

Emilio could now tell Lolita and Roberto of his sleepless night looking for a way to save her baby.

"I read everything I could find in regard to not being able to find a baby's heartbeat even though the mother can feel it moving and the baby continues to grow. I finally found the probable cause—anterior placenta!" Emilio said enthusiastically.

"This is where the placenta moves around to the front of the belly and makes it very difficult to hear the baby's heartbeat. I took all my research to Dr. Simpson early this morning. That is why he ordered the X-rays."

Lolita and Roberto looked at each other in amazement and gratitude for Emilio's determination to follow his instincts and save their baby's life.

"Emilio, you are the best brother anyone could hope for. If you had not done this, my procedure would have already been finished and my baby would be gone. Thank you for working hard to prove what you and I both knew to be true. I am so thankful you were able to speak with Dr. Simpson before he went ahead with his plans. After the worst month of my life waiting for the D&C today, this is a miracle!" said Lolita as tears streamed down her face. Her words came intermittently, broken up by her deep sobs.

Emilio smiled and said, "Everything will be fine."

Lolita took a tissue and dried her tears. She carefully got up from the bed and took her clothes from the closet with her to change in the bathroom. In the meantime, Emilio helped Roberto gather Lolita's things and placed them in her small, tan, hard-sided suitcase. They had never been more anxious to get back to their home.

Roberto called Angela and gave her the amazing news. She was overcome with emotion and couldn't wait to hug Lolita after this terrifying experience. He told her they would be on their way home as soon as Lolita was ready. As the three of them drove up to the house, they could see Angela and the girls sitting in the courtyard to their home, waiting for them.

Angela had not been able to sleep either. Praying fervently throughout the night, she'd asked God for a miracle, and it seemed she had been granted one.

Although overjoyed with Emilio's findings and knowing her baby was alive, Lolita worried that something may still be wrong with her baby when it was born. She was especially worried about the baby's heart and wondered if the doctors were not able to hear the heartbeat because there may also be a defect.

The next few months were incredibly difficult and sad for Lolita and Roberto. They weren't sure of the problems their baby may have, so they prayed that it would be healthy and strong. Their church joined them in prayer for a good pregnancy and delivery and for a healthy baby.

With her family to care for and preparations to be made for the new baby, the last few months of Lolita's pregnancy seemed to go by quickly. Physically, she felt strong, but emotionally, Lolita couldn't let go of her fear that something could still happen to her baby before, during, or after the birth. This was not something she had ever felt with her two previous pregnancies.

At the end of January, Lolita visited Dr. Simpson because she had started experiencing mild contractions. Although she knew this was normal at thirty-nine weeks, she wanted reassurance that everything was still fine with the baby.

"You are only one centimeter dilated, and everything appears to be good," said the doctor. "We still have a little time. Take care of anything you need to do before the baby is born because you will be back here soon."

A few days later, on an early February afternoon, Lolita took Angela and the girls for their weekly grocery shopping trip to Food Giant. They walked up and down every aisle, picking up the things they needed, including short-grain white rice and bags of black and red beans to make the Cuban meals they were so accustomed to.

Each of the girls had a favorite cereal, so Lolita had always bought them their own box. Cristina reached up to get her favorite, Sugar Corn Pops, and then she grabbed Isabela's favorite, Frosted Flakes. She put both boxes into the shopping cart, which was starting to fill up.

As Lolita and Angela stood talking and looking for the self-rising flour to make Angela's tropical lime pound cake, Lolita felt the familiar rush of warm water running down her legs, into her brown suede shoes, and onto the floor. Angela and the girls looked at the small puddle forming by Lolita's feet and Angela knew her water had just broken.

"What is that, *Mami*?" asked Isabela. "Do you need to go to the bathroom?"

"No, this just means the baby will be here soon. We have to go home to get my suitcase, and your father will take me to the hospital," said Lolita as she pushed the cart full of groceries to the side. While every step for Lolita felt uncomfortable, they all quickly walked to the car.

"Lolita, give me your keys," said Angela.

"No, I am fine to drive," replied Lolita.

"Lolita, it would be better if I drive and you sit on the passenger side. You could begin to cramp any minute. *Give me the keys*," said Angela more forcefully.

Lolita handed the keys over to her mother. After making sure the girls were seated, she closed their door and walked around to the other side of the car. She sat in the front seat, closing the door after herself. Angela cautiously drove through the parking lot of the grocery store and made a right-hand turn onto the main road.

The trip home was only about ten minutes, but Lolita asked Angela to pull into the next gas station so she could call Roberto from a payphone and ask him to meet her at the house right away. Roberto and Lolita spoke for just a minute, and they knew it was time to implement the plan they had discussed. He hung up the phone and quickly called his business manager, Walter, informing him of the situation. He ran to get in the car and drive home, forgetting to take his clean uniforms.

Lolita had kept her suitcase packed from her previous trip to the hospital a few months earlier, so now she only needed to get her toothbrush and toothpaste, and she was ready to go. She could feel her emotions building up in her chest. Her hands were shaky as she closed the suitcase. Roberto walked into the room and hugged Lolita. He felt nervous but didn't want her to see him like this.

"How do you feel?"

"I'm ready to go to the hospital, but I want so much for this baby to be okay," said Lolita with a trembling voice.

"It will be. I just know it," said Roberto. Although he too was fearful for the safety of their baby, he wanted to comfort Lolita.

"I will take your suitcase," said Roberto as he picked it up and walked out of the room. He took it to the car and placed it in the trunk.

Lolita was saying goodbye to Angela, Cristina, and Isabela when Roberto came back into the house. The girls were excited, knowing *Mami* and *Papi* would be bringing a new baby home.

"I will be praying for you and the baby," Angela said with conviction in her voice. "God will take care of you both."

Lolita hugged them all one last time and gathered her purse and coat before leaving to go to the car with Roberto. He walked ahead of her and opened the front passenger door.

"*Gracias, mi amor,*" said Lolita.

Once she was seated, Roberto closed the car door and went around to get in the driver's seat. He turned the ignition key and they were on their way. During the drive, Lolita practiced the breathing exercises for expecting mothers she had read in the brochure from the doctor's office. Lolita and Roberto talked about some trivial things to ease their worries.

"Don't forget to call Mrs. Stewart in the morning to let her know that I will not be able to go on the field trip to Mathis Dairy with Isabela's class tomorrow," Lolita reminded Roberto.

"I will do that first thing in the morning," Roberto assured her.

"Also, please call Graciela to let her know that Cristina will not be there tomorrow evening for her piano lesson," said Lolita.

"I will do that too. Please, don't worry about these things. I will take care of them."

The trip to the hospital took them close to thirty minutes. But it was made tolerable for Lolita, as they focused on lighter conversation and the tasks for which Lolita needed Roberto's help. As for Roberto, he tried to keep her mind focused on this moment. As they passed the sign announcing Georgia Baptist Hospital, Lolita put her black leather purse on her arm and prepared to get out of the car.

Roberto drove directly to the emergency parking area. He dropped Lolita and her suitcase off by the door so she wouldn't have to walk back from wherever he could find a parking spot.

"I'll be right back. Sign in, find a seat, and wait for me inside the sitting area," said Roberto.

Fortunately for Lolita, the wait to be seen in the emergency room was only about twenty minutes. While she waited for Roberto to return, she filled out all of her admission forms. As she was completing the last one, Roberto stepped through the sliding glass doors into the waiting area.

"Can you please take these to the front desk for me?" Lolita asked as she raised the papers.

As Roberto approached the desk to return the forms, he heard Lolita's name called over the loudspeaker. He hurried back to where Lolita was sitting to watch her suitcase while she went back to be evaluated.

Lolita carefully stood with her back to the bright blue wheelchair and placed her hands on the arms of the chair to steady herself before slowly lowering into the seat. A portly old nurse with a kind face turned and whisked her away.

After a little more than an hour, Dr. Simpson came out to speak with Roberto.

"We are going to admit Lolita and keep her under observation. Once her contractions start to get stronger, we will take her back to the operating room, administer the sedative though an IV, and deliver your baby as we had planned," he said with his usual dry demeanor. "Do you have any questions?"

"When can I see her?" asked Roberto.

"The labor and delivery nurse will let you know once we send Lolita to her assigned room so you can take her things and stay with her."

"Thank you, doctor," said Roberto.

The preparations for Lolita's delivery had begun. The nurses and the attending staff were showing her extra attention by keeping her comfortable and taking her vitals often. Dr. Simpson had been on the brink of making a deadly error in judgment with this pregnancy, so he knew that every single person caring for Lolita needed to execute flawlessly. This baby would need to have all available life-saving equipment should the need arise.

Sooner than anyone expected, Lolita's contractions started coming closer together. Her hands cradled her swollen and tight belly—she prayed that everything would go smoothly. Within a few minutes, it was time for the nurse to take Lolita's vital signs and check on how her labor was progressing.

"Lolita, your contractions are now coming five minutes apart, so we are taking you to the operating room momentarily to prepare you for the delivery of your baby," said the nurse.

Dr. Simpson explained that when the contractions became stronger and closer together, Lolita was to be wheeled back to the OR so they could begin sedation in preparation for the delivery. Lolita began active labor, writhing in intense pain. The nurse tried to comfort Lolita, but she couldn't focus on anything other than the intense pain. When the time came, they asked her to count backward from ten. She was asleep in an instant.

When she woke up, the nurse was beside her bed holding the baby.

"It's a boy, ma'am. You have a perfectly healthy baby boy," said the nurse.

"Are you sure? Is he okay?" asked Lolita desperately.

"Yes. Your delivery went well, and your new baby boy is doing great. His heartbeat is strong—and as you can hear from his cries, his lungs are strong too. He is healthy," said the nurse.

Roberto and Emilio were waiting in the lobby with the other expectant fathers and family members. They spoke softly about how the last few months awaiting the baby's arrival had been grueling. Roberto expressed gratitude toward Emilio and his instinct to investigate the doctor's initial findings. If not for Emilio, they would not be here today.

A few more hours passed as they sat, nervously awaiting any news about Lolita and the baby. Soon, a nurse appeared and shared the news that Lolita had a successful delivery and a healthy baby boy. Both were overjoyed.

They gathered their belongings and followed the nurse back to the room where Lolita and this baby that had been so hoped for were resting. Dr. Simpson was still in the room when Roberto and Emilio arrived.

It was as if the entire world had disappeared and all they could see were Lolita and this perfect baby boy. Roberto and Emilio couldn't take their eyes of them. Lolita and Roberto had decided to name him Roberto Emilio Alejandro, and they would call him Alex. He weighed seven pounds, four ounces and measured twenty-one inches long. He had the cutest little dimples on his tiny cheeks, just like his older sister, Cristina. Roberto, Emilio, and Lolita were so thankful for this moment. Their feelings were almost too much to even express.

The doctor watched this scene unfold and was relieved at the delivery of the healthy baby boy. He shuddered to think what could have happened. This whole situation had caused him to question everything he knew about medicine, but he was the type of man who would never let an ounce of weakness show. He congratulated the new family in a dry and monotone voice and went back to his day of seeing patients.

There were happy tears of relief and gratitude at seeing this beautiful brown-eyed baby boy and knowing he was perfectly healthy.

It was the miracle they had long awaited.

CHAPTER TWENTY-ONE

ATLANTA, GEORGIA

MAY 1974

Finally, at thirty-seven years old, Emilio was accepted to *la Universidad Autónoma de Guadalajara* in Mexico—the oldest and most prestigious medical school in the country.

Lolita and Roberto committed to helping Emilio and Ana financially, and even though they had not been in their new house very long, that summer, they refinanced it and gave them money for the trip and to establish themselves.

Emilio and Ana, along with their two young girls, Lily and Marisol, moved to Mexico in mid-August. They hated to leave, but nothing would stand in the way of Emilio's dreams.

The journey was almost two thousand miles and took close to a week by car. Near the end of the trip, along a winding and dusty road, a cow crossed their path. Emilio did all he could to avoid hitting the massive animal, but he couldn't react in time. The car was damaged, but they were all safe. The trip was delayed a few days while the car was being repaired. They got back on the road and arrived in Guadalajara the week before Emilio was to begin classes. He had worked so hard, and his dreams of becoming a doctor were coming true.

They settled into a small, beautiful row house in a neighborhood near the university with lots of children for the girls to play with. Ana didn't work outside the home, so she could take care of the girls. Lolita and Roberto agreed to send them money every month for their living expenses for the next six years, as Emilio would complete medical school and then begin earning money during his residency. It wasn't easy. Roberto and Lolita sacrificed daily to support two families. Roberto continued to work long hours at the service station, despite the changing seasons and freezing temperatures. In the winter, the constant exposure from the elements as he went between the gasoline pumps and the car repair bays would dry his skin to the point of cracking and bleeding. In the summer, the heat was sweltering.

But Roberto never once complained. He made a good living for his family and was grateful for the opportunity to live and work in a free country. His job was physically demanding, and the days were long, but he wouldn't have traded this for anything.

★

In September of 1974, as Lolita was preparing the girls' breakfasts before school on a cool Thursday morning, she relished in the stunning view outside her kitchen window. The fall leaves were turning beautiful shades of red and gold. Lolita never tired of this gorgeous change each year. She loved the crispness in the air and even more, experiencing the four seasons in the southern U.S. In contrast, the subtropical climate in Cuba keeps the temperatures around seventy-eight degrees year-round. The winter months are slightly cooler, and the summers are made for hot, lazy days at the beach. The heat and humidity can be stifling at the peak of the summer months, but the cool trade winds bring a nice breeze to the island.

Lolita had many great memories of trips to the beach with her friends as she was growing up and of the warm, clear, turquoise-colored water year-round, but since the seasons aren't remarkably different, one could change into the next without anyone being fully aware. When she was finally able to bundle up with a thick coat, scarf, boots, and lined gloves on a cold day, it was still something she looked forward to with great anticipation.

Lolita had prepared breakfast for herself and Roberto earlier this morning so they could have a few moments of conversation while enjoying their meal before the children awakened. Lolita enjoyed cooking and often made "early breakfast"—something they both enjoyed while still in their pajamas. Today, she served eggs scrambled with smoked gouda cheese, diced ham, and a small amount of sautéed chopped onion. Roberto and Lolita had discovered grits, a new staple in their Cuban-American kitchen, since moving to the United States. In the southern part of the country, this was a popular dish, and Roberto, who also enjoyed cooking, had put his own special twist on them. He used whole milk to cook the grits with a mixture of butter, cream cheese, salt, and fresh cracked pepper. He topped it with a small amount of shredded cheddar cheese. It reminded them of mashed potatoes but had that distinctive texture of grits. It paired perfectly with the eggs. Of course, they had a Cuban *cortadito* as they did every day. This was a little piece of the home they left behind and their favorite way to drink Cuban coffee.

Lolita would start making the foam by whisking a few tablespoons of sweet granulated cane sugar with an equal part of espresso until the sugar dissolved and a light brown foam formed. Next, she set it aside and poured the fragrant brewed Cuban espresso into the dainty coffee cups and mixed it with a little steamed milk to cut the bitterness of the coffee. She would top it all off with the sweetened foam.

It was heavenly.

Lolita also served fresh-squeezed orange juice. She had always loved it, so it was no trouble for her to make it when she had the time.

They talked and laughed as they ate the tasty meal Lolita had prepared. The time passed quickly and when they finished, Roberto stood from the table to shower and get dressed so he could drop the girls off at school on his way to work.

"*Muchas gracias, mi amor*," said Roberto. "I enjoy it when we have time for our special morning meal. Everything you made today was wonderful, but the oranges for the juice were remarkably sweet and delicious."

"*Sí!* I enjoyed everything as well, but I think the juice was my favorite part of the meal today, too!" said Lolita.

Roberto gently kissed Lolita on the forehead and smiled on his way to the bedroom to get ready for the day. He knew he had been blessed with a wonderful wife and family. His heart was full.

Lolita cleared the dirty dishes and rushed to reset the table for the girls. She quickly prepared their food, and as she took it to the table, she called out for them.

"Cristina, Isabela—your breakfast is ready. Please come eat. We don't want to be late for school."

"*Ahora, Mami*. We will be right there," Cristina replied loudly.

Lolita had prepared the girls's favorite breakfast, *café con leche* with fresh Cuban bread and softened butter. This was a traditional Cuban breakfast that Angela had served her for as long as she could remember while growing up. Now, her girls loved it too.

After only a few moments, Cristina and Isabela ran into the kitchen, kissed their mother on the cheek, and expectantly sat at the table.

"*Gracias, Mami!*" they both exclaimed.

"*De nada*. I'm so glad you like your breakfast, girls," Lolita said with a smile.

The girls were ready for the day, so they finished their breakfast and washed their hands.

"Can we have our special vitamins?" asked Cristina.

Lolita had started giving the girls Flintstone vitamins after they had seen them on TV last year. Cristina liked the yellow ones and

Isabela, the purple ones. "Here you go. One for you and one for you," said Lolita as she handed one to each girl.

Cristina picked up her book bag and the lunch Lolita had packed for her in the new Holly Hobbie metal lunch box she had gotten for the beginning of the school year.

Isabela was only five and her kindergarten served lunch and snacks for the kids, so Lolita didn't need to prepare anything for her to eat.

Right then, Roberto came into the kitchen to say goodbye to Lolita and to take the girls to the car for their ride to school. Lolita hugged and kissed them all and said, "I love you very much! I hope you all have a great day. I will be waiting in the car rider's line to pick you girls up at 2:30 this afternoon."

They all put on their coats and walked out the front door. Lolita closed the door and walked over to the living room window to watch them leave. She pulled back the sheer gold curtain covering the window and waved to them. They waved back as Roberto put the car in reverse and rolled out of the driveway as they headed to school.

Lolita went back into the kitchen to clean up all the breakfast dishes before feeding baby Alex. As she ran the warm water and picked up the dishwashing detergent, she looked out the kitchen window again. Her eyes drifted to the driveway on the side of the house. She smiled as she saw the shiny 1974 coppery-brown Cadillac Coupe DeVille with the sand-colored roof that was now hers. Roberto had purchased this car, their first-ever brand new one, and had given it to Lolita as a gift to celebrate becoming citizens of the United States of America a few months earlier.

Citizenship in this new country had been a dream for them since they arrived from Spain five years earlier. The U.S. had opened its arms to them and given them a chance at a better life. Owning a new luxury car was outside of the realm of possibility only a few years earlier as they waited for their exit visas from Cuba to appear in their mailbox. Their life was completely different now, and for this, her gratitude was ever-present.

Lolita and Roberto followed in the steps of Emilio, Ana, and Angela and submitted their applications for citizenship not long after Alex was born in February of 1974. After waiting several months, they received a reply from the office of the United States Immigration and Naturalization Service outlining all the requirements needed to become citizens. Reading over the enclosed material, they knew the process would be lengthy, but they were prepared to do whatever was needed to become U.S. Citizens.

The next step was to attend an interview in which an immigration representative would ask them questions to determine if they would be admitted to sit for their citizenship tests.

The letter included the date and time for their meeting. It was exactly ten days away, and this brought up feelings of nervousness and excitement for them. Despite a slight language barrier, everything went well, and they left the interview feeling confident that they would be moved forward for the final step—passing an English and a civics test. Not having grown up in the U.S., Lolita and Roberto studied together every evening after they had put the children to bed. On the day of the test, they felt prepared, but the butterflies in their stomachs confirmed for them that they were stepping into the next important milestone of embracing their new country. The studying paid off—within a few weeks, they received the invitation to attend the oath ceremony at the federal building downtown, where they would take the Oath of Allegiance to the United States of America.

They dressed in their Sunday best. Roberto wore a dark gray wool suit, a starched white button-down shirt, and a thin, solid yellow tie. Lolita wore a midnight blue mid-length skirt with a tailored jacket and high-heeled shoes that she had bought for this special day. She combed her pretty brown hair into a French twist and took extra care to apply her makeup. This day and what it meant for them was indeed an incredible honor and privilege that those born in the United States could not comprehend. They arrived early to ensure nothing would get in the way of fulfilling this dream. The parking spots surrounding the federal building were all taken, so they circled and noticed the entrance to a parking garage. At the top, a dark blue sign with big white letters read U.S. District Court Parking. They drove into the garage and circled until they found an empty parking place on the fifth floor. When they stepped out of their car, the clear blue sky was bright, and the sunshine warmed their skin. They exchanged excited looks and Roberto said, "This is really happening!" They both knew it was going to be a life-changing day in the best way possible and their exuberance was palpable.

As Lolita and Roberto walked up the stairs to the entrance of the courthouse, they marveled at the tall columns and impressive architectural details on the building. Roberto opened the heavy oversized brass and glass doors for Lolita to pass through. He was always a gentleman; Lolita loved that about him. They went directly to room 148 as the letter had instructed.

The door to the room was propped open and upon stepping inside, they noticed many international faces and knew they were in the right place. They could hear people speaking in different languages and in English with many foreign accents. The room was filled with a beautiful and melodic cacophony of conversations. Lolita and Roberto smelled a mix of perfume, spices, cigarettes, and musty clothes. Being in this room was overwhelming to their senses, but they wanted to take in everything. They knew they would remember this day for as long as they lived.

As they looked around, Roberto noticed a family of six standing close to them. They appeared to be a father and mother with their three teenage children and what looked to be a grandmother. The women were dressed in beautifully patterned sarees in deep blues, greens, and white with gold trim. The two teenage girls also wore sarees, but their colors were solid and muted. One wore a combination of blush and white and the other a mix of pale blue and yellow. The girls were laughing and talking with their brother. The adults around them were speaking among themselves in hushed tones.

On the other side, Lolita saw a couple that appeared to be a husband and wife, mostly silent—waiting patiently. They were very tall with alabaster skin. Lolita imagined they were from somewhere in Europe, perhaps Scandinavia. The clothing they were wearing also seemed heavier than that of the rest of the people in the room. The weather outside was glorious so there was no need for this type of clothing. Perhaps it was just habit, or maybe it was all they owned.

Everywhere Lolita and Roberto turned, the looks of relief and nervous optimism were on the faces of young and old.

The sights, sounds, and smells of this room were some they would never forget. As officials began to gather on the stage, Roberto looked at Lolita and pointed to the front of the room. The ceremony was about to begin.

Many countries were represented here, but they were surprised to learn that the number was actually forty-three countries when the immigration official gave his opening remarks. Once he concluded his short comments to welcome the candidates for citizenship and had set the agenda for the ceremony, he motioned for the group to form a line and file to the far-left wall. They were then to turn and stand facing the front of the room.

Lolita and Roberto had waited five years for this day and could hardly contain the pride they felt. Their mouths were dry, and their hearts were racing.

It was a momentous occasion when they, along with the room full of people from around the world, raised their right hands and with words that were cracked with emotion, pledged their allegiance and loyalty as they recited the Oath of Allegiance.

"I hereby declare, on oath, that I absolutely and entirely renounce and abjure all allegiance and fidelity to any foreign prince, potentate, state, or sovereignty, of whom or which I have heretofore been a subject or citizen; that I will support and defend the Constitution and laws of the United States of America against all enemies, foreign and domestic; that I will bear true faith and allegiance to the same; that I will bear arms on behalf of the United States when required by the law; that I will perform noncombatant service in the Armed Forces of the United States when required by the law; that I will perform work of national importance under civilian direction when required by the law; and that I take this obligation freely, without any mental reservation or purpose of evasion; so help me God."

Once this part of the ceremony was completed, the official read a proclamation from U.S. President Richard Nixon before they each received their Certificate of Naturalization. After the ceremony and with a smile, they waved their new tiny American flags and drove home elated knowing they had finally become official citizens of the United States of America. This privilege extended to any minor children not born in the U.S., and as Cristina was only seven years old, she too became a U.S. citizen that day.

They knew this was a privilege they would forever treasure.

CHAPTER TWENTY-TWO

ATLANTA, GEORGIA; GUADALAJARA
MEXICO; AUGUSTA, GEORGIA;

WEST NEW YORK, NEW JERSEY
AND LA PALMA,
PINAR DEL RIO, CUBA

1975 — 1979

Becoming U.S. citizens was a major milestone in the family's journey. Their business was thriving, and their family was doing well in school and in their community, but this was the final piece that needed to be put into place before they could fully enjoy life in the United States as Americans.

Emilio and Ana were doing well in Mexico. Emilio excelled in medical school and Ana enjoyed supporting him and taking in Mexican culture with the girls whenever she could. Angela missed Emilio, Ana, and the girls very much and wished she could see them.

"Lolita," said Angela. "Do you think we could plan a trip to see Emilio and his family? I really miss them."

"Yes, it would be wonderful to see them," said Lolita. "I miss them too. I have also always been fascinated with Mexican culture and traditions. I will have to speak with Roberto and see when he thinks we could plan this."

Lolita and Roberto researched flights and purchased tickets flying into Miguel Hidalgo y Costilla International Airport in Guadalajara. They planned a wonderful two-week trip. It would be the first time on an airplane for Isabela and Alex, and they loved the adventure. Lolita dressed the children in their Sunday best for the big trip. Flying was a huge extravagance—especially to another country—and she wanted to be sure they all looked their best when they landed in Mexico. Ana and the girls picked up the family and they drove the short trip back to their house. Emilio was still in school but made it home in time for the whole family to enjoy dinner together. It was a joyous reunion. They spent the evening reminiscing, catching up, sharing new and old stories, and just enjoyed being in one another's company again. Before they knew it, it was close to midnight, and some of the children had fallen asleep on the living room floor. Ana and Emilio carried the girls to bed and Lolita, Roberto, Angela, and the children settled into two small guest rooms for the night.

They awoke to the sun shining brightly through the sheer curtains. Lolita stepped out of bed and could see a beautiful courtyard lined with native plants and flowers. It was a quaint space with colorful ceramic pots, and a bistro set to enjoy a *cafécito* in the morning. Lolita was already smitten with Mexico. It just felt different and special. It felt like home away from home.

Everyone woke to the smells of breakfast cooking. Ana had prepared a traditional Mexican meal including various egg dishes, fresh corn tortillas, ripe tropical fruits, freshly squeezed orange juice, hot chocolate, and everyone's favorite buttery *pan dulce*—sweet soft bread with a crunchy sugar-coated topping.

After a filling breakfast, they all loaded into Emilio's car and visited the Guadalajara Zoo, the largest zoo in all of Mexico. The variety of animal species was amazing. The children were beside themselves with all there was to see. The favorite among them all was the white Bengal tigers. They were majestic and beautiful. They also visited the aviary with dozens of species of birds, the aquarium featuring many types of sharks and fishes, and finished the day off in the gift shop. Emilio allowed each of the children to pick their favorite stuffed animal. All the girls chose fluffy white polar bears and Alex chose the white Bengal tiger.

A few days into the trip, Lolita and Roberto took a flight into Mexico City. The children stayed back with Angela and Ana so they could enjoy time alone together. Lolita was immediately taken with the sights, smells, and sounds of Mexico City. They enjoyed eating at sidewalk cafes, listening to the traveling mariachi bands, and shopping at local stores. The night before they were due to fly back to Guadalajara, Lolita and Roberto attended a special dinner show with the Mexico City Philharmonic Orchestra accompanied by traditional Mexican dancers. The dancing and music were spectacular. Lolita was in heaven.

She was still excited the following morning but began feeling ill after breakfast. They boarded the plane, but Lolita was sure to have the flight attendants bring her a few bags just in case she was to become sick in the air. She was fine on the flight, but as soon as they landed, her symptoms intensified. When they got back to the house, she had to run to the restroom to be sick. She couldn't leave the restroom for several hours. Ana and Angela became concerned and asked Roberto to try to get in touch with Emilio. When Emilio arrived home, he took one look at Lolita and could see she was extremely dehydrated.

"We need to take her to the hospital, Roberto," said Emilio. "She is not doing well. Help me lift her up and put some shoes on her."

Roberto and Angela reached around Lolita's back to help her sit up while Emilio swung her legs around so Ana could slip on some flats. They braced themselves so she could just lean back as they slowly walked her to the car. She could barely stand, but they managed. Once they arrived at the hospital, the doctors and nurses immediately began running tests. She continued to get sick and the nurses started an IV drip to relieve her dehydration. The results of the tests showed Lolita had picked up a parasite, likely from the water. She would need to stay in the hospital for a few hours until she could keep a small amount of food and water down. She went home with medicine to help with her nausea and it took her a few weeks to feel completely herself again.

The last few days in Guadalajara were spent sightseeing, enjoying cooking special Mexican cuisine, and preparing to return home to Atlanta. It was a great trip and they couldn't wait to go back again.

When they arrived back home, Roberto returned to business as usual and Lolita, Angela, and the children fell back into their daily routines. With only a few weeks until school would start back again, they enjoyed playing outside from sunup to sundown, riding their bicycles in the cul-de-sac, and eating long picnic lunches on the lawn.

Cristina especially loved taking care of her pet rabbits, who lived in the backyard. They each had their own living space in a large custom-built rabbit habitat. She would fill the floors with hay, carrot shavings, lettuce, and any other food scraps she thought they would enjoy. Tragedy struck one day when a huge neighborhood dog took advantage of an open gate. That night when Cristina went to check on her rabbits, she was shocked to find one missing. She noticed drops of blood on the concrete and then on the open gate and immediately burst into tears. She knew it was the neighbor's dog. She was devastated for weeks.

The beginning of school helped to get her mind off the dead rabbit she so loved. Cristina continued playing the piano and for the first time, she also began competing in the National Piano Auditions sponsored by the National Guild of Piano Teachers. Her skills were improving with every practice and she enjoyed playing whenever she had free time. A favorite pastime was visiting the local music store to pick out the latest sheet music. Cristina enjoyed all types of music—everything from classical to pop to holiday to hymns. When she first started taking piano lessons, she would spend hours writing the names on every single note—Do, Re, Mi, Fa, Sol, La, Si. Cristina was detail-oriented from day one. Although she played by ear, it was important to her to be able to read music. In order to be competitive, she had to know the notes.

Cristina was asked to play in the 1976 Christmas recital at church. She practiced for weeks and chose three songs: "Angels We Have Heard on High," "Silent Night," and "Away in a Manger." The crowd loved her playing and even began singing along toward the end of her performance. For a nine-year-old, Cristina played so well and was as poised as a seasoned pianist.

Lolita began preparing for Christmas morning a few weeks ahead because she had something very special planned for the children this year. Instead of having all the gifts wrapped under the tree, the children awoke to one small wrapped gift with a note revealing a clue about the next present's location. They were so excited. They squealed with joy with every gift—it was the most special Christmas scavenger hunt. The morning turned to day and the children had unwrapped dolls, train sets, lip balms, new clothes, cars, books, a kitchen set, a baseball, glove and bat, and matching baby doll cribs and highchairs. They were thrilled and stayed in their pajamas all day playing with their new toys and snacking on treats.

That winter was cold and rainy for Atlanta. The kids weren't able to play outside as much. The basement became their new favorite place to play. They would play school—Cristina was always the teacher and taught Isabela how to read and do simple math. Cristina would gather everyone together and read stories to them, acting out all the voices of the characters. Isabela and Alex loved this time with Cristina the most.

Finally, the weather gave way to spring, and Lolita and Roberto began planning for Easter. Lolita loved finding matching outfits for her girls. She especially loved matching Easter dresses. This year she found the most precious dresses in lavender with a delicate floral print. The sleeves were made from white pleated voile creating a bell shape—fitted at the shoulder and wider at their hands. The outfit was complete with white tights and white patent leather Mary Jane shoes. They also each had white wrist-length gloves and a tiny white purse. The girls's hair was perfectly styled with matching lavender barrettes. Alex wore a tiny three-piece suit with a vest and striped brown tie and spit-shined leather wing-tipped shoes. Easter was a huge celebration in the church community. After Sunday morning services, everyone gathered for lunch at the house. Angela and Lolita had cooked a full meal the day before including ham, scalloped potatoes, green beans, and rolls. No meal was complete without rice and black beans. They feasted and Lolita and Roberto hosted a neighborhood Easter egg hunt for all the children. It was the most fun; the children competed to find the golden egg, which was filled with special candies and a crisp twenty-dollar bill. It was a thrill for all the children.

Ana and Emilio shared the news that they would be expecting a new baby in August. They invited the whole family to visit again around the baby's due date. Lolita and Roberto began planning the trip for later in the summer. This time they would drive their brand-new, pale-yellow 1977 Buick Estate station wagon with wood paneling. The 1,800-mile trip from Atlanta to Guadalajara took over five days of driving. They stopped to sleep at night and visited a few tourist attractions along the way, including a monument at the Tropic of Cancer in Zacatecas, Mexico.

They finally arrived and settled in for a longer stay. During this visit, a lot of their time was spent helping Ana with the girls and preparing for the new baby. Lolita was out shopping with Ana one day when she spotted the most perfect little pair of cowboy boots for Alex and quilted denim purses with a cherry pattern for the girls. They loved their gifts and Alex immediately slipped into his new boots. He was in love. He wore them every moment of every day, even while he slept. Lolita would sneak into the room to try to gently take them off his feet, but he would awaken and protest to the point where she just stopped trying. *He'll grow out of them eventually*, she thought.

Lolita and Roberto's children were so excited to meet their new baby cousin as Ana's due date approached.

They spent the last few days in Mexico exploring and getting to know Ana and Emilio's neighbors, who also had young children. One afternoon, several of the neighborhood children were playing outside. Alex, just three at the time, was trying to impress the neighborhood children with his command of the English language. He wanted Lolita and Roberto to bring a bicycle down from the tiered patio in the front yard. He confidently shouted in Spanish with an English accent, "*Bajar biciclet!*"— bring down my bicycle. The children all roared with laughter. They all understood what he said, of course. He had tricked no one. To this day, no one has forgotten the story of *bajar biciclet* and the family uses it often as an inside joke.

The following day, after spending the afternoon at a local park with the children, Lolita and Ana wanted to relax at home for a bit while the children played outside. A few minutes later, Lily ran inside to announce that the man pushing his cart with frozen treats would be passing their house soon.

"Can we please have *paletas*?" asked Lily.

These were cream or water-based popsicles with pieces of fresh fruit, and the variations were endless.

"We haven't had them in a few days, and I would love the mango-flavored one," said Ana. "I need something to cool off from being out in the sun today. Would you like one, Lolita?"

"Yes, I would love one," she said. "Stay here, Ana, and I will get the children their *paletas* and bring ours back."

"Thank you," said Ana. "I'm worn out."

Lolita went back to the guest bedroom and reached inside the dresser for her wallet. When she stepped outside, the children were already crowding around the man and his small white cart. They were yelling out the flavors they each wanted—banana, strawberry, guava, lemon, and watermelon—with excitement.

Lolita paid for the *paletas* and went back inside. The children sat on the stoop and enjoyed their cold treats as the juice ran down their little arms. They laughed and carried on—brushing their arms on their clothes, using them as napkins. The cousins loved sharing this time with each other and they wished they all could live here.

Ana and Lolita were comfortably sitting in the air-conditioned living room, savoring their *paletas*, when Emilio burst in the front door.

"Elvis is dead."

"What did you say? What happened?" asked Lolita, astonished by the news.

"Elvis died today but the news didn't say how he died," said Emilio. "Some friends at the university were talking about it this afternoon. I was surprised to hear it too."

She couldn't believe what she was hearing. She had loved Elvis since she was a young girl in Cuba. *How could this be? He was only forty-two years old,* she thought.

Lolita could feel a lump in her throat. She almost felt embarrassed when her eyes filled with tears. She loved Elvis's music, but more than that, he was a connection to her adolescence—he had always been one of her favorites.

"I am so sad and at the same time, angry with myself," said Lolita.

"Why would you say that?" asked Ana.

"Last summer, one of my friends called to tell me she had two tickets to see Elvis perform that night at the Omni Coliseum in downtown Atlanta," said Lolita. "She couldn't use them and offered them to me. I told her I was tired from being out all day with the children, but I appreciated her kindness and that I would love to see him some other time. Now that will never happen."

Lolita began sobbing as she told the story.

"I am sorry you are so sad," said Ana.

"Thank you," said Lolita. "I think it was just a shock hearing he had died and then thinking that I will never go to one of his concerts now.

"I know how much you loved him, even as a girl in Cuba," said Emilio.

"I did and I still do," said Lolita. She had nothing else to say—only to absorb the news Emilio had shared.

Angela made a dinner of homemade mashed potatoes, baked chicken, and an avocado and tomato salad. She was a great cook and Ana was glad she didn't have to cook for the family tonight. After dinner, everyone was exhausted from the day and got to bed early. The next morning, they would wake refreshed and Lolita could have some perspective around yesterday's bad news.

Lolita and Roberto had planned the trip for six weeks so they could be there for the baby's birth. The due date came and went and still, there was no baby. They had no choice. They could not stay longer because the school year would be starting. Within a week of leaving, the baby was finally born on August 29—Camila, another little girl. She was precious with dark brown hair and eyes. Emilio and Ana sent photos and videos of the new baby and all the girls together. Their family was complete.

When Halloween came around, Lolita knew exactly how she would dress the girls. She loved Mexican culture so she gathered all her traditional Mexican garb and dressed the girls head to toe with colorful Mexican attire. They each wore long black full skirts, a brightly colored blouse, and big Mexican hats—Cristina wore a black velvet one with gold sequins and Isabela wore a turquoise one with silver sequins. Lolita also made a long braid for each girl using black yarn and placed it on the center of their heads before securing the hats in place. Cristina carried a guitar and Isabela shook maracas in the air. The girls wore the costumes to school on the day of the Fall Festival. There was no question. They both won first prize for their grades and Cristina won the overall contest. She received a small certificate to commemorate her win.

The following spring, after completing medical school in Guadalajara, Emilio still had one year before he could earn his MD degree. He needed to complete the Fifth Pathway program, which was a one-year supervised clinical training program for students who have completed four years at a foreign medical university to finish his MD degree. He applied to the Medical College of Georgia and was accepted. He, Ana, and the three girls moved to Augusta, Georgia so he could begin the program.

Ana invited Cristina and Isabela to come to spend a week with her and Emilio and their cousins during summer vacation. The girls were so excited. They had never slept away from home. Lolita packed shorts, T-shirts, sandals, and their swimsuits. Ana had mentioned that she would be taking Lily and Marisol to swim lessons at the YMCA. Lolita wanted Cristina and Isabela to learn how to swim. It would be a fun getaway for the girls.

On the drive down, Lolita realized she forgot to pack the girls their pajamas. She saw a sign advertising a K-Mart a few exits down the road. She and the girls jumped out to quickly buy those and get back to their trip. Each girl chose a new pajama—Cristina got one with a blue cloud pattern and Isabela liked one with pink flowers. On their way to the register, Lolita noticed some cute hairbrushes.

I'll pick one up for each of the girls and surprise them, thought Lolita.

She selected a pale pink one for Isabela and a light blue one for Cristina. Lolita always bought them those colors so there was no mistaking who the item belonged to. When they got back in the car, Lolita was happy to give her girls this little treat.

"Here you go, Cristina," said Lolita as she handed her the blue brush. "Isabela, here is yours." Lolita stretched her hand to give her the pink brush. Then she steered the car out of the parking lot and back onto I-20 East.

"We love these," exclaimed Isabela.

"Thank you, *Mami*," said Cristina. "Can I please have the pink one? I am tired of always getting all of the blue things."

"No, the pink one is mine," cried Isabela.

"Give it to me," yelled Cristina.

The girls started to fight, and Lolita was not going to have it.

"Cristina, Isabela, please let me see the brushes," said an aggravated Lolita. "I will hold onto them for you."

The girls reluctantly handed the brushes to Lolita, who calmly rolled down the driver's side window, and at fifty-five miles per hour, flung the hairbrushes into the grassy median. The girls started crying and screaming. Lolita didn't care. She was not going to spend one minute longer listening to them fuss.

"Now, if you don't stop crying," said Lolita. "You will each get a spanking when we get to your aunt and uncle's house."

The girls composed themselves but learned a valuable lesson that day. Lolita would not put up with ill-behaved children.

Ana had already signed the girls up for daily swim lessons. On Monday morning, they all loaded into Ana's car and drove to the swimming pool. They were so excited to meet their swim teacher, Rosie. She was a sweet teenage girl who loved teaching young kids how to swim. She would have her hands full with this crew. Cristina, being the oldest, was apprehensive about swimming. Rosie was trying to teach Cristina to dive. Instead of tucking and rolling into the water, Cristina grabbed Rosie and pulled her into the water with her. Rosie was not amused. Eventually, everyone learned to swim, and they enjoyed their summer days at the pool. Cristina and Isabela were not ready to go home after their visit, but school would be starting soon.

Emilio completed his program and was ready to graduate from medical school. The ceremony was set for August 5, 1979. It seemed surreal to Emilio that at forty-two, he had finally achieved his dream of becoming a doctor. Lolita, Roberto, and Angela joined Ana with all the children to celebrate this tremendous accomplishment. Emilio felt such pride and gratitude to receive his medical degree from the Medical College of Georgia. He was ready for the next step, but first, he would need to prepare for and pass the FLEX (Federation Licensing Examination) before he could begin his family practice residency.

The following week, Emilio, Ana, and the girls packed a U-Haul truck and moved back to Atlanta, into Roberto and Lolita's home, while he researched the best preparation programs.

Lolita and Roberto were thrilled to welcome Emilio and Ana and the children. The house accommodated everyone very comfortably. It was full of joy and laughter as they all enjoyed being together once again. Emilio gave himself six months to find the right fit while he was interning at Georgia Baptist Hospital. He applied to several programs, but he had his heart set on the Kaplan course offered in West New York, New Jersey.

After only a few weeks, he received a letter letting him know he had been accepted into the six-month Kaplan course and classes would be starting the following month.

Emilio went ahead of Ana and the girls and found a small apartment where they could live for the time being. Rent was high in the area; all they could afford was a one-bedroom apartment. The girls were now eight, six, and two years old, but Ana and Emilio weren't able to rent a place with an extra bedroom for them. They placed Camila's crib in the bedroom with them and Lily and Marisol slept on the pull-out couch in the tiny family room. Even though Emilio was still deep in the process, and years away from being able to practice on his own, he and Ana were happy with the life they were building. He could see the future and knew everything would turn out just the way it should.

★

LA PALMA, PINAR DEL RÍO, CUBA
1979

Tending to La Paloma had been Daniel's existence for longer than he could remember, and it had long since lost its novelty. Years upon years had taken a toll, and Daniel was tired of this life he once loved.

When he and Gabriela moved to La Paloma, he had so many hopes and dreams for their lives. As the years passed, his prolonged sadness changed him in so many ways. Daniel's muscular physique and the big, beautiful, green eyes that captivated Gabriela and persuaded her to fall in love with him were now just a memory. Daniel's eyes had turned cloudy, and the hollow expression on his face haunted him. His frame had become thin and frail, and his sunken face betrayed everything he tried to hide.

This humid late August morning was like any other in many respects. The air hung heavy, and the heat had already begun to take hold.

He awoke in the darkness well before dawn and whispered the prayer he had said each morning since he was a boy.

"God, I ask you today to guide my hands and my feet in your service to others. I pray that my heart will be open to know where I can be a blessing and share your love."

Daniel pulled the covers to the side and sat up on the bed. As he swung his feet around and placed them on the floor, Daniel rubbed his eyes and wished he could just fall back asleep. He wanted to forget his troubles for at least a few more hours. He had a long day ahead of him, so he got up, got dressed, and stepped his aching feet into his black work boots. He picked up the small, black plastic comb from the dresser and slowly walked to the mirror. He started to run it through his thinning hair but paused for a moment when he didn't recognize the man looking back at him.

The reflection showed a man much older than his years. His exposure to the hot Caribbean sun every day of his life had given his face a leathery appearance with deep, tanned wrinkles. His full, wavy, black hair was now graying and had been cut short long ago. He examined his scarred and age-spotted hands from all the years of laboring on his farm and thought, *Who is this man?*

Daniel had once been a happy family man and *campesino*—a rural farmer—but that season of his life was now just a distant memory. He now only had a few animals to care for and a small garden to tend.

Daniel prepared a quick breakfast of *café con leche* with toasted bread on which he generously spread fresh butter. This simple meal warmed his belly and gave him the strength he needed to begin his pre-dawn routine. He walked outside and went through the chicken coop first to collect the eggs. He continued down the green grassy hill to milk the cows and set up their feed. These daily laborious tasks were made easier when his children were still around to help. He missed having their help on the farm, but even more, he missed having them all sitting around the dinner table, recounting their day and enjoying each other's company as they laughed and shared their stories. Now he ate alone, in silence. The isolation was heart-wrenching.

While the sky was still dark and filled with glimmering stars, he filled up the animals' heavy watering containers. He continued on to the far end of the property, where he would gather red, green, and yellow tomatoes, bright orange carrots, and a few other ripe vegetables from his garden.

Walking back toward the house, he knew his aging neighbor, Señora López, would be counting on him to share his daily pickings. He took the well-worn path from the farm to her small, yellow concrete home. She greeted him at the door with an easy smile and thanked him for his kindness.

"How are you feeling today, Daniel?" asked Señora Lopez. Her smiling grey eyes shone with gratitude. "I can't tell you how much I appreciate that you always find it in your heart to stop by and bring me some wonderful things from your garden." It had been a little more than a year since Señor Lopez passed away, and Daniel felt he needed to look after his elderly neighbor.

The families had lived next door to each other for the last forty-three years. They had a close relationship, but he respected her and had always addressed her in a formal manner. Señora Lopez had been a beauty in her day. She was still very attractive even though her bright blue eyes had faded, and her skin was no longer that of a young woman.

Taking care of Señor Lopez since he was diagnosed with lung disease a few years earlier had taken a lot out of her. He had smoked for many years and continued until his last day. His doctor never mentioned anything to him or asked him to stop smoking. No one warned him this could further damage his lungs. Señora Lopez did everything she could to take care of him, but in the process, she lost herself.

Many years ago, Señora Lopez had shown Daniel and Gabriela a color magazine in which she had been featured at the age of sixteen. She posed along with a dozen other girls in the latest swimsuits at the water's edge at *Playa Varadero*. The fine, white sand and the crystal clear, blue water were perfection. The midday sun was reflecting on the water, and their radiant smiles jumped off the pages of the magazine. They were running and frolicking in the warm surf, and you could see they were genuinely enjoying themselves. This was a day that they would remember forever. She was proud of that experience and had been happy to share it with them. She now used a cane to help with her balance, and arthritis had deformed her hands. But the stunning girl from the magazine still lived inside this lovely woman.

"I've seen better days, Señora Lopez," he said with a heavy sigh. There was sorrow in his deep-set eyes.

Daniel began to make his way back home as he did every day—but today would be different.

As the pink morning light started to illuminate the horizon, he shuffled down to the barn where the horses were beginning to awaken. Daniel brushed each of the horses with a firm but tender touch. He loved them all, but he couldn't deny that his favorite was *Mantequilla*—butter—a perfect name for a golden horse. She was already standing in her stall, waiting for him. Her soft, tawny fur and gentle caramel eyes melted his heart every time he saw her. *Mantequilla* knew the sorrows of his soul.

"How is the most beautiful girl in all of Cuba?" he asked her.

As Daniel brushed *Mantequilla's* silky mane, he remembered how Gabriela always said that this golden-hued horse with the soulful eyes had stolen her heart. Daniel missed Gabriela terribly. He missed the way she looked at him with so much love in her soft amber eyes. Lately, with her gone, he grew more melancholic with each passing day.

The dense air in the barn was uniquely heavy today.

Streams of golden sun made their way through the windows, but nothing could lighten the darkness and emptiness Daniel felt inside. His mind was swirling as he thought about the last twenty-six years since Gabriela's passing. They had been difficult and lonely years. At times, his despair was unbearable.

His life felt hopeless, his existence meaningless. Sorrow escaped from every pore of his skin.

He lit a cigarette, took a long inhale, and began to gather his supplies for the day. He looked for a few things that weren't in his usual toolbox. He took the heavy harness off of a bale of hay with great care. Daniel had done this very same task when he was a boy, but in his haste wasn't careful and the harness snapped, almost decapitating him.

Carrying the harness with him, he walked over to a high shelf near the feeding troughs. He ran his weathered hand along the rough surface of the wooden board until he found a long and thick rope he had used when training his horses.

Daniel continued toward the darkness of the back of the barn, where he found the old wooden step stool that he used when milking the cows before Gabriela found three newer and more sturdy ones at the Agricultural Fair of 1952. He carried the worn-out step stool and positioned it below the center beam of the barn, using the harness to secure it to a sturdy stall door. With sweaty palms and an eerie sense of calm, he tossed the rope over the beam and carefully tied a tight knot. He looked around one final time, taking it all in. The fading memories of his family were too painful for him to bear. He longed for the incessant aching in his heart to cease.

With his beloved Gabriela gone and his children scattered to the wind, he couldn't muster the strength to go on.

In his last moments, Daniel silently prayed. "*Dios mio*. The promise of heaven is too great, and my sorrow too overwhelming. My soul longs for peace. Amen."

CHAPTER TWENTY-THREE

ATLANTA, GEORGIA

1979 — 1983

The golden light of the late afternoon sun had started to fade behind the tall pine trees in Roberto and Lolita's backyard. The family enjoyed spending time outside, and with only a few days before the children went back to school, Lolita decided to serve dinner on the patio. She made a wonderful meal of homemade hamburgers and fresh-cut French fries with *natilla de leche*—custard pudding—for dessert.

"*Natilla* is my favorite," said Alex.

"Mine too," said Isabela.

"You can both have some as soon as you finish your dinner," said Lolita.

Lolita and Roberto loved to watch their children laugh and enjoy a family meal around their new black wrought-iron table overlooking their beautifully landscaped backyard. It was starting to get dark when they finished eating, so the children helped by taking their plates to the sink.

In La Palma, Señora Lopez's hands trembled as she dialed Roberto and Lolita's phone number. This was a phone call she never could have imagined she would need to make. Through the years, she and Roberto had kept in touch, but she knew this call would break his heart. Just as Lolita dipped her hands into the warm soapy dishwater, the phone rang.

She and Roberto looked at each other and wondered who would be calling them after 9 p.m. on a Saturday night. Roberto still had a few remaining items to pick up from the table, so Lolita rinsed her hands and dried them off with a dishtowel. She walked to the far wall to pick up the phone.

"Hello," said Lolita.

"*Sí, hola*, Lolita. This is Consuelo Lopez."

"*Hola*, Señora Lopez," said Lolita. "Nice to hear from you. *Como está?*"

"I am doing well. But I have some sad news to share with you and Roberto about Daniel."

"Oh, my goodness," said Lolita. "What has happened?"

"I would like to speak with Roberto so I can tell him myself," said Señora Lopez. "Is he there?"

"Yes, please hold for just a moment," said Lolita as Roberto walked back into the kitchen with the remaining dishes.

"Roberto, Señora Lopez is on the line and wants to speak with you," said Lolita as she handed him the phone. "It's about your father."

"Señora Lopez, what has happened to my father?" asked Roberto nervously.

"As we've discussed before, your father had not been doing well for a long time," she said with sadness in her voice. "His depression . . . "

"What do you mean *had*?" asked Roberto as he started to panic.

"Well, his depression had worsened recently. This morning, his woeful expression hurt my heart when he stopped by to bring me some fresh vegetables from his garden, as he always did," said Señora Lopez.

"Around midday, I went to the house to ask him over for lunch and to see if he wanted to talk. I looked around the house, but I didn't find him. I thought he may be in the barn. I walked through the stalls and when I stepped around to the back, I found him—he had . . . he had taken his own life."

"Oh, no, no, no," said Roberto as he raised his hand to his head in horror. His heart was pounding. His mouth became parched and the lump in his throat gave way to a torrent of tears.

"How can this be? What happened?" asked Roberto, his head swirling with confusion and shock.

"I'm so sorry, Roberto," said Señora Lopez through her sobs. "He hanged himself from one of the beams in the very back of the barn earlier today."

"What? I can't believe this," said Roberto as the tears fell uncontrollably. "He seemed to be okay when I spoke with him last month."

"He had good days and bad days but lately, they've mostly been bad," said Señora Lopez.

"Daniel was a special man," said Señora Lopez. "His love for you and your brothers and sisters never faded. He loved and honored your mother with such deep devotion. Your father was never the same after she passed away and your family was separated.

"Thank you for letting me know," said Roberto.

His mind was reeling with the devastating news.

"I would like to send you money for his funeral."

"The government covers those expenses, so no need to send me anything," said Señora Lopez.

"Okay, I will send you some money . . . " said Roberto. "So you can buy additional food or anything you need once your government ration ends for the month."

"Thank you so much, Roberto," said Señora Lopez. "I would appreciate anything you could spare. The rations are never enough, and sometimes, I go hungry."

"I will send it to you," said Roberto. "Thank you again for letting me know about my father. Goodbye."

Roberto's father had always been his hero. During the last twelve years, although they had been separated, Roberto spoke with him monthly. He had always held out hope that he would see his father again one day, and now, his dreams of reuniting with him were crushed.

Lolita embraced Roberto as he hung up the phone. She knew the terrible pain of losing your father. They stood there for a moment as Roberto tried to make sense of his terrible loss—he couldn't. Roberto grieved for lost time with his beloved father and for the future they would never have.

★

Emilio's and Ana's life in New Jersey during the winter months was nothing like they had experienced before. The temperatures regularly dipped below freezing and the big snowfalls would keep Ana and the girls in the apartment for days at a time. The snow, icy temperatures, and wind were a brutal combination. They had only one car, so Ana had to wait for Emilio to come home before she could go out and pick up groceries, diapers, and anything else they needed.

Roberto continued to send them money each month. Every morning, Ana ticked the days off a white wall calendar in the kitchen until Emilio would take the exam. Finally, at the end of February 1980, Emilio sat for the exam and passed it on his first try. They were elated—he would now be able to apply for a residency away from the cold weather of the northeastern United States. They also hoped to rent a place with more room for their family.

Within a few weeks, Emilio was accepted into the three-year family practice residency program at Gadsden Baptist Hospital in Gadsden, Alabama. He and Ana found a cute, white two-bedroom house that had been built in the 1940s to call home. It was on a tree-lined street in a neighborhood only minutes from the hospital. There was a fenced-in yard for the girls to play, and at last, Ana could feel settled long enough to set up a home and make it their own.

The girls loved the house and the backyard but still preferred to sleep in their parents' bed if they could get away with it. Emilio loved his girls, but he had to rest, and they needed to learn to sleep in their own beds. He came up with a sweet little song with a catchy tune and lyrics that encouraged the girls to sleep in their own beds.

The girls loved to hear him sing and his song made them feel comforted and loved. As soon as they would hear the song, they knew it was bedtime and learned to stay in their beds like big girls.

Papi tiene tres niñas muy linda	*Papi* has three beautiful girls
Que duermen solas en sus camitas	That sleep alone in their little beds
Quieren mucho a Mami y a Papi	They love *Mami* and *Papi* a lot
Y le dan mucha felicidad	And they give them lots of joy
Ta ta ta…	Ta ta ta…

Emilio and Ana were so proud of the girls. They were growing up and they loved watching their personalities shine through.

The family had wonderful neighbors, like Mr. and Mrs. Bobo. They were grandparents and loved to visit with Ana and Emilio, occasionally bringing the girls small gifts and candy.

Emilio would work at the hospital during the week, and on Friday afternoon, after he finished his shift, he would drive close to an hour and a half to work in an emergency room at a small hospital in Rockmart, Georgia for the weekend. Emilio was exhausted by Sunday evening when he made the drive back home. After a few hours of sleep, Emilio would return to his residency at the hospital at 6 a.m. the following day.

This was the first time since he began his medical studies in the United States that he was able to make a living from his medical career. He and Ana celebrated this major milestone—they no longer needed Lolita and Roberto to send them money. Emilio was finally at a place where he could begin to pay Lolita and Roberto back for all the money they had loaned him and his family throughout the years. Emilio calculated the interest based on the current rates and added it to each payment. He felt like he was one step closer to achieving his dreams.

Early spring in Atlanta was delightful—warmer weather, more sunshine as the days grew longer, beautiful dogwood trees in bloom, and the outdoor activities with friends—they were all back.

It was also only a few weeks before a layer of yellow pollen covered everything in sight and the nonstop sneezing started.

"Ahchoo! Ahchoo!" sneezed Lolita as she walked into the service station.

"*Salud*—God bless you," said Roberto. "The pollen seems high today. My eyes are itchy, and I've been sneezing too."

"Thank you," said Lolita. "Yes, I saw the news this morning on Channel 2 before I dropped the children off at school, and the weatherman said that the pollen was going to be very high today."

"That explains it," said Roberto with an eye roll.

"I grabbed a bite for us," said Lolita. "Your favorite—Burger King."

"Thank you, *mi amor*," said Roberto.

"I'll meet you in the office so we can sit down for a quick lunch and you can give me any last-minute updates before I run payroll this afternoon," said Lolita. "I will also go through the mail and run accounts payable."

"That sounds good," said Roberto as he headed to the restroom to wash his hands before sitting down to eat with Lolita.

Lolita stayed in the office after lunch to get her work done, while Roberto went back to the service bays. He needed to make sure the mechanics were staying on task as the shop was busy, and they had several customers waiting on their repairs.

Lolita opened the second drawer on the left side of the brown wooden desk and eyed the stack of mail piled on top of the company checkbook. She had not been there since last week, so she was prepared to tackle it today.

She noticed an envelope from Union Oil with the distinctive navy blue and orange logo in the top left corner. She was curious to see what the letter contained.

Dear Roberto,

Thank you for being a valued part of the Union Oil Company. We appreciate the effort that our General Managers invest into the success of our organization and are excited to present a new contest to recognize our top performers. The contest will reward the GMs with the most tire sales from June 1st until June 30th. The grand prize is set at $10,000 in cash for our first-place winner! We will award a cash prize of $5,000 for the second-place winner and the third-place finisher will receive $3,000 in cash. We will also have many smaller prizes to award the top one hundred GMs. Please plan for this period to have a high volume of tire orders. More importantly, make sure you share your excitement about the great deals we will be offering when speaking with your customers. We can't wait to reward you for your great work.

Sincerely,
Sidney K. Jones
Vice President, Global Sales

Lolita reread the letter. Their service station already had a high volume of tire sales, and this contest made her very excited, thinking of all the things they could do with the $10,000 grand prize. Before she started spending the money they hadn't won yet, she took the letter and ran to find Roberto.

"Roberto," Lolita called out as she walked toward the front counter. "Roberto."

He didn't answer, so she glanced outside to see if he was at the gas pumps. She saw Steve, their part-time employee, helping an elderly woman but no sign of Roberto. She kept walking out to the service area, and near the tall garage doors, Roberto was explaining to a customer the work that his car needed. Lolita didn't want to interrupt him, so she waited until he finished. As she walked up to speak with him, she extended her hand and gave him the letter.

"Take a look at this," said Lolita with excitement in her voice. "Union Oil is having a contest to see which location sells the most tires during the month of June, and the prizes are fantastic."

Roberto took his time to read the letter, and when he looked up, he had a smile on his face. He knew he and his team could potentially win the grand prize. And if not the grand prize, one of the two other cash prizes. He would have to beat out several hundred other Union Oil locations around the country, but he was confident he and Lolita could do this.

"This is fantastic," said Roberto. "We have to find a way to get more customers in the door to increase our already great tire sales."

"We need to think about how we can best market this promotion. We have a few weeks before we have to start planning something to bring the traffic into the shop."

"Yes, let's think about this and come up with something outstanding that will help us earn the first-place prize," said Lolita.

During the next few weeks, Roberto and Lolita put together a plan to have a big tire sale event on June 7, 1981, the first Saturday of the month. They decided to start the event at 8 a.m. and go until 6 p.m. Now that these details were set, it was time to start planning the event.

★

Roberto and Lolita liked to stay up each night and watch the late news at 11. They were loyal to Channel 2 Action News and had been watching the newscast since they arrived in Atlanta. It kept them informed and helped them learn English. They were shocked as they watched the lead story.

It was about Cuba.

Amid the growing discontent over the even further degraded economy in Cuba, Castro had announced the day before that anyone who wanted to leave the island for the United States could leave. Immediately, people began creating makeshift boats using boards from their houses, inner tubes tied together with twine, and anything else they thought might allow them to make the ninety-mile trip to Florida.

No one was sure they would make it through the shark-infested waters, but they were desperate to finally be free of the Cuban government's tyranny. Tens of thousands flocked to the Port of Mariel to begin their perilous journey. The first of the immigrants began arriving on the Florida shores today. Lolita and Roberto were dumbfounded as they watched thousands of Cubans launching out to sea in the hopes of making it to freedom. The ramshackle boats were loaded down—some with as many as twenty-seven people aboard. Hundreds of lives were lost as many of the boats were not seaworthy and failed. People were swallowed up by the sea.

The Cuban government was throwing away its people. Castro and his criminal regime cleared mental health facilities and prisons and offered them a one-way ticket out of Cuba. Everyone gathered at the port in the search for a better life. Roberto and Lolita could see the desperation on the faces of the men, women, and children as they stepped out of the waters onto U.S. soil. They were both overtaken by emotion seeing fellow Cubans arriving in Florida. Between April and October of 1980, 125,000 people would leave Cuba and eventually reach the United States. This event would come to be known as the Mariel boatlift.

A family friend called Lolita the very next day to let her and Roberto know that Angela's sister Elsa, her husband Max, their adult son Teodoro, his wife Juanita, and their two small children, Alina and Esteban, had left Cuba earlier that morning on an overloaded raft filled with neighbors and friends. As soon as they received the call, Lolita and Roberto began packing everything and planning their trip to Miami to hopefully meet them when they arrived.

They set out the next morning, making the twelve-hour drive, not really knowing if and where they would find the family. Once in

Miami, they heard that all the refugee families were being taken to the Orange Bowl, a large stadium with tremendous capacity to process the immigrants. Lolita and Roberto made their way there and volunteered, helping process the immigrants in the hopes of finding Angela's sister and her family. It took the family a full day and a half to reach Florida. They arrived terribly dehydrated with scorched skin and blistered lips.

After three days, Teodoro called Lolita and Roberto's home to let them know that he and his family had arrived in the U.S. safely. When Angela was almost to the phone, she fell and broke her leg. As she lay on the floor in immense pain, she asked Cristina to bring the phone close to where she had fallen on the floor and spoke with Teodoro. He told her he was at a resettlement camp at a military base. They had been moved to Fort Chaffee, Arkansas.

Angela had Cristina hang up the phone and asked her to call a neighbor for help. The man next door quickly ran over and called an ambulance. While they were waiting for the ambulance, Lolita called to see if she had heard anything. Angela told her about Teodoro's call and about her fall. Lolita and Roberto were relieved to hear the family was safe but were very worried about Angela. The ambulance arrived and took Angela to Georgia Baptist Hospital. She was admitted and had surgery the next day.

Lolita and Roberto jumped in the car and drove the twelve hours back home, and after sleeping there one night and gathering clean clothes and supplies, they took off driving to Arkansas with just a map. The trip took them eight hours.

There were tens of thousands of people walking around. Lolita and Roberto had no way to find them. They walked around for less than thirty minutes when Lolita saw a man with a small child on his hip and walking with a slight limp. She recognized Teodoro and yelled out his name. They reunited and it seemed like a miracle to find him on this property with hundreds and hundreds of acres. The rest of the family members had agreed to meet Teodoro in the area and within a few minutes, the whole family was together again.

Lolita and Roberto filled out the papers to sponsor them. They left to go back home and waited until the government had processed their paperwork. Teodoro and his family were desperate and called Lolita every single day. There was nothing she could do to get them out. Finally, all of their paperwork was approved, and the government put them on a plane to Atlanta. Lolita and Roberto went to welcome them at the airport. They were the first Cuban family to leave the military base in Arkansas and move to Georgia. The *Atlanta Journal-Constitution* published a story about their harrowing journey from Cuba to Atlanta.

Teodoro and his family moved in with Lolita and Roberto when they arrived in Atlanta. After a month, Lolita and Roberto set the family up with an apartment, furnishings, clothes, and food, using their own money as well as donations from their church. Lolita and Roberto gave them an older used car, a green station wagon, to get around. They were very appreciative and worked hard to start building a new life. They were able to begin paying back Lolita and Roberto after just a few months.

Teodoro and Juanita were thankful to be raising their family in the freedom of the United States. Within a few years, they learned they would be having their third baby—another little girl to love. They named her Patricia. She had fair skin, light brown hair, and big brown eyes. She was precious. Alina and Esteban were the best big brother and sister. They loved taking care of her and were a tremendous help to Juanita. Their family was complete.

When Lolita and Roberto had gotten Teodoro and his family settled, Lolita started planning for the big tire sale. She had a local print shop design and print flyers for Steve to distribute within a three-mile radius the week before the big event. She ordered orange and navy triangle pennant flags to hang from the top of the building, and Roberto attached them with a stake to the ground at the front of the property. Lolita placed an order for bright orange polo shirts, with big navy letters reading "TIRE SALE" on the back, which each of the employees wore.

She also found a small red Coca-Cola trailer with a little prep area inside and windows to serve customers. Cristina, Isabela, and Alex wore the branded shirts and worked inside the trailer most of the day. It was a hot day with temperatures in the mid-nineties. The children didn't care. They gave away hot dogs and Cokes to anyone who stopped in. Roberto hired a photographer to document the day because, even if they didn't win, he wanted something to remind them of the tremendous event they pulled together and the energy everyone on the team put into making it a great day.

The total investment for this event came to $650. More than two hundred people stopped in, and the tire sales for the day totaled more than their highest monthly sales historically. Roberto and Lolita were ecstatic and couldn't wait to see the final numbers for the entire month of June. The winners would be announced on August 1. After an incredible day and surpassing their previous record, they were all ready to get something to eat, shower, and get in bed early.

"Can we please go to Shakey's Pizza for dinner?" Isabela asked her mom. "*Please?*"

"I'll check with your dad, but I think it will be okay because I am too tired to cook," said Lolita.

When they got into the car a few minutes later, Roberto agreed that Isabela had a good idea. They ordered two large pizzas, pepperoni and Hawaiian, and enjoyed their dinner. Soon, they were ready to go home.

The children were exhausted, and after Angela helped them with a quick bath, they slipped into their pajamas and went off to sleep.

★

Summer arrived and the kids were busy enjoying a vacation to the beach, church camps, picnics, swimming lessons, and late nights catching lightning bugs in Mason jars. The summer flew by and Lolita and Roberto were anxiously awaiting news if they had won the top prize for the Union Oil Tire Contest. Finally, the day arrived. The mailman made a special trip inside the shop to deliver a certified letter.

Lolita and Roberto nervously opened the envelope and were ecstatic when they read the news. They had won the contest and the $10,000 top prize for sales. The letter congratulated them on their incredible job—they far surpassed the second-place winner. It informed them they would be receiving a check and a marble plaque within the week. They couldn't believe it. They had all worked so hard and it had paid off. They were excited to share the news with their employees, friends, and patrons of the shop who had made the award possible.

The following spring of 1982, Lolita and Roberto began planning a new custom-built home in the Smoke Rise area of Atlanta. Once again, Lolita chose the most beautiful fixtures and appliances. She began selecting tasteful and modern furnishings for the new home. It would be two stories with a soaring foyer and grand staircase. No detail was spared.

Lolita and Roberto made up for years of scarcity with lavish homes and vacations. This home would cost them $250,000. Lolita and Roberto's work ethic and ambition were unmatched. They knew what it felt like not to be able to build a life of their choosing, so they were more determined than even their American counterparts to succeed.

While the house was being built, they purchased a brand new 1982 Brown Cadillac Sedan DeVille and took Cristina, Isabela, and Alex on a three-week summer vacation to Canada. Again, no expense was spared—they stayed in the most upscale hotels and resorts, ate at wonderful restaurants, and visited all of the greatest tourist attractions from Toronto to Ottawa to Montreal to Quebec City.

Some of the highlights included a visit to Niagara Falls with a cruise on the Maid of the Mist to the base of the falls, a ride to the top of the CN Tower complete with a full sit-down lunch, a stay at the Château Frontenac, overlooking the St. Lawrence River, and a coast down the Rideau Canal. Lolita and Roberto treated the children to a full shopping spree at one of the most high-end shopping malls in

Toronto. The girls chose trendy Izod Lacoste clothing items and Alex chose some toys, including a red double-decker self-propelled bus. He was so excited. Everywhere they went Alex would pull back the bus and let it fly, knocking over glasses and careening into dishes while the family was trying to enjoy lunch. Roberto and Lolita regretted this purchase and finally, Roberto couldn't take it any longer and grabbed the bus. With one crack, he broke it in two. Alex was crushed and couldn't contain his tears as Cristina and Isabela snickered under their breath.

After an amazing vacation, it was time to head back home to Atlanta. After two days of travel, it was late when the family arrived home. They went straight to bed, waiting to unpack the next day. They all slept in late and enjoyed a slow morning unpacking and looking over their souvenirs. Lolita found a small pouch of cash in Alex's bag. She began counting it and it added up to several hundred dollars. She was in shock. She yelled out for Roberto and Alex.

"What is this . . . Alex, where did you get all of this money?" implored Lolita.

"You and Daddy left money on the tables after we ate and I wanted to be sure you didn't forget about it," cried Alex.

Lolita and Roberto looked at one another in horror. They were realizing that every single place they dined had been left without a tip. They were embarrassed and never imagined that at eight years old, Alex would be able to get away with this for the entire trip.

"This is money for the men and women who took care of us at all those fancy restaurants," said Roberto.

Alex broke down in tears.

"I didn't know. You just left it behind, and I thought I was helping," wailed Alex.

"Thank you for being so thoughtful," reassured Lolita, as she reached down and hugged him. We are not upset with you; we are just sad that the wonderful people that helped us didn't receive their tips."

"Can we mail it to them?" asked Alex.

"No, but just remember from now on that when you visit a restaurant, you always want to thank the servers for their good service with a nice tip," said Lolita.

Alex never forgot this lesson.

That fall, the children went back to school and builders were putting the finishing touches on the new house. They were preparing it for the family to move in just before the Christmas holidays. As they were packing boxes and getting ready to move, Lolita received a phone call from Roberto's little sister Elisa in Cuba. She called to ask Roberto to sponsor her, her husband Bernardo, and their two children Marta and Jorge.

The conditions in Cuba had further deteriorated since the Mariel boatlift a few years earlier. They were desperate to get out of Cuba. Roberto and Lolita agreed to sponsor them, and they began the necessary paperwork. Within a few months, Elisa and her family arrived in Atlanta. Roberto and Lolita did the same they had done with Teodoro and his family. After living with them for a month, Lolita and Roberto helped them finance their own apartment and furnishings. They were incredibly grateful and made it a priority to start paying them back as soon as possible.

★

The next few years were filled with the everyday things of American life. Cristina kept playing piano, Isabela was a cheerleader, and Alex took karate lessons.

The family continued to evolve into American culture. They had been in the United States for only fourteen years, but they were fitting right in and making a place for themselves in their community. They took advantage of every opportunity they would have never had under the Cuban communist government. All they needed was the opportunity to thrive, and they persevered by working incredibly hard, sacrificing, and staying determined to make their dreams come true.

The day finally came when Emilio was able to open his own medical practice, making his dream of becoming a doctor a reality. It was in Atalla, Alabama, but it wasn't like any other medical practice in Alabama. Every detail of the office was incredibly beautiful and planned by a team of highly regarded professional decorators. The walls displayed large framed prints of bald eagles. The bald eagle represented everything he held dear—courage, strength, bravery, perseverance, resolve, and determination. Emilio's hard work paid off and his practice soon began to flourish.

He was a well-respected man and physician and people would come from all over to be under his care. Patients would bring baked goods, produce from their farms, handwritten poems, and cross-stitched artwork. One afternoon, Emilio received a call that took him by total surprise. It was Dr. Moore, the physician who had kicked the cot he was sleeping on while he was a lab technician at Georgia Baptist Hospital. Emilio had never forgotten this moment of humiliation.

Dr. Moore carried on in conversation without addressing how he had treated Emilio. He acted as if nothing had ever happened. Being the gentleman he was, Emilio graciously let bygones be bygones and invited him to visit his new practice. Dr. Moore arrived and was taken aback by Emilio's new office. He couldn't believe how far he had come and what a success he had made of himself.

As he was preparing to leave, Dr. Moore asked if Emilio might have a need for another physician in his thriving practice. Emilio was again gracious and replied that he didn't have any openings at the time but would keep him in mind for the future as the practice grew.

He had indeed come a long way from that young man sleeping on a cot in the back of the lab. In only a few short years, his practice had grown beyond his expectations and he and Ana began looking for a new home. They found a beautiful colonial-style house situated on a large lot by the Gadsden Country Club. It had a circular driveway and tall white columns across the large front porch. They wanted to add something for the young girls to enjoy, so they had a custom pool built, complete with a waterslide and hot tub, in the picturesque backyard. It was perfect.

CHAPTER TWENTY-FOUR

ATLANTA, GEORGIA

1983 — 1992

Cristina soon met the man of her dreams while attending church camp. It was the summer of 1983, and she knew she would marry Andrés as soon as she saw him. He was tall with dark brown hair and eyes. He was also from a Cuban family and was a few years older. It took a while for Andrés to realize his feelings for Cristina were more than just friendly, and they began dating the following summer after attending a mutual friend's wedding. Roberto and Lolita loved Andrés and welcomed him into the family from the very start of their relationship. Roberto and Lolita surprised Cristina for her sixteenth birthday with a new black Chevy Camaro Z28. Cristina and Andrés would spend hours driving around with the T-tops off and listening to Van Halen, Whitney Houston, Phil Collins, Chicago, Sting, Madonna, and so many other unmatched bands of the 1980s.

After a year of getting to know each other, Andrés proposed to Cristina on Christmas Eve. Soon thereafter, Cristina began dreaming about her big day. Their families were thrilled. Although it seemed much too soon to all their American friends, it was Cuban tradition for couples to marry at a young age.

In the spring of 1985, Cristina graduated from high school and began planning the details of her and Andrés's wedding. It would be magical. They set the date for April of 1986. A few months before the wedding, Cristina and Andrés bought their first home. It was a new two-story house with light gray siding and a navy-blue front door on a quiet cul-de-sac. It was the perfect first home for them, and Cristina enjoyed filling it with beautiful furnishings and decorations in shades of blue, gray, and blush, creating a relaxing and warm environment.

Cristina and Andrés's big day finally arrived. It was a gorgeous spring day to celebrate the wedding of the year for the Hispanic community in Atlanta. Cristina's gown was custom-made with a sweetheart neckline and fitted bodice. Imported lace from Spain covered the sleeves and A-line satin skirt. She wore a pearl necklace that Angela had given her for this special day, and her hair and makeup were impeccable. She was a stunning bride.

The nine bridesmaids were dressed in mauve gowns with a ruched waistline. Roberto beamed with pride as he walked Cristina down the aisle. They were surrounded by all their friends and family, who had embraced them when they came to America with nothing. He and Lolita were both overjoyed. They never could have envisioned this day back when they were holding little Cristina on their flight out of Cuba. The ceremony was beautiful. After exchanging vows and sharing their first kiss as husband and wife, they walked down the aisle to Jeremiah Clarke's "Prince of Denmark March," also known as "Trumpet Voluntary." The ceremony was followed by a huge reception with a sit-down dinner for three hundred people. Again, Lolita and Roberto spared no expense for their little girl. There was a parquet dance floor, and a DJ spun tunes late into the night. The most amazing day of Cristina's and Andrés's lives was followed by a ten-day honeymoon in Honolulu on the island of Oahu, in Hawaii.

Because they were both young and had never traveled far away from their families, it was an exciting time for them. They were in awe of the spectacular scenery around every bend on the island—the views of the sparkling blue ocean, the lush green trees and mountains, and the fields of pineapples as far as the eye could see were incredible. Each day was filled with new adventures—a visit to the Polynesian Cultural Center, a breathtaking drive to Diamond Head Crater, a catamaran cruise to the Pearl Harbor Memorial, and sunny days sipping Blue Hawaii cocktails on Waikiki Beach. Their honeymoon had exceeded all of their expectations, but it was finally time to go home.

Cristina squeezed all of the souvenirs they had bought into their suitcases and they waited for a taxi to take them to the airport. They checked their luggage then waited at the gate to board a Delta Airlines jet for the ten-hour flight back to Atlanta.

Lolita, Roberto, Isabela, and Alex were waiting to pick them up at Atlanta's Hartsfield International Airport. As soon as Cristina saw her family, she waved and smiled and ran to greet them. Andrés followed her. It warmed Lolita and Roberto's heart to see their girl so happy. On the drive home, Cristina and Andrés told stories of all the interesting and fun things they had seen and done.

"It was a tropical paradise," said Cristina. "The natural beauty was overwhelming."

"We rented a red convertible mustang and drove all over the island," said Andrés.

"We loved being there every single day," said Cristina. "The food was wonderful, and everyone was so nice."

"Sounds like you guys had an amazing honeymoon," said Lolita.

"We did," said Cristina as she smiled and looked at Andrés. "It was an awesome trip."

"Yes, it was beyond anything I could have imagined," said Andrés.

Roberto and Lolita pulled into the driveway of Cristina and Andrés's new house and helped them unload their bags. As Cristina was showing Lolita some of the souvenirs, Roberto invited Andrés to the living room.

"There's something I'd like to share with you," said Roberto.

"Sure, what's going on?" asked Andrés.

"Well, I've been in conversations with Union Oil about purchasing the property where the service station is now," said Roberto. "I've also spoken to our CPA and to our business advisor. They both feel the deal is structured fairly. It will give us the opportunity to expand the service areas, which is where we generate the most revenue."

"That is really great news, Roberto," said Andrés. "I am happy to see the success you've had so far—I think this will be a great move forward."

"Thank you, Andrés," said Roberto. "I feel like this is a great opportunity that I can't pass up. That is why I wanted to speak with you. I know you are getting ready to start working on your MBA, but I could sure use your skills to help us grow to the next level. I know you are on the management fast-track with Davidson's, but you can help me run the business and learn how to be an entrepreneur."

"Wow," said Andrés with a look of surprise. "Thank you so much for asking me to join the company. I would like to speak with Cristina about this. Can I let you know in the next few days?"

"Yes, of course," said Roberto. "I will compensate you more than fairly and would love for you to come on board as soon as possible."

"Thank you again," said Andrés. "I promise to let you know very soon."

They joined Lolita and Cristina as the women were talking about the incredible days Cristina and Andrés had spent in Hawaii.

"I know you both must be tired from the long flight. We are going to head home so you can get some rest," said Lolita.

"Thank you for picking us up," said Cristina.

"Yes, we really appreciate it," said Andrés.

They hugged goodbye and Roberto and Lolita were on their way. Roberto told Lolita that he talked with Andrés about coming to work with him at the shop as they had discussed earlier.

"What did he say?" asked Lolita.

"He wants to speak with Cristina and will let us know in the next few days.

"I can understand that," said Lolita.

Two days passed before Roberto heard back from Andrés. Roberto wasn't sure if this was something Andrés wanted, but he knew it would be good for the business to have someone he could trust in a key role.

"Roberto, Cristina and I have considered your offer and I would like to accept it," said Andrés. "I am excited about the potential of what we can build together."

"That is wonderful news, Andrés," said Roberto. "When do you go back to work at Davidson's?"

"I will be back at work on Monday and will turn in my notice then," said Andrés. "I would like to work out my two weeks there, so I don't leave them in a bad position."

"Of course," said Roberto. "It is what I would expect from you."

"Thank you," said Andrés. "I will be able to start in two Mondays. I am really looking forward to it."

"Yes, Andrés," said Roberto. "I am looking forward to it as well."

The next few months were filled with all of the preparations to close the deal with Union Oil. Roberto and Lolita had secured a loan for $100,000 for the purchase of the property. They began planning to tear down the service station and remove the gasoline pumps and tanks. In its place, they would build a brand-new service center. The Small Business Administration loaned them $200,000 for the new construction.

Lolita and Roberto had already custom built and designed two homes, so they decided they wanted to do the same for the new structure. It would be a two-story, fourteen thousand-square-foot building with eleven service bays. The showroom and waiting area would be on the lower level, adjacent to the work areas, and the offices would take up the top floor.

In late June, the property was cleared of the existing building. They moved two of the car lifts to where the gasoline pumps had previously stood and continued working to maintain sales the best they could. When Lolita and Roberto broke ground for the new building, it was a momentous occasion. They never imagined when they arrived in the United States eighteen years earlier how their lives would change for the better.

Within the first week, the contractor they had hired and that had been verified by the bank withdrew the first $50,000 to begin construction. Lolita and Roberto waited for him on the morning they had agreed to start the project. When he didn't show up, they thought something may have happened, and that he would have an explanation for them. They dialed his number throughout the day but there was no answer. The later it became, the more concerned they grew.

"You don't think this man is going to run off and not do the work we've hired him for, do you?" asked Lolita.

"I am hoping he has just had an emergency, but I am worried," said Roberto. "This is very unprofessional."

The next day, and the next few days, they couldn't get in touch with him and decided to contact the police. When they explained the situation to the officer, he suggested they file a police report.

Another few days passed, and the project was at a standstill. Lolita and Roberto were discussing their options when the phone rang.

"Hello," said Roberto as he picked up the receiver.

"Hello, this is Officer Williams with the DeKalb County Police Department. I wanted to give you an update on the report you filed last week. The company you contracted has numerous claims against them and the owner has twenty-one lawsuits pending," said the officer.

"How is that possible?" asked Roberto. "The bank verified him and his company before we signed the contract with them."

"I don't know how they could have verified him, as he's had lawsuits filed against him with the earliest being more than five years ago. We will issue an arrest warrant, but as far as the money he took, you'll need to go back to the bank and see if they can help you since they verified him."

"Thank you, officer," said Roberto.

Roberto was stunned. He couldn't believe what he had just heard. He knew at that moment that he had lost the $50,000. After he told Lolita, she was in tears. They had worked so hard for this day and now their future was uncertain—but giving up wasn't an option. They discussed what they should do next.

They went to the bank to ask them for the $50,000 that had been stolen by the contractor the bank had approved. The bank manager was very apologetic but did not accept any responsibility. After much discussion, the only option he offered Roberto and Lolita was to loan them another $50,000. Their loan would now come to $250,000. This was a huge financial blow, but one they knew they would overcome. Lolita and Roberto went directly to the Small Business Administration for recommendations of reputable contractors and received a few names. After speaking with each of them, they hired one they felt comfortable with.

The construction went as planned, and on November 16, 1986, Lolita, Roberto, and Andrés, along with three service technicians, opened the doors to European Specialists of Atlanta. They were thrilled. After they had gone through so much, their beautiful new facility was a reality. The business specialized in foreign cars—Volvo, Mercedes, BMW, and others. They quickly grew their clientele and the business took off. They were hiring new service technicians every few weeks until all eleven bays were filled. The business continued to grow and thrive. Lolita and Roberto were able to double up on payments some months in order to pay down the balance of their loans.

Their business was growing at such a rapid pace that Lolita and Roberto asked Cristina to come on board to help with the bookkeeping and advertising. She loved working with her dad, he paid her quite well, and her schedule was very flexible.

Andrés was doing well in his MBA program and began encouraging Cristina to think about applying to Georgia State University to work toward an undergraduate degree. After some thought, Cristina enrolled in the college of education to become a kindergarten teacher. She soon learned this was not a good fit for her. Andrés suggested she explore business, and Cristina declared an accounting major, like her father. Cristina began to see that her small private school education hadn't prepared her for college-level math courses. She struggled in her first few semesters with poor grades and was eventually placed on academic probation. Cristina was devastated but took the time to think about the future and what she really would like to study when she returned to school. In the meantime, she threw herself into continuing to grow the business. Lolita and Roberto saw how effective Cristina and Andrés were at running the business and were very proud of them. Lolita and Roberto had hopes and dreams of beginning to travel the world now that their family and business were falling into place.

Lolita and Roberto soon began to plan a three-week vacation around Europe in the spring of 1987. The family traveled together to many wonderful places throughout France, Germany, and Spain. In France, they visited Napoleon's tomb and the Eiffel Tower in Paris. They ate croissants in sidewalk cafes and took in the culture of the French people. They enjoyed dinner at Maxim's, a premier French restaurant in Paris since 1893. Maxim's was a landmark French eatery known throughout the world for its refined French classics in an art nouveau setting. They dined on an eight-course menu boasting caviar, mixed soups and fine salads, seafood, and prime beef entrees, and delectable French pastries. They capped off each course with a tasting of fine champagnes from the top vineyards in the Champagne region. It was the most unforgettable meal, totaling $600. Lolita and Roberto wouldn't typically splurge on a meal like this, but they knew it was a once-in-a-lifetime opportunity to enjoy such amazing local cuisine as a family.

In Germany, the family arrived in Munich and were met by a limousine driver holding a sign with their last name. The driver loaded their bags and made his way onto the notorious Autobahn. Lolita thought this would be the end of her life and she would never see Cristina and Andrés again. The driver sustained speeds of around 150 miles per hour for the entire trip to the hotel. They were all clutching one another and trying not to be sick.

"We are going so fast," said Lolita. "Are there a lot of accidents here?"

"There are rarely accidents here. But when they do happen, they are always fatal," said the driver. "No one survives."

Lolita was never so glad to reach a destination safely. The children were wide-eyed, and Roberto looked green in the face.

They visited top tourist attractions all throughout Germany including the Black Forest, one of the most visited mountain ranges in all of Europe. The densely forested region is filled with tiny villages, thermal baths, mountains and pastures, lakes, waterfalls, and breathtaking views. The town squares welcomed tourists with museums, cafes serving black coffee drinks, tart cherry pastries, and fine German chocolates. It was a favorite among the amazing destinations they visited throughout Europe.

In Spain, they visited Madrid. This city held so many special memories for Lolita and Roberto. Arriving there flooded their minds with so many emotions as they recalled their time there under such different circumstances. Lolita especially recalled the night they were to celebrate her twenty-third birthday in a special restaurant in the city center. They had spent the little money they had at the thrift shop buying outfits for the big night. They arrived downtown and soon realized they wouldn't have enough money to eat dinner. It was a heartbreaking moment for both of them. They made their way back home with dreams of a better future.

Now here they were—nearly twenty years later—and so much had changed. They were totally different people, now with three children, a beautiful home, and a thriving business. Instead of a hostel, they had a spacious and luxurious room at a five-star hotel. Lolita had always held the dream that she would one day return and be able to shop to her heart's content at *El Corte Inglés* in Madrid. So many years ago, she and Angela stood inside the store surrounded by lovely things and no way to purchase anything. She was devastated then. This time she arrived with a list of items to purchase. She bought everything from handmade fine linens for the dining room table, cashmere scarves, buttery soft Spanish leather pumps in nude and black, makeup items from the best cosmetic houses in Europe, and fine gold and silver jewelry adorned with beautiful sapphires and diamonds. She left the store with arms full of bags and a full heart. Roberto was so happy to see her enjoying what he could not give her eighteen years ago.

After three weeks, the family returned home to Atlanta. Andrés had kept the business going while they were away. Roberto was so pleased to have someone he could trust. He was impressed to find that sales had increased under Andrés's management. Aside from continuing to build the business, the family kept up with all their many activities, including school, karate, cheerleading and church events, and functions. Angela had recently been diagnosed with type 2 diabetes and Lolita had begun spending more time caring for her. Her health had begun to decline after the diagnosis. Diabetes compounded other health issues, and she was also dealing with the symptoms of congestive heart failure. She was slowing down, rarely spending time at her sewing machine as she had in years past.

Emilio was busy in Alabama building his medical practice but he, Ana and the children visited Lolita and Roberto whenever they had an opportunity. They celebrated Christmas of 1987 together as a family. It was a tradition they cherished, and the children, who were now all teenagers, loved spending the holidays with their cousins.

At the beginning of the next year, Cristina returned to school. This time, she chose a major aligned with what she truly loved. She enrolled in the Department of Communications with the hopes of pursuing a journalism degree. This time around she excelled in her studies, making straight As.

That spring, Isabela graduated with the class of 1988 from Mountainside Christian High School. She knew she wanted to study home economics and had fallen in love with the Samford University campus in Birmingham, Alabama.

That fall Lolita and Roberto moved her into the Beeson Woods dorm where she quickly acclimated to college life. Now it would be just Alex at home. Angela continued to decline in health over the next few months, and Lolita and Roberto began feeling as though these would be their last holidays together as a family.

Cristina and Andrés had planned a weekend ski trip to Sugar Mountain in North Carolina just after the new year. It was the first time skiing for both of them, but they enjoyed this new sport and spent the evenings sipping hot chocolate by the fire pit. One morning, Andrés surprised Cristina with a sleigh ride through the snowy pastures behind the resort. It was a wintry scene from a vintage postcard, and Cristina could not have been happier.

When they returned home, Andrés went back to work, but Cristina was not feeling well. She thought perhaps she had a touch of the flu, so she decided to rest at home for a few days. Instead of feeling better, she started having intense nausea and suspected she may be pregnant. The following day, she was visiting Andrés's mother in the hospital after routine surgery and decided to stop by the lab with his sister, Lourdes, for a pregnancy test before heading home. In less than ten minutes they drew her labs and shortly thereafter gave her the results. The test confirmed it—she was pregnant. She and Lourdes couldn't contain their excitement. Andrés was over the moon when Cristina told him the news. The whole family was thrilled to be welcoming the first grandchild. Angela was spending time at Emilio and Ana's home and was happy to hear the news that she would soon have a great-grandbaby. She had a dream that Cristina would deliver a beautiful baby girl with a head full of dark curly hair.

Everyone was so happy for Cristina and Andrés, but Angela's health took a quick turn for the worse. Ana noticed Angela was lethargic and seemed confused. When Ana began to take her pulse, she noticed the extreme swelling in her legs, ankles, and feet. Ana was startled and quickly took Angela's pulse. Her heart rate was incredibly fast, which panicked Ana. She knew these symptoms signaled a very serious condition. Ana immediately dialed Emilio, who asked her to bring Angela to see him at the clinic right away. As soon as Emilio saw her and took her vitals, he called 911 for an ambulance to take her to Gadsden Memorial Hospital. He stepped into the ambulance with her with Ana following closely in her car. Angela was admitted and officially diagnosed with end-stage congestive heart failure. There was nothing they could do, other than drain the fluid from her lungs and keep her comfortable. In only a couple of days, Angela slipped into unconsciousness and never woke back up. She passed away on March 10, 1989. The family, devastated by the loss, would take a while to grieve her absence. The hope of a new baby helped as everyone began planning for the birth of Cristina and Andrés's baby in the fall.

Andrés was near completing his MBA program and was learning so much about the world of business. He was contributing business principles and best practices he had learned while in school. This led to continued growth and increased sales and profitability. In May, Andrés earned his MBA from the Robinson College of Business at Georgia State University and Cristina was so proud of him.

After working so hard, Andrés and Cristina decided to get away for a bit and visit Lolita and Roberto's beach condo in Florida. They had purchased it the year before. It was a fun place for the family to gather with room enough for everyone. It was beautifully decorated with a beachside theme. It was inviting and relaxing with pale yellows, blues, soft white, and traditional beach-inspired decor. Every evening after dinner, Andrés and Cristina took long walks along the beach.

Cristina's pregnancy progressed without any complications until one evening, a few weeks before her due date, she became extremely ill after attending a friend's wedding. She was up sick all night long and into the next day. She was weak, dehydrated, and exhausted. Andrés called the doctor and he told him to bring Cristina into Northside Hospital right away to be examined. Their best efforts weren't enough to stop the contractions brought on by food poisoning. The baby began showing signs of distress, and the doctor decided to perform an emergency C-section.

It all happened so quickly. The family all began praying, and the pastor came to sit with them as they awaited news. On October 15, 1989, before they knew it, Cristina and Andrés were parents to a tiny baby girl. She had beautiful light brown eyes and dark curly hair, just as Angela had dreamed. She only weighed six pounds and ten ounces, but she was perfectly healthy. They fell in love with her instantly. Once the nurse had cleaned her up and placed her on her mother's chest, Cristina gently kissed her tiny cheek and whispered, "I loved you before I met you." Cristina was overcome with emotion—this new baby had stolen her heart. It was such a special time for Cristina, Andrés, and their baby. They named her Alejandra Hope, after her uncle, Alex, and she was perfect.

The first Christmas with Alejandra was so special. She was only a few months old, but Cristina insisted on a picture with Santa at the local mall. Alejandra was not too happy to be in the lap of a strange bearded man, and she got so upset that she threw up all down her brand new little red Christmas dress. The pictures still turned out to be adorable and the whole family celebrated together with Roberto and Lolita buying the most gifts for Alejandra. They loved spoiling their first grandbaby and were happy when Alejandra started talking and began calling them Alita and Papa.

The following spring, in April of 1990, Emilio called Cristina to tell her he had a surprise for her and Isabela.

"I want you to plan to come visit Ana and me one day next week," said Emilio. "We have a surprise for you and Isabela."

"What? That is so exciting. Can you tell me what it is? Is it another little donut?" asked Cristina, giggling.

"No, it is not a donut, but I think you will like it even more," said Emilio with so much excitement in his voice.

"That sounds great," exclaimed Cristina. "I will talk with Isabela and let you know which day we can drive there."

"I can't wait to see you both," said Emilio.

"Me too," replied Cristina. "I am excited to see you, Ana, and the girls."

Emilio lived to surprise and delight everyone he loved. In appreciation for Lolita and Roberto's support and love for so many years, he gifted Cristina and Isabela full dress presidential gold Rolexes. He gave Alex a stainless and gold men's Datejust Rolex. These gifts were extravagant and expensive, but Emilio had achieved all of his dreams and could now afford them. Gifts were how he chose to express his deep gratitude for the sacrifices that Lolita and Roberto had made for close to a decade.

Cristina and Isabela were flabbergasted when they opened the navy-blue leather jewelry boxes with a tiny gold key that was topped with the Rolex crown. Inside the box was a beautiful, colorful silk scarf with jewel-tone designs and images of the watch throughout. There was a small lid that revealed a tan suede watch pillow. On top of the pillow sat the Rolex watch with twinkling diamonds set at each hour and a bezel with a ring of sparkling diamonds around the face of the watch. It was absolutely magnificent. The girls were overtaken with joy and Emilio was filled with pride to see their excitement. He had also purchased the same watch for Ana and each of his three girls. He wanted to shower them all with his love and affection. Cristina still has her watch and treasures it to this day.

After graduating from high school, Lily and Marisol joined Isabela at Samford University, and the three cousins loved spending time together as young adults. Alex was busy finishing high school and playing baseball. Lolita and Roberto, who would soon be empty nesters, began keeping a list of the places they would visit around the world.

★

Roberto and Alex had always shared a love of baseball. In October of 1991, the Atlanta Braves were in the World Series, so Roberto was doing his best to find tickets to surprise Alex. Due to the large auto part orders that Roberto's business placed each month, one of the suppliers called to offer him two tickets to game five of the World Series.

The game was amazing. Roberto and Alex enjoyed their time together, cheering on the Braves and snacking on their favorite ballpark treats, including hot dogs, nachos, and huge soft pretzels. The Braves won that night over the Minnesota Twins with a score of 14-5 and advanced to the next game of the series. The Braves lost the next two games of the series to the Twins, and the Twins took home the trophy. Roberto and Alex would always remember this night and for years wished they could recreate the magical experience they shared.

During Christmas break, Isabela and a few friends had made plans to celebrate the holiday season together with an afternoon of shopping, followed by a nice dinner. They found beautiful accessories, candles, and specialty items in cute boutiques as they strolled around the quaint downtown area of Roswell. The girls sipped on hot apple cider and enjoyed looking at the twinkling lights on the trees that lined the sidewalk. They talked and laughed and had a memorable afternoon. When it was time for dinner, they had all been wanting to try a trendy new pizzeria, Pie Bar. It served traditional wood-fired, baked crust pies as well as pies with interesting combinations, like gorgonzola and pear and fig and blue cheese. They ordered several pies to share and loved the unique toppings. The girls had a terrific evening. When it was time to leave, Isabela's best friend, Lori, didn't want the night to end.

"Would any of you like to get a drink at the bar next door before we head home?" she asked.

"I'm too tired," said one of the girls.

"Me too," chimed in another.

"How about you, Isabela?" asked Lori with a smile.

"Well, okay," said Isabela. "Just one."

The girls had all enjoyed a wonderful time, and after hugs and kisses, Isabela and Lori walked next door. The others left to go home.

Isabela and Lori found an open table and took a seat. They each ordered a glass of Belle Glos Pinot Noir and were catching up on some of the plans for the rest of the season when Isabela noticed a handsome man standing at the bar staring at her. She shyly looked down at the table and giggled.

"What is it?" asked Lori. "Why are you laughing?"

"That guy at the end of the bar was looking at me," said Isabela.

Lori looked to see who she was talking about, and yes, he was definitely looking at her. She noticed he wouldn't take his eyes off her.

"He's cute," said Lori.

"He is," said Isabela as she smiled at Lori and then glanced his way again before composing herself.

"Don't look now, Isabela," said Lori. "I think he's walking this way."

"Oh, wow," said Isabela smiling. She turned to look as he was approaching the table.

"Hi, my name is Preston. And I have to tell you, you are beautiful," he said.

"Thank you," said Isabela.

"Pardon me for interrupting," said Preston, "but do you mind if I get your number? I'd like to take you out sometime."

Isabela wasn't sure if she should give him her phone number. She didn't know him, but her first impression was that he seemed like a good guy.

"Sure, here you go," said Isabela, handing him a napkin with her number.

As he made his way back to the bar, the girls commented on Preston's beautiful green eyes, and Isabela was excited to see him again. A few days later, Preston called Isabela. They talked on the phone for hours. He asked her if she would like to go to dinner with him and she said yes. They made plans for the following weekend. One date led to another and then another. They loved being with each other and the following year, he proposed with a beautiful diamond engagement ring—which she gladly accepted.

★

Lolita and Roberto were out for their twenty-eighth wedding anniversary dinner with dear friends Laura and Alfredo when Roberto began sweating profusely. Alfredo was a physician and knew immediately something was very wrong. He attempted to take Roberto's pulse, but it was weak to the point of being almost undetectable. They all jumped in Alfredo's car and drove directly to Georgia Baptist Medical Center. Roberto was admitted through the Emergency Department so they could run additional tests. By the next morning, they had determined Roberto would need quadruple bypass surgery. They were all shocked. He was only fifty-three years old and was in relatively good health. This was a daunting diagnosis and would be a difficult surgery. The doctors scheduled it for early the next morning. The whole family gathered together the evening before the surgery to spend time with him and pray that all would go well with the surgery. The operation lasted five hours. Afterward, the doctors came to speak with Lolita and the children and assured them that everything went well, and Roberto should have a complete recovery. Over the next few months, he went to rehab four times a week to gain strength and mobility and increase his endurance.

The following May, it was all the more sweet to see Alex graduate from Parkland High School. They all cheered as Alex walked across the stage as part of the class of 1992, to receive his diploma. His plans were to attend Samford University in the fall.

It was an amazing feeling for Lolita and Roberto to have all three of their children grown and graduated from high school, starting their lives as young adults. The years had been kind to them, and they looked forward to all that was in store for them in the years to come.

Lily was invited to intern at the George H.W. Bush White House and would be starting in the fall. She would take a year off from Samford and return after the conclusion of the internship. She loved politics, and the White House was the perfect experience for her to learn the ins and outs of government. Her role was in the Office of Public Liaison working with African-American, small business, and women's issues. She returned calls, managed schedules, drafted letters, and other administrative tasks. She enjoyed every bit of the work and living in D.C.

Emilio and Ana were also incredibly proud of Lily, Marisol, and Camila. They were all growing into smart, confident, well-educated young ladies who would continue to make the family so proud of how far they had come.

CHAPTER TWENTY-FIVE

ATLANTA, GEORGIA
AND MIAMI, FLORIDA
1993

Roberto had never forgotten his younger sister and always longed to know her. He had tried many times before to locate her to no avail. He had always imagined that she had moved to Miami when she left Cuba. On the many family vacations to visit relatives, he would make frequent trips to Dadeland Mall in south Miami, just hoping for a chance encounter. He held hope in his heart for so many years that they would one day meet again. Even though they never really knew one another, Roberto always held a special place in his heart for María de los Angeles. She was a reminder of his late mother, whom he adored and lost too soon.

Roberto had had an unusually busy day at work and arrived home hours past dinner time on this Thursday in late January. As he and Lolita sat at the table having a Cuban coffee, the marigold phone on the wall rang. They looked at each other and wondered who would be calling them this late. Lolita stood to answer it, and on the other end of the line was the most unexpected voice.

"*Hola, sí* . . . yes, this is Lolita. Hector, yes, he is sitting right here. Would you like to speak with him?"

"Hector Santiago wants to speak with you," said Lolita.

Roberto stood, stunned, and took the phone from Lolita. He cleared his voice.

"Hello, Hector . . . it's been so long . . . is everything okay?"

Hector's voice trembled—he had so much to share and didn't know where to begin.

"I am very sick, Roberto . . . the cancer has taken hold and I fear I don't have much time left. I cannot go to my grave without telling you about your sister, María de los Angeles."

"Is there something the matter with her?" asked Roberto.

"No, she is doing fine," said Hector.

"I have always known that you deserved to be reunited with the baby you last saw almost forty years ago, and I want to help you find her. I am sorry that I have not given you the information you needed to find her, but I never wanted to damage the loving relationship she had with her father, Dr. Sánchez," said Hector.

Tears of joy were brimming from Roberto's eyes and he began sobbing, his voice barely a whisper.

"I can't believe what you are saying. I am very sorry you are ill, and I want to thank you for sharing this with me at this time," said Roberto.

"I want you to know that not only do I know she is here in Miami, but my daughter, Lucía, works at a law firm that employs private investigators. She has shared your story with her boss, and they have committed to donating the resources to help find María de los Angeles," said Hector.

Roberto was taken aback, and his knees felt as though they would buckle beneath him. Lolita came to his side and he steadied himself as she took his hand in hers.

"I have been waiting my whole life for this moment. I am beyond words," said Roberto.

Roberto's heart was racing, and his mind was spinning with the possibility that he would once again lay eyes on his beloved baby sister.

"Thank you, my friend. Thank you is all I can say . . . I can't thank you enough," said Roberto through tears and ragged breaths. "Please, tell me what I need to do."

"As I mentioned, Lucía was waiting until I spoke with you before beginning the search for her. I will let her know that she can move forward now," said Hector. "I will reach back out to you as soon as I hear back from her. It may be days or weeks or more. We don't know, but they are professionals and will do their best to find her."

"Again, thank you is all I can say, and I will be waiting for your call," said a shocked Roberto.

He turned to look at Lolita and she was in tears. They had finally come the closest they had ever been to finding the girl he had searched for her entire lifetime. Lolita and Roberto embraced, and cried tears of joy mixed with tears from the past that Roberto could never express. It was a moment that they would never forget, and they would share this story with their family for decades to come.

In a split second their whole lives had changed. It was late and they were both exhausted, but sleep eluded them. Roberto went into the kitchen to prepare a cup of tea hoping this would calm his nerves. He sat at the kitchen table and thought about his life and wondered about the life of María de los Angeles. It was a sleepless night, but Roberto relished the time thinking about his father, his siblings, and his mother, whom he wished could know that while life had been challenging for him, he was now a happy man with a full life.

The following days were filled with hopes, questions, excitement, and fear at this incredible surprise that he never imagined would happen. Each evening around the dinner table, Lolita, Roberto, and the children were hopeful the day would come when they would hear back from Hector that María de los Angeles had been found. They knew it could take some time. On the fourth day, early in the morning, the phone rang. Lolita and Roberto once again looked at each other and with puzzled looks, wondered who would be calling this early in the morning.

"Hello?" said Roberto.

"*Hola*, Roberto," said Hector. "I have news for you."

Roberto's heart began to race, and his hands turned ice cold. He was nervous to hear the news that Hector had to share.

"Last night, I received a call from Lucía that the investigators have located María de los Angeles here in Miami," said an animated Hector.

"What?" yelled Roberto. He couldn't believe what he was hearing.

"Yes, she lives here with her husband and three small children."

"I have a million questions, but the most pressing one is do you think she wants to meet me? How can I meet her?" asked Roberto.

"I will have Lucía call you to figure out the details, but she will help you plan a reunion very soon."

"I can't express my gratitude for helping to bring us back together after almost four decades," said Roberto.

He hung up the phone and sunk into the sofa. He could barely speak. Lolita sat by his side. She knew the words of his heart without having to hear them. The joy spiked with sorrow was overwhelming. He was still in a daze as he left for work for the day. He knew it would be a long day as he processed all the scenarios that may finally come to fruition.

A few more restless days passed, and he finally heard from Lucía.

The phone rang once again in the early evening before dinner. Both Lolita and Roberto knew this was the call they had been waiting for.

"Go ahead, *mi amor* . . . this call is for you," said Lolita.

"*Hola*, this is Roberto."

"Mr. Martínez de Osaba," this is Lucía Santiago Gonzalez, Hector Santiago's daughter. I believe you have been waiting to hear from me. I am calling with more good news and details about María de los Angeles," said Lucía.

"I know my father shared that she lives in Miami with her family. She goes by the name María de los Angeles Gómez. Her husband, Dr. Rafael Gómez, is a pediatrician. She works with him in his office. We have the address for you, and I will help set up a meeting as soon as you can make the trip to Miami," Lucía said, getting more excited with each word.

Roberto had been silent up to this point and it was almost too much to make sense of. *She knows where María de los Angeles is and is going to help me meet her.* His thoughts felt as if they were a movie playing in slow motion while at the same time racing around in a blur.

"We can be there tomorrow if that works for you," said an elated Roberto.

"Tomorrow is Saturday, so the doctor's office is closed," said Lucía. "Would you be able to travel to Miami on Monday? If you can do that, we can meet at my home to put our plan together for the following day. In only a few days, you will meet the sister you have been looking for."

"Does she know about me?" Roberto asked in barely a whisper.

"No," said Lucía, "she does not."

Roberto took a deep breath.

"She grew up as an only child, and from what I know her parents never shared her past with her. This will be a shock as it has been for you as well. Please prepare yourselves for anything. This will be overwhelming for her in so many ways. Her whole life is about to change in ways we cannot even imagine," said Lucía.

"*Gracias.* We will prepare everything and leave at dawn on Monday. The drive will take us about twelve hours, so we can be at your home around six," said Roberto.

"That would work for Samuel and me. Please plan to have dinner with us, and we'll work out the details for the following day," said Lucía.

"I am so happy that you are making this meeting possible," said Roberto. "The words *thank you* don't feel as if they are enough to tell you how grateful I am for you and your father." Roberto grabbed the pen from his front pocket and scratched down Lucía's address on a nearby piece of scrap paper.

"Goodbye for now," he said.

"Goodbye," said Lucía.

The weekend crawled by as their anticipation mixed with so many questions and emotions. They spent hours carefully selecting the clothes they would wear to meet María de los Angeles.

"Should I wear a suit and tie, or should I wear something more casual?" asked Roberto.

"I think you should wear your brown suit and a white shirt with your new red and blue patterned tie," said Lolita. "You will look so handsome. This will be such a special day in both of your lives, and I want you to look your best."

Lolita and Roberto held each other's gaze, and a nervous smile parted their lips before Roberto replied, "Yes, I think that is a very good idea. That is what I will wear."

Lolita wanted to wear a special outfit for the occasion too and pulled several dresses from the closet. She held each one up and looked at her reflection in the mirror, trying to decide which one would be just right. She wanted to look beautiful but not be the center of attention. She chose a modest ivory dress with a small floral print and a flattering belted waistline.

They had each decided the special outfit that they would wear, and after packing and unpacking a few other items, they zipped their bags and placed them by the front door for their early departure.

After a few hours of fitful sleep, they were both awake well before dawn. Lolita prepared a small breakfast of toasted Cuban bread and filled a thermos with *café con leche* for the trip. They loaded their bags, two pillows, and a few small blankets into the back of the white Chevy Suburban and drove away to what they knew would be a life-changing trip.

As they headed south out of Atlanta, the stars were still twinkling in the night sky. The sun began to rise a few hours later, and before they knew it, the twelve-hour drive had passed, and the Miami skyline came into full view. Their excitement filled the car to overflowing as they pulled into Lucía's long driveway. Lucía held the key to all the answers for the questions he had carried around his entire lifetime.

They hurried out of the car to the front door and rang the bell. Lucía opened the door with a wide smile and open arms. Her joy in bringing this brother and sister together after all these years was palpable. After tight hugs and a few tears, everyone gathered around the dinner table and enjoyed a delicious homemade meal. Roberto and Lolita were grateful for Lucía and Samuel's hospitality.

After dinner, they moved to the living room to discuss their plans for the following day. The four of them agreed they would go to Dr. Gómez's office just after lunch. Lucía would ask for María de los Angeles, explaining she was an old friend.

They all expected the process would be simple, and within minutes the moment Roberto had been dreaming about since he was thirteen years old would come true. Thinking about the reunion made him feel like that same teenage boy today. The plans were set, and now it was time to rest from a long day of travel for the momentous day that awaited them in the morning.

Lolita and Roberto checked into their hotel and quickly unpacked. They were exhausted and sleep finally took over that night. For Roberto, sleep came with beautifully vivid dreams of his childhood home at La Paloma and the love that surrounded his family before the death of his mother. He dreamt through the night—one dream more splendid than the next—and awoke to the Florida sun peeking through the blinds.

Lolita and Roberto passed the morning hours by walking on the beach and looking in a few shops along the boardwalk. They chatted about their hopes for the afternoon, each expressing both excitement and anxiety.

They had a light lunch at the hotel and prepared to leave to meet Lucía at the office of María de los Angeles's husband. They arrived at the same time as Lucía and Samuel. They greeted one another and nervously walked in together.

The office was fairly empty at this hour and Lucía was able to walk straight up to the sliding glass window. Lolita and Roberto anxiously stood behind her as she patiently waited for the woman behind the window to complete her task. She finally looked up and made eye contact with Lucía and slowly slid open the window.

"How can I help you, ma'am?" she asked as she noticed Lolita and Roberto standing behind her. She began to grow nervous at the sight of four grown adults, with no children, standing behind the window.

"My name is Lucía Santiago Gonzalez. We are here to see María de los Angeles Gómez. I was told she may also work here, helping with her husband's practice."

"What is this about, ma'am?" asked Eva nervously.

The tension in the room began to grow.

They could tell immediately Eva was uncomfortable. She shuffled papers anxiously and squirmed in her seat, trying to figure out what she was going to do. She knew this was what they had always warned her against. She was told never to allow anyone she did not know to have access to María de los Angeles.

Lucía said, "I am an old friend of hers. I am in town with friends and I wanted to say hello."

Eva drew in a deep breath before sliding the window closed without a word. She slowly stood up and walked to the back of the office.

They all stood in confusion, knowing something did not feel right about Eva's behavior.

A few minutes passed as they stood in silence waiting for Eva to return. Instead, the door to the waiting room flew open and Dr. Rafael Gómez appeared.

"How can I help you? What business do you have with my wife?" He shuddered, visibly shaken. Lucía looked at Roberto.

"Tell him," she said.

Roberto cleared his throat and stood up straight to meet Dr. Gómez's stare.

"Your wife is my younger sister," Roberto spat out.

The room grew silent once again. Everyone was overwhelmed by the tension.

"This cannot be," said Dr. Gómez confidently. "My wife is an only child. I have been married to her for fifteen years. I was extremely close to her father, Dr. Joaquin Sánchez, and he never spoke a word of this to me."

Roberto tried to get a word in, but Dr. Gómez interrupted him.

"Are you implying that my wife's father or mother had an affair?"

"No. Not at all," said Roberto. "María de los Angeles is my youngest sister. I was thirteen years old when our mother died and our family of ten was split apart."

Dr. Gómez continued to stare at him in disbelief.

"I am telling you the truth, sir. We want nothing from you—we brought copies of our bank statements and photos of our family business—I just want to see my sister. If you don't believe me, you can draw my labs right now. I promise you, I am her brother." Dr. Gómez knew Roberto was serious about making such an offer. At this time, DNA testing was not commonplace, but for someone to be that secure and that confident in their truth made Dr. Gómez consider that this, in fact, could be his brother-in-law.

After a few minutes, the doctor agreed that he would tell his wife and gave Roberto his word as a man and as a doctor that he would contact him the following day to let him know if she would agree to meet with them.

Dr. Gómez immediately decided he would cancel all of his afternoon appointments and close his office to learn the truth from the only person who would know: his mother-in-law, Señora Margarita Sánchez.

After closing up and sending Eva home, he went to the back office, where María de los Angeles was waiting anxiously to know the identity of the strangers asking for her.

Before he could say a word, María de los Angeles asked, "Was that my brother?"

Dr. Gómez was stunned. He asked, "Why would you ask that?"

"I have always felt that someday, someone would come looking for me—as if a piece of me was out there somewhere. Deep inside, I've always wondered why my mother and I have always been so distant. Our personalities couldn't be more different. It's hard to explain . . . I have always suspected there was something my parents were hiding from me."

"I've never seen any pictures of my mother when she was pregnant with me. So this, along with all the other deep feelings, made me feel that one day someone would show up to help me put together all the missing pieces I have felt inside."

"I understand. But we need to go talk to your mother to get the truth," said Dr. Gómez.

The Gómezes quickly made arrangements for their children to be picked up from school and called Señora Sánchez to let her know about the visitor and that they were on their way to her house to get the answers they needed. They did not give her any details about the visitors, but Margarita began adamantly denying any knowledge of the stranger. She knew in her heart exactly who this person could be. The day she had been dreading for the last thirty-nine years was happening.

When they arrived at her mother's house, María de los Angeles stood outside the courtyard surrounded by a wrought iron fence. She shouted for her mother to come open the courtyard gate. Margarita stayed just inside the door to her home, peering through a small opening.

"Please come let us in. We have something important that we need to speak with you about," said Dr. Gómez.

"Whatever you need to tell me, you can tell me from there," said an agitated Margarita.

"Is it true that I have a brother?" asked María de los Angeles.

"I don't know what you are talking about," said Margarita. "Why would you ask me something like that?"

"Why won't you come speak to us? You are acting so strange. I feel like you know something. Please come talk to us," pleaded María de los Angeles. Margarita knew this conversation could only end one way—with the truth. Even still, she continued to deny what she knew for close to an hour. She remained half-hidden inside the door the whole time until finally admitting that María de los Angeles was adopted at birth and she had many siblings.

"I have told you what it is you want to know," said Margarita. "I will never speak of this again."

The truth coming to light now was especially difficult for Margarita as her husband, Joaquin, had passed away four years earlier. He adored María de los Angeles, and he had moved heaven and earth to protect his precious daughter from the truth.

That evening María de los Angeles had a lot to think about. After several hours of soul-searching and talking, María de los Angeles told her husband that now that she knew the truth, she wanted to finally meet her brother after thirty-nine years. In the midst of all of this, she had volunteered to chaperone a field trip to the zoo for her son Diego's kindergarten class in the morning. They planned for her to go on the field trip and for Dr. Gómez to call Roberto and Lolita and let them know that they would meet them for lunch at the hotel.

The following morning, Roberto and Lolita were anxiously waiting for any type of news from Dr. Gómez or María de los Angeles. They wanted to see if the man they met yesterday would live up to his word. This trip had been physically and mentally draining for both of them, and they needed to have resolution for something that had been building up inside for nearly four decades.

As the morning drew on, no news arrived. The more time passed, the more discouraged and disheartened they became. It was getting close to noon, and they needed to check out of the hotel. When they reached the front desk and gave their name, the manager breathed a sigh of relief.

"Mr. Martínez de Osaba, I have been trying to call your room, but we have been having trouble with the phone lines. I have a message for you."

He handed Roberto the slip of paper and written in blue ink was Dr. Gómez's message. He and María de los Angeles would be there to meet them for lunch.

Roberto and Lolita embraced and knew that in a few minutes, a lifetime of searching would come to an end. They waited in the lobby of the hotel for what seemed like an eternity. They both were relieved that this day had come, but at the same time, they were nervous and anxious, not knowing how this day would end up.

Roberto turned and saw a shiny black sports car drive up to the entrance of the hotel. He saw the profile of María de los Angeles and his heart knew her instantly. She stepped out of the car. She was tall and slender, beautiful and graceful just like their mother, Gabriela. She was her mother's daughter.

When María de los Angeles walked in with Dr. Gómez, there was not a dry eye in the lobby. They had shared with the manager the meaning of the message and he and a few members of his staff were discretely witnessing this lovely occasion.

"*Hola*," said María de los Angeles with an unexpected joy that surprised her.

Approaching Lolita first, she opened her arms to embrace her and asked, "Are you my sister-in-law?"

"Yes! Yes!" said Lolita.

"Where is my brother?" asked María de Los Angeles.

Roberto had been overwhelmed with emotion at seeing his sister arrive and found a small bench near the front door to sit and watch as she walked into the hotel.

"Your brother is right over there," said Lolita, smiling through her tears.

Roberto and María de los Angeles locked eyes, and all of the missing pieces finally came together at that moment.

After long overdue hugs, many tears, some laughter, and conversation, they were ready to sit down to a meal together. They shared a lifetime over lunch—telling stories, sharing memories, looking at photos of their children—it was as if no time or space had ever separated them. The bond between brother and sister remained after all these years.

CHAPTER TWENTY-SIX

ATLANTA, GEORGIA
1993 — 1996

One never knows how someone will react when their life gets turned upside down. To find out what you have believed to be the truth for your entire life was a fabrication could have created so many negative feelings of resentment and loss. For María de los Angeles, it was a wonderful turn of events in her life, and this validated what her soul had been longing for for thirty-nine years. She had lived a charmed life with loving parents and the best of everything at her fingertips. She had no reason to look beyond the family she had in search of a family she thought may be. But now that she knew the truth, she embraced everyone and everything about this new life with her entire being. She was gracious and kind, loving and caring, funny, joyful—and she completed the puzzle of Roberto's family.

After a wonderful time together in Miami, Lolita and Roberto returned home to Atlanta with hearts bursting with joy. They told anyone and everyone who would listen about the story of María de los Angeles. Roberto would begin each time and be reduced to tears within minutes as he shared his heart and his overwhelming joy at the miracle of finding his baby sister all these years later.

Lolita and Roberto looked forward to bringing María de los Angeles and her entire family to Atlanta. They knew her fortieth birthday was in April, so they wanted to throw an amazing party for her at the house. When they asked her if this was something she would like, she tearfully told them it would be a wonderful gift to celebrate her birthday with her new family.

When María de los Angeles and her husband Dr. Gómez arrived at the airport, the whole family was waiting anxiously at the gate to greet them. As she walked off the jetway, Cristina and Isabela were overtaken by how beautiful she was. To them, she looked like a model or a movie star. They had not imagined she was such a stunning woman.

Lolita and Roberto planned every single detail—they had delicious catered food, a DJ, endless beer, wine, and cocktails, and they invited all of their friends to celebrate with them. They danced late into the night—no one wanted the celebration to end. After the party, María de los Angeles and Rafael stayed in Atlanta for a few days to continue visiting with the family. They grew close right away and looked forward to many more years of get-togethers and celebrations as a big happy family.

Plans began right away to get together in Miami. Lolita and Roberto were so happy to see their families bond so easily. Cristina, Andrés, and Alejandra spent a week at María de los Angeles's house. The children were close in age to Alejandra—the oldest, Elena, was eight, Daniella was six, and Diego was three. They were beautiful and well-behaved children. It was the perfect fit for Alejandra, who was now four years old. The children played so well together like they were immediately family and Cristina and Andrés loved spending time with María de los Angeles and Rafael.

Over the next few years, the family gathered as often as they could, visiting each other's homes, Disney World, Cape Canaveral, and other destinations for families with small children. Each time they were together was a wonderful experience for everyone.

★

In May, the Georgia Hispanic Chamber of Commerce put out an announcement seeking nominations for the Hispanic Business of the Year. There were hundreds of submissions of worthy businesses and entrepreneurs. The winner would be announced at the Annual Awards Gala in June. Lolita and Roberto were excited to submit their story for consideration. The board of directors met to review all of the nominations. After much consideration of the more than twenty finalists, Lolita and Roberto were notified that European Specialists of Atlanta would receive this honor at the yearly celebration. They were beside themselves. This was the culmination of all of their hard work for the last twenty-five years. They had started from nothing and now, they were being recognized as the top company among so many successful businesses.

It was a black-tie event. The whole family attended. The girls wore fancy ball gowns and the men wore tuxedos. The local newspaper, the *Atlanta Journal-Constitution*, covered the event and showcased an 8 x 10 photo of the family, with Roberto proudly holding the trophy and smiling ear to ear. Roberto couldn't believe how much all of his hard work had paid off over the years. He was filled with immense gratitude to be recognized as a successful business owner in his community.

Roberto and Lolita's girls had now graduated college within months of one another. It was a huge achievement for Cristina as she was balancing being a new wife, mother, and student. She graduated from Georgia State University with a Bachelor of Arts in Communications, minoring in Broadcast Journalism and Criminal Justice. The university honored its graduates along with those who helped them achieve their degrees with a special breakfast and award. Lolita and Roberto attended as Lolita had spent so many days and hours watching Alejandra so Cristina could finish her degree. Lolita walked across the stage, received her award, and took a nice photo as she shook the hand of the dean of the School of Journalism.

Isabela's graduation from Samford University was a wonderful occasion for the family to gather together again to celebrate. Lolita and Roberto were so proud of their girls and their dedication to their studies. The girls would be the first college graduates, besides Emilio, to earn their degrees. Isabela had worked hard to excel in her studies and was ready to use her degree in the hospitality field. This was the perfect fit for her.

Everyone was thriving. Emilio's practice was growing to the point of needing a second location. He opened the sister location on Bay Street in downtown Gadsden. It was a smaller clinic, but just as beautiful.

★

Fourth of July was just around the corner and Lolita and Roberto were planning to visit Emilio and Ana at their home in Gadsden. They had a huge fourth of July celebration and Emilio wowed everyone with fireworks. He was a bit of a daredevil, lighting and running away as the fireworks flew and exploded in a beautiful display of colorful bursts. The party was in full swing when Emilio accidentally lit a firework and it backfired, flying toward his face, skimming the skin between his eyes and his eyeglasses. It shot right through that tiny space. It was a miracle he was not hurt or blinded. Emilio, always the life of the party, just kept lighting fireworks and entertaining the kids.

The rest of the summer was spent preparing for Isabela and Preston's wedding. It was a gorgeous wedding, and María de Los Angeles and her husband attended the formal wedding. Isabela was a stunning bride. She wore a long-sleeved gown with an eight-foot train. Her olive skin looked flawless set against the white off-the-shoulder dress. Her chestnut hair was in a perfect updo with a princess tiara and imported lace veil.

The bridesmaids wore fuchsia dresses in a luxurious raw silk fabric with an off-the-shoulder design. Alejandra was the flower girl and wore a white satin dress with tiny white pearls scattered on the skirt. She was adorable. Following the ceremony, family and friends gathered at the country club for a lavish reception. It was a fairytale wedding and reception followed by an exquisite tropical honeymoon.

Alex was attending classes at Samford that winter and was modeling part-time for magazines, TV, and catalogs in the southeast. A modeling scout took an interest in him, and he received an invitation to model in Milan, Italy. After discussing it with Lolita and Roberto, they decided it would be a good opportunity for him. He worked for many fashion houses while in Milan, modeling clothing and representing men's fine fragrance and high-end watches. He would resume his classes at Samford when the European fashion season was over.

The new year began, and life was unfolding nicely for everyone. Roberto and Lolita were continuing to build the company and the girls were enjoying domestic life.

Cristina was still overseeing all of the office responsibilities at the business and staying busy with Alejandra, who was going to be starting kindergarten in the fall. One afternoon, Cristina noticed a few drops of blood dripping from her nose. She didn't think much of it and did all of the things to try to get it to stop. After twenty minutes, the blood flow became increasingly heavy so she called 911 for assistance. An ambulance and fire engine were dispatched and arrived minutes later. Before they addressed the bleeding, they took her vitals and were shocked to find her blood pressure at 140/110. After a few minutes, they were finally able to get the blood to clot and suggested Cristina follow up with a specialist to see why her blood pressure was so high. The following week she had made an appointment with a cardiologist. When he examined her, all seemed to be in order. Cristina's blood pressure was 121/72, and she had no other symptoms. He told her to call his office if she had any other problems and to monitor her blood pressure. Cristina was feeling well and maintained her duties at work and was planning a summer vacation at the family beach condo for the beginning of June.

On a Friday morning a few weeks later, Cristina awoke with every single part of her body in pain. Her joints ached terribly. Her shoulders and hips felt as if they were being pulled apart. The bottoms of her feet felt like she was stepping on broken glass. It was intense pain like nothing she had ever felt before. At twenty-seven years old, she should not be feeling any of this. Cristina knew something was really wrong when she went to the restroom. Her urine was the color of black coffee. Cristina was terrified and yelled out for Andrés.

"What is happening to me . . . look in the toilet . . . it's black!" shouted Cristina.

"I don't know, but this can't be good," said Andrés, beginning to panic.

Cristina had never experienced this before and started to cry.

"Here, don't cry," said Andrés as he pulled her in for a hug. "It will be okay."

"Call the doctor, please, right now," said Cristina through her tears.

Andrés didn't want Cristina to see him like this, but he was very concerned. He immediately dialed Cristina's doctor who advised him to bring her into the hospital right away so he could run some tests. Andrés helped Cristina get out of bed as she was unable to walk down the stairs on her own. She had to sit down and shimmy herself down the stairs. From there, she leaned on Andrés to get to the car. The ride to the hospital was excruciating. Once they arrived at the hospital, Cristina was in such terrible agony they had to bring a wheelchair out to transport her inside. After the doctor examined her, he drew labs. He wasn't sure what was going on, but he didn't find anything else of concern, other than a low-grade fever. The doctor prescribed NSAIDs, non-steroidal anti-inflammatory drugs, to reduce the inflammation in her body and asked her to come back on Monday for additional tests. Clearly, the doctor was not trained in issues involving the kidney. The dark urine was a clear sign of a problem with the kidneys, and

NSAIDs are known to cause additional damage to the already compromised kidneys.

Cristina did as he asked and took the prescription over the weekend. She felt so much better and her fever was gone by Monday morning. She questioned if she needed to go back to the doctor for additional tests as she had a lot of things planned for the week. Andrés told her she needed to make sure she was okay and to go to her visit as scheduled. When the doctor drew the bloodwork at her appointment, he was aghast at seeing her results. Cristina had lost two-thirds of her kidney function over the weekend. The nephrons, or filters, in the kidney do not regenerate and he let her know she would need to see a nephrologist as soon as possible. He gave her a recommendation for a specialist in the same building. Cristina stopped by to make an appointment on her way out and was relieved that she could get in to see him the following week. She and Andrés weren't overly concerned as they didn't know what the consequences of the lab work could be.

The day of the appointment arrived, and Cristina went to work as usual. She left at lunchtime so she wouldn't be late for her visit. The specialist reviewed her labs and examined her. In a very matter-of-fact way, he delivered the terrible news.

"I have looked over all of the test results, and you are in the early stages of kidney failure," said the doctor.

"What does that mean," asked Cristina as her hands started to shake.

"It means that you will continue to lose kidney function until you need a kidney transplant," said the doctor. "It will be in about ten years."

"What? I don't understand," said Cristina as tears began to well in her eyes. "I am healthy and young, and I feel great again. How could this be?"

"We don't always know what causes this," said the doctor. "I would like to schedule you for a kidney biopsy to determine the best course of treatment. We want to preserve your kidney function as long as possible."

"I don't know anything about kidney disease," said Cristina. "What do I need to do to preserve it?"

"I will set you up to see a nutritionist who specializes in helping nephrology patients," said the doctor. "I will have my receptionist call you when we schedule you for the biopsy. You will have to be admitted to the hospital, and we will have to put you under anesthesia."

"What are you going to do?" asked Cristina. "What will the biopsy tell you?"

"It will give us more information as to the origin of your condition and we can then develop a plan for you," said the doctor.

"I would also like you to be tested for lupus," added the doctor. "Lupus can cause kidney failure and I want to rule it out."

Cristina left the doctor's office and before she made it to the parking garage, she burst out crying. She didn't know much about kidney failure but the news of needing a kidney transplant was devastating. She thought about her little girl, who was only four years old. Cristina wanted to watch Alejandra grow up and the uncertainty of what she had been told to this point broke her heart. For her. For her daughter. For her family.

Cristina opened her car door and slid into her seat but didn't turn the ignition to start up her car. She lowered her forehead onto the steering wheel and took a few minutes to think about what she had just heard. She tried to pull herself together, but she was scared, and this felt like a death sentence.

How long will I feel good until I get very sick?

Will I have the energy to play with Alejandra?

Am I going to see her graduate from high school or even from kindergarten?

These were all questions swirling in her head. Her mind was racing, and she was overwhelmed with her new diagnosis. Cristina drove to the shop to tell Andrés and her father. She hoped Lolita would be there too. When she arrived, Veronica, the front desk manager and Lolita and Roberto's trusted right-hand person, told her that her parents were meeting in the upstairs office with their CPA. Veronica noticed Cristina's bloodshot eyes.

"Is everything okay?" asked Veronica.

"I don't know," said a tearful Cristina. "Do you remember when I was sick last week? I had labs drawn, and then I met with a specialist to review the results today. He told me I was in kidney failure and would need a transplant . . . in . . . ten . . . years."

Cristina could hardly finish her sentence. Veronica came around from behind her desk and embraced her friend.

"I'm so sorry to hear this, Cristina," said Veronica with concern in her voice.

"Thank you," said Cristina. "I'm not sure what this all means right now but I will be going to the hospital for additional testing soon, and we will know more then."

"Is there anything you need right now?" asked Veronica. "What can I help you with?"

"There's nothing we can do except wait, but thank you," said Cristina. "I need to speak with Andrés. Is he here?"

"He went on a test drive a few minutes ago but should be back any time," said Veronica.

"Thank you," said Cristina.

"I will wait in the break room for Andrés and for my parents to finish," said Cristina.

"Okay, I will let them know as soon as I see them that you want to speak with them," said Veronica.

While Cristina was waiting for her parents and Andrés, she called Emilio at his office.

"Hi, *Tio*—uncle. Do you have a few minutes to talk?" asked Cristina.

"Yes, I have a couple of minutes before I have to see my next patient," said Emilio.

"I wanted to let you know that I met with the specialist today that I had mentioned to you last week, and he reviewed the results of my bloodwork with me," said Cristina. "He told me I was in the early stages of kidney failure and that I would need a kidney transplant in ten years," said Cristina as her voice started to quiver.

"Please don't cry," said Emilio. "Everything will be fine. First, we need to see exactly what the findings show so we will know the best course of action. Can you please ask the doctor to send me all the results?"

Emilio gave Cristina his fax number and asked for them to be sent as soon as possible. He tried to hide the concern and nervousness in his voice, but Cristina could sense it. Emilio had loved Cristina since the first time he held her, minutes after she was born. Emilio would do anything to ensure he understood all the facts of her diagnosis and that Cristina received the best medical treatment available.

"Yes, I will call them this afternoon and will let you know when to expect them," said Cristina.

Just then, Lolita walked into the break room.

"*Tio*, I have to go now. Thank you for trying to help me," said Cristina.

"Hey, Mom," said Cristina.

"Hey, what is going on?" asked Lolita. "I noticed that Veronica had a very serious look on her face when we came downstairs. "Is she okay?"

"Yes, she is okay, Mom," said Cristina. "Where is Dad?"

"He should be down any moment," said Lolita. "Why?"

"I want to speak with you both about the results the specialist reviewed with me today," said Cristina.

"Are you okay?" asked Lolita. "I was thinking your appointment was tomorrow and I was going to ask you if you would like for me to go with you."

"I'm not okay," said Cristina as the lump in her throat gave way to hot tears. "The specialist told me I am in the beginning stages of kidney failure and I will need a kidney transplant in about ten years. I don't know much about any of this but I'm terrified."

Roberto stood in the doorway with a growing look of concern. He heard what Cristina had said. Roberto looked at Lolita and then back at Cristina.

Their world just stopped.

Lolita put her arm around Cristina, and Roberto embraced them both. No one in the family had ever had a medical diagnosis like this, and they weren't sure of the long-term prognosis.

"Just before you came in here, I called *Tio* to tell him what the doctor told me," said Cristina. "He said not to worry right now as we don't have the complete story. He asked to have all of the test results faxed to him so he can review them."

"Not because he is my brother, but Emilio truly is one of the most gifted and knowledgeable doctors I know," said Lolita. "Let's wait until he assesses everything and tells us what we should do next."

"I trust him completely," said Roberto. "Yes, let's wait until we know what we are dealing with so we can decide how to best treat it."

"Okay," said Cristina. "You are right. I agree that until we know more, there's nothing we can do."

Just then, Andrés stepped into the break room and was surprised to see Roberto, Lolita, and Cristina with somber looks on their faces. He could tell from their tear-stained cheeks they had been crying.

"What's happened?" asked Andrés.

Cristina explained the results the specialist had shared with her and that although she was frightened, she told him Emilio was going to review them and see what the next step should be. Andrés's hands started to shake. He wasn't expecting Cristina's medical incident from a few weeks ago to result in this diagnosis. He knew they had to find the best treatment for her. Andrés had loved Cristina since they were kids, and this news was devastating to him. He needed her. Alejandra needed her. He wrapped his arms around her and held her tightly. They would face this together and he would do everything to ensure she received the best treatment available.

The next few days were a blur as Cristina tried to process her new reality.

I am a healthy twenty-seven-year-old and I feel great. How can this be?

As Emilio pored over the results, his heart sank. He could find nothing to contradict the specialists' findings. *I want to run all of these tests again and have a nephrologist at the Kirklin Clinic at the University of Alabama at Birmingham review them,* he thought.

The hospital system at UAB had always been on the leading edge of organ transplants, and if the results showed this was where Cristina was headed, he wanted the best doctors to evaluate her. Emilio called Cristina and told her he didn't find anything different from what the specialist had told her, and he wanted her to be seen by a doctor at UAB.

"I know they will run more in-depth studies and give us the complete picture," said Emilio. "We will then know with certainty what we should do next. Don't worry, Cristina. We are going to get to the bottom of this."

"I'm really scared," said Cristina.

"We don't know all of the facts yet, so don't spend too much time worrying about something that may not be what we imagine or may not even come to pass," said Emilio.

"You are right," said Cristina. "Although it may be difficult, I will try to keep myself occupied with Alejandra and everything else going on in my life."

"I think that is a good plan," said Emilio. "I always say, 'Procrastinate your anxiety,' because there is no need to fear the worst when we don't fully understand the situation. I will call the Kirklin Clinic now and see how quickly they can get you in to see a nephrologist. As soon as they can schedule an appointment for you, I will let you know."

"Thank you, *Tío*," said Cristina. "I am relieved you are taking control to help me find answers."

Emilio called the clinic as soon as he finished his conversation with Cristina. He was able to secure an appointment for three weeks out. Although he was concerned, he knew she would have the best doctors reviewing her case.

Three weeks later, the nephrologist at UAB confirmed the original specialists' findings. Cristina also underwent tests for lupus, but the findings showed no evidence of it. The doctor who performed the lupus tests prescribed a large dose of steroids to try to decrease the inflammation and stop additional damage to her kidneys. The final test was a biopsy of the kidney to determine the cause of the failure and determine the best course of treatment. The results came back a few days later, and they were inconclusive. Her diagnosis was "unspecified glomerulonephritis." She would need to have blood work every three months to ensure there were no changes. Once the tests were all run and she knew the medical plan, Cristina was able to relax a bit about the diagnosis, especially since she was feeling so well.

She changed some elements of her diet, but overall Cristina's life carried on as normal. She did take the time to educate herself by reading books and speaking with other transplant patients. She came across a book called *The Kidney Patient's Book* at the local library. The foreword was written by Doctor William E. Mitch at Emory University Hospital in Atlanta. Cristina was so taken by what he wrote that she decided to call Emory, hoping to be able to speak with him.

Dr. Mitch took Cristina's call. He was an incredible man and so kind to talk with her about her diagnosis. He was so reassuring and put her mind at ease. He agreed to see her when her condition progressed, but for the time being, he encouraged her to continue taking care of herself. Cristina was even more relieved after speaking with Dr. Mitch. She trusted his advice and was comforted to know he would be her doctor when the time came.

Life returned to normal, besides the addition of high blood pressure medication and steroids. The doctors advised her of the side effects of the medications. Many she never experienced, but the side effects she did experience were the result of the high dose of steroids—and those were very unpleasant. Cristina gained weight, had frequent emotional ups and downs, developed acne on her face and had insomnia. She learned to live with the side effects, and life went on, as it does. Because kidney disease usually has no outward symptoms, no one could believe her diagnosis. She looked healthy and her energy level was the same as it had always been. Her condition sort of faded into the background of life, and Cristina continued to build her life with her family.

After a difficult year, the family gathered together to celebrate Lily's graduation from Samford with a Bachelor of Arts in International Relations and a concentration in History and Political Science. It was exactly what everyone needed after a trying time.

CHAPTER TWENTY-SEVEN

ATLANTA, GEORGIA AND THE CARIBBEAN SEA
1996 — 2022

The following year, Lolita and Roberto surprised Cristina and Isabela and their husbands along with María de los Angeles and Rafael with an all-expenses-paid seven-day luxury cruise. They had an amazing time together soaking in the sea, the warm tropical sunshine, and all the lavish amenities aboard the ship. The spa services and food were incredible, the shopping opportunities were endless, and the ports of call were all around the Caribbean islands of Turks and Caicos, the Cayman Islands, and Grand Bahama Island. The bonding time among the girls with María de los Angeles was priceless. They had just met her three years prior, and this trip allowed them all to get to know one another better. They laughed, took tons of photos, shared stories, and expressed so much gratitude for the man who brought María de los Angeles back into their family.

It was a very busy summer for the family. In May, Marisol graduated from Samford with a Bachelor of Science in Biology, and she had her sights set on Boston University's School of Dental Medicine. She had dreamed of being a dentist all her life and wanted to be a doctor like her father, Emilio. She wanted nothing more than to make him proud. Camila also graduated from high school in May. She was so excited to follow in her sisters's and cousins's footsteps and attend Samford University in the fall. The 1996 Summer Olympics were being held in Atlanta. It brought so much excitement to the city and it was amazing to see all of the action up close. Many attended events such as gymnastics, swimming, diving, and volleyball. The gymnastic events were especially exciting as the "Magnificent Seven" competed as Team USA coached by the famous Béla Károlyi. During the summer games, Kerri Strug helped the U.S. clinch its very first gold medal of the games after she landed a nearly perfect vault on a severely sprained ankle. The world watched in awe as she clearly was hurt but was determined to stick the landing. The crowd went wild as she landed on one foot before falling to the ground in pain.

Two days after the closing ceremonies of the Olympic games, Isabela gave birth to a beautiful little girl named Scarlett. She had soft black hair and big brown eyes. Isabela and Preston were over the moon. Lolita and Roberto waited in the room for hours and were elated when they saw this precious new baby. They were proud grandparents and couldn't wait to spoil her the way they had always done with Alejandra.

When the spring term was over at Samford, Alex decided to move to Nashville. He loved to sing in addition to his modeling, and he wanted to pursue his dreams of becoming a star. Lolita and Roberto were wary but agreed to support his decision. He quickly secured an agent and spent his time writing songs for a music publishing company before cutting his own record. He also spent time modeling and attending auditions for acting jobs. He lived there for four years before moving back to the Atlanta area to marry his high school sweetheart, Heather.

Marisol soon met her husband, Charles, while on a visit home from her studies in the dental program at Boston University. It was love at first sight. They married in a beautiful ceremony the following year around the holidays. Everything was decorated in snow white, gold, and red. It was a winter wonderland, and she was a gorgeous bride. She wore a slender-cut sheath dress that flattered her hourglass figure. Her piercing hazel green eyes were accentuated by a fingertip veil atop a delicate pearl and gold tiara. After the honeymoon, Charles moved to be with Marisol as she was about halfway through her program.

The following spring, Emilio, knowing how much Alejandra loved medical topics, invited her to spend her spring break shadowing him at the practice. She was only in fourth grade but already had dreams of working in the medical field. She spent all of her allowance on medical books designed for children when the yearly Scholastic book fair was held at the elementary school. Rather than a trip to the beach or Disney World, Alejandra wanted nothing more than to spend her break learning from her great uncle. Emilio ordered her a small white lab coat with her name embroidered on the front. Alejandra was thrilled and to this day remembers it as one of the best spring breaks ever.

Lolita and Roberto's business saw continued growth, and Andrés, having implemented so many new programs, policies, and best practices, caught the eye of a recruiter from a Fortune 500 company. They offered him a great position as a sales leader with potential for advancement, where he would develop and grow a team of sales representatives. He hated to leave Roberto, but the business was on very solid ground with a great number of loyal clients and customers, and he knew the business would continue to do well. Cristina was on board and excited to see Andrés moving up in the corporate world. Lolita and Roberto were sorry to see him go, but were so proud of him and excited that he had this amazing opportunity.

Emilio and Ana were so proud to see Marisol graduate from dental school in May of 2000. Emilio knew the endless rewards of being a doctor and was so happy to see his daughter follow in his footsteps. Marisol and Charles were excited to see where life would take them next. She knew she wanted to be close to family, so she began researching the possibilities of working as a dentist in Alabama.

The excitement continued as Camila graduated from Samford University with a Bachelor of Science in Human Development and Family Studies. She went on to earn a Master's degree in Marriage and Family Therapy. Emilio and Ana loved seeing their three girls living the life of their dreams. Happiness is all they ever wanted for their family—seeing their girls become highly educated successful young women was more than they could have ever dreamed of.

Another sweet baby joined the family that fall when Isabela and Preston welcomed a new little girl, Jacqueline. She had the most beautiful olive skin with precious dimples on her sweet little cheeks. Scarlett was so excited to be a big sister to this adorable new baby. Lolita and Roberto were thrilled to have another little girl to love.

The family continued thriving. Emilio and Ana were doing great and Emilio's practice was a staple in the Gadsden community. Roberto and Lolita's lives were full and exciting. They were taking more and more time away from the business to travel the world. They were enjoying destinations like Alaska and Brazil and would continue traveling for many years, well into retirement, visiting amazing places like Argentina, Russia, Colombia, Panama, Costa Rica, Hawaii, Puerto Rico, England, Italy, Sweden, Finland, and Chile. They loved traveling—the flights, the cruises, visiting new and old friends around the world—every bit of it was magical to them.

Alex's black-tie wedding in 2002 to Heather was an extravagant celebration. The two families spared no expense throwing the wedding of Heather's dreams. The reception was fit for royalty, held at the Georgian Terrace Hotel across from Atlanta's Fox Theatre. The hotel has a long history of lavish affairs, and this was no exception. The guests swooned over every detail and loved knowing that Margaret Mitchell's "Gone With the Wind" had its star-studded debut at the Georgian Terrace Hotel in 1939.

Later that year, on a warm spring day, Camila married her soulmate, Jack. It was a simple but elegant wedding and she looked radiant in a white satin, strapless dress and a long veil covered with tiny luminescent pearls. They couldn't stop smiling and knew they would remember this day for the rest of their lives. All their family and friends came to celebrate their love and it was a joy for Emilio to give away his baby girl.

To add to the joy, within a few years, both Marisol and Camila each welcomed a baby girl. Elizabeth looked just like Marisol with light hazel eyes and fair skin. She looked like a little porcelain doll. Allison was a perfect combination of Camila and Jack. She had the best features of each, and her tiny little mouth formed a sweet smile.

Roberto and Lolita were excited to welcome yet another grandchild. After a few years of marriage, Alex and Heather welcomed their first baby—finally, a boy! They named him Dylan after Alex's love of the singer-songwriter Bob Dylan. He was so tiny and wrapped in a soft baby blue blanket. No one could take their eyes off of him. He was a perfect shade of pink and had long dark eyelashes. Alex and Heather loved being new parents and doted on him day and night.

Cristina loved being an aunt to Isabela's girls and couldn't wait to love on her first nephew. He was a good baby and rarely cried. Although she felt great, her regular doctor's appointments and labs began slowly showing a decline in her kidney function. In order to be prepared, the doctors began the work up for Cristina for a future kidney transplant. They would have to find a donor, and the doctors gave her the option of having family members tested to see if they were a match. Lolita was the first to step up to be evaluated. After months of testing, she was devastated to find out that while healthy for her age, her kidney function was not sufficient to be a donor. Alex wanted to be tested next. He was young, healthy, and more than willing to do this for his big sister. Though Cristina didn't want him to have to go through this at such a young age, he began the rigorous testing process. Several months later they got the results that Alex was a perfect match for Cristina. They were all so relieved to know they had a living donor ready when the time came. Now it was just a matter of waiting.

Lily had met her match in a man named Stephen. They were introduced at a business networking function and shared a love of current events, trivia, politics, and pop culture. Their dating story is one for the ages, and after years of friendship and dating off and on they decided they belonged with one another. They had a summer wedding in a lovely church they both attended with many friends and family. The flowers were divine in shades of coral, pink, and blush. The bridesmaids wore periwinkle blue floor-length gowns. Lily wore a strapless satin dress and a sheer shoulder covering with baby blue beading matching the bridesmaid's gowns. The bride and groom walked the aisle after becoming husband and wife to an orchestral piece from *Return of the Jedi*. They settled into married life after a honeymoon in Las Vegas. Their stay at the Venetian resort had made them truly feel as though they were in Venice, Italy. It was beautiful.

The next year brought three times the joy with three precious new babies coming into the family. Alex and Heather were thrilled to welcome a sweet baby boy they named Parker. He had light eyes and hair like Heather's side of the family. This baby had the cutest little dimples on his chubby little cheeks, and they fell in love with him instantly. Lily and Stephen added to the girls with the birth of Noelle. She was a fair-skinned beauty from the very start. Her dark blonde hair and brown eyes were mesmerizing. They were beyond happy to welcome their firstborn. Marisol and Charles were enamored with their new baby boy and his strikingly beautiful blue eyes. They named him Lucas. Elizabeth was so excited to have a little brother. Emilio and Ana were thrilled with two precious new babies to spoil.

★

In January of 2007, Cristina went in for a routine appointment, and her doctor expressed concern over her diminishing kidney function. He broke the news that it was time to begin planning for the kidney transplant in the next few months. Cristina's fear rose again, but the doctor talked her through every detail and once again eased her mind that all would be well.

Emory University Hospital was one of the leading transplant centers in the country, performing multiple kidney transplants each week. She was in the best of hands, but it was still very nerve-wracking to know that very soon she would be undergoing major surgery.

The surgery was scheduled for Tuesday, March 20, 2007. The doctor had told her she would be in the hospital for about five days, so Cristina went on a shopping spree and bought all sorts of special things. Pajamas, fancy slippers, electric curlers, and makeup—none of which she would use. Cristina and Alex were feeling good and confident but the same could not be said for Lolita and Roberto. They were a mess. They couldn't believe that two of their children would soon be undergoing major surgery at the same time.

Cristina and Alex were asked to be at the hospital at 6 a.m. to check in on the day of surgery. Cristina was feeling great in her high heels, cute sweater, and slim-fitting black pants. She still could not believe what was about to happen. It was so surreal. She felt so healthy and wondered again and again how this could be happening right now. Andrés was by Cristina's side. He was so nervous that he was grinding his teeth and chipped a tooth. Cristina took his hand and comforted him, telling him everything would be just fine and not to worry.

The doctors took Alex back first. They could not prepare Cristina until they confirmed Alex's kidney was healthy and viable for the transplant. They each had their own transplant team, and once the doctors made the confirmation that it was an optimal kidney, Cristina was taken into surgery. Alex's kidney was considered a "super filtrator," and Cristina couldn't have been luckier to receive such a healthy kidney.

Lolita and Roberto had close to fifty friends and family join them at the hospital to sit with them and pray. They were a nervous wreck. Time seemed to stand still. The surgeries took all day. They were desperate to get any word. Finally, the team of doctors came to speak to Lolita and Roberto. The surgeries both went extremely well. Lolita and Roberto were beyond relieved and couldn't wait to see them once they got out of recovery.

After a few hours in recovery, Lolita and Roberto were allowed to visit with Cristina and Alex in their individual rooms. Both were groggy but in good spirits. The days in the hospital passed pretty quickly. Three times a day, Cristina and Alex were to walk laps around the hospital floor to keep up their strength and to avoid blood clots. Alex's recovery was rough. He was in a great deal of pain for about three weeks. Cristina fared better. She had very little pain.

The following week, Cristina was asked to be at the Emory Transplant Center each morning for labs to be sure everything was going as planned. Andrés took time out of his busy schedule to take her each day. At the end of the week, Roberto and Lolita asked Andrés if they could take her in for her tests. He thought Cristina would like that and told them it was a good idea. They were happy to spend this time with her and when they left the clinic, Lolita asked her if she would like to walk around the mall and have lunch. Cristina loved the idea; they decided to go to Phipps Plaza and have lunch at the Nordstrom Cafe. It felt wonderful for Cristina to have the transplant behind her. She was relieved to be feeling so great so soon after her surgery.

When Cristina left the hospital, she had been given materials and resources for organ transplant recipients, among them, a brochure for the Georgia Transplant Foundation. It listed some of the services the organization offered transplant patients. Additionally, she saw that the yearly transplant conference was scheduled for a few weeks later. She was interested in attending and wanted to participate in some of the breakout sessions to learn more about how to best take care of her new kidney. On the day of the conference, Cristina looked forward to spending time meeting other transplant patients and understanding more about aftercare. While she stood in line at the registration desk, she overheard two women talking in Spanish behind her. They mentioned that they had not seen any material in Spanish and neither of them spoke English. Cristina had learned that minorities were at higher risk for uncontrolled high blood pressure, leading to kidney failure. She approached a woman with a GTF nametag and introduced herself. She told her about the conversation she had overheard.

"Are any of the materials available in Spanish?" asked Cristina.

"No, at this time we don't have any, and unfortunately, we don't have it in our budget for this year," she replied.

"I've learned that minorities have a higher incidence of kidney failure, and I'm wondering, how do they get information on how to take care of their health?" asked Cristina.

"I imagine they get that information from a doctor or local clinic," she said.

"I have an idea," said Cristina. "What if I volunteered to translate all of the material to Spanish? I'm a native speaker and work with several translators at my job that will gladly help us, as they know of my experience."

Within a few weeks, Cristina had facilitated having all of the materials translated into Spanish. They were so pleased with this new offering and Cristina's past experience serving on volunteer boards that they asked her to serve on the Board of Directors for the Georgia Transplant Foundation. It was an immense honor for Cristina to be able to give back to an organization that does such amazing things.

The whole transplant experience opened Cristina's eyes to the bigger story at play. Her selfless brother had graciously given her a gift that no amount of money could buy—the gift of life. It wasn't lost on her that the only reason he was alive to save her life is that many years ago, Emilio had done the seemingly impossible and saved Alex's life, even before he was born. God had blessed this family beyond measure.

★

Alex returned home from the hospital and while he was recuperating at home, Heather gave birth to their last little boy. They named him Matthew. He had chocolate brown eyes and was as cute as a button.

He took on the nickname "Peanut" because he could not have been any more adorable. Their family was now complete.

Roberto had been in negotiations with the state of Georgia, fighting an eminent domain order. The business property sat on a desired piece of land and the state wanted to take possession to expand the entrance onto the freeway. After months of discussion, they agreed on a fair settlement and Roberto began making plans to retire. In a surprising turn of events, months after the final settlement, the state returned the land to Roberto and Lolita after making the necessary improvements. The state of Georgia had taken thirty of the fifty parking spaces in their expansion, making it challenging for customers bringing their cars in for repairs to find parking.

Lolita and Roberto decided they were ready to retire. Alex studied for his commercial real estate license and passed the test with flying colors. He was able to find a buyer who was very familiar with the automobile industry and saw much value in the location and the business. He made them an offer they couldn't refuse, and within a few months, Roberto and Lolita were ready to continue traveling the world. At sixty-seven and sixty-two, they began reaping the fruits of their labor. All of this was possible only because the United States had welcomed them and they had worked diligently day after day to build a life for themselves and their family. They came here with nothing and were truly living the American Dream.

The day Cristina thought she would never see arrived—Alejandra's high school graduation. It was held outdoors in the courtyard of her private school. She graduated with high honors and the whole family was in attendance. Seeing her walk across the stage and receive her diploma filled Cristina with so much gratitude and pride.

Alex returned to his studies and graduated from Oglethorpe University with a Bachelor of Arts in Business Marketing only two months after the transplant. Life was looking up for everyone. Both Alex and Cristina were healing and were feeling better and better every day. The whole family celebrated these milestones with a Caribbean cruise that summer.

The following October, the family would receive devastating news. Isabela discovered a lump in her breast and made an appointment to see her doctor immediately. The doctor found another tumor and told her it did not look good. When preparing the surgical plans, they discovered she had three small tumors in that breast. After they biopsied several of the tumors, thirty-seven-year-old Isabela was diagnosed with Stage II breast cancer as it had already reached her lymph nodes. They didn't waste any time and scheduled her for a complete double mastectomy with reconstruction within a few days. The surgeon ended up removing twenty-eight lymph nodes from her left armpit and arm.

After the surgery, she would undergo four rounds of chemotherapy and thirty-three doses of radiation that left her so weak that many times Lolita would have to take her back to the hospital. Due to the chemotherapy treatments, hair loss was inevitable. She lost all of her long, beautiful thick hair. Her body could not withstand the harsh chemicals and radiation. After many grueling treatments, she was finally declared cancer-free and to this day remains free of cancer. Isabela was able to regrow her hair thicker and fuller than before.

She eventually rebounded and knew she wanted to help other breast cancer patients. One hardship that was particularly difficult was the drains and the lack of drain management systems on the market. She could not easily shower or dress to leave the house for weeks after the surgery. The drains were unruly and unmanageable. Isabela designed a drain management garment to be worn in the shower that fits easily and comfortably, with pouches on either side to manage the drains. The "Pink Pouch" is designed with comfort and dignity in mind. Isabela patented the product sold by her company, Life in the Pink, which continues to help women recovering from breast cancer.

Isabela's recovery was difficult, but she started to see improvement as time passed. She regained her strength slowly but surely and emerged as a stronger, more determined woman filled with gratitude and courage.

In the spring, Alejandra graduated with a Bachelor of Science in Exercise Science from Samford University. This was another day

Cristina thought she would never experience. The day was incredibly meaningful on so many levels. As the family celebrated, Cristina recalled the day when the doctor told her that her future was unknown. She was now healthier than ever, and seeing Alejandra one step closer to living the life of her dreams was extraordinary.

Alex and Heather decided to end their marriage. They had tried to make it work, but in the end, they decided it was best for both them and the children.

Soon more babies made their way into the family. Marisol and Charles had another baby girl and named her Emilia, in honor of her grandfather, Emilio. She had light blue eyes and fair porcelain skin. She was a beautiful baby and completed their family. Camila and Jack welcomed a second little girl named Marie. She was adorable, and Allison was instantly in love with her baby sister. They were so happy with their growing family that within a year, they decided to try for one more, hoping for a boy. They were delighted to welcome James to the family in 2013. He had huge blue eyes and was the perfect bookend to their family.

The biggest surprise of all came from Lily and Stephen. After thinking they would be parents to an only child for many years, Lily discovered she was expecting a baby the following summer. Caroline was born and had blonde hair and her grandmother Ana's striking green eyes. She was precious. Noelle was thrilled as she never thought she would be a big sister. Caroline was the perfect gift they didn't know they wanted.

The following year, the family would grow even more. María de los Angeles and Rafael's oldest daughter, Elena, married her high-school sweetheart, Mateo, in a made-for-Hollywood wedding at Douglas Entrance, a historic venue in Coral Gables, Florida. Elena and Mateo chose their special day to be December 4 as a way to honor her parent's love for each other on their thirty-fourth wedding anniversary. Elena wore an ivory strapless silk gown with her long black hair pulled up in a chignon. She was breathtaking. Her delicate tulle veil brushed past her shoulders and looked as if it were floating when she walked down the aisle on the arms of both María de los Angeles and Rafael. The ceremony honored the Jewish traditions of Rafael's family in a beautiful chuppah covered in white orchids and roses. Elena and Mateo recited lovely vows they had written for each other. The rabbi offered them a metal engraved kiddush cup of red wine to share as he blessed their union. He then asked Elena to circle around her groom seven times, representing the new family they were forming and creating a wall of protection around them. Their final step before becoming husband and wife was the smashing of the glass, which was inside a cloth bag. Mateo stomped on the glass, looked up at Elena, and they both smiled and knew their future awaited. Their reception was elegant and reminiscent of high-society weddings of the 1950s. After dancing the night away to big band music, the newlyweds set off on a one-month European honeymoon to Paris, London, Geneva, Rome, and Venice. Their wedding and honeymoon were the fairytale Elena had always dreamed of. They settled into married life and were blessed with two precious boys, Joseph and Aiden, a few years apart. They had dark hair and eyes and the most incredible long eyelashes. They got them from their mother—they almost didn't look real. Everywhere they went, people would notice and compliment the adorable boys.

Scarlett graduated from high school that summer. She would go on to attend college along with her high school sweetheart, Andrew. Scarlett would eventually earn a Bachelor of Business Administration and Andrew would earn a Bachelor of Exercise Science from Georgia Southern University. The family was so proud of Scarlett and of Andrew, who had become like a son to them. Their future was bright.

Elena's younger sister, Daniela, was busy finishing her college degree in education when she was invited to attend a weekend BBQ at a friend's house. She was happy to take a break from her final projects before graduation. Daniela was in the backyard when she heard a familiar voice. She turned around and was surprised to see her first love from high school standing there. She and Anthony had dated on and off, and life had taken them down separate paths. She couldn't believe her eyes. She had thought about him through the years, but things never worked out to reconnect and rekindle their relationship.

After hugs and laughter, they sat in a corner of the patio in a small loveseat and talked until nightfall, not paying attention to anyone else at the party. Now that she was an adult, Daniela knew that she had found the love of her life. He was attentive, kind, funny, and enjoyed the simple yet meaningful things in life, just like her. They got to know each other all over again at a more mature level, and over time, they knew they wanted to spend the rest of their lives with one another. Unlike the grand celebration held for her sister's wedding, Daniela wanted a private ceremony. They ultimately decided to elope, and afterward, they took a wonderful two-week honeymoon to Europe, visiting Florence, Rome, Pisa, Tuscany, and charming small towns like San Gimignano in Italy. They also traveled to England and rang in the new year with a spectacular firework display in the city center of London. It was a dream come true for them.

Soon after they returned from their honeymoon, Daniela and Anthony were thrilled to learn they would be having a baby in the fall. Daniela would spend most of her pregnancy feeling sick and exhausted. Right around her due date, all the Miami TV stations had wall-to-wall coverage that Hurricane Irma was barreling toward South Florida. With the news of a massive storm forecasted to hit land within days, Daniela's doctor scheduled her to be induced. She and Anthony were concerned at first and then began to panic as homes and businesses lost power. They made their way to Baptist Hospital, and after a difficult labor, they welcomed a sweet little girl named Grace Eliza. She had a fair complexion with green eyes and brown hair. She was beautiful. Daniela and Anthony couldn't take their eyes off this new life they were blessed with. Their little family grew again a few years later when they had a precious baby boy. They named him Jordan, and he had green eyes and light brown hair. Daniela had been told she would need a cesarean section because this baby would weigh more than nine pounds. The moment she saw him, she fell in love with this cuddly baby. He was a very good baby and slept through the night after a few months. He never cried unless it was time for a feeding. Grace loved helping Daniela take care of him and declared that he was her baby too.

María de los Angeles and Rafael's son, Diego, was a smart, thoughtful, and fun-loving young man. He studied accounting at Florida International University with dreams of one day becoming a CPA. He was ambitious and had several jobs while in school. He worked at an accounting firm several times a week on the days he didn't have classes. In the evenings, he would wait tables at a sushi restaurant in the Doral area of Miami and enjoyed the interaction with people from all over the world. In his free time, he liked to play basketball, golf, travel and spend time with his friends. His hard work in school paid off and he opened his own accounting firm to much success soon after becoming a CPA.

María de los Angeles and Rafael's children were becoming successful and independent young adults with children of their own. The families continued to get together as often as they could. The children all got along well and remain very close to this day.

Alejandra had been working in healthcare at a clinic that specialized in helping under-insured patients. She loved this work. It was her passion and her lifelong purpose. She knew she would need a higher level of education to pursue her calling at a greater capacity. After working at the clinic for several years, she applied to the Accelerated Masters in Nursing Pathway at the University of Alabama at Birmingham. The program was designed for students with a Bachelor's degree in another field to receive their Bachelor's and Master's in Science consecutively.

Alejandra excelled in the program and graduated with honors as a family nurse practitioner. She would go on to become manager of clinical operations at a clinic serving the population she loves the most—underserved patients—in Indianapolis, Indiana. Cristina could hardly contain her joy at seeing her daughter earn a Master's degree and working in a field that she loved. She was once again so grateful for the blessing of being here, healthy, and watching her only daughter achieve her dreams.

Alex found love again with Emma. They were a match made in heaven. They tied the knot in 2018, and within the year they welcomed a sweet little boy with butterscotch brown eyes and a headful of curly brown hair, named Marco. His older brothers doted over him and having a baby around again brought so much joy and fun.

Lolita and Roberto were smitten with this new baby. Alex would send videos to their phones of Marco playing, eating, and eventually talking and running around. They were delighted and would watch them often—which always brought a smile to their faces.

★

Jacqueline's high school graduation in 2020 was unlike any other. The Covid-19 pandemic impacted all American schools, and many events were now being held with Covid restrictions. She was fortunate to be able to have an in-person graduation, but everyone sat six feet apart, wearing masks. It had a totally different feel than what she expected. Jacqueline had big dreams of a huge graduation party with her friends and family and now she found herself unable to have a big celebration. The family was so proud of her and celebrated with a small gathering at a high-end restaurant that would still make the day feel very special. Jacqueline would leave for college in a few months, following in Scarlett's footsteps. She would attend Georgia Southern University, declaring a major in Marketing to earn a Bachelor's in Business Administration as well.

2020 was a year of global suffering due to the Covid-19 pandemic. It was filled with so much loss, uncertainty, fear, and so many feelings of helplessness. For the family, their losses, tragedies, and grief were compounded when María de los Angeles passed away on August 15 from complications of Alzheimer's at the age of sixty-seven. The family grieved for this beautiful light that had gone out. Roberto had tirelessly searched for her for many years and had finally found her, only to lose her to this terrible disease. The most painful part of all was that due to the coronavirus, this wife, mother, sister, and friend who was so loved, was in isolation at the hospital when she died, with no one by her side. Rafael had cared for her for many years with unsurpassed dedication. She was the love of his life and he had done everything possible to keep her healthy. Everyone should be so fortunate to find a once-in-a-lifetime love like the one María de los Angeles and Rafael shared. It was what every love story aspires to be. In the end, he and the children were not allowed to be with her. They learned of her death when they received a phone call from the hospital, bringing additional suffering to the family because of the pandemic. She was buried in a ceremony upholding traditional Jewish customs and only close family was permitted to attend. All others joined in a video conference. Her warmth, beauty, and generosity of spirit will live in the hearts of all those that loved her.

Only six weeks later, on October 1, Emilio succumbed to the ravages of Parkinson's disease a few days before his eighty-third birthday. His decline had been gradual over the years, but the last few weeks of his life were excruciating for the family as they watched this intelligent, vivacious, and loving husband, father, brother, uncle, and friend slip away. After several days in the hospital with end-of-life symptoms, the doctors sent him home for comfort care. They ordered a hospital bed that arrived by the time he was transferred home. He was made as comfortable as possible, and in less than twenty-four hours, he passed peacefully into eternity. He was surrounded by his entire family, and Lily's beautiful soft voice sang him into heaven with traditional hymns and a song called "In the Presence of Jehovah" at the moment of his passing. The void this amazing man left in all who knew him was enormous. His humor, kindness, fierce loyalty, and love for life will be missed and treasured by everyone who knew him. Emilio and Ana had celebrated their fiftieth wedding anniversary in July, only a few months before his death. Theirs was a deep and abiding love that only grew stronger with each year that passed. Emilio lived life on his own terms and lived it to the fullest. Not many people can say they have been invited to two dinners at the White House hosted by Presidents

Ronald Reagan and George H. W. Bush. Or that they've flown on Air France's Concorde from New York to London on a flight lasting just under three hours on the supersonic jet, compared to a subsonic jet at seven to eight hours. Or that they traveled to Kuwait for a business opportunity with a medical supply company. Or, more grand than any other achievement, attained their lifelong dream, which for Emilio, was to be a doctor for thirty-six years, until his retirement in 2018. In his later years, his three daughters and eight grandchildren brought him and Ana great happiness. Even with the struggles of his condition, he persevered and never lost his positive attitude and love for life.

★

The summer of 2021 brought an event Lolita and Roberto thought they would never see. The Cuban citizens planned massive peaceful protests across the island after sixty-two years of oppression, scarcity, and isolation from the world. They were met with violence, kidnappings, and imprisonments from government enforcers just for expressing their desire to be free after so many years of suffering. Some global media outlets focused on this event, but the U.S. media sadly relegated it to the sidelines. It still remains a massive humanitarian crisis, as the unarmed citizens have no viable way of overthrowing the oppressive government. Their weapons were taken away at the start of the revolution, enabling the communist government to perpetrate human rights violations through the decades, never allowing the citizens to decide for themselves as there are no free elections. Lolita and Roberto watched in disbelief and sadness knowing that nothing will ever change unless an outside entity steps in to defend a defenseless population.

That fall, Scarlett and Andrew had the magical wedding they had been waiting for since they fell in love in seventh grade. No expense was spared. Isabela and Preston wanted it to be the perfect day for their daughter. It was the social event of the year. Scarlett looked amazing. She wore an ivory lace dress with a plunging neckline and fitted bodice and skirt that flared out just above the knee. Her long dark hair was perfectly styled under a simple veil with a long train. The weather on that October day was perfect for an outdoor wedding. Blue skies and warm temperatures made for a gorgeous ceremony under a formal altar surrounded by columns. The bridal party was huge, with twelve bridesmaids and twelve groomsmen. The whole affair was fit for royalty. The reception included a full sit-down dinner, craft cocktails, and a live band. They honeymooned in Punta Cana, a beautiful resort town in the Dominican Republic. Scarlett and Andrew enjoyed many adventures—zip lining, snorkeling with sharks, riding horses on the beach, and relaxing at the resort with good food and cocktails. Lolita and Roberto and the entire family were so excited to finally see Scarlett and Andrew become husband and wife.

★

A few weeks later, the Atlanta Braves had once again made it to the World Series. The city of Atlanta was in a frenzy. Roberto felt like a little boy again, playing baseball with his friends in La Palma. He was so excited, and every time he spoke with Alex he would update him on all of the most current stats in the series. Alex wanted nothing more than to surprise his father with tickets to game four of the series being played at Truist Park in Atlanta against the Houston Astros. Several years earlier, Roberto had been diagnosed with the beginning stages of dementia, but he never missed a baseball game on television. He continued to be a die-hard Atlanta Braves fan and remembered clearly when the Braves made it to the World Series in 1991. The game was an experience of a lifetime with his son, and he thought about that day often. Alex had never forgotten their time together at the '91 series and searched for the best tickets he could get to see the Braves play in the World Series. He finally found the perfect seats and was able to give his father the amazing news that they would be going to the World Series again together. Roberto was ecstatic and waited for Alex to pick him up on game day. They drove to the park early and secured their seats before standing in line for all of their favorite ballpark treats—hot dogs, nachos, and huge soft pretzels. The smells, sights, and sounds brought back a flood of memories for them both from their time together at the '91 game. They had an amazing night, and this time, the Braves won the game and went on to win the Series. The Atlanta Braves were World Series Champions again, and Alex would not have traded this night for anything. It was a full-circle moment, one that neither of them would ever forget.

★

Roberto and Lolita's children were now grown with families of their own. They were so proud of the life and education they had provided for their children. In only one generation, they had changed the course of their family.

The years had passed quickly. Roberto and Lolita's fifty-fifth wedding anniversary was a joyful milestone in 2020. They had planned something special to celebrate their marriage with an elaborate trip to the Amalfi Coast of Italy. But in an unprecedented turn of events, the Covid-19 pandemic struck the world and put all of their plans on hold. They were finally able to reschedule their trip for November of 2021, though. As they waited for the taxi to the airport, Roberto thought of that day fifty-three years ago when he and Lolita were waiting for another taxi that would take them to a different airport and a new life.

There, they would take a flight that would forever change them. They had been two kids that left everything they had in search of freedom, with nothing but a dream.

The days they spent in little Italian cafes and relaxing on the terrazza of their beautiful villa were a dream come true for them. Every night before they tucked into bed, they would open all the windows and the sound of the waves crashing against the cliffs would send them peacefully off to sleep.

On the last evening of this most memorable trip, the sun was setting over the Mediterranean Sea as Roberto and Lolita were finishing their anniversary dinner. The view of the sapphire water against the fiery sunset was breathtaking, and a warm breeze danced around them. They stayed at the table long after eating their wonderful meal. They drank wine, laughed, and reminisced on a life full of love and adventure.

Tonight, when they were back in their villa, they opened the windows and stood there for a moment. Lolita and Roberto looked in wonder at the nighttime sky. They marveled at the millions of twinkling stars above them and knew the greatness of God's hand had guided them throughout their lives.

As Lolita thought about the last fifty-five years, she was reminded of a quote from her favorite book, *The Alchemist* by Paulo Coelho. "It's the possibility of having a dream come true that makes life interesting."

She turned to Roberto and said, "Thank you for sharing my dreams and for creating a *most* interesting life for us, *mi amor*."

They embraced under the canopy of stars, and for a few precious moments, they felt like the only two people in the entire world.

CHAPTER TWENTY-EIGHT

ATLANTA, GEORGIA
2022

Day turned to evening and evening turned to night as Cristina sat in complete awe of all that her father shared with her about her family. The hours had passed in a heartbeat. She was enraptured by the stories of her family's past.

Cristina had spent the last few weeks so wrapped up in her own heartache and pain that she had forgotten just how much life was worth living despite all of its challenges.

"Thank you for sharing the story of your life, *Papi*," said Cristina as she wiped tears from her eyes.

"It has been my pleasure, *muñeca*—doll," replied Roberto as he reached over to lovingly wipe a tear away from Cristina's cheek. "Sometimes in life, we have to look back in order to move forward," Roberto continued.

"You come from a long line of strong men and women. We have all faced insurmountable challenges that have tested our character, but we've learned to look for the blessings in everything," said Roberto. "You are no different, *mi amor*. You will look back on this time one day and see that all along, you were becoming the woman and mother you were always meant to be."

Lolita looked at her husband and daughter, feeling all of the love between them and the love that had been passed down by each generation. Lolita was proud of their family's history of courage and determination.

Through her sadness, Cristina mustered the words, "Why does it hurt so badly right now? Will it always feel this way?"

"It hurts so deeply because you have given of yourself and you have known great love. You are grieving a great loss and that takes time. But I promise you that it won't always hurt this badly," said Roberto.

"How do you know?" asked Cristina.

"I know because I have been in your position many times in my life—heartbroken, lost, confused—but time has a way of working out our sufferings. And each time, we grow stronger. You don't feel it now, but you will. You will, *mi amor*," reassured Roberto.

"Your father is right. The tough times expand our capacity for gratitude, purpose, and resilience," said Lolita. "These are the moments that show us what we are made of."

"I understand, *Mami*," said Cristina. "I just wish I could be on the other side of this pain. But I hope from the stories I've heard today, I will come out stronger than I was before."

"Yes, you will, my girl," said Roberto.

"I am going to prepare some *manzanilla* tea for us and will be back in a few minutes," said Lolita.

As Lolita made her way to the kitchen, Roberto took Cristina's hand in his. There was no need for words. They sat quietly as the beauty of their treasured family stories surrounded them. The stories had now found a home inside Cristina's heart. She was grateful to learn so much about the strength and bravery each and every generation brought forward with them to the next.

Lolita walked back into the living room with a wooden tray holding three green and gold porcelain cups on delicate saucers. The tea was an amber color with piping ribbons of steam wafting into the air. The smell reminded Lolita of when she was a young woman and Angela would make tea for the two of them to sit and catch up at the end of the day. Lolita missed her mother. There wasn't a day she didn't think of the strong mother whose qualities she embodied. Lolita offered the cups to Cristina and Roberto, and they continued to talk while highlights of the stories milled around Cristina's mind.

Each story her father told deeply resonated with different parts of her heart—the love between her grandparents, Daniel and Gabriela, reminded her of her own mother and father's love for one another and their deep dedication to their children and family. Cristina had at times taken this level of love for granted as most children do of their parents, but hearing these stories gave her a new perspective on what love truly means.

"Although I never had the opportunity to meet some of our family members, the enduring qualities they passed down to future generations have given us so much—including one of the most important qualities, the strength to persevere in the face of adversity," said Cristina. "I also think about the lifelong struggles my grandfather Daniel endured and how he never gave up on his family. Everything he did, he did for them."

"He was a man of strong faith and family values. His influence has had an incredible ripple effect on each of us," said Lolita.

"Yes, he had a huge heart," said Cristina.

"I remember throughout our lives how you both have come back from defeats and failures that would have devastated others with such resilience and determination. I admire you more than you could ever know," said Cristina. "Your devotion to our family and to each other during these times has been the gift you have given us all."

"In our minds, there was no other way to handle difficult situations," said Lolita. "We had to find a solution when the odds were stacked against us."

"I can now see how my grandmother Angela instilled these same values in you, *Mami*. Her quiet strength and sense of purpose always guided her decisions. She encouraged you and my uncle Emilio to always follow your dreams," said Cristina. "I remember as a young girl when he, my aunt Ana, and their two little girls moved to Mexico from the United States for him to begin medical school. He was incredibly brave to do this at thirty-seven. It showed me that nothing could interfere with the pursuit of his dreams. It was a tremendous sacrifice but one he knew he had to make. He was an extraordinary uncle, a protective brother, a devoted husband, an adoring father, a gifted physician, and a loyal friend to everyone he met. I miss him terribly."

Lolita's eyes welled with tears at the thought of having lost him just a little over a year ago at the age of eighty-two. A gentle smile crossed her lips when she remembered the good times she had shared with her irreplaceable brother and best friend. Cristina placed her hand on Lolita's shoulder and gently comforted her.

"His dreams were bold, and he had the courage to make them come true," said Cristina.

"He was a trailblazer," said Lolita, wiping away a tear.

"Yes, he was," said Cristina. "It amazes me the level of dedication and heart he and so many others displayed to achieve their own dreams. When I think of Dr. and Señora Sanchez, we have so much to be thankful for. Although not part of our family, they selflessly stepped in when my grandfather needed them most. Their willingness to help led them to achieve their dream of having their own family. They raised María de los Angeles in a loving home and gave her a charmed life—they adored her. She grew into a kind and beautiful woman—a loving aunt, a caring daughter, a faithful wife, a dedicated mother, a dear sister, and a delightful friend. Her heart expanded to fit a lifetime of love she graciously received and so freely returned to the family she didn't know she had. Your bond was forged the first time your eyes met—she had found her missing piece."

"Yes, I vividly remember when we saw each other for the first time," said Roberto with a faraway look in his eyes. "It was the moment I had been waiting for all my life. She had a light in her eyes that was magic. I feel her absence every day."

The tears streamed down Lolita, Roberto, and Cristina's cheeks. The mixed emotions they felt were all because of love—the love of family—those that are no longer here and those we are fortunate enough to still have with us. Cristina was sitting between her parents and stretched out her arms to bring them both in for a hug. They stayed there for a moment and Lolita and Roberto were thankful for the opportunity to share these amazing memories with Cristina. The account of their family's history had now been passed down to the next generation. Cristina was now the keeper of these special stories.

"I can't begin to tell you how extraordinary it has been to spend the day with you both and learn the details of the courageous, strong, determined, and loving family we belong to," said Cristina as she stood from her chair. "Listening to the many stories of bravery and the challenges so many of our loved ones have overcome, I know I can't give up on my life and on my dreams. I am going to gather my things and go back home. I don't know what will happen, but I have a legacy to uphold."

Roberto and Lolita looked at each other with slightly raised eyebrows and smiled gingerly—it was the look of optimism. They wanted the best for Cristina and her family and were happy to see her follow in the footsteps of so many that faced adversity and were victorious in the past.

"I spoke with Alejandra this morning, and she and Andrés had planned to have pizza and watch a movie at home tonight," said Cristina. "If she calls here, please do not say anything to her."

"We will not say anything," said Lolita.

Cristina quickly walked back to her childhood bedroom. It only took her a few minutes to pack her clothes, shoes, toiletries, and her small brown leather journal. Every day since she was in seventh grade, Cristina had been keeping a diary that later became a journal. All of her secrets were kept in the dozens of notebooks stored in the cedar chest at the foot of the bed. They were safe, and it gave her a sense of nostalgia to know her thoughts and musings from so many years ago were there for her anytime she wanted to read them. Cristina threw everything in the bag she had brought with her and took it to the front door. She then went to the kitchen to get her car keys and give her parents each a hug. This morning when she awakened, she couldn't have imagined today would hold so much emotion and pride in her family. She would always remember everything about this day.

"I am so grateful for the time we've shared," said Cristina. "May I take the photo of my grandmother to share with Alejandra?"

"Yes, you may. It was a very special day for us to share with you, *mi amor*," said Roberto.

"*Gracias, Papi*," I will call you once I speak with Alejandra and Andrés."

"That sounds very good. I will look forward to hearing from you," said Lolita.

Cristina gave them one last hug and placed her bag in the trunk of her sleek charcoal gray BMW. They waved to her as she backed out of the driveway and she waved goodbye. During the drive home, Cristina felt nervous but knew she had to bravely face her future. She turned into their neighborhood and felt her pulse quicken. It was elevated in equal parts hope and fear. Hope for her future and fear of the unknown. It was a chance she had to take. She was nervous and her hands had grown cold. Her heart felt wide open—more so than it had ever been. If anyone would have told her just last week that she would be in this position, she would have never believed it. She circled her car around the back of their elegant home and pulled up to her side of the garage. The carriage-style garage door was closed, and she knew as soon as she pressed her opener, Alejandra and Andrés would be startled by the noise and open the door leading from the house to the garage.

Cristina hesitated for a moment. She knew that once the garage door started to lift, her life would be different—one way or another. She slowly raised her trembling hand and gently touched the button on the opener. Before the garage door reached the top, she could see the door leading to the house had been opened. Andrés and Alejandra were standing there with puzzled looks on their faces.

Cristina parked her car and opened the door. Alejandra came running to hug her mother.

"Mom!" said Alejandra. "You're home!"

"I didn't know you would be coming home tonight," said Andrés.

"Neither did I," said Cristina with a faint smile. "I've learned some things about my family from my parents today that have made me think about our marriage and our family—all that we have been through together."

"I'd love to hear more," said Andrés.

"It's late and I'm very tired. Can we talk about it tomorrow?" asked Cristina.

"Of course," said Andrés.

Cristina took her bag from the trunk of her car and rolled it inside. She reached for a glass from the cabinet and filled it with water to take with her to the guest bedroom.

"I was just getting ready to leave," said Alejandra.

"I'm so glad I got to see you, my girl," said Cristina as she pulled her in for another hug. "I'm going to make breakfast in the morning. Can you come by around 11:00?"

"Yes, I can be here then," said Alejandra. "Will you be here too, Dad?"

"I will be here, sweetheart," said Andrés with a smile.

Alejandra hugged her father and left with a hopeful heart.

The next morning, the smell of a *cafécito* Cubano brewing awakened Andrés. The delicious aroma brought back warm feelings of the good times they had shared in their many years of marriage. He wanted his thoughts to linger here in the happy moments, but his mind went to the arguments and hurtful words they had said to each other before she left. He regretted them once he was alone with his thoughts, but he knew she needed time to think things through at her parents' home this past week. He rolled out of bed and slipped on a pair of red plaid pajama pants and an old T-shirt. After brushing his teeth and running his fingers to tame his wavy hair, he walked downstairs, barefoot and hungry.

"Good morning, how did you sleep?" asked Cristina.

"I tossed and turned some but finally was able to get a few hours of rest," said Andrés as he walked to the stovetop and poured himself a small cup of Cuban coffee. "How about you?"

"I was exhausted. As soon as my head hit the pillow, I was out and I didn't wake up until just a little while ago," said Cristina.

"I'm glad you got to rest. It's good to have you home and I know we need to talk, but can we save that for later, after Alejandra leaves today?" asked Andrés.

"Yes, of course," said Cristina as she opened the refrigerator and reached for the ingredients she needed to cook breakfast. "I'm preparing breakfast," said Cristina. "Would you like for me to make enough for you?"

"Yes, please," said Andrés.

He sat at the kitchen table and leafed through the Atlanta Business Chronicle as he sipped his cafecito. He enjoyed his Sunday morning routine.

The smells coming from the kitchen were delectable—the sizzling bacon, the fluffy scrambled eggs, and the buttery croissants. They put a smile on Alejandra's face as she opened the door to her parent's home.

"Something smells wonderful," said Alejandra. "It's a good thing I'm hungry."

Cristina, Andrés, and Alejandra sat around the table enjoying the delicious meal Cristina had prepared and catching up. In some ways, it felt like old times to Cristina, but she knew that she and Andrés had many things they needed to talk about. The food and conversation were a good place to start reconnecting so they could communicate in a caring space.

When it was time to get ready for the day, Alejandra helped Cristina wash the breakfast plates, while Andrés went upstairs to shower. Cristina and Alejandra loved having a few minutes to themselves for girl talk. It only took them a few minutes to wrap up the leftovers, put everything in the dishwasher, and wipe down the counters. The kitchen was spotless, so they opened the French doors leading to the outdoor patio and sat on the soft tan cushions of the oversized brown wicker chairs to enjoy the cool fall weather. They talked and laughed and loved spending this time together. Before they realized it, more than an hour had passed and when Alejandra looked at her watch, she said, "Oh no, I am going to miss my massage and facial appointments at the spa this afternoon if I don't leave in the next few minutes. I only have thirty minutes to get there, park, and be ready."

"I wish you could stay," said Cristina.

"Me too, Mom," said Alejandra. "I am so happy that I was able to join you and Dad for breakfast. By the way, what's going on with you guys?"

"I'm not really sure, honey," said Cristina.

"I know things had gotten pretty bad before you left, but I've seen Dad a few times this week and he seemed sad. He told me that he wished things had not escalated to the point where you would leave. He said that he didn't know if you and he could ever go back to what you had, but being without you this week for the first time in your marriage has made him realize that he at least wanted to talk and see if your relationship could be salvaged."

"He told you that?" asked Cristina.

"Yes, I think that his fear of losing you felt real this past week," said Alejandra.

"I'm surprised to hear that," said Cristina. "Our last argument was very hurtful. I would like for us to talk too once he comes back downstairs."

"You mentioned last night that you had spent the day with my grandparents, Alita and Papa, and they had shared stories from our family's history," said Alejandra. "I want you to tell me some of those stories."

"I can't wait to tell you of the incredible courage, perseverance, and love that guided so many in our family through terrible situations," said Cristina. "They also told me stories of hope, happiness, and healing that were woven through the generations. The experiences were both unbelievable and inspirational."

"I will be finished at the spa at 5 p.m.," said Alejandra. "I want to come back and at least hear some of the stories that have touched you so deeply."

"Yes, I would love that," said Cristina. "I will be making lasagne this evening, so why don't you come back and help me prepare it?"

"Yes, that sounds good. I'll be back as soon as I'm finished," said Alejandra. "I'm so happy you were able to spend this special time with Alita and Papa and learn about our ancestors."

"I can't wait to tell you the stories that inspired so much courage and made me feel optimistic about my future—and the future of our family," said Cristina. "I know that it won't be an easy road, but our family has never backed away from adversity."

"I know you are fearless and give your entire self to everything you do," said Alejandra. "You inspire me, and I can't wait to come back home," said Alejandra. She gave Cristina a quick kiss on the cheek and swung her purse onto her shoulder before leaving.

Cristina loved the closeness she shared with Alejandra. They were best friends. They not only loved to spend time together, but they were each other's greatest supporters. Cristina felt happy that Alejandra would be back soon. In the meantime, the weather was too wonderful to stay indoors so she took a book her mother had given her from her purse, *The Alchemist*, and a plush cream-colored blanket and settled in the same comfy chair she had used before. She began reading and was pulled into the story within the first few pages. She was immersed in this magical tale when she heard the door leading out to the patio open. She looked back and saw Andrés standing there with a pensive but soft expression on his face. Cristina placed her bookmark on the page she was reading and closed the book before sliding it onto the coffee table.

"Why don't you have a seat?" asked Cristina.

Andrés wanted to wrap his arms around her and hug her for days. She had always been his soft place to land, but this past week had been a glimpse into what his life would be without Cristina. It was something he hoped would never come to pass. He held his emotions close to his heart and slowly sat in the chair across from Cristina.

"What have you been doing this afternoon?" asked Cristina.

"I was going to read for a little while and ended up taking a nap," said Andrés. "The last few weeks at work have been stressful and the tension between us kept me from sleeping well."

"I spent the week mostly in bed at my parents' house," said Cristina. "It was a very tough week after the fights we had and the terrible things we said to each other."

"I just want to tell you that I have felt awful about the things I said to you. I know we had been having problems for a long time, but you didn't deserve my anger and my disrespect," said Andrés. "I am sorry for pushing you away. I'm glad that you are back home. We truly need to think about what our future will look like. We have to decide if we will find happiness together or apart. Whichever it is, we should be respectful of each other's decisions."

"I am prepared to have the difficult conversations," said Cristina. "That is the only way we will know. Over the past week, my thoughts were filled with anger, despair, and profound sadness. The last thing in the world I would ever imagine is that we would be here today—talking with you in a much different way from the night I left. I know neither of us wants to throw away our relationship but we each have to do some soul searching."

They talked for hours.

"I'm willing to try if you are," said Andrés, as he leaned forward and took Cristina's hand in his. Cristina looked away and then gazed into Andrés's eyes. She wasn't sure they could ever make it work. She loved him and she knew that he loved her. They both adored their only daughter and for many years, they had been happy—maybe they could find that happiness again.

"Yes, Andrés," said Cristina. "We have been through a lot together. We have known both joy and pain and all of the emotions in between. I am not sure how I feel, but I think it may be too late to save our marriage. We have grown apart and are different people. My mindset has changed from being hurt and angry to wanting to move forward with all of the love and respect we have always shared in order for each of us to find our forever happiness."

Andrés looked down at the ground. He slowly stood from his chair. He embraced Cristina with his whole heart. It felt like the first time he had put his arms around her so many years ago. They stayed there without saying a word for a long time. They both knew that there would be no fixing their marriage, but perhaps a beautiful friendship would remain.

"Mom, Dad," called out Alejandra. "Are you home?"

"Yes, we are on the patio," said Andrés.

They met in the kitchen and Alejandra could tell something was different

"What happened?" asked Alejandra with a confused look on her face.

"We've talked about our relationship and our family and how we want to move forward," said Andrés. "We have weathered many storms together and we want to be able to give each other the gifts of grace, of forgiveness, of patience, and, most importantly, the gift of happiness. Your mother and I have decided after much discussion to continue to care and love for each other but to go our separate ways. We are dedicated to our family and you no matter what."

"I was afraid that you would tell me that," said Alejandra. "I'm happy to know you will both remain committed to our family. I know relationships are complicated, but the love that we share as a family is special. You have to do whatever you can to find happiness."

Andrés pulled both of his girls into a tight hug—they were his world. Today had been unexpected. It was not the outcome he was hoping for, but he respected Cristina's need to live the life she wanted. After a moment, Cristina was the first to step back. She felt a sense of hope that had been missing for so long.

"I am going to start preparing dinner before it gets too late," said Cristina. "It will be ready soon."

"I'm going upstairs to collect my thoughts and change for dinner," said Andrés.

"A homemade dinner sounds so good, and lasagna is my favorite," said Alejandra.

"Why don't you help me set the table while I start cooking?" asked Cristina.

"Sure, I'm glad to do it," said Alejandra.

It wasn't long before they were once again sitting around the table to a delicious meal and enjoying each other's company—laughing, reminiscing, and telling wonderful stories of their own family, despite their decision today. After dinner, Alejandra wasn't ready for this time with her parents to end. She had seen their struggles in recent years, and although it was sad to see her parent's marriage end, she was hopeful they would remain a tight-knit family.

"This was all so good, Mom," said Alejandra. "Thank you for preparing it for us."

"Your lasagna has always been the best," said Andrés. "I wouldn't trade it for one from the best Italian restaurant in all of Atlanta."

"Thank you," said Cristina. "It makes me happy that you both loved it."

"How about we help clear the table and then we can all watch a movie?" asked Alejandra.

Cristina and Andrés exchanged glances and then looked at Alejandra. They knew she wasn't ready to leave. As much as Cristina wanted to spend time with her, the last two days had been a whirlwind. After lying in bed for a week, her energy was zapped. She wasn't sure how long she would be able to stay awake.

"I'm down for a movie," said Andrés.

"I don't know," said Cristina. "I'm kind of tired from everything that has happened since yesterday morning."

"Come on, Mom," said Alejandra in a drawn-out tone.

"Okay, as long as I can get into some comfy clothes," said Cristina as she started up the stairs. "Come with me, Alejandra. There is something I want to show you."

Alejandra followed her mother into the guest bedroom and sat on the bed. Cristina's suitcase lay open on the floor in their guest bedroom. She sat down and felt around for her soft black leggings and light blue T-shirt. She carefully unfolded the T-shirt to reveal a beautiful vintage picture inside a pewter picture frame.

"What is that?" asked Alejandra, coming in closer to see the picture.

"It is something very special," said Cristina. "It is a picture of Papa's mother, your great-grandmother. Her name was Gabriela, and she was a soft-spoken and brave woman. She was the loving wife to your great-grandfather Daniel and the dedicated mother to Papa and his nine siblings."

"Where did you get this?" asked Alejandra.

"I asked Papa to let me bring it home so I could share it with you," said Cristina. "He and Alita told me stories of so many in our family throughout the generations who faced adversities and tragedies that would break most people. They lived through tremendous joys and persevered through deep sorrows. Our family's heritage of love, strength, and determination is something we must keep close to our hearts."

"I want to know more about my great-grandmother and the others..." said Alejandra. "I would love to hear these stories that mean so much to Alita and Papa and now to you."

"It will take us a while, so I'm guessing you are okay with skipping the movie tonight?" asked Cristina.

"Absolutely," said Alejandra as she sat on the floor across from her mother.

Cristina wasn't sure where she would start to tell the incredible stories of their family's history. She would now be passing these down to her daughter.

"I never got to meet them, but Papa told me so many stories of how our family was full of love for one another," said Cristina. "Alita and Papa had this picture of his mother and another of his father restored. He couldn't remember the last time he had seen a picture of his parents. He said it brought him so much joy to see them after all these years."

"I would love to see more pictures and hear the stories of our family from long ago," said Alejandra curiously. "I want to know what stories he told you that inspired you and gave you so much hope. Can you tell me more about our family?"

"Well, let's go back to 1936 . . . ."

ACKNOWLEDGMENTS

My heart swells with inexplicable gratitude and love for my ancestors and family members for having the courage to face and overcome adversity and for never giving up on their dreams. I am and will be forever grateful for the love they held in their hearts and passed down through each generation. I will keep the stories I've learned in *my* heart for the rest of time.

Gracias infinitas to my parents, Loida and Roberto Osaba, for your love, support, and encouragement through my entire life but especially so during the writing of this memoir. Your patience in telling me your experiences, which became so many of the stories in this book, was limitless. After all these years, I've come to fully understand your love and absolute dedication to our family and the immense sacrifices you made. You risked everything for our freedom, and for that gift, I will be eternally grateful.

Many thanks to my brother, Robb Osaba, and my sister, Suzette Osaba Bryan. You are and have always been my best friends, confidants, and sounding boards for everything. We have laughed, cried, and laughed until we cried. I treasure you both.

Very special thanks to my daughter, Lindsey Pimentel, for being my biggest cheerleader and supporter in writing this book and in life. You inspire me every day with your kind and beautiful heart. You are my greatest blessing. I love you to the moon and back.

I would like to express my sincere gratitude to my A-team, whose talent, dedication, and tireless efforts helped me bring my family's story to life. I am thankful for the countless hours you all invested into our shared vision of this project. Meredith Dunn with Freedom Press, my consultant and content editor extraordinaire. Your compassion and guidance helped me tell this story in a way that would make my ancestors and family proud. Charissa Newell, my cover and interior designer. You are a true artist and captured the feelings and emotions of my family's stories in your artwork beautifully. Steph Spector, my wonderful editor. You did an amazing job editing a partially bilingual book, including accents, without knowing how to speak Spanish.

A special note of appreciation to Ozzie Areu, Ralph de la Vega, Judith Martínez-Sadri, Dr. Pierluigi Mancini, Isabel González Whitaker, Christian Espinosa, Brandon Andress, Lia Valencia Key, Dr. Jason Young, Tim Drake, and Robyn Benincasa for your enthusiasm and support. I am humbled and honored to have these shining stars in their own right believe in me and in my family's story.

Many thanks to my friends, family, and colleagues for your never-ending support, interest, and excitement to read our story.

Thank you to the members of my weekly writing group. You have inspired and challenged me with constructive feedback, spirited discussions, and friendship.

I wish to thank those family members who are no longer with us for the example they set for us all. I so wish they could have read the complete stories of our family and seen all the beauty that dwells in the lives they created. The love they so freely gave lives on in all of us.

To my favorite authors, Paulo Coelho and Andre Dubus III, and to my favorite screenplay writer, Roberto Benigni, I want to thank you for inspiring me and teaching me how to tell a story.

I thank God, for without Him, none of this would have been possible.

I have dreamed of this heartfelt and emotional retelling of my family's journey for many years and am thrilled to share it with you now.

RECIPES

LOLITA'S CUBAN PICADILLO
(SEASONED GROUND BEEF)

1 tbsp olive oil

½ large chopped onion

½ large chopped bell pepper

2 cloves of garlic, minced

½ cup dry white wine

8 oz can tomato sauce

¼ cup raisins (or more to taste)

10 medium whole green olives stuffed with pimento

1 tbsp olive juice

1 tsp ground cumin

1 lb lean ground beef

2 large potatoes, peeled and cut into very small pieces

½ cup water

Salt and pepper to taste

In a large skillet, heat olive oil on medium heat. Cook and stir onion, bell pepper, and garlic in hot oil until soft. Add dry cooking wine, tomato sauce, raisins, olives, cumin, and salt. Add ground beef and stir until browned completely and mixed with the other ingredients. Add water and potatoes and stir to incorporate into the ground beef mixture. Cover the skillet and reduce heat on low for 15-20 minutes until potatoes are tender. Raise to medium heat and cook uncovered for another five minutes. Serve over white rice.

ANA'S ARROZ CON LECHE
(RICE PUDDING)

1 ½ cups of rice (short grain)

2 ½ cups of water

1 stick of cinnamon

¼ - ½ tsp salt

1 ½ cups of whole milk

1 can of condensed milk

1 can of evaporated milk

¼ cup of sugar

½ stick of butter

1 tsp vanilla

Place rice, water, cinnamon, and salt in a large pot on medium heat on the stove.

Cook until soft (approx. 20 minutes), stirring occasionally. Drain excess water.

Remove the cinnamon stick. Stir in the whole milk, condensed milk, evaporated milk, sugar, and butter. Keep on medium heat and continue stirring until the liquid ingredients have been absorbed and the mixture has the consistency of pudding. Place in individual serving bowls and top with ground cinnamon.

Refrigerate before serving.

DANIEL'S BATIDO DE MAMEY
(MAMEY MILKSHAKE)

2 cups fresh mamey, cubed or frozen pulp, thawed and broken up to fit blender

2 cups cold whole milk

⅓ cup sweetened condensed milk

⅓ cup sugar (or to taste)

pinch of salt

⅓ cup crushed ice

Place all ingredients into the blender and process until smooth. Serve in a tall glass.

EMILIO'S CUBAN SANDWICH

1 loaf Cuban bread

1 lb sweet ham

½ lb lechón asado (Cuban style pork)

½ lb Swiss cheese

3 tbsp butter

dill pickle slices

yellow mustard

Cut the bread into four equal sections. Slice each section lengthwise and add a little butter and mustard to both sides. Place cheese on each side and add ham, pork and pickles. Spread butter evenly on the outside of each sandwich and place in a panini or sandwich press for 2-3 minutes, until the cheese is melted. You can also use a griddle with a cast iron pan to press the sandwich down, flipping it halfway through. Press with enough pressure so the sandwich will be about half of its regular size, but not too much more, as the bread will become soggy from the mustard and juices. Slice diagonally to serve.

ANGELA'S CUBAN CHICKEN NOODLE SOUP

2 chicken breasts, with skin and bone-in

1 lime

1 tbsp olive oil + 1 tbsp olive oil

2 tbsp mojo (La Lechonera or another brand)

1 tbsp garlic powder

1 tsp cumin

8 oz can tomato sauce

1 onion, medium, cut into large pieces

½ bell pepper, seeded and cut into large pieces

1 tomato, large, cut into large pieces

3 cups water

2 potatoes, medium, peeled, and cut into small cubes

1 tsp yellow food coloring

8 oz or ½ packaged bag spaghetti noodles

salt and pepper to taste

In a small bowl, marinate chicken breasts with lime juice, 1 tbsp olive oil, mojo, garlic powder, and cumin. Let stand for 30 minutes.

In a large pan, cook the remaining 1 tbsp olive oil, tomato sauce, onion, bell pepper, and tomato on medium heat—this is sofrito, the seasoning base for the soup. Stir until cooked, approximately 5 minutes.

In a large pot over low-medium heat, add water, chicken breasts, and sofrito. Cook for approximately 45 minutes or until chicken breasts are fully cooked and tender.

Place the chicken on a plate to cool. Remove the skin and bones and discard. Shred chicken and set aside.

Drain the pot of broth to remove vegetables and return broth to the pot. Set vegetables aside to use in another recipe or discard.

Add potatoes to the pot and cook until soft, approximately 15-20 minutes.

Add chicken, noodles, and yellow food coloring to broth when potatoes are cooked.

Add salt and pepper to taste.

Lower heat and simmer uncovered for 20 minutes or until the potatoes are cooked and the noodles are soft.

FOR MORE RECIPES

visit www.madaymartinezdeosaba.com

Made in United States
Troutdale, OR
01/05/2024